ABRAHAM LINCOLN, 1864

ABRAHAM LINCOLN
AND MEN OF WAR-TIMES

SOME PERSONAL RECOLLECTIONS OF
WAR AND POLITICS
DURING THE LINCOLN ADMINISTRATION

A. K. McClure

FOURTH EDITION

Introduction to the Bison Books Edition
by James A. Rawley

UNIVERSITY OF NEBRASKA PRESS
LINCOLN AND LONDON

Introduction © 1996 by the University of Nebraska Press
Manufactured in the United States of America

⊖ The paper in this book meets the minimum requirements of
American National Standard for Information Sciences—Permanence
of Paper for Printed Library Materials, ANSI Z39.48-1984.

First Bison Books printing: 1996
Most recent printing indicated by the last digit below:
10 9 8 7 6 5 4 3 2 1

Library of Congress Cataloging-in-Publication Data
McClure, Alexander K. (Alexander Kelly), 1828–1909.
Abraham Lincoln and men of war-times: some personal recollections
of war and politics during the Lincoln administration / A. K. McClure;
introduction to the Bison Books ed. by James A. Rawley.—4th ed.
p. cm.
Includes bibliographical references and index.
ISBN 0-8032-8228-1 (pbk.: alk. paper)
1. United States—History—Civil War, 1861–1865—Biography.
2. United States—Politics and government—1861–1865. 3. Lincoln,
Abraham, 1809–1865—Friends and associates. 4. Presidents—
United States—Biography. I. Title.
E467.M43   1996
973.7′092′2—dc20
96-22221 CIP

Reprinted from the fourth edition (1892) by the Times Publishing
Company, Philadelphia.

To—

Andrew Gregg Curtin,
the Great War
Governor of the
Union; Patriot
Statesman, Friend;
this volume is
affectionately
dedicated

A. K. McClure

INTRODUCTION

James A. Rawley

Alexander Kelly McClure—"Aleck" to his friends—was an active participant and sharp observer of mid-nineteenth century American politics. Editor, legislator, orator, attorney for a member of John Brown's band, eyewitness to the battle of Antietam, victim of a Confederate raid on his hometown of Chambersburg, Pennsylvania, state party chairman, assistant adjutant general, and friend to mighty Civil War figures, the Pennsylvanian was on occasion in Washington discussing crises and policies with President Abraham Lincoln. Lincoln was told by the Philadelphia editor, John W. Forney, "McClure is a man of power, talent, wealth, and sagacity, and should always be so regarded."

A prolific writer, he brought out his *Abraham Lincoln and Men of War-Times* in 1892. An instant success, it ran through four editions in that year. A century and more later it continues to hold value for biographers and historians. McClure further added to Lincoln literature and lore with an anecdotal work entitled *Old Time Notes of Pennsylvania* in 1905. The saying attributed to Lincoln, "It is true that you may fool all the people some of the time; you can even fool some of the people all the time; but you can't fool all the people all the time," is traceable to McClure's book, *"Abe" Lincoln's Yarns and Stories*, first published in 1901.

Born on his family's mountainous farm in Perry County, Pennsylvania, in 1828, Alexander McClure was descended from Scotch-Irish ancestors. After being educated at home, he was apprenticed to a tanner and simultaneously learned the printing trade. Publishing and public office occupied his early years as he worked as editor of southern Pennsylvania papers and served on the governor's staff as colonel and later as deputy United States marshal.

He rose to prominence in his state in the 1850s, becoming owner of the widely influential *Franklin Repository*, published in Chambersburg. His race for auditor general in 1853 as a Whig candidate failed. Selling the *Repository* in late 1855, he and a friend immediately bought the *Harrisburg Telegraph*, giving him a voice in the state capital. He devoted special attention to legislative sessions and appealed to both "American" (Know Nothing) and Republican readers, hoping for a union of the two anti-Democratic political parties. In 1856 he was admitted to the bar, a well-traveled path to political office.

McClure, an ardent enemy of the "Democracy" (as the opposing party was often called), attended the first Republican national nominating convention in June 1856, which to his dismay passed over the conservative John McLean, justice of the Supreme Court, the only person he believed capable of carrying the state against the Democratic nominee, the Pennsylvanian James Buchanan. McClure "had no faith in Frémont, either as a candidate or as a President," he later wrote, and considered the pathfinder's nomination by the Republicans political suicide. Not long after, McClure sold the *Telegraph* and turned to the law and politics, establishing his law office in Chambersburg.

In 1857 McClure became an elected official, winning a seat in the state house of representatives as a Union party member. Two years later he was elected to the state senate on the People's party ticket. (Both of these party names—Union and People's—drew back from using the name Republican, which party leaders deemed less inclusive and less likely to attract anti-slavery Democrats, former Whigs, and Know Nothings.) As a state lawmaker he established a reputation as an advocate of business enterprise, especially of a protective tariff. In 1859 he served briefly as attorney for John Cook, a captured member of John Brown's raiders. The episode, related in *Lincoln and Men of War-Times*, revealed McClure's sympathy with plans to have his client escape rendition to Virginia for trial.[1]

The year 1860 stood as perhaps the most important in McClure's long career. The United States was to elect a president after six years of national turmoil, and Pennsylvania was to elect a governor in a tangled party setting. Opponents of the "Democracy" discovered they were an element in a four-cornered presidential race; and the People's party underwent a bitter internal contest for control. On the national scene the Democrats divided, as Northerners nominated Stephen A. Douglas and Southerners, John C. Breckinridge, Buchanan's vice president. The Constitutional Union party attracted former Whigs and conservatives and nominated John Bell. In Pennsylvania the People's party was torn between two factions. Simon Cameron, influential and ambitious politician with a tarnished reputation, aspired to win his state's endorsement as presidential nominee. Andrew Gregg Curtin, former Whig of untarnished reputation, aspired to the governor's chair and control of the party.

McClure disliked Cameron and admired Curtin. At the People's party state convention in February 1860, McClure unsuccessfully opposed Cameron's endorsement and successfully strove to secure Curtin's nomination. In this twisted situation McClure accepted appointment as chairman of the People's State Committee.

Wholeheartedly committed to the Curtin cause, distrustful of Cameron, he was a delegate to the Republican national convention in Chicago. Like most of the Pennsylvania delegates, he believed the leading contender for the presidential nomination was too extreme. William H. Seward, as governor of New York, had displayed a sympathy with Roman Catholics that might alienate Know Nothings, numerous in Philadelphia, a bloc the People's Party hoped to capture. As United States senator, Seward had declared there is a "higher law" than the Constitution, frightening slaveholders and others who relied on the Constitution to protect their interests.

Pennsylvania's support seemed crucial, first to the nomination and later to the election. Second to New York in the size of its electoral vote, Pennsylvania normally voted Democratic, was the home state of the incumbent president, James Buchanan, and in

1856 had been pivotal in defeating the Republicans. In that election the Democrats had polled 231,000 votes; the Republicans, 148,000 and the Americans or Know Nothings, 82,000. The combined Republican and American vote equaled the Democratic total. With the Republican, or People's Party, divided between the Cameron and Curtin factions and the Americans an uncertain factor, Pennsylvania in 1860 kindled anxiety among Lincoln's backers. Curtin and his friends not only did not want Cameron to win the Republican nomination but also did not believe that Curtin himself could be elected governor should Seward become the nominee.

At the Chicago convention, McClure and Curtin labored to undermine whatever strength Cameron's candidacy possessed. An all-night caucus of the Pennsylvania delegates at least agreed to give Cameron support on the first ballot, Justice John McLean on the second, and Lincoln on the third. As it worked out, the arrangement shifted Pennsylvania's support to Lincoln rather than Seward. Cameron obtained a poor third place on the first ballot, McLean a poorer fifth rank. With Pennsylvania's fifty-two votes for Lincoln on the third ballot, the gain helped impel the convention to name Lincoln as the party's choice. Pennsylvania's vote, in collaboration with Indiana's, had been significant, though perhaps not as significant as McClure's account claims, in preventing Seward's nomination, in achieving Lincoln's victory.[2]

Success in Chicago was one thing, success in the national election another. As state chairman, McClure bore the burden of securing his state's popular vote for Lincoln. Cameron, desiring to control the state organization, remained a problem for McClure. In an amusing incident McClure and the Curtinites retained control. The night before the first state committee meeting, McClure seized advantage of a late-night drinking spree on the part of the Cameron members. The next morning the sober Curtinites controlled the meeting, with more than twenty Cameronites missing.

Holding the party's state canvass in his hands, McClure expertly transformed a "loose aggregation," as he said, into a network that for the first time extended to "every election district" in the diverse state, he informed Lincoln. He kept in touch with the national committee chairman, Edwin D. Morgan, governor of New York, from whom he solicited funds, and, most importantly, with Abraham Lincoln.

The Lincoln-McClure relationship in 1860 is well documented, as correspondence between the two politicians proliferated. McClure reported efforts of the three anti-Republican elements— Douglas Democrats, Breckinridge Democrats, and Fillmore Americans—to fuse. He continued sanguine about Lincoln's chances.[3]

Disturbing reports reached Lincoln about discord between the Cameron and Curtin elements. He dispatched his close friends, Leonard Swett and Judge David Davis, to Pennsylvania to investigate the canvass. Both Lincoln and the Curtinites who feared he would side with the Cameron faction were relieved when the Illinoisans reported favorably on McClure. Emphasizing a protective tariff more than antislavery, he sought support from German-Americans through a speechmaking tour by Carl Schurz and from American party members through one by a former American party leader, Daniel Ullman. Adding his own powerful oratory to the chorus, he saw Curtin and the Republicans prevail in the gubernatorial election in October.

On October 9 he triumphantly telegraphed Lincoln: "state safe by ten thousand" votes, and the following day: "Curtin elected by over twenty-five thousand." In November, Pennsylvania and the other free states made Lincoln president.

Lincoln's victory over his opponents and Curtin's over Cameron were followed by Lincoln's offer, after an importunate visit from Cameron, of a cabinet post to Cameron, fulfilling an assurance that McClure alleges was made by Lincoln's manager in return for Cameron's support. Because of Cameron's soiled reputation, the offer provoked an indignant outcry. McClure wired his own protest, saying the appointment would destroy the party in Pennsylvania, and in return received an invitation to come see Lincoln in Springfield.

McClure immediately entrained for Springfield, and upon arriving there went straight to Lincoln's house. For two hours they discussed the "Cabinet imbroglio," as McClure described it, and the national crisis as slave states were proceeding to secede. The next day Lincoln withdrew he cabinet offer to Cameron, in part because of his talk with McClure.

Lincoln continued to ponder the appointment until he arrived in Washington, when he appointed Cameron secretary of war, informing McClure what he was doing. It was a fateful act, as Cameron's incompetence as war minister was revealed in the first months of the Civil War.

Two days after Fort Sumter surrendered to the Confederacy, Governor Curtin and McClure met with Lincoln in Washington to ascertain Pennsylvania's role in the war. McClure was chairman of the Military Committee of the Pennsylvania senate. It was the beginning of McClure's service to the Union during the war. During the next four stormy years, when his state became the scene of the Civil War's most famous battle at Gettysburg and his own home at Chambersburg was burned by Confederates, he was a keen-eyed observer of the president and of a galaxy of generals and politicians.

In the war's second year, when enthusiasm for volunteering cooled, Lincoln and Curtin asked McClure to execute a draft of men. Draft resistance flared, causing McClure to telegraph Lincoln for advice. Putting nothing on the record, the president discreetly sent assistant adjutant-general Townsend to carry an oral message, "It might be well, in an extreme emergency, to be content with the appearance of executing the laws; I think McClure will understand." McClure accordingly adjusted some draft quotas and further rebellion was averted.

In the course of the 1862 state draft, McClure also encountered resistance from the commanding officer at Harrisburg. Very slow in mustering men, he was impeding the draft. As thousands of men waited to be mustered into service, McClure hastened to Washington to see Lincoln. After hearing McClure's story Lincoln immediately appointed him assistant adjutant-general of the United States, with the rank of major, outranking the Harrisburg captain. The draft went forward and when it was completed McClure resigned his commission.

Such adroitness formed a part of the portrait of Lincoln that McClure knew. In his first acquaintance with Lincoln, McClure met a man dressed in "snuff-colored and slouchy pantaloons; open black vest, held by a few brass buttons; straight or evening dress-coat, with tightly fitting sleeves to exaggerate his long, bony arms, and all supplemented by an awkwardness." McClure recollected, "Before half an hour had passed I learned not only to respect but, indeed, to reverence the man."

Later conversations, some at great length, helped fill out the portrait. McClure beheld the president as a master politician, "one of the greatest of American statesmen," endowed with exceptional common sense, "a peculiarly receptive and analytical mind," un-changing in purpose once he had made up his mind, self-reliant, free from arrogance, patient, and above all guided by the will of the people.

He found Lincoln, with all his readily apparent traits, to be a Sphinx, never revealing the inner man. On one occasion, after half an hour of conversation in which McClure gave Lincoln his views, he asked the president for his views. Lincoln answered, "Well McClure, the fact is I'm 'shut pan' on that question."

McClure's account of Lincoln and emancipation is rich in un-derstanding and insight. McClure recognized that early on Lin-coln opposed slavery but was not "a sentimental abolitionist." At the same time the president knew that slavery caused the war and if fighting persisted the institution must be destroyed. McClure noted the president's patience, efforts to promote state emancipation, re-luctance to use his power to free rebels' slaves, the Union-saving aim, and the religious element of emancipation. The analysis of both the preliminary and formal Emancipation Proclamation is keen.

McClure does not attempt a biography of the sixteenth presi-dent, but conforms to his title, *Lincoln and Men of War-Times*. Beyond his arresting chapters on Lincoln, he limns interesting relationships between Lincoln and notable Civil War leaders— political and military. Many of them are Pennsylvanians of whom McClure had opportunities to have first-hand knowledge: Simon Cameron and Edwin Stanton, Lincoln's secretaries of war; Generals George B. McClellan and George G. Meade; ex-president James B. Buchanan; Governor Andrew Gregg Curtin; the Republican radical Thaddeus Stevens; and lesser lights.

Amidst these portraits runs a strain of impartiality, surprising from the pen of a partisan Republican and Lincoln admirer. McClure is sympathetic to the beleaguered Buchanan's plight during the secession crisis and lauds the former president's support of Lincoln during the war as a Union Democrat. In the twice-dismissed and controversial McClellan, McClure discerns a military genius and "one of the most loyal of men."

Many of McClure's pen strokes are striking. Of Salmon P. Chase he wrote, "One of the greatest intellects among all the Republican leaders, he was an absolute failure as a politician." Horace Greeley he judged "the most brilliant and forceful editor the country has every produced." Regarding U. S. Grant, he acknowledges, "For twelve years I cherished a personal prejudice against Grant because of his supposed want of fidelity to Lincoln that I now believe to be wholly unjust."

In an interpretation that anticipates a future academic judgment of Thaddeus Stevens, often regarded as an antagonist of Lincoln, McClure asserted, "Stevens was ever clearing the underbrush and preparing the soil, while Lincoln followed to sow the seeds that were to ripen in a regenerated Union." Taking note of Edwin Stanton's abrasive personality, McClure records his own belief "that at no period during the war after Stanton had entered the Cabinet, did Lincoln feel that any other man could fill Stanton's place with equal usefulness to the country."

General George G. Meade, victor at Gettysburg, is described as one of "our unrewarded heroes." McClure attributes this neglect to the failure of Meade after Gettysburg to capture Lee and his retreating army. When McClure asked Lincoln whether he was not satisfied with the general's accomplishment, the president answered, "I am profoundly grateful down to the bottom of my boots for what he did at Gettysburg, but I think if I had been General Meade I would have fought another battle."

The most controversial part of McClure's book is his assertion that Lincoln in 1864 desired to drop Hannibal Hamlin as his running mate and to make Andrew Johnson his vice president. McClure documents a portion of this heated argument in an appendix detailing his disagreement with the denials of Lincoln's secretary and biographer, John George Nicolay. For more than a century most historians sided with McClure. More recent scholarship has thrown doubt on McClure's reliability on the question, citing the weakness of his evidence that Hamlin was dropped at Lincoln's behest and the credibility of his reminiscences. His case stands unproved.[4]

The point of credibility is well taken. Reminiscences written decades after the event are subject to question; and all the more so when the narrator puts himself at the center of the story. McClure's claims of closeness to Lincoln are best documented for the year 1860, when a paper trail of correspondence connected the candidate in Springfield and the campaign manager in Harrisburg. This documented relationship is a staple for historians of the campaign and the subsequent Cameron appointment. The less full record for succeeding years may in part be attributable to the burning of his home in Chambersburg in 1864, which destroyed his correspondence with Lincoln, he said.

McClure's *Recollections* stands as a good read. Immersed in the throbbing politics of the Civil War era, he held responsible offices and knew many of the figures he wrote about. Historians and biographers see him as a significant source.

NOTES

1. The only full-length study of McClure is William Henry Russell, "A Biography of Alexander K. McClure," Ph.D. diss., University of Wisconsin, 1953.

2. Reinhard Luthin, *The First Lincoln Campaign* (Cambridge, MA: Harvard University Press, 1944) contains a good account of Pennsylvania's role in 1860.

3. Robert Todd Lincoln Papers, Library of Congress, has the Lincoln-McClure correspondence.

4. Don E. Fehrenbacher, "The Making of a Myth: Lincoln and the Vice-Presidential Nomination in 1864," *Civil War History* 41 (December 1995): 273–90. See also Brooks D. Simpson, "Alexander McClure on Lincoln and Grant: A Questionable Account," *Lincoln Herald* 95 (fall 1993): 83–86.

PREFACE.

THE chapters in this volume make no pretensions to give either a biography of Abraham Lincoln or a history of his memorable Administration. They were written amidst the constant pressure of editorial duties simply to correct some popular errors as to Lincoln's character and actions. So much has been written of him by persons assuming to possess information obtained in the inner circle of his confidence, and such conflicting presentations of his personal attributes and private and public acts have been given to the public, that I have deemed it a duty to contribute what little I could from personal knowledge, to correct some common errors in estimating his character, ability, and efforts.

The closest men to Abraham Lincoln, both before and after his election to the Presidency, were David Davis,

Leonard Swett, Ward H. Lamon, and William H. Herndon. Davis and Swett were his close personal and political counselors; Lamon was his Marshal for Washington and Herndon had been his law-partner for twenty years. These men, who knew Mr. Lincoln better than all others, unite in testifying that his extreme caution prevented him from making a personal confidant of any one; and my own more limited intercourse with him taught me, in the early period of our acquaintance, that those who assumed that they enjoyed Lincoln's confidence had little knowledge of the man. It is the generally honest but mistaken belief of confidential relations with Lincoln on the part of biographers and magazine and newspaper writers that has presented him to the public in such a confusion of attitudes and as possessing such strangely contradictory individual qualities.

I saw Mr. Lincoln many times during his Presidential term, and, like all of the many others who had intimate relations with him, I enjoyed his confidence only within the limitations of the necessities of the occasion. I do not therefore write these chapters assuming to have been the confidant of Mr. Lincoln; but in some things I did see him as he was, and, from necessity, knew what he did and why he did it. What thus happened to come under my own observation and within my own hearing often related to men or measures of moment then and quite as momentous now, when the events of the war are about to be finally crystallized into history.

My personal knowledge of occurrences in which Mr. Lincoln and other great actors in the bloody drama of our Civil War were directly involved enables me to present some of the chief characteristics of Mr. Lincoln, and to support them by facts and circumstances which are conclusive. I have, therefore, written only of Lincoln and his relations with the prominent chieftains and civilians with whom I had more or less intimate personal acquaintance. The facts herein given relating to leading generals and statesmen are presented to illustrate in the clearest manner possible the dominating characteristics of Mr. Lincoln. They may or may not be accepted by the public as important, but they have the one merit of absolute truthfulness.

Abraham Lincoln achieved more in American statesmanship than any other President, legislator, or diplomat in the history of the Republic; and what he achieved brought no borrowed plumes to his crown. Compelled to meet and solve the most momentous problems of our government, and beset by confused counsels and intensified jealousies, he has written the most lustrous records of American history; and his name and fame must be immortal while liberty shall have worshipers in any land. To aid to a better understanding of this "noblest Roman of them all" is the purpose of these chapters; and if they shall, in the humblest degree, accomplish that end, I shall be more than content.

———

The portraits in these chapters have been selected with scrupulous care and executed in the best style. The frontispiece portrait of Lincoln is the only perfect copy of his face that I have ever seen in any picture. It was

taken in March, 1864, on the occasion when he handed
Grant his commission as lieutenant-general. Two nega-
tives were taken by the artist, and only one of them
"touched up" and copies printed therefrom at the time.
The other negative remained untouched until a few
months ago, when it was discovered and copies printed
from it without a single change in the lines or features
of Lincoln's face. It therefore presents Lincoln true to
life. The other portraits of Lincoln present him as he
appeared when he delivered his speech in Cooper Institute, New York, in 1859, with the cleanly-shaven face
that was always maintained until after his election to the
Presidency, and as he appeared when studying with his
son "Tad" at his side. These portraits I have selected
because they give the most accurate presentations of the
man, and to them are added a correct picture of the
humble home of his early childhood; of his Springfield
home of 1860; of the tomb in which his dust reposes
near Springfield, Ill.; and a fac-simile of his letter of
acceptance in 1860.

I am greatly indebted to the Lives of Lincoln given by
Nicolay and Hay—the most complete and accurate record
of dates and events, military and civil, relating to Lincoln—by Mr. Herndon, by Mr. Lamon, by Mr. Arnold,
and by Mr. Brooks, and to Mr. Blaine's "Twenty Years
in Congress," for valuable information on many points
referred to in these chapters.

A. K. McCLURE.

PHILADELPHIA, 1892.

CONTENTS.

LIST OF ILLUSTRATIONS.

Springfield, Ill., May 23. 1860

Hon: George Ashmun.
  President of the Republican National Convention.
    Sir:
        I accept the nomination tendered
me by the Convention over which you preside, and
of which I am formally apprized in the letter of yourself and others, acting as a Committee of the Convention, for that purpose.

        The declaration of principles and sentiments,
which accompanies your letter, meets my ▬▬
approval; and it shall be my care not to violate,
or disregard it, in any part —

        Imploring the assistance of Divine Providence,
and with due regard to the views and feelings
of all who were represented in the Convention;
to the rights of all the states, and territories, and
people of the nation; to the inviolability of the
Constitution, and the perpetual union, harmony, and
prosperity of all, I am most happy to co-operate for
the practical success of the principles declared by the
Convention —   Your obliged friend, and fellow citizen
                                    A. Lincoln

FAC-SIMILE OF LINCOLN'S LETTER OF ACCEPTANCE.

[Copied from "Abraham Lincoln; A History," by permission of its authors.]

LINCOLN IN 1860.

I T was the unexpected that happened in Chicago on that fateful 18th of May, 1860, when Abraham Lincoln was nominated for President of the United States. It was wholly unexpected by the friends of Seward; it was hoped for, but not confidently expected, by the friends of Lincoln. The convention was the ablest assembly of the kind ever called together in this country. It was the first national deliberative body of the Republican party that was to attain such illustrious achievements in the history of free government. The first national convention of that party, held in Philadelphia in 1856, was composed of a loose aggregation of political free-thinkers, embracing many usually denominated as "cranks." The party was without organization or cohesion; its delegates were self-appointed and responsible to no regular constituency. It was the sudden eruption of the intense resentment of the people of the North against the encroachments of slavery in Northern Territories, and neither in the character of its leaders nor in the record of its proceedings did it rank as a distinctively deliberative body. It nominated a romantic adventurer for President—a man untried in statesmanship and who had done little to commend him to the considerate judgment of the nation as its Chief Magistrate in a period of uncom-

mon peril. The campaign that followed was one of
unusual brilliancy, and resulted in anchoring nearly all
of the old Democratic States of the West in the Republican column. In 1860 the principles of the Republican
party had been clearly defined; its organization had been
perfected in every Northern State, and each delegate
to that convention at Chicago was regularly chosen and
represented a great party inspired by a devotion to its
faith that has seldom been equaled and never surpassed
in all our political history. The halo of romance that
encircled General Fremont, "the Pathfinder," four
years before had perished, and he was unthought of as
a candidate.

For nearly two years before the meeting of the Chicago
Convention in 1860 the Republican party had one pre-
eminent leader who was recognized as the coming candidate for President. The one man who had done most
to inspire and crystallize the Republican organization
was William H. Seward of New York. Certainly, two-
thirds of the delegates chosen to the convention preferred him for President, and a decided majority went
to Chicago expecting to vote for his nomination. Had
the convention been held in any other place than
Chicago, it is quite probable that Seward would have
been successful; but every circumstance seemed to con-
verge to his defeat when the delegates came face to face
in Chicago to solve the problem of a Republican national
victory. Of the 231 men who voted for Lincoln on the
third and last ballot, not less than 100 of them voted
reluctantly against the candidate of their choice. It
was a Republican-Seward convention; it was not a Sew-
ard-Republican convention. With all its devotion to
Seward it yielded to a higher devotion to Republican
success, and that led to the nomination of Abraham
Lincoln.

I have read scores of magazine and newspaper articles assuming to explain how and why Lincoln was nominated at Chicago in 1860. Few of them approach accuracy, and no one of them that I can recall tells the true story. Lincoln was not seriously thought of for President until but a few weeks before the meeting of the National Convention. Blaine has truly said that the State Convention of Illinois, held but a short time before the meeting of the National Convention, was surprised at its own spontaneous and enthusiastic nomination of Lincoln. He had been canvassed at home and in other States as a more than possible candidate for Vice-President. I well remember Lincoln mentioning the fact that his own delegation from Illinois was not unitedly in earnest for his nomination, but when the time came for casting their votes the enthusiasm for Lincoln in Chicago, both inside and outside the convention, was such that they could do no less than give him the united vote of the State. Leonard Swett, who was one of the most potent of the Lincoln leaders in that struggle, in a letter written to Mr. Drummond on the 27th of May, 1860, in which he gives a detailed account of the battle made for Lincoln, states that 8 of the 22 delegates from Illinois "would gladly have gone for Seward." Thus, not only in many of the other States did Lincoln receive reluctant votes in that convention, but even his own State furnished a full share of votes which would have been gladly given to Seward had he been deemed available.

The first breach made in the then apparently invincible columns of Seward was made by Horace Greeley. His newspaper, the *Tribune*, was then vastly the most influential public journal on the continent, and equaled in the world only by the *Times* of London. His battle against Seward was waged with tireless energy and consummate skill. It was not then known that he had separated from immediate political association with Seward and Weed. Had his relations with those gentlemen been fully understood then, as they were soon after the convention, when Greeley's memorable letter of political dissolution was given to the public, it would have greatly impaired his influence in opposing Seward. But I think it just to Greeley to say that, independent of all real or imaginary wrongs from Seward and Weed, he was honestly convinced that Seward was not an available candidate in 1860. He espoused the cause of Edward Bates of Missouri, who was a man of most distinguished character and ability, and whose record appealed very strongly to the more conservative elements of the party. Indeed, the nomination of Bates would have been within the lines of possibility, instead of the nomination of Lincoln, had the convention been surrounded by local influences in his favor as potent as were the local influences for the successful candidate. The Pennsylvania delegation in determining its final choice gave Lincoln barely four majority over Bates, and but for the fact that Indiana had decided to give unanimous support to Lincoln at an early stage of the contest, Bates would have been a much more formidable candidate than he now appears to have been by the records of the convention.

The defeat of Seward and the nomination of Lincoln were brought about by two men—Andrew G. Curtin of Pennsylvania, and Henry S. Lane of Indiana, and neither accident nor intrigue was a material factor in the struggle.* They not only defeated Seward in a Seward con-

---

* Mrs. Henry S. Lane to the Author, September 16, 1891 : "I read with the greatest interest your excellent article in the St. Louis *Globe-Democrat*, giving a history of the convention which nominated Lincoln. I thank you for the kindly mention of Mr. Lane's name in that memorable convention. So many different versions of the same have been given the public (with many mis-

vention, but they decided the contest in favor of Lincoln against Bates, his only real competitor after Seward. Curtin had been nominated for Governor in Pennsylvania and Lane had been nominated for Governor in Indiana. The States in which their battles were to be fought were the pivotal States of the national contest. It was an accepted necessity that both Pennsylvania and Indiana should elect Republican Governors in October to secure the election of the Republican candidate for President in November. Curtin and Lane were naturally the most interested of all the great host that attended the Chicago Convention in 1860. Neither of their States was Republican. In Pennsylvania the name of Republican could not be adopted by the party that had chosen Curtin for Governor. The call for the convention summoned the opposition to the Democratic party to attend the People's State Convention, and all shades of antagonism to the administration then in power were invited to cordial and equal participation in the deliberations of that body. The Republicans had made a distinct battle

---

takes) that I was glad to see a true one published to vindicate the truth of history.

"I was with my husband in Chicago, and may tell you now, as most of the actors have 'joined the silent majority,' what no living person knows, that Thurlow Weed, in his anxiety for the success of Seward, took Mr. Lane out one evening and pleaded with him to lead the Indiana delegation over to Seward, saying they would send enough money from New York to ensure his election for Governor, and carry the State later for the New York candidate.

"His proposal was indignantly rejected, as there was neither money nor influence enough in their State to change my husband's opinion in regard to the fitness and availability of Mr. Lincoln for the nomination, and with zeal and energy he worked faithfully for his election, remained his firm friend through his administration till the end came and death crystallized his fame. With sincere thanks, respectfully."

for Governor three years before, with David Wilmot as
their candidate, against Isaac Hazelhurst, the American
candidate, and William F. Packer, the Democratic candidate. The result was the election of Packer by a
majority over the combined votes of both the opposing
nominees. The American organization was maintained
in Philadelphia and in many of the counties of the State.
Fillmore had received a large majority of the votes cast
for the Fremont-Fillmore Fusion Electoral ticket in 1856
in various sections. These elements had been combined
in what was then called the People's party in Pennsylvania in the State elections of 1858 and 1859, and the
Democrats had been defeated by the combination, but
the American element remained very powerful and quite
intense in many localities. Without its aid the success
of Curtin was simply impossible. A like condition of
things existed in Indiana. The American element had
polled over 22,000 votes for Fillmore in 1856, and in
1858, when the same effort was made in Indiana to unite
all shades of opposition to the Democracy, the combination was defeated by a small majority. While the anti-
slavery sentiment asserted itself by the election of a
majority of Republicans to Congress in 1858, the entire
Democratic State ticket was successful by majorities
varying from 1534 to 2896. It was evident, therefore,
that in both Pennsylvania and Indiana there would be a
desperate battle for the control of the October election,
and it was well known by all that if the Republicans
failed to elect either Curtin or Lane the Presidential
battle would be irretrievably lost.

Both of the candidates presented in these two pivotal
States were men of peculiar fitness for the arduous task
they had assumed. Both were admittedly the strongest
men that could have been nominated by the opposition
to the Democracy, and both were experienced and con-

summate politicians. Their general knowledge of politics and of the bearing of all political questions likely to be felt in the contest made them not only wise counselors, but all appreciated the fact that they were of all men the most certain to advise solely with reference to success. Neither of them cared whether Seward, Lincoln, Bates, or any of the other men named for President should be nominated, if the man chosen was certain to be the most available. They were looking solely to their own success in October, and their success meant the success of the Republican party in the nation. With Lane was John D. Defrees, chairman of his State committee, who had been called to that position because he was regarded as best fitted to lead in the desperate contest before him. I was with Curtin and interested as he was only in his individual success, as he had summoned me to take charge of his October battle in Pennsylvania. The one thing that Curtin, Lane, and their respective lieutenants agreed upon was that the nomination of Seward meant hopeless defeat in their respective States. Lane and Defrees were positive in the assertion that the nomination of Seward would lose the Governorship in Indiana. Curtin and I were equally positive in declaring that the nomination of Seward would defeat Curtin in Pennsylvania.

There was no personal hostility to Seward in the efforts made by Curtin and Lane to defeat him. They had no reason whatever to hinder his nomination, excepting the settled conviction that the nomination of Seward meant their own inevitable defeat. It is not true, as has been assumed by many, that the objection to Seward was because of his radical or advanced position in Republican faith. It was not Seward's "irrepressible conflict" or his "higher-law" declarations which made Curtin and Lane oppose him as the Republican candidate. On the

3

contrary, both of them were thoroughly anti-slavery men, and they finally accepted Lincoln with the full knowledge that he was even in advance of Seward in forecasting the "irrepressible conflict." Lincoln announced in his memorable Springfield speech, delivered on the 17th of June, 1858, "'A house divided against itself cannot stand;' I believe this Government cannot endure permanently half slave and half free," and Seward's "irrepressible-conflict" speech was not delivered until the 25th of October.* Lincoln was not only fully abreast with Seward, but in advance of him in forecasting the great battle against slavery. The single reason that compelled Curtin and Lane to make aggressive resistance to the nomination of Seward was his attitude on the school question, that was very offensive to the many thousands of voters in their respective States, who either adhered to the American organization or cherished its strong prejudices against any division of the school fund. It was Seward's record on that single question when Governor of New York that made him an

---

* It is an irrepressible conflict between opposing and enduring forces, and it means that the United States must and will, sooner or later, become either entirely a slaveholding nation or entirely a free-labor nation.—*Seward's speech at Rochester*, October 25, 1858.

But there is a higher law than the Constitution which regulates our authority over the domain and devotes it to the same noble purposes. The territory is a part, no inconsiderable part, of the common heritage of mankind bestowed upon them by the Creator of the universe. We are His stewards, and must so discharge our trust as to secure, in the highest obtainable degree, their happiness.—*Seward's Senate speech*, March 11, 1850.

"A house divided against itself cannot stand." I believe this Government cannot endure permanently one half slave and one half free. I do not expect the Union to be dissolved; I do not expect the house to fall; but I do expect it will cease to be divided. It will become all one thing or all the other.—*Lincoln's Springfield speech*, June 17, 1858.

impossible candidate for President in 1860, unless he was to be nominated simply to be defeated. Had he been nominated, the American element in Pennsylvania and Indiana would not only have maintained its organization, but it would have largely increased its strength on the direct issue of hostility to Seward. It was not an unreasonable apprehension, therefore, that inspired Curtin and Lane to protest with all earnestness against the nomination of Seward. There could be no question as to the sincerity of the Republican candidates for Governor in the two pivotal States when they declared that a particular nomination would doom them to defeat, and it was Andrew G. Curtin and Henry S. Lane whose earnest admonitions to the delegates at Chicago compelled a Seward convention to halt in its purpose and set him aside, with all his pre-eminent qualifications and with all the enthusiastic devotion of his party to him.

It was Curtin and Lane also who decided that Lincoln should be the candidate after Seward had been practically overthrown. When it became known that Seward's nomination would defeat the party in Pennsylvania and Indiana, the natural inquiry was, Who can best aid these candidates for Governor in their State contests? Indiana decided in favor of Lincoln at an early stage of the struggle, and her action had much to do in deciding Pennsylvania's support of Lincoln. The Pennsylvania delegation had much less knowledge of Lincoln than the men from Indiana, and there were very few original supporters of Lincoln among them. Wilmot was for Lincoln from the start; Stevens was for Judge McLean; Reeder was for General Cameron. The delegation was not a harmonious one, because of the hostility of a considerable number of the delegates to Cameron for President, and it was not until the first day that the convention met that Pennsylvania got into

anything like a potential attitude. At a meeting of the
delegation it was proposed that the first, second, and
third choice of the delegates for President should be
formally declared. It is needless to say that this proposition did not come from the earnest supporters of
Cameron, but it was coupled with the suggestion that
Cameron should be unanimously declared the first choice
of the State; which was done. Stevens was stubbornly
for McLean, and had a considerable following. He
asked that McLean be declared the second choice of the
State, and, as McLean was then known to be practically
out of the fight, he was given substantially a unanimous
vote as the second choice. The third choice to be expressed by the delegation brought the State down to
practical business, as it was well known that both the
first and second choice were mere perfunctory declarations. The battle came then between Bates and Lincoln, and but for the facts that Indiana had previously
declared for Lincoln, and that Curtin and Lane were
acting in concert, there is little reason to doubt that
Bates would have been preferred. Much feeling was
exhibited in deciding the third choice of the State, and
Lincoln finally won over Bates by four majority. When
it became known that Pennsylvania had indicated Lincoln as her third choice, it gave a wonderful impetus to
the Lincoln cause. Cameron and McLean were not
seriously considered, and what was nominally the third
choice of the State was accepted as really the first choice
among possible candidates. The slogan of the Lincoln
workers was soon heard on every side, "Pennsylvania's
for Lincoln," and from the time that Pennsylvania
ranged herself along with Indiana in support of Lincoln
not only was Seward's defeat inevitable, but the nomination of Lincoln was practically assured. Thus did
two men—Curtin and Lane—not only determine Sew-

ard's defeat, but they practically determined the nomination of Lincoln.

Notwithstanding the substantial advantages gained by the supporters of Lincoln in the preliminary struggles at Chicago, the fight for Seward was maintained with desperate resolve until the final ballot was taken. It was indeed a battle of giants. Thurlow Weed was the Seward leader, and he was simply incomparable as a master in handling a convention. With him were such able lieutenants as Governor Morgan, and Raymond of the New York *Times*, with Evarts as chairman of the delegation, whose speech nominating Seward was the most impressive utterance of his life. The Bates men were led by Frank Blair, the only Republican Congressman from a slave State, who was nothing if not heroic, aided by his brother Montgomery, who was a politician of uncommon cunning. With them was Horace Greeley, who was chairman of the delegation from the then almost inaccessible State of Oregon. It was Lincoln's friends, however, who were the "hustlers" of that battle. They had men for sober counsel like David Davis; men of supreme sagacity like Leonard Swett; men of tireless effort like Norman B. Judd; and they had what was more important than all—a seething multitude wild with enthusiasm for Abraham Lincoln. For once Thurlow Weed was outgeneraled just at a critical stage of the battle. On the morning of the third day, when the final struggle was to be made, the friends of Seward got up an imposing demonstration on the streets of Chicago. They had bands and banners, immense numbers, and generous enthusiasm; but while the Seward men were thus making a public display of their earnestness and strength, Swett and Judd filled the immense galleries of the wigwam, in which the convention was held, with men who were ready to shout to the echo for Lincoln whenever opportunity offered. The result was that when the Seward men filed into the convention there were seats for the delegates, but few for any others, and the convention was encircled by an immense throng that made the wigwam tremble with its cheers for the "rail-splitter."

Twelve names had been put in nomination for President, but the first ballot developed to the comprehension of all that the struggle was between Seward and Lincoln. Seward had received 173½ votes and Lincoln 102. The other votes scattered between ten candidates, the highest of whom (Cameron) received 50½, all of which were from Pennsylvania with the exception of 3. Cameron's name was at once withdrawn, and on the second ballot Seward rose to 184½, with Lincoln closely following at 181, but both lacking the 233 votes necessary to a choice. The third ballot was taken amid breathless excitement, with Lincoln steadily gaining and Seward now and then losing, and when the ballot ended Lincoln had 231½ to 180 for Seward. Lincoln lacked but 2½ votes of a majority. His nomination was now inevitable, and before the result was announced there was a general scramble to change from the candidates on the scattering list to Lincoln. Cartter of Ohio was the first to obtain recognition, and he changed four Ohio votes from Chase to Lincoln, which settled the nomination. Maine followed, changing ten votes from Seward to Lincoln. Andrew of Massachusetts and Gratz Brown of Missouri next came with changes to the Lincoln column, and they continued until Lincoln's vote was swelled to 354.*

---

* The following were the ballots for President:

	First.	Second.	Third.
Lincoln	102	181	231½
Seward	173½	184½	180

As soon as Ohio gave the necessary number of votes to Lincoln to nominate him a huge charcoal portrait of the candidate was suddenly displayed from the gallery of the wigwam, and the whole convention, with the exception of the New York delegation, was whirled to its feet by the enthusiasm that followed. It was many minutes before the convention could be sufficiently calmed to proceed with business. The New York delegates had kept their seats in sullen silence during all this eruption of enthusiasm for Lincoln, and it was long even after quiet had been restored that Evarts' tall form was recognized to move that the nomination be declared unanimous. He was promptly seconded by Andrew of Massachusetts, who was also an ardent supporter of Seward, and the motion was adopted with a wild hurrah that came spontaneously from every part of the convention excepting the several lines of seats occupied by the seventy delegates from New York. Mr. Evarts' motion for a recess was unanimously carried, and the convention and its vast audience of spectators hurried out to make

	First.	Second.	Third.
Cameron	50½*	2	. .
Bates	48	35	22
Chase	49	42½	24½
McLean	12	8	5
Dayton	14	10	1
Collamer	10*	. .	. .
Wade	3*	. .	. .
Read	1	. .	. .
Sumner	1	. .	. .
Fremont	1	. .	. .
Clay	. .	2	1

Before the third ballot was announced changes were made to Lincoln, giving him 354 votes, or 120 more than the number necessary to nominate.

* Withdrawn.

the streets ring with shouts for the Illinois candidate for President.

Until after the nomination of Lincoln little attention had been given to the contest for Vice-President. Had Seward been nominated, Lincoln would have been unanimously tendered the second place on the ticket, but with Lincoln nominated for the first place the leading friends of Lincoln at once suggested to the friends of Seward that they should name the candidate for the Vice-Presidency. Mr. Greeley was sent to Governor Morgan to proffer the nomination to him if he would accept it, or in case of his refusal to ask him to name some man who would be acceptable to the friends of Seward. Governor Morgan not only declined to accept it himself, but he declined to suggest any one of Seward's friends for the place. Not only Governor Morgan, but Mr. Evarts and Mr. Weed, all refused to be consulted on the subject of the Vice-Presidency, and they did it in a temper that indicated contempt for the action of the convention. Hamlin was nominated, not because Seward desired it, for New York gave him a bare majority on the first ballot, but because he was then the most prominent of the Democratic-Republicans in the East. The contest was really between Hamlin and Cassius M. Clay. Clay was supported chiefly because he was a resident of a Southern State and to relieve the party from the charge of presenting a sectional ticket; but as there were no Southern electoral votes to be fought for, Hamlin was wisely preferred, and he was nominated on the second ballot by a vote of 367 to 86 for Clay.* Not-

---

* The following were the ballots for Vice-President:

	First.	Second.
Hamlin	194	367
Clay	101½	86
Hickman	58	18

withstanding Governor Morgan's keen disappointment at the defeat of Seward, he was easily prevailed upon to remain at the head of the National Committee, thus charging him with the management of the national campaign.

I called on Thurlow Weed at his headquarters during the evening after the nominations had been made, expecting that, with all his disappointment, he would be ready to co-operate for the success of the ticket. I found him sullen, and offensive in both manner and expression. He refused even to talk about the contest, and intimated very broadly that Pennsylvania, having defeated Seward, could now elect Curtin and Lincoln. Governor Curtin also visited Mr. Weed before he left Chicago, but received no word of encouragement from the disappointed Seward leader.* Weed had been defeated in his greatest effort, and the one great dream of his life had perished. He never forgave Governor Curtin until the day of his death, nor did Seward maintain any more than severely civil relations with Curtin during the whole time that he was at the head of the State Department. I called on

	First.	Second.
Reeder	51*	. .
Banks	38½*	. .
Davis (Henry Winter) . . .	8*	. .
Dayton	3	. .
Houston	3	. .
Read	1	. .

* Withdrawn.

* I called on Morgan the night after the nomination was made. He treated me civilly, but with marked coolness, and I then called on Weed, who was very rude indeed. He said to me, "You have defeated the man who of all others was most revered by the people and wanted as President. You and Lane want to be elected, and to elect Lincoln you must elect yourselves." That was all, and I left him.—*Governor Curtin's Letter to the Author,* August 18, 1891.

Seward but once after the organization of the Lincoln Cabinet, and not for the purpose of soliciting any favors from him, but he was so frigid that I never ventured to trespass upon him again. Three months after the Chicago convention, when the battle in Pennsylvania was raging with desperation on both sides, I twice wrote to Weed giving the condition of affairs in the State and urging the co-operation of himself and Chairman Morgan to assure the success of the ticket in October. He made no response to either letter, and it so happened that we never met thereafter during his life.

The contest in Pennsylvania was really the decisive battle of the national campaign. A party had to be created out of inharmonious elements, and the commercial and financial interests of the State were almost solidly against us. I cannot recall five commercial houses of prominence in the city of Philadelphia where I could have gone to solicit a subscription to the Lincoln campaign with reasonable expectation that it would not be resented, and of all our prominent financial men I recall only Anthony J. Drexel who actively sympathized with the Republican cause. Money would have been useless for any but legitimate purposes, but the organization of a great State to crystallize incongruous elements was an immense task and involved great labor and expense. I visited Chairman Morgan in New York, presented the situation to him, but he was listless and indifferent, and not one dollar of money was contributed from New York State to aid the Curtin contest in Pennsylvania. The entire contributions for the State committee for that great battle aggregated only $12,000, of which $2000 were a contribution for rent of headquarters and $3000 were expended in printing. Three weeks before the election, when I felt reasonably confident of the success of the State ticket, I again visited Governor Morgan, and met with him Moses Taylor and one or two others, and they were finally so much impressed with the importance of carrying a Republican Congress that they agreed to raise $4300 and send it direct to some six or seven debatable Congressional districts I indicated. Beyond this aid rendered to Pennsylvania from New York the friends of Mr. Seward took no part whatever in the great October battle that made Abraham Lincoln President. Curtin was elected by a majority of 32,164, and Lane was elected in Indiana by 9757. With Curtin the Republicans carried 19 of the 25 Congressmen, and with Lane the Republicans of Indiana carried 7 of the 11 Congressmen of that State. Thus was the election of a Republican President substantially accomplished in October by the success of the two men who had defeated William H. Seward and nominated Abraham Lincoln at Chicago.

A VISIT TO LINCOLN.

I NEVER met Abraham Lincoln until early in January, 1861, some two months after his election to the Presidency. I had been brought into very close and confidential relations with him by correspondence during the Pennsylvania campaign of 1860. His letters were frequent, and always eminently practical, on the then supreme question of electing the Republican State ticket in October. It was believed on all sides that unless Pennsylvania could be carried in October, Lincoln's defeat would be certain in November. Pennsylvania was thus accepted as the key to Republican success, and Lincoln naturally watched the struggle with intense interest. In accordance with his repeated solicitations, he was advised from the headquarters of the State Committee, of which I was chairman, of all the varied phases of the struggle. It soon became evident from his inquiries and versatile suggestions that he took nothing for granted. He had to win the preliminary battle in October, and he left nothing undone within his power to ascertain the exact situation and to understand every peril involved in it.

The Republican party in Pennsylvania, although then but freshly organized, had many different elements and bitter factional feuds within its own household, and all who actively participated in party efforts were more or less involved in them. I did not entirely escape the bit-

(Photo by Brady, Washington.)

ABRAHAM LINCOLN, 1859.

terness that was displayed in many quarters. Had I been simply a private in the ranks, it would have been of little consequence to Lincoln whether I was competent to conduct so important a campaign or not; but when he was advised, not only from within the State, but from friends outside the State as well, that the party organization in Pennsylvania was not equal to the pressing necessities of the occasion, he adopted his own characteristic methods to satisfy himself on the subject.

I had met David Davis and Leonard Swett for the first time at the Chicago Convention, and of course we knew little of each other personally. Some time toward midsummer, when the campaign in Pennsylvania was well under way, Davis and Swett entered my headquarters together and handed me a letter from Lincoln, in which he said that these gentlemen were greatly interested in his election—that they were on East looking into the contest generally, and he would be pleased if I would furnish them every facility to ascertain the condition of affairs in the State. I was very glad to do so, and they spent two days at my headquarters, where every information was given them and the methods and progress of the organization opened to them without reserve. They saw that for the first time in the history of Pennsylvania politics the new party had been organized by the State Committee in every election district of the State, and that everything that could be done had been done to put the party in condition for a successful battle.

After Davis and Swett had finished their work and notified me of their purpose to leave during the night, they invited me to a private dinner at which none were present but ourselves. During the course of the dinner Swett informed me that they were very happy now to be able to tell me the real purpose of their mission—that had their information been less satisfactory they would have returned without advising me of it. He said that they had been instructed by Lincoln to come to Pennsylvania and make personal examination into the condition of affairs, especially as to the efficiency of the party organization of the State, and that his reason for doing so was that he had been admonished that the direction of the campaign by the State Committee was incompetent and likely to result in disaster. They added that, inasmuch as their answer to Lincoln must be that the organization was the best that they had ever known in any State, they felt entirely at liberty to disclose to me why they had come and what the result of their inquiry was.

After their return to Illinois letters from Lincoln were not less frequent, and they were entirely confident in tone and exhibited the utmost faith in the direction of the great Pennsylvania battle. I twice sent him during the campaign—once about the middle of August, and again in the latter part of September—a carefully-prepared estimate of the vote for Governor by counties that had been made up by a methodical and reasonably accurate canvass of each election district of the State. The first gave Governor Curtin a majority of 12,000, leaving out of the estimate a considerable doubtful vote. The last estimate gave Curtin a majority of 17,000, also omitting the doubtful contingent. The result not only justified the estimates which had been sent to him in the aggregate majority, but it justified the detailed estimates of the vote of nearly or quite every county in the State

Curtin's majority was nearly double the last estimate given him because of the drift of the doubtful vote to our side, and, being successful in what was regarded as the decisive battle of the campaign, Lincoln accorded me more credit than I merited. From that time until the day of his death I was one of those he called into coun-

sel in every important political emergency. Much as I
grieved over the loss of the many to me precious things
which I had gathered about my home in Chambersburg,
and serious as was the destruction of all my property
when the vandals of McCausland burned the town in
1864, I have always felt that the greatest loss I sustained
was in the destruction of my entire correspondence with
Abraham Lincoln.

About the 1st of January, 1861, I received a telegram
from Lincoln requesting me to come to Springfield. It
is proper to say that this invitation was in answer to a
telegram from me advising him against the appointment
of General Cameron as Secretary of War. The factional
feuds and bitter antagonisms of that day have long since
perished, and I do not purpose in any way to revive
them. On the 31st of December, Lincoln had delivered
to Cameron at Springfield a letter notifying him that he
would be nominated for a Cabinet position. This fact
became known immediately upon Cameron's return, and
inspired very vigorous opposition to his appointment, in
which Governor Curtin, Thaddeus Stevens, David Wilmot, and many others participated. Although the Senate, of which I was a member, was just about to organize,
I hastened to Springfield and reached there at seven
o'clock in the evening. I had telegraphed Lincoln of
the hour that I should arrive and that I must return at
eleven the same night. I went directly from the dépôt
to Lincoln's house and rang the bell, which was answered
by Lincoln himself opening the door. I doubt whether
I wholly concealed my disappointment at meeting him.
Tall, gaunt, ungainly, ill clad, with a homeliness of
manner that was unique in itself, I confess that my heart
sank within me as I remembered that this was the man
chosen by a great nation to become its ruler in the gravest period of its history. I remember his dress as if it

were but yesterday—snuff-colored and slouchy pantaloons; open black vest, held by a few brass buttons;
straight or evening dress-coat, with tightly-fitting sleeves
to exaggerate his long, bony arms, and all supplemented
by an awkwardness that was uncommon among men of
intelligence. Such was the picture I met in the person
of Abraham Lincoln. We sat down in his plainly furnished parlor, and were uninterrupted during the nearly
four hours that I remained with him, and little by little,
as his earnestness, sincerity, and candor were developed
in conversation, I forgot all the grotesque qualities which
so confounded me when I first greeted him. Before half
an hour had passed I learned not only to respect, but,
indeed, to reverence the man.

It is needless to give any account of the special mission on which I was called to Springfield, beyond the
fact that the tender of a Cabinet position to Pennsylvania
was recalled by him on the following day, although renewed and accepted two months later, when the Cabinet
was finally formed in Washington. It was after the
Pennsylvania Cabinet imbroglio was disposed of that
Lincoln exhibited his true self without reserve. For
more than two hours he discussed the gravity of the situation and the appalling danger of civil war. Although
he had never been in public office outside the Illinois
Legislature, beyond a single session of Congress, and had
little intercourse with men of national prominence during the twelve years after his return from Washington,
he exhibited remarkable knowledge of all the leading
public men of the country, and none could mistake the
patriotic purpose that inspired him in approaching the
mighty responsibility that had been cast upon him by
the people. He discussed the slavery question in all its
aspects and all the various causes which were used as
pretexts for rebellion, and he not only was master of the

4

whole question, but thoroughly understood his duty and was prepared to perform it. During this conversation I had little to say beyond answering an occasional question or suggestion from him, and I finally left him fully satisfied that he understood the political conditions in Pennsylvania nearly as well as I did myself, and entirely assured that of all the public men named for the Presidency at Chicago he was the most competent and the safest to take the helm of the ship of State and guide it through the impending storm. I saw many dark days akin to despair during the four years which recorded the crimsoned annals from Sumter to Appomattox, but I never had reason to change or seriously question that judgment.

I next met Abraham Lincoln at Harrisburg on the 22d of February, 1861, when he passed through the most trying ordeal of his life. He had been in Philadelphia the night before, where he was advised by letters from General Winfield Scott and his prospective Premier, Senator Seward, that he could not pass through Baltimore on the 23d without grave peril to his life. His route, as published to the world for some days, was from Philadelphia to Harrisburg on the morning of the 22d; to remain in Harrisburg over night as the guest of Governor Curtin; and to leave for Washington the next morning by the Northern Central Railway, that would take him through Baltimore about midday. A number of detectives under the direction of President Felton of the Philadelphia, Wilmington, and Baltimore Railroad, and Allan Pinkerton, chief of the well-known detective agency, were convinced from the information they obtained that Lincoln would be assassinated if he attempted to pass through Baltimore according to the published programme. A conference at the Continental Hotel in Philadelphia on the night of the 21st, at which

Lincoln was advised of the admonitions of Scott and Seward, had not resulted in any final determination as to his route to Washington. He was from the first extremely reluctant about any change, but it was finally decided that he should proceed to Harrisburg on the morning of the 22d and be guided by events.

The two speeches made by Lincoln on the 22d of February do not exhibit a single trace of mental disturbance from the appalling news he had received. He hoisted the stars and stripes to the pinnacle of Independence Hall early in the morning and delivered a brief address that was eminently characteristic of the man. He arrived at Harrisburg about noon, was received in the House of Representatives by the Governor and both branches of the Legislature, and there spoke with the same calm deliberation and incisiveness which marked all his speeches during the journey from Springfield to Washington. After the reception at the House another conference was held on the subject of his route to Washington, and, while every person present, with the exception of Lincoln, was positive in the demand that the programme should be changed, he still obstinately hesitated. He did not believe that the danger of assassination was serious.

The afternoon conference practically decided nothing, but it was assumed by those active in directing Lincoln's journey that there must be a change. Lincoln dined at the Jones House about five o'clock with Governor Curtin as host of the occasion. I recall as guests the names of Colonel Thomas A. Scott, Colonel Sumner, Colonel Lamon, Dr. Wallace, David Davis, Secretary Slifer, Attorney-General Purviance, Adjutant-General Russell, and myself. There were others at the table, but I do not recall them with certainty. Of that dinner circle, as I remember them, only three are now living—Governor

Curtin, Colonel Lamon, and the writer hereof. Mr. Judd was not a guest, as he was giving personal attention to Mrs. Lincoln, who was much disturbed by the suggestion to separate the President from her, and she narrowly escaped attracting attention to the movements which required the utmost secrecy.

It was while at dinner that it was finally determined that Lincoln should return to Philadelphia and go thence to Washington that night, as had been arranged in Philadelphia the night previous in the event of a decision to change the programme previously announced. No one who heard the discussion of the question could efface it from his memory. The admonitions received from General Scott and Senator Seward were made known to Governor Curtin at the table, and the question of a change of route was discussed for some time by every one with the single exception of Lincoln. He was the one silent man of the party, and when he was finally compelled to speak he unhesitatingly expressed his disapproval of the movement. With impressive earnestness he thus answered the appeal of his friends: "What would the nation think of its President stealing into the Capital like a thief in the night?" It was only when the other guests were unanimous in the expression that it was not a question for Lincoln to determine, but one for his friends to determine for him, that he finally agreed to submit to whatever was decided by those around him.

It was most fortunate that Colonel Scott was one of the guests at that dinner. He was wise and keen in perception and bold and swift in execution. The time was short, and if a change was to be made in Lincoln's route it was necessary for him to reach Philadelphia by eleven o'clock that night or very soon thereafter. Scott at once became master of ceremonies, and everything that was done was in obedience to his directions. There was a crowd of thousands around the hotel, anxious to see the new President and ready to cheer him to the uttermost. It was believed to be best that only one man should accompany Lincoln in his journey to Philadelphia and Washington, and Lincoln decided that Lamon should be his companion. Colonel Sumner, who felt that he had been charged with the safety of the President-elect, and whose silvered crown seemed to entitle him to precedence, earnestly protested against Lincoln leaving his immediate care, but it was deemed unsafe to have more than one accompany him, and the veteran soldier was compelled to surrender his charge. That preliminary question settled, Scott directed that Curtin, Lincoln, and Lamon should at once proceed to the front steps of the hotel, where there was a vast throng waiting to receive them, and that Curtin should call distinctly, so that the crowd could hear, for a carriage, and direct the coachman to drive the party to the Executive Mansion. That was the natural thing for Curtin to do—to take the President to the Governor's mansion as his guest, and it excited no suspicion whatever.

Before leaving the dining-room Governor Curtin halted Lincoln and Lamon at the door and inquired of Lamon whether he was well armed. Lamon had been chosen by Lincoln as his companion because of his exceptional physical power and prowess, but Curtin wanted assurance that he was properly equipped for defense. Lamon at once uncovered a small arsenal of deadly weapons, showing that he was literally armed to the teeth. In addition to a pair of heavy revolvers, he had a slung-shot and brass knuckles and a huge knife nestled under his vest. The three entered the carriage, and, as instructed by Scott, drove toward the Executive Mansion, but when near there the driver was ordered to take a circuitous route and to reach the railroad dépôt within half an hour. When Curtin and his party had gotten fairly away from the hotel I accompanied Scott to the railway dépôt, where he at once cleared one of his lines from Harrisburg to Philadelphia, so that there could be no obstruction upon it, as had been agreed upon at Philadelphia the evening before in case the change should be made. In the mean time he had ordered a locomotive and a single car to be brought to the eastern entrance of the dépôt, and at the appointed time the carriage arrived. Lincoln and Lamon emerged from the carriage and entered the car unnoticed by any except those interested in the matter, and after a quiet but fervent "Good-bye and God protect you!" the engineer quietly moved his train away on its momentous mission.

As soon as the train left I accompanied Scott in the work of severing all the telegraph lines which entered Harrisburg. He was not content with directing that it should be done, but he personally saw that every wire was cut. This was about seven o'clock in the evening. It had been arranged that the eleven o'clock train from Philadelphia to Washington should be held until Lincoln arrived, on the pretext of delivering an important package to the conductor. The train on which he was to leave Philadelphia was due in Washington at six in the morning, and Scott kept faithful vigil during the entire night, not only to see that there should be no restoration of the wires, but waiting with anxious solicitude for the time when he might hope to hear the good news that Lincoln had arrived in safety. To guard against every possible chance of imposition a special cipher was agreed upon that could not possibly be understood by any but the parties to it. It was a long, weary night of fretful anxiety to the dozen or more in Harrisburg who had knowledge of the sudden departure of Lincoln. No one attempted to sleep. All felt that the fate of the nation hung on the safe progress of Lincoln to Washington without detection on his journey. Scott, who was of heroic mould, several times tried to temper the severe strain of his anxiety by looking up railway matters, but he would soon abandon the listless effort, and thrice we strolled from the dépôt to the Jones House and back again, in aimless struggle to hasten the slowly-passing hours, only to find equally anxious watchers there and a wife whose sobbing heart could not be consoled. At last the eastern horizon was purpled with the promise of day. Scott reunited the broken lines for the lightning messenger, and he was soon gladdened by an unsigned dispatch from Washington, saying, " Plums delivered nuts safely." He whirled his hat high in the little telegraph office as he shouted, " Lincoln's in Washington," and we rushed to the Jones House and hurried a messenger to the Executive Mansion to spread the glad tidings that Lincoln had safely made his midnight journey to the Capital.

I have several times heard Lincoln refer to this journey, and always with regret. Indeed, he seemed to regard it as one of the grave mistakes in his public career. He was fully convinced, as Colonel Lamon has stated it, that "he had fled from a danger purely imaginary, and he felt the shame and mortification natural to a brave man under such circumstances." Mrs. Lincoln and her suite passed through Baltimore on the 23d without any sign of turbulence. The fact that there was not even a curious crowd brought together when she passed through the city—which then required considerable time, as the cars were taken across Baltimore by horses—confirmed Lincoln in his belief. It is needless now to discuss the question of real or imaginary danger in Lincoln passing through Baltimore at noonday according to the original programme. It is enough to know that there were reasonable grounds for apprehension that an attempt

might be made upon his life, even if there was not the
organized band of assassins that the detectives believed
to exist.   His presence in the city would have called out
an immense concourse of people, including thousands of
thoroughly disloyal roughs, who could easily have been
inspired to any measure of violence.   He simply acted
the part of a prudent man in his reluctant obedience to
the unanimous decision of his friends in Harrisburg
when he was suddenly sent back to Philadelphia to take
the midnight train for Washington, and there was no
good reason why he should have regretted it; but his
naturally sensitive disposition made him always feel
humiliated when it recurred to him.

The sensational stories published at the time of his
disguise for the journey were wholly untrue.   He was
reported as having been dressed in a Scotch cap and
cloak and as entering the car at the Broad and Prime
station by some private alley-way, but there was no truth
whatever in any of these statements.   I saw him leave
the dining-room at Harrisburg to enter the carriage with
Curtin and Lamon.   I saw him enter the car at the Harrisburg dépôt, and the only change in his dress was the
substitution of a soft slouch hat for the high one he had
worn during the day.   He wore the same overcoat that
he had worn when he arrived at Harrisburg, and the
only extra apparel he had about him was the shawl that
hung over his arm.   When he reached West Philadelphia
he was met by Superintendent Kenney, who had a carriage in waiting with a single detective in it.   Lincoln
and Lamon entered the carriage and Kenney mounted
the box with the driver.   They were in advance of the
time for the starting of the Baltimore train, and they
were driven around on Broad street, as the driver was
informed, in search of some one wanted by Kenney and
the detective, until it was time to reach the station.

When there they entered by the public doorway on Broad street, and passed directly along with other passengers to the car, where their berths had been engaged. The journey to Washington was entirely uneventful, and at six in the morning the train entered the Washington station on schedule time. Seward had been advised, by the return of his son from Philadelphia, of the probable execution of this programme, and he and Washburne were in the station and met the President and his party, and all drove together to Willard's Hotel. Thus ends the story of Lincoln's midnight journey from Harrisburg to the National Capital.

(Photo by Brady, Washington.)

LIEUT.-GENERAL WINFIELD SCOTT, 1861.

LINCOLN'S SORE TRIALS.

ABRAHAM LINCOLN arrived in Washington on the 23d of February, 1861, to accept the most appalling responsibilities ever cast upon any civil ruler of modern times. If he could have commanded the hearty confidence and co-operation of the leaders of his own party, his task would have been greatly lessened, but it is due to the truth of history to say that few, very few, of the Republican leaders of national fame had faith in Lincoln's ability for the trust assigned to him. I could name a dozen men, now idols of the nation, whose open distrust of Lincoln not only seriously embarrassed, but grievously pained and humiliated, him. They felt that the wrong man had been elected to the Presidency, and only their modesty prevented them, in each case, from naming the man who should have been chosen in his stead. Looking now over the names most illustrious in the Republican councils, I can hardly recall one who encouraged Lincoln by the confidence he so much needed. Even Seward, who had been notified as early as the 8th of December that he would be called as Premier of the new administration, and who soon thereafter had signified his acceptance of the office and continued in the most confidential relations with Lincoln, suddenly, on the 2d of March, formally notified Lincoln of his reconsideration of his acceptance. The only reason given was that circumstances had occurred since his acceptance which seemed to render it his duty "to ask leave to withdraw that consent." The circumstances referred to were the hopeless discord and bitter jealousies among party-leaders both in and out of the Cabinet.

Lincoln found a party without a policy; the strangest confusion and bitterest antagonisms pervading those who should have been in accord, not only in purpose, but in earnest sympathy, with him in the discharge of his great duties, and he was practically like a ship tempest-tossed without compass or rudder. Even the men called to his Cabinet did not give Lincoln their confidence and co-operation. No two of them seemed to have the same views as to the policy the administration should adopt. Seward ridiculed the idea of serious civil war, and then and thereafter renewed his bond for peace in sixty days, only to be protested from month to month and from year to year. Chase believed in peaceable disunion as alto-gether preferable to fraternal conflict, and urged his views with earnestness upon the President. Cameron, always eminently practical, was not misled by any senti-mental ideas and regarded war as inevitable. Welles was an amiable gentleman without any aggressive quali-ties whatever, and Smith and Bates were old and con-servative, while Blair was a politician with few of the qualities of a statesman.

A reasonably correct idea of the estimate placed upon Lincoln's abilities for his position may be obtained by turning to the eulogy on Seward delivered by Charles Francis Adams in 1873. Adams was a Republican mem-ber of Congress when Lincoln was chosen President, and he was Lincoln's Minister to England during the entire period of the war. In eulogizing Seward as the master-spirit of the administration and as the power behind the throne stronger than the throne itself, he said: "I must affirm, without hesitation, that in the history of our government down to this hour no experiment so rash has ever been made as that of electing to the head of affairs a man with so little previous preparation for his task as Mr. Lincoln." Indeed, Lincoln himself seems to have been profoundly impressed with his want of fitness for the position when he was first named as a candidate from his State. In 1859, after he had attained national reputation by his joint discussion with Douglas in the contest for Senator, Mr. Pickett, the editor of an Illinois Republican journal, wrote to him, urging that he should permit the use of his name for President. To this he answered: "I must in candor say I do not think myself fit for the Presidency. I certainly am flattered and gratified that some partial friends think of me in that connection, but I really think it best for our cause that no concerted effort, such as you suggest, should be made." Seward evidently agreed with his eulogist, Mr. Adams. That is clearly shown by the fact that in less than one month after the administration had been inaugurated he wrote out and submitted to the President a proposition to change the national issue from slavery to foreign war, in which he advised that war be at once declared against Spain and France unless satisfactory explanations were promptly received, and that the enforcement of the new policy should be individually assumed by the President himself or devolved on some member of his Cabinet. He added that while it was not in his special province, "I neither seek to evade nor assume the responsibility." In other words, Seward boldly proposed to change the national issue by a declaration of war against some foreign power, and to have himself assigned practically as Dictator. He assumed that the President was incompetent to his task, that his policy, if accepted, would be committed to himself for execution, and that he meant to be Dictator is clearly proved by the fact that in his formal proposition he provides that the policy "once adopted, the debates on it must end and all agree and abide."

Outside of the Cabinet the leaders were equally discordant and quite as distrustful of the ability of Lincoln to fill his great office. Sumner, Trumbull, Chandler, Wade, Henry Winter Davis, and the men to whom the nation then turned as the great representative men of the new political power, did not conceal their distrust of Lincoln, and he had little support from them at any time during his administration. Indeed, but for the support given him by the younger leaders of that day, among whom Blaine and Sherman were conspicuous, he would have been a President almost without a party. The one man who rendered him the greatest service of all at the beginning of the war was Stephen A. Douglas, his old competitor of Illinois. When the Republican leaders were hesitating and criticising their President, Douglas came to the front with all his characteristic courage and sagacity, and was probably the most trusted of all the Senators at the White House. It is not surprising that there was great confusion in the councils of the Republican leaders when suddenly compelled to face civil war, but it will surprise many intelligent readers at this day to learn of the general distrust and demoralization that existed among the men who should have been a solid phalanx of leadership in the crisis that confronted them. It must be remembered that there were no precedents in history to guide the new President. The relation of the States to the National Government had never been defined. The dispute over the sovereignty of the States had been continuous from the organization of the Republic until that time, and men of equal intelligence and patriotism widely differed as to the paramount authority of State and Nation. Nor were there any precedents in history of other civilizations that could throw any light upon the dark path of Lincoln. There have been republics and civil wars, but none that furnish any rule that could be applied to the peculiar condition of our dissevered States. The President was therefore compelled to decide for himself in the multitude of conflicting counsels what policy the administration should adopt, and even a less careful and conservative man than Lincoln would have been compelled, from the supreme necessities which surrounded him, to move with the utmost caution.

Lincoln could formulate no policy beyond mere generalities declaring his duty to preserve the integrity of the Union. He saw forts captured and arsenals gutted and States seceding with every preparation for war, and yet he could take no step to prepare the nation for the defense of its own life. The Border States were trembling in the balance, with a predominant Union sentiment in most of them, but ready to be driven into open rebellion the moment that he should declare in favor of what was called "coercion" by force of arms. Coercion and invasion of the sacred soil of the Southern States were terms which made even the stoutest Southern Union man tremble. As the administration had no policy that it could declare, every leader had a policy of his own, with every invitation to seek to magnify himself by declaring it. The capital was crowded with politicians of every grade. The place-seekers swarmed in numbers almost equal to the locusts of Egypt, and the President was pestered day and night by the leading statesmen of the country, who clamored for offices for their henchmen. I well remember the sad picture of despair his face presented when I happened to meet him alone for a few moments in the Executive Chamber as he spoke of the heartless spoilsmen who seemed to be utterly indifferent to the grave dangers which threatened the government. He said: "I seem like one sitting in a palace assigning apartments to importunate applicants while the structure is on fire and likely soon to perish in ashes."

Turn where Lincoln might, there was hardly a silver lining to the dark cloud that overshadowed him. The Senate that met in Executive session when he was inaugurated contained but 29 Republicans to 32 Democrats, with 1 bitterly hostile American, and 4 vacancies from Southern States that never were filled. It was only by the midsummer madness of secession and the retirement of the Southern Senators that he was given the majority in both branches of Congress, and when he turned to the military arm of the government he was appalled by the treachery of the men to whom the nation should have been able to look for its preservation. If any one would study the most painful and impressive object-lesson on this point, let him turn to Greeley's *American Conflict* and learn from two pictures how the stars of chieftains glittered and faded until unknown men filled their places and led the Union armies to victory. In the first volume of Greeley's history, which was written just at the beginning of the war and closed with the commencement of hostilities, there is a page containing the portraits of twelve men, entitled "Union Generals." The central figure is the veteran Scott, and around him are Fremont, Butler, McDowell, Wool, Halleck, McClellan, Burnside, Hunter, Hooker, Buell, and Anderson. These were the chieftains in whom the country then confided, and to whom Lincoln turned as the men who could be entrusted with the command of armies. In the second volume of Greeley's history, published after the close of the war, there is another picture entitled "Union Generals," and there is not one face to be found in the

last that is in the first. Grant is the central figure of
the Heroes of the Union at the close of the war, with
the faces of Sherman, Sheridan, Thomas, Meade, Hancock, Blair, Howard, Terry, Curtis, Banks, and Gilmore
around him. In short, the military chieftains who saved
the Union in the flame of battle had to be created by
the exigencies of war, while the men upon whom the
President was compelled to lean when the conflict
began one by one faded from the list of successful
generals.

The ability of the government to protect its own life
when wanton war was inaugurated by the Southern Confederacy may be well illustrated by an interview between
the President, General Winfield Scott, Governor Curtin,
and myself immediately after the surrender of Sumter.
The President telegraphed to Governor Curtin and to me
as Chairman of the Military Committee of the Senate to
come to Washington as speedily as possible for consultation as to the attitude Pennsylvania should assume in the
civil conflict that had been inaugurated. Pennsylvania
was the most exposed of all the border States, and, being
the second State of the Union in population, wealth, and
military power, it was of the utmost importance that she
should lead in defining the attitude of the loyal States.
Sumter was surrendered on Saturday evening, the 13th
of April, 1861, and on Monday morning Governor Curtin and.I were at the White House to meet the President
and the Commander-in-Chief of the armies at ten o'clock
in the morning. I had never before met General Scott.
I had read of him with all the enthusiasm of a boy, as
he was a major-general before I was born, had noted
with pride his brilliant campaign in Mexico, and remembered that he was accepted by all Americans as the Great
Captain of the Age. I assumed, of course, that he was
infallible in all matters pertaining to war, and when I

5

met him it was with a degree of reverence that I had seldom felt for any other mortal.

Curtin and I were a few minutes in advance of the appointed time for the conference, and as the Cabinet was in session we were seated in the reception-room. There were but few there when we entered it, and a number of chairs were vacant. We sat down by a window looking out upon the Potomac, and in a few minutes the tall form of General Scott entered. In the mean time a number of visitors had arrived and every chair in the room was occupied. Scott advanced and was cordially greeted by Governor Curtin and introduced to me. He was then quite feeble, unable to mount a horse by reason of a distressing spinal affection; and I well remember the punctilious ideas of the old soldier, who refused to accept either Curtin's chair or mine because there were not three vacant chairs in the room, although he could not remain standing without suffering agony. We presented the ludicrous spectacle of three men standing for nearly half an hour, and one of them feeble in strength and greatly the senior of the others in years, simply because there were not enough chairs for the entire party. With all his suffering he was too dignified even to lean against the wall, although it was evident to both of us that he was in great pain from his ceremonial ideas about accepting the chair of another. When we were ushered into the President's room the practical work of our mission was soon determined. The question had been fully considered by the President and the Secretary of War, who was a Pennsylvanian. Governor Curtin speedily perfected and heartily approved of the programme they had marked out, and we had little to do beyond informing them how speedily it could be executed. How quickly Pennsylvania responded to the request of the government will be understood when I state that in a single day a bill embracing all the features desired was passed by both branches and approved by Governor Curtin.

It was only after the work of Pennsylvania had been defined and disposed of that I began to get some insight into the utterly hopeless condition of the government. I found General Scott disposed to talk rather freely about the situation, and I ventured to question him as to the condition of the capital and his ability to defend it in case of an attack by General Beauregard. The answer to the first question I ventured was very assuring, coming from one whom I supposed to know all about war, and to one who knew just nothing at all about it. I asked General Scott whether the capital was in danger. His answer was, "No, sir, the capital is not in danger, the capital is not in danger." Knowing that General Scott could not have a large force at his command, knowing also that General Beauregard had a formidable force at his command at Charleston, and that the transportation of an army from Charleston to Washington would be the work of only a few days, I for the first time began to inquire in my own mind whether this great Chieftain was, after all, equal to the exceptional necessities of the occasion. I said to him that, if it was a proper question for him to answer, I would like to know how many men he had in Washington for its defense. His prompt answer was, "Fifteen hundred, sir; fifteen hundred men and two batteries." I then inquired whether Washington was a defensible city. This inquiry cast a shadow over the old veteran's face as he answered, "No, sir; Washington is not a defensible city." He then seemed to consider it necessary to emphasize his assertions of the safety of the capital, and he pointed to the Potomac, that was visible from the President's window. Said he: "You see that vessel?—a sloop of war, sir, a sloop of war." I looked out and saw the vessel, but I could not help thinking, as I looked beyond to Arlington Heights, that one or two batteries, even of the ineffective class of those days, would knock the sloop of war to pieces in half an hour.

As Johnson, Cooper, and a number of other able soldiers had left the army but a short time before, I felt some anxiety to know who were commanding the forces under General Scott in Washington. He gave me their names, and within three days thereafter I saw that two of them had resigned and were already in Richmond and enlisted in the Confederate service. My doubts multiplied, and a great idol was shattered before I left the White House that morning. I could not resist the conviction that General Scott was past all usefulness; that he had no adequate conception of the contest before us; and that he rested in confidence in Washington when there was not a soldier of average intelligence in that city who did not know that Beauregard could capture it at any time within a week. My anxiety deepened with my doubts, and I continued my inquiries with the old warrior by asking how many men General Beauregard had at Charleston. The old chieftain's head dropped almost upon his breast at this question, and a trace of despair was visible as he answered in tremulous tones: "General Beauregard commands more men at Charleston than I command on the continent east of the frontier." I asked him how long it would require Beauregard to transport his army to Washington. He answered that it might be done in three or four days. I then repeated the question, "General, is not Washington in great danger?" The old warrior was at once aroused, straightened himself up in his chair with a degree of dignity that was crushing, and answered—"No, sir, the

capital can't be taken; the capital can't be taken, sir."
President Lincoln listened to the conversation with evident interest, but said nothing. He sat intently gazing
at General Scott, and whirling his spectacles around in
his fingers. When General Scott gave the final answer
that the capital could not be taken, Lincoln, in his
quaint way, said to General Scott, "It does seem to me,
general, that if I were Beauregard I would take Washington." This expression from the President electrified
the old war-lion again, and he answered with increased
emphasis, "Mr. President, the capital can't be taken,
sir; it can't be taken."

There was but one conclusion that could be accepted
as the result of this interview, and that was that the
great Chieftain of two wars and the worshiped Captain
of the Age was in his dotage and utterly unequal to the
great duty of meeting the impending conflict. Governor
Curtin and I left profoundly impressed with the conviction that the incompetency of General Scott was one of
the most serious of the multiplied perils which then confronted the Republic. I need not repeat how General
Scott failed in his early military movements; how he
divided his army and permitted the enemy to unite and
defeat him at Bull Run; how General McClellan, the
Young Napoleon of the time, was called from his victories in Western Virginia to take command of the
army; how that change reinspired the loyal people of
the nation in the confidence of speedy victories and the
overthrow of the rebellion; how he and his Chief soon
got to cross purposes; and how, after months of quarrel,
the old Chieftain was prevailed upon to resign his place.
The inside history of his retirement has never been written, and it is best that it should not. President Lincoln,
Secretary Cameron, and Thomas A. Scott were the only
men who could have written it from personal knowledge,

They are dead, and an interesting chapter of history has perished with them.

Such was the condition of the government at the opening of our civil war. A great soldier was at the head of our army, with all his faculties weakened by the infirmities of age, and we were compelled to grope in the dark day after day, week after week, month after month, and even year after year, until chieftains could be created to lead our armies to final victories. It must be remembered also that public sentiment had at that time no conception of the cruel sacrifices of war. The fall of a single soldier, Colonel Ellsworth, at Alexandria cast a profound gloom over the entire country, and the loss of comparatively few men at Big Bethel and Ball's Bluff convulsed the people from Maine to California. No one dreamed of the sacrifice of life that a desperate war must involve. I remember meeting General Burnside, General Heintzelman, and one or two other officers of the Army of the Potomac at Willard's Hotel in December, 1861. The weather had been unusually favorable, the roads were in excellent condition, and there was general impatience at McClellan's tardiness in moving against Manassas and Richmond. I naturally shared the impatience that was next to universal, and I inquired of General Burnside why it was that the army did not move. He answered that it would not be a difficult task for McClellan's army to capture Manassas, march upon Richmond, and enter the Confederate capital; but he added with emphasis that he regarded as conclusive that "It would cost ten thousand men to do it." I was appalled to silence when compelled to consider so great a sacrifice for the possession of the insurgents' capital. Ten times ten thousand men, and even more, fell in the battles between the Potomac and Richmond before the stars and bars fell from the Richmond State House, but in the fall of 1861 the proposition to sacrifice ten thousand lives to possess the Confederate capital would have been regarded by all as too appalling to contemplate. Indeed, we were not only utterly unprepared for war, but we were utterly unprepared for its sacrifices and its bereavements; and President Lincoln was compelled to meet this great crisis and patiently await the fullness of time to obtain chieftains and armies and to school the people to the crimsoned story necessary to tell of the safety of the Republic.

LINCOLN'S CHARACTERISTICS.

ABRAHAM LINCOLN was eminently human. As the old lady said about General Jackson when she had finally reached his presence, "He's only a man, after all." Although much as other men in the varied qualities which go to make up a single character, taking him all in all, "none but himself can be his parallel." Of all the public men I have met, he was the most difficult to analyze. His characteristics were more original, more diversified, more intense in a sober way, and yet more flexible under many circumstances, than I have ever seen in any other. Many have attempted to portray Lincoln's characteristics, and not a few have assumed to do it with great confidence. Those who have spoken most confidently of their knowledge of his personal qualities are, as a rule, those who saw least of them below the surface. He might have been seen every day during his Presidential term without ever reaching the distinctive qualities which animated and guided him, and thus hundreds of writers have assumed that they understood him when they had never seen the inner inspirations of the man at all. He was a stranger to deceit, incapable of dissembling; seemed to be the frankest and freest of conversationalists, and yet few understood him even reasonably well, and none but Lincoln ever thoroughly understood Lincoln. If I had seen less of him

(Photo by Gutekunst, Philadelphia.)

ABRAHAM LINCOLN AND HIS SON TAD.

I might have ventured with much greater confidence to attempt a portrayal of his individuality, but I saw him many times when Presidential honors were forgotten in Presidential sorrows, and when his great heart throbbed upon his sleeve. It was then that his uncommon qualities made themselves lustrous and often startled and confused his closest friends.

I regard Lincoln as very widely misunderstood in one of the most important attributes of his character. It has been common, during the last twenty-five years, to see publications relating to Lincoln from men who assumed that they enjoyed his full confidence. In most and perhaps all cases the writers believed what they stated, but those who assumed to speak most confidently on the subject were most mistaken. Mr. Lincoln gave his confidence to no living man without reservation. He trusted many, but he trusted only within the carefully-studied limitations of their usefulness, and when he trusted he confided, as a rule, only to the extent necessary to make that trust available. He had as much faith in mankind as is common amongst men, and it was not because he was of a distrustful nature or because of any specially selfish attribute of his character that he thus limited his confidence in all his intercourse with men. In this view of Lincoln I am fully sustained by those who knew him best. The one man who saw more of him in all the varied vicissitudes of his life from early manhood to his elevation to the Presidency was William H. Herndon, who was his close friend and law-partner for a full score of years. In analyzing the character of Lincoln he thus refers to his care as to confidants: "Mr. Lincoln never had a confidant, and therefore never unbosomed himself to others. He never spoke of his trials to me, or, so far as I knew, to any of his friends." David Davis, in whose sober judgment Lincoln had more confidence than in that of his other friends, and who held as intimate relations to him as was possible by any, says: "I knew the man so well; he was the most reticent, secretive man I ever saw or expect to see."

Leonard Swett is well known to have been the one whose counsels were among the most welcome to Lincoln, and who doubtless did counsel him with more freedom than any other man. In a letter given in Herndon's *Life of Lincoln* he says: "From the commencement of his life to its close I have sometimes doubted whether he ever asked anybody's advice about anything. He would listen to everybody; he would hear everybody; but he rarely, if ever, asked for opinions." He adds in the same letter: "As a politician and as President he arrived at all his conclusions from his own reflections, and when his conclusions were once formed he never doubted but what they were right." Speaking of his generally assumed frankness of character, Swett says, "One great public mistake of his [Lincoln's] character as generally received and acquiesced in is that he is considered by the people of this country as a frank, guileless, and unsophisticated man. There never was a greater mistake. Beneath a smooth surface of candor and apparent declaration of all his thoughts and feelings he exercised the most exalted tact and wisest discrimination. He handled and moved men remotely as we do pieces upon a chessboard. He retained through life all the friends he ever had, and he made the wrath of his enemies to praise him. This was not by cunning or intrigue in the low acceptation of the term, but by far-seeing reason and discernment. He always told only enough of his plans and purposes to induce the belief that he had communicated all; yet he reserved enough to have communicated nothing."

Mr. Herndon, in a lecture delivered on Lincoln to a

Springfield audience in 1866, said: "He [Lincoln] never revealed himself entirely to any one man, and therefore he will always to a certain extent remain enveloped in doubt. I always believed I could read him as thoroughly as any man, yet he was so different in many respects from any other one I ever met before or since his time that I cannot say I comprehended him." Mr. Lamon, who completes the circle of the men who were closest to Lincoln, the man who was chosen by Lincoln to accompany him on his midnight journey from Harrisburg to Washington, and whom he appointed Marshal of the District of Columbia to have him in the closest touch with himself, thus describes Lincoln in his biography: "Mr. Lincoln was a man apart from the rest of his kind—unsocial, cold, impassive; neither a good hater nor fond friend." And he adds that Lincoln "made simplicity and candor a mask of deep feelings carefully concealed, and subtle plans studiously veiled from all eyes but one."

I have seen Lincoln many times when he seemed to speak with the utmost candor, I have seen him many times when he spoke with mingled candor and caution, and I have seen him many times when he spoke but little and with extreme caution. It must not be inferred, because of the testimony borne to Lincoln's reticence generally and to his singular methods in speaking on subjects of a confidential nature, that he was ever guilty of deceit. He was certainly one of the most sincere men I have ever met, and he was also one of the most sagacious men that this or any other country has ever produced. He was not a man of cunning, in the ordinary acceptation of the word; not a man who would mislead in any way, unless by silence; and when occasion demanded he would speak with entire freedom as far as it was possible for him to speak at all. I regard him as one who believed that the truth was not always to be spoken, but who firmly believed, also, that only the truth should be spoken when it was necessary to speak at all.

Lincoln's want of trust in those closest to him was often a great source of regret, and at times of mortification. I have many times heard Mr. Swett and Mr. Lamon, and occasionally Mr. Davis, speak of his persistent reticence on questions of the gravest public moment which seemed to demand prompt action by the President. They would confer with him, as I did myself at times, earnestly advising and urging action on his part, only to find him utterly impassible and incomprehensible. Neither by word nor expression could any one form the remotest idea of his purpose, and when he did act in many cases he surprised both friends and foes. When he nominated Mr. Stanton as Secretary of War there was not a single member of his Cabinet who had knowledge of his purpose to do so until it was done, and when he appointed Mr. Chase Chief-Justice there was not a man living, of the hundreds who had advised him and pressed their friends upon him, who had any intimation as to even the leaning of his mind on the subject. I remember on one occasion, when we were alone in the Executive Chamber, he discussed the question of the Chief-Justiceship for fully half an hour; named the men who had been prominently mentioned in connection with the appointment; spoke of all of them with apparent freedom; sought and obtained my own views as to the wisdom of appointing either of them,—and when the conversation ended I had no more idea as to the bent of his mind than if I had been conversing with the Sphinx. I suggested to him, in closing the conversation, that his views on the subject were very much more important than mine, and that I would be very glad to have them, to which he gave this characteristic answer: "Well, McClure, the fact is I'm 'shut pan' on that question."

Lincoln's intellectual organization has been portrayed by many writers, but so widely at variance as to greatly confuse the general reader. Indeed, he was the most difficult of all men to analyze. He did not rise above the average man by escaping a common mingling of greatness and infirmities. I believe he was very well described in a single sentence by Mr. Herndon when he said: "The truth about Mr. Lincoln is, that he read less and thought more than any man in his sphere in America." Tested by the standard of many other great men, Lincoln was not great, but tested by the only true standard of his own achievements, he may justly appear in history as one of the greatest of American statesmen. Indeed, in some most essential attributes of greatness I doubt whether any of our public men ever equaled him. We have had men who could take a higher intellectual grasp of any abstruse problem of statesmanship, but few have ever equaled, and none excelled, Lincoln in the practical, common-sense, and successful solution of the gravest problems ever presented in American history. He possessed a peculiarly receptive and analytical mind. He sought information from every attainable source. He sought it persistently, weighed it earnestly, and in the end reached his own conclusions. When he had once reached a conclusion as to a public duty, there was no human power equal to the task of changing his purpose. He was self-reliant to an uncommon degree, and yet as entirely free from arrogance of opinion as any public man I have ever known.

Judged by the records of his administration, Lincoln is now regarded as the most successful Executive the Republic has ever had. When it is considered what peculiarly embarrassing and momentous issues were presented to him for decision, and issues for which history had no precedents, it is entirely safe to say that no man has ever equaled him as a successful ruler of a free people. This success was due chiefly to one single quality of the man—the will of the people was his guiding star. He sprang from the people and from close to Mother Earth. He grew up with the people, and in all his efforts, convictions, and inspirations he was ever in touch with the people. When President he looked solely to the considerate judgment of the American people to guide him in the solution of all the vexed questions which were presented to him. In all the struggles of mean ambition and all the bitter jealousies of greatness which constantly surged around him, and in all the constant and distressing discord that prevailed in his Cabinet during the dark days which shadowed him with grief, Lincoln ever turned to study with ceaseless care the intelligent expression of the popular will.

Unlike all Presidents who had preceded him, he came into office without a fixed and accepted policy. Civil war plunged the government into new and most perplexing duties. The people were unschooled to the sad necessities which had to be accepted to save the Republic. Others would have rushed in to offend public sentiment by the violent acceptance of what they knew must be accepted in the end. These men greatly vexed and embarrassed Lincoln in his sincere efforts to advance the people and the government to the full measure of the sacrifices which were inevitable; but Lincoln waited patiently—waited until in the fullness of time the judgment of the people was ripened for action, and then, and then only, did Lincoln act. Had he done otherwise, he would have involved the country in fearful peril both at home and abroad, and it was his constant study of, and obedience to, the honest judgment of the people of the nation that saved the Republic and that enshrined him in history as the greatest of modern rulers.

If there are yet any intelligent Americans who believe that Lincoln was an innocent, rural, unsophisticated character, it is time that they should be undeceived. I venture the assertion, without fear of successful contradiction, that Abraham Lincoln was the most sagacious of all the public men of his day in either political party. He was therefore the master-politician of his time. He was not a politician as the term is now commonly applied and understood; he knew nothing about the countless methods which are employed in the details of political effort; but no man knew better—indeed, I think no man knew so well as he did—how to summon and dispose of political ability to attain great political results; and this work he performed with unfailing wisdom and discretion in every contest for himself and for the country.

A pointed illustration of his sagacity and of his cautious methods in preventing threatened evil or gaining promised good is presented by his action in 1862 when the first army draft was made in Pennsylvania. There was then no national conscription law, and volunteering had ceased to fill up our shattered armies. A draft under the State law was necessary to fill a requisition made upon Pennsylvania for troops. The need for immediate reinforcements was very pressing, and in obedience to the personal request of both Lincoln and Governor Curtin I accepted the ungracious task of organizing and executing the draft under the State laws. How promptly the task was executed may be understood when I say that within sixty days the entire State was enrolled, quotas adjusted, the necessary exemptions made, the draft executed, and seventeen organized regiments sent to the front, and without a dollar of cost to either the State or National Governments for duties performed in my office beyond the salaries of two clerks. While there were mutterings of disloyalty in a very few sections of Pennsylvania, and they only within a very limited circle, there was one sore spot where open rebellion was threatened. That was Cass township, Schuylkill county. The Mollie Maguires were then just approaching the zenith of their criminal power, and Cass township was the centre of that lawless element. Thirteen murders had been committed in that district within a few years, and not one murderer had been brought to punishment. This banded criminal organization was as disloyal to the government as it was to law, and it was with the utmost difficulty that even an imperfect enumeration had been made and the quota adjusted to be supplied by draft. The draft was made, however, and on the day fixed for the conscripts to take the cars and report at Harrisburg the criminal element of the district not only refused to respond to the call, but its leaders came to the station and drove other conscripts violently from the dépôt.

It was open, defiant rebellion. I at once reported the facts to Secretary Stanton, who promptly answered, directing that the draft should be enforced at every hazard, and placing one Philadelphia regiment and one regiment at Harrisburg subject to the orders of the Governor, with instructions to send them at once to the scene of revolt. Fearing that the Secretary did not fully comprehend the peril of a conflict between the military and the citizens, Governor Curtin directed me to telegraph more fully to Secretary Stanton, suggesting his further consideration of the subject. His answer was promptly given, repeating his order for the military to move at once to Cass township and enforce the law at the point of the bayonet. The regiments were given marching orders, and reached Pottsville on the following day. I felt that a conflict between the military and citizens in any part of the State

6

must be very disastrous to the loyal cause, and after full consultation with Governor Curtin, in obedience to his directions, I telegraphed to Lincoln in cipher asking him to consider the subject well. This was in the early part of the day, and I was surprised and distressed when evening came without any reply. When I entered the breakfast-room of the hotel the next morning I saw seated at the table Assistant Adjutant-General Townsend of the United States Army. I knew him well, and when he saw me he beckoned me to his side and asked me to breakfast with him. We were out of hearing of any others at the table, and he at once stated to me the purpose of his visit. He had arrived at three o'clock in the morning, and was waiting to see me as soon as I should appear. He said: "I have no orders to give you, but I came solely to deliver a personal message from President Lincoln in these words: 'Say to McClure that I am very desirous to have the laws fully executed, but it might be well, in an extreme emergency, to be content with the appearance of executing the laws; I think McClure will understand.'" To this General Townsend added: "I have now fulfilled my mission; I do not know to what it relates."

I of course made no explanation to General Townsend, but hurried from the breakfast-table to summon Benjamin Bannan from Pottsville to Harrisburg as speedily as possible. He was the commissioner of draft for that county, a warm friend of the President, and a man of unusual intelligence and discretion. He reached Harrisburg the same day, and Lincoln's instructions were frankly explained to him. No one had any knowledge of them but ourselves and the Governor. Commissioner Bannan appreciated the necessity of avoiding a collision between the military and the citizens of Cass township, but, said he, " How can it be done? How can the laws even appear to have been executed?" I told him that in a number of cases evidence had been presented, after the quotas had been adjusted and the draft ordered, to prove that the quotas had been filled by volunteers who had enlisted in some town or city outside of their townships. In all such cases, where the evidence was clear, the order for the draft was revoked because the complement of men had been filled. I said only by such evidence from Cass township could the order for the draft be revoked and the arrest of the conscripted men for service be avoided. He intuitively comprehended the gravity of the situation, and took the first train home. By the next evening he was back and laid before me a number of affidavits in regular form, apparently executed by citizens of Cass township, which, if uncontradicted, proved that their quota was entirely full. I asked no explanations, but at once indorsed upon the testimony that as the quota of Cass township had been filled by volunteers, the draft was inoperative in that district and its conscripts would not be held to service.

I have never made inquiry into the method of obtaining those affidavits, and there is none now living who could give any information about it, as Mr. Bannan has long since joined the great majority beyond. The Governor had, in the mean time, halted the troops at Pottsville, and as the laws seemed to be executed in peace, the regiments were ordered back by the Governor and the conflict between the military and the Mollie Maguires was averted. Stanton never had knowledge of Lincoln's action in this matter, nor did a single member of his administration know of his intervention. Had Stanton been permitted to have his sway, he would have ruled in the tempest, and Pennsylvania would have inaugurated a rebellion of her own that might have reached fearful proportions, and that certainly would have greatly paralyzed the power of the loyal people of the State. I am quite sure that not until after the war was ended, and probably not for years thereafter, did any but Lincoln, Curtin, Bannan, and myself have any knowledge of this important adjustment of the Cass township rebellion.

LINCOLN IN POLITICS.

IF Abraham Lincoln was not a master politician, I am
entirely ignorant of the qualities which make up such
a character. In a somewhat intimate acquaintance with
the public men of the country for a period of more than
a generation, I have never met one who made so few
mistakes in politics as Lincoln. The man who could
call Seward as Premier of his administration, with Weed
the power behind the Premier, often stronger than the
Premier himself, and yet hold Horace Greeley even
within the ragged edges of the party lines, and the man
who could call Simon Cameron to his Cabinet in Pennsylvania without alienating Governor Curtin, and who
could remove Cameron from his Cabinet without alienating Cameron, would naturally be accepted as a man of
much more than ordinary political sagacity. Indeed, I
have never known one who approached Lincoln in the
peculiar faculty of holding antagonistic elements to his
own support, and maintaining close and often apparently
confidential relations with each without offense to the
other. This is the more remarkable from the fact that
Lincoln was entirely without training in political management. I remember on one occasion, when there was
much concern felt about a political contest in Pennsylvania, he summoned half a dozen or more Pennsylvania
Republicans to a conference at the White House. When

LINCOLN'S HOME IN CHILDHOOD.

LINCOLN'S HOME IN SPRINGFIELD.

we had gathered there he opened the subject in his quaint way by saying: "You know I never was a contriver; I don't know much about how things are done in politics, but I think you gentlemen understand the situation in your State, and I want to learn what may be done to ensure the success we all desire." He made exhaustive inquiry of each of the persons present as to the danger-signals of the contest, specially directing his questions to every weak point in the party lines and every strong point of the opposition. He was not content with generalities; he had no respect for mere enthusiasm. What he wanted was sober facts. He had abiding faith in the people, in their intelligence and their patriotism; and he estimated political results by ascertaining, as far as possible, the popular bearing of every vital question that was likely to arise, and he formed his conclusions by his keen intuitive perception as to how the people would be likely to deal with the issues.

While Lincoln had little appreciation of himself as candidate for President as late as 1859, the dream of reaching the Presidency evidently took possession of him in the early part of 1860, and his first efforts to advance himself as a candidate were singularly awkward and infelicitous. He had then no experience whatever as a leader of leaders, and it was not until he had made several discreditable blunders that he learned how much he must depend upon others if he would make himself President. Some Lincoln enthusiast in Kansas, with much more pretensions than power, wrote him in March, 1860, proposing to furnish a Lincoln delegation from that State to the Chicago Convention, and suggesting that Lincoln should pay the legitimate expenses of organizing, electing, and taking to the convention the promised Lincoln delegates. To this Lincoln replied that

"in the main, the use of money is wrong, but for certain objects in a political contest the use of some is both
right and indispensable." And he added, "If you shall
be appointed a delegate to Chicago I will furnish $100 to
bear the expenses of the trip." He heard nothing further
from the Kansas man until he saw an announcement in
the newspapers that Kansas had elected delegates and
instructed them for Seward. This was Lincoln's first
disappointment in his effort to organize his friends to
attain the Presidential nomination, but his philosophy
was well maintained. Without waiting to hear from his
friend who had contracted to bring a Lincoln delegation
from Kansas he wrote him, saying, "I see by the dispatches that since you wrote Kansas has appointed delegates instructed for Seward. Don't stir them up to
anger, but come along to the convention, and I will do
as I said about expenses." It is not likely that that
unfortunate experience cost Lincoln his $100, but it is
worthy of note that soon after his inauguration as President he gave the man a Federal office with a comfortable salary.

When he became seriously enlisted as a candidate for
the Presidential nomination, he soon learned that while
he could be of value as an adviser and organizer, the
great work had to be performed by others than himself.
He gathered around him a number of the ablest politicians of the West, among whom were Norman P. Judd,
David Davis, Leonard Swett, O. M. Hatch, and Mr.
Medill of the Chicago *Tribune*. These men had, for the
first time, brought a National Convention to the West,
and they had the advantage of fighting for Lincoln on
their own ground with the enthusiasm his name inspired
as a potent factor in their work. They went there to
win, and they left nothing undone within the range of
political effort to give him the nomination. Two posi-

tions in the Cabinet, one for Pennsylvania and one for Indiana, were positively promised by David Davis at an early period of the contest, when they feared that there might be serious difficulty in uniting the delegations of those States on Lincoln. It is proper to say that Lincoln had no knowledge of these contracts, and had given no such authority, and it is proper, also, to say that the contracts were made in both cases with comparatively irresponsible parties who had little power, if any, in guiding the actions of their respective delegations. Certainly Lane and Curtin, who were the most important factors in bringing their States to the support of Lincoln, not only were not parties to these contracts, but were entirely ignorant of them until their fulfillment was demanded after Lincoln's election. I have good reason to know that in the case of Pennsylvania that contract, while it did not of itself make General Cameron Secretary of War, had much to do with resolving Lincoln's doubts in favor of Cameron's appointment in the end.

There were no political movements of national importance during Lincoln's administration in which he did not actively, although often hiddenly, participate. It was Lincoln who finally, after the most convulsive efforts to get Missouri into line with the administration, effected a reconciliation of disputing parties which brought Brown and Henderson into the Senate, and it was Lincoln who in 1863 took a leading part in attaining the declination of Curtin as a gubernatorial candidate that year. Grave apprehensions were felt that Curtin could not be re-elected because of the bitterness of the hostility of Cameron and his friends, and also because there were 70,000 Pennsylvania soldiers in the field who could not vote. Lincoln was Curtin's sincere friend, but when Curtin's supporters suggested that his broken health called for his retirement, Lincoln promptly agreed to tender Curtin a first-class foreign mission if he decided to decline a re-nomination. Curtin accepted the proffered mission, to be assumed at the close of his term, and he published his acceptance and his purpose to withdraw from the field for Governor.

Curtin's declination was responded to within a week by a number of the leading counties of the State per-emptorily instructing their delegates to vote for his re-nomination for Governor. It soon became evident that the party would accept no other leader in the desperate conflict, and that no other candidate could hope to be elected. Curtin was compelled to submit, and he was nominated on the first ballot by more than a two-thirds vote, although bitterly opposed by a number of promi-nent Federal officers in the State. Lincoln was disap-pointed in the result—not because he was averse to Cur-tin, but because he feared that party divisions would lose the State. Both Lincoln and Stanton made exhaustive efforts to support Curtin after he had been nominated, and all the power of the government that could be wielded with effect was employed to promote his elec-tion. The battle was a desperate one against the late Chief-Justice Woodward, who was a giant in intellectual strength, and who commanded the unbounded confidence and enthusiastic support of his party, but Curtin was elected by over 15,000 majority.

One of the shrewdest of Lincoln's great political schemes was the tender, by an autograph letter, of the French mission to the elder James Gordon Bennett. No one who can form any intelligent judgment of the polit-ical exigencies of that time can fail to understand why the venerable independent journalist received this mark of favor from the President. Lincoln had but one of the leading journals of New York on which he could rely for positive support. That was Mr. Raymond's

New York *Times.* Mr. Greeley's *Tribune* was the most widely read Republican journal of the country, and it was unquestionably the most potent in moulding Republican sentiment. Its immense weekly edition, for that day, reached the more intelligent masses of the people in every State of the Union, and Greeley was not in accord with Lincoln. Lincoln knew how important it was to have the support of the *Herald*, and he carefully studied how to bring its editor into close touch with himself. The outlook for Lincoln's re-election was not promising. Bennett had strongly advocated the nomination of General McClellan by the Democrats, and that was ominous of hostility to Lincoln; and when McClellan was nominated he was accepted on all sides as a most formidable candidate. It was in this emergency that Lincoln's political sagacity served him sufficiently to win the *Herald* to his cause, and it was done by the confidential tender of the French mission. Bennett did not break over to Lincoln at once, but he went by gradual approaches. His first step was to declare in favor of an entirely new candidate, which was an utter impossibility. He opened a leader on the subject thus: "Lincoln has proved a failure; McClellan has proved a failure; Fremont has proved a failure; let us have a new candidate.'' Lincoln, McClellan, and Fremont were then all in the field as nominated candidates, and the Fremont defection was a serious threat to Lincoln. Of course, neither Lincoln nor McClellan declined, and the *Herald*, failing to get the new man it knew to be an impossibility, squarely advocated Lincoln's re-election.

Without consulting any one, and without any public announcement whatever, Lincoln wrote to Bennett, asking him to accept the mission to France. The offer was declined. Bennett valued the offer very much more than the office, and from that day until the day of his death he was one of Lincoln's most appreciative friends and hearty supporters on his own independent line. The tender of the French mission to Bennett has been disputed, but I am not mistaken about it. W. O. Bartlett, a prominent member of the New York bar, and father of the present Judge Bartlett of the Supreme Court of that State, had personal knowledge of Lincoln's autograph letter that was delivered to Bennett, and Judge Bartlett yet has the original letter, unless he has parted with it within the last few years. Bennett was not only one of the ablest and one of the most sagacious editors of his day, but he was also one of the most independent, and in controversy one of the most defiant. He was in a position to render greater service to Lincoln and to the country in its desperate civil war than any other one man in American journalism. He did not pretend to be a Republican; on the contrary, he was Democratic in all his personal sympathies and convictions, but he gave a faithful support to the war, although often freely criticising the policy of the administration. He had no desire for public office, but he did desire, after he had acquired wealth and newspaper power, just the recognition that Lincoln gave him, and I doubt whether any one thing during Bennett's life ever gave him more sincere gratification than this voluntary offer of one of the first-class missions of the country, made in Mr. Lincoln's own handwriting, and his opportunity to decline the same. Looking as Lincoln did to the great battle for his re-election, this was one of the countless sagacious acts by which he strengthened himself from day to day, and it did much, very much, to pave the way for his overwhelming majority of 1864.

That Lincoln understood practical politics after he had been nominated for a second term is very clearly illustrated in the letter he wrote to General Sherman on the 19th of September, 1864. The States of Indiana, Ohio, and Pennsylvania then voted in October for State offices, and Indiana was desperately contested. Ohio was regarded as certain, and Pennsylvania had only Congressmen and local officers to elect. The soldiers of Indiana could not vote in the field, and Lincoln's letter to Sherman, who commanded the major portion of the Indiana troops, appeals to him, in Lincoln's usual cautious manner, to furlough as many of his soldiers home for the October election as he could safely spare. His exact language is: "Anything you can safely do to let your soldiers, or any part of them, go home to vote at the State election will be greatly in point." To this he adds: "This is in no sense an order; it is simply intended to impress you with the importance to the army itself of your doing all you safely can, yourself being the judge of what you can safely do." While this was "in no sense an order," it was practically a command that Sherman promptly and generously obeyed, and the result was that Morton was elected Governor by some 22,000 majority. It was at Lincoln's special request that General Logan left his command and missed the march to the sea, to stump Indiana and Illinois in the contest of 1864. He was one of the ablest and most impressive of all the campaigners of the West, and it was regarded by Lincoln as more important that Logan should be on the hustings than in command of his corps.

I recall a pointed illustration of Lincoln's rare sagacity when confronted with embarrassing political complications that occurred in 1862, when I was in charge of the military department of Pennsylvania pertaining to the draft for troops made under the State law. Harrisburg was an important centre of military supplies, as well as the political centre of the State. Immense army contracts were there awarded and executed under officers assigned to duty at that place. After the draft had been made the conscripts began to pour into the capital by thousands, and, as the demand for reinforcements in the field was very pressing, I called upon the military officer of the city and urged upon him the necessity of mustering the new men as promptly as possible. To my surprise, he mustered only two companies the first day out of a thousand men. On the second day, notwithstanding my earnest appeal to him, he mustered no more than two companies, and on the third day, when I had over 5000 men in camp, a mere mob without organization or discipline, the same tedious process of mustering was continued. I telegraphed Secretary Stanton that I had many men in camp, and that they were arriving in large numbers, but that I could not have them mustered—that I could forward a regiment of troops every day if the government would furnish the officers to muster and organize them. A prompt answer came that it would be done. The following morning a new officer appeared, of course subordinate to the commandant of the place who had charge of the mustering, and he promptly mustered an entire regiment the first day. On the following morning he was relieved from duty and ordered elsewhere, and the mustering again fell back to two companies a day.

In the mean time over 7000 men had been gathered into the camp, and it was evident that the question of supplying the camp and the interests of contractors had become paramount to the reinforcement of the army. I telegraphed Lincoln that I would see him in Washington that night, and hurried on to correct the evil by personal conference with him. The case was a very simple one, and he readily took in the situation. He knew that I had labored day and night for two months, without compensation or the expectation of it, to hasten the Pennsylvania troops to the aid of our soldiers in the field, and I said to him that if he would send mustering officers to organize them promptly, I would return and finish the work; if not, I would abandon it and go home. Lincoln was greatly pained at the development, but he understood that a change of military officers at Harrisburg, such as this occasion seemed to demand, would involve serious political complications. He was of all things most desirous to strengthen our shattered armies, and it was evident very soon that he meant to do so in some way, but without offense to the political power that controlled the military assignments at Harrisburg. Without intimating his solution of the problem, he rang his bell and instructed his messenger to bring Adjutant-General Thomas to the Executive Chamber. Soon after the Adjutant-General appeared, and Lincoln said: "General, what is the military rank of the senior officer at Harrisburg?" To which the Adjutant-General replied: "Captain, sir," and naming the officer. Lincoln promptly said in reply: "Bring me a commission immediately for Alexander K. McClure as Assistant Adjutant-General of the United States Volunteers, with the rank of major." The Adjutant-General bowed himself out, when I immediately said to Lincoln that I could not consent to be subject to arbitrary military orders—that I desired no compensation for the work I performed, and I must decline the honor he proposed to confer upon me. In his quiet way he replied: "Well, McClure, try my way; I think that will get the troops on without delay and without treading on anybody's toes. I think if you will take your commission back to Harrisburg, call upon the captain in command there to muster you into the service of the United States, and show him your assignment to duty there, you will have no trouble whatever in getting the troops organized and forwarded as rapidly as you wish. Now try it, won't you?"

I saw the wisdom of the suggestion, and well understood why the President desired to avoid the offense that would have been given by the removal of the military officers, and I agreed to try his plan. When I returned to Harrisburg the next day I sent for the senior officer to come to my office. He came in with all the dignity and arrogance of an offended Cæsar and spoke to me with bare civility. I quietly handed him my commission, requested him to muster me into the military service, and also exhibited the order assigning me for duty at Harrisburg. When he saw my commission his hat was immediately removed and he was as obsequious as he had been insolent before. When he had finished mustering me into the service I said to him, "I presume you understand what this means. I don't propose to make any display of military authority or to interfere with anything except that which I have immediately in hand. There must be a regiment of troops mustered and forwarded from this State every day until the troops in camp are all sent to the field. Good-morning." He immediately bowed himself out, saluting in military style as he did so—a grace that I had not yet mastered sufficiently to return—and from that day until the camp was emptied of conscripts a regiment of troops was mustered daily and forwarded to Washington. That was the only military authority I ever exercised, and few knew of the military dignity I had so suddenly attained. When the troops were forwarded to the field and the accounts settled I resigned my commission as quietly as I received it and sent my resignation to the President, who, as he had voluntarily promised, ordered its immediate acceptance. The officer who was thus so unexpectedly superseded, and who was so promptly made to render efficient service to the country by Lincoln's admirable strategy, is no longer among the living, and I· omit his name. He learned how Lincoln could discipline a soldier, and he profited by the lesson.

7

LINCOLN AND EMANCIPATION.

ABRAHAM LINCOLN was not a sentimental Abolitionist. Indeed, he was not a sentimentalist on
any subject. He was a man of earnest conviction and
of sublime devotion to his faith. In many of his public
letters and State papers he was as poetic as he was epi-
grammatic, and he was singularly felicitous in the pathos
that was so often interwoven with his irresistible logic.
But he never contemplated the abolition of slavery until
the events of the war not only made it clearly possible,
but made it an imperious necessity. As the sworn Executive of the nation it was his duty to obey the Constitution in all its provisions, and he accepted that duty
without reservation. He knew that slavery was the immediate cause of the political disturbance that culminated
in civil war, and I know that he believed from the beginning that if war should be persisted in, it could end only
in the severance of the Union or the destruction of slavery. His supreme desire was peace, alike before the war,
during the war, and in closing the war. He exhausted
every means within his power to teach the Southern people that slavery could not be disturbed by his administration as long as they themselves obeyed the Constitution
and laws which protected slavery, and he never uttered
a word or did an act to justify, or even excuse, the South

LINCOLN'S TOMB AT SPRINGFIELD.

in assuming that he meant to make any warfare upon
the institution of slavery beyond protecting the free Territories from its desolating tread.

It was not until the war had been in progress for
nearly two years that Lincoln decided to proclaim the
policy of Emancipation, and then he was careful to assume the power as warranted under the Constitution only
by the supreme necessities of war.   There was no time
from the inauguration of Lincoln until the 1st of January, 1863, that the South could not have returned to the
Union with slavery intact in every State.   His preliminary proclamation, dated September 22, 1862, gave notice
that on the 1st of January, 1863, he would by public
proclamation, "warranted by the Constitution upon
military necessity," declare that "all persons held as
slaves within any State, or designated part of the State,
the people whereof shall then be in rebellion against the
United States, shall be thenceforward and for ever free."
Every insurgent State had thus more than three months'
formal notice that the war was not prosecuted for the
abolition of slavery, but solely for the restoration of the
Union, and that they could, by returning and accepting
the authority of the National Government at any time
before the 1st of January, 1863, preserve slavery indefinitely.   Lincoln's letter to Horace Greeley, written just
one month before his preliminary Emancipation Proclamation, presents in the clearest and most concise manner
Lincoln's views on the subject of slavery and the Union.
After saying that if he could save the Union without
freeing any slaves he would do it; that if he could save
it by freeing all the slaves he would do it; and that if
he could save it by freeing some and leaving others
he would also do that, he adds: "What I do about
slavery and the colored race I do because I believe it
helps to save this Union, and what I forbear I forbear

because I do not believe it would help to save the Union.''

As President of the Republic, Lincoln was governed at every step by his paramount duty to prevent the dismemberment of the nation and to restore the Union and its people to fraternal relations. The best expression of his own views and aims in the matter is given in a single brief sentence, uttered by himself on the 13th of September, 1862, only nine days before he issued the preliminary proclamation. It was in response to an appeal from a large delegation of Chicago clergymen, representing nearly or quite all the religious denominations of that city, urging immediate Emancipation. He heard them patiently, as he always did those who were entitled to be heard at all, and his answer was given in these words: ''I have not decided against the proclamation of liberty to the slaves, but hold the matter under advisement, and I can assure you the matter is on my mind by day and by night more than any other. Whatever shall appear to be God's will I will do.'' However Lincoln's religious views may be disputed, he had a profound belief in God and in God's immutable justice, and the sentence I have just quoted tells the whole story of Lincoln's action in the abolition of slavery. He did not expect miracles —indeed, he was one of the last men to believe in miracles at all—but he did believe that God overruled all human actions; that all individuals charged with grave responsibility were but the means in the hands of the Great Ruler to accomplish the fulfillment of justice. Congressman Arnold, whom Lincoln once declared to me to be the one member of the House in whose personal and political friendship he had absolute faith, speaking of the earnest appeals made to Lincoln for Emancipation, says: ''Mr. Lincoln listened not unmoved to such appeals, and, seeking prayerful guidance of Almighty God, the Proclamation of Emancipation was prepared. It had been, in fact, prepared in July, 1862.''

Thus from July until September, during which time there was the greatest possible pressure on Lincoln for an Emancipation policy, his proclamation had been formulated, but his usual caution had prevented him from intimating it to any outside of his Cabinet. It was the gravest step ever taken by any civil ruler in this or any other land, and military success was essential to maintain and execute the policy of Emancipation after it had been declared. Had McClellan been successful in his Peninsula campaign, or had Lee been defeated in the second conflict of Manassas, without bringing peace, the proclamation would doubtless have been issued with the prestige of such victory. Under the shivering hesitation among even Republicans throughout the North, Lincoln felt that it needed the prestige of a military victory to assure its cordial acceptance by very many of the supporters of the government. The battle of Antietam, fought by the only general of that time who had publicly declared against an Emancipation policy, was the first victory the Army of the Potomac had achieved in 1862, and five days after the Antietam victory the preliminary proclamation was issued.

Only the careful student of the history of the war can have any just conception of the gradual manner in which Lincoln approached Emancipation. He long and earnestly sought to avoid it, believing then that the Union could be best preserved without the violent destruction of slavery; and when he appreciated the fact that the leaders of the rebellion were unwilling to entertain any proposition for the restoration of the Union, he accepted the destruction of slavery as an imperious necessity, but he sought to attain it with the least possible disturbance.

The first direct assault made upon slavery was by Secretary Cameron's overruled annual report in December, 1861, in which he advised the arming of slaves. The first Congress that sat during the war made steady strides toward the destruction of slavery by the passage of five important laws. The first abolished slavery in the District of Columbia; the second prohibited slavery in all the Territories of the United States; the third gave freedom to the escaped slaves of all who were in rebellion; the fourth gave lawful authority for the enlistment of colored men as soldiers; and the fifth made a new article of war, prohibiting any one in the military or naval service from aiding in the arrest or return of a fugitive slave under pain of dismissal. Slavery was abolished in the District of Columbia as early as April, 1862, the act having passed the Senate by 29 to 6, and the House by 92 to 38. A bill prohibiting slavery in the Territories was passed on the 19th of June, and a bill giving freedom to slaves of rebellious masters who performed military service was passed on the 17th of July.

Thus was Congress steadily advancing toward Emancipation, and as early as March, 1862, Lincoln had proposed his plan of compensated Emancipation. On the 6th of March he sent a special message to Congress recommending the adoption of the following joint resolution:

RESOLVED, That the United States ought to co-operate with any State which may adopt gradual abolishment of slavery, giving to such State pecuniary aid, to be used by such State, in its discretion, to compensate for the inconvenience, public and private, produced by such change of system.

His message very earnestly pressed upon Congress the importance of adopting such a policy, and upon the country the importance of accepting it, North and South. His concluding sentence is: "In full view of my great responsibility to my God and to my country, I earnestly beg the attention of Congress and the people to the subject." Again, when revoking General Hunter's order of the 9th of May, 1862, declaring all slaves free within his military district, Lincoln made a most impressive appeal to the people of the South on the subject of compensated Emancipation. He said: "I do not argue; I beseech you to make the argument for yourselves. You cannot, if you would, be blind to the signs of the times. . . . The change it contemplates would come gently as the dews of heaven, not rending or wrecking anything. Will you not embrace it? So much good has not been done by any one effort in all past time as, in the providence of God, it is now your high privilege to do. May the vast future not have to lament that you have neglected it." Soon after this Lincoln had an interview with the Congressional delegations from the Border Slave States, at which he again earnestly urged them to accept compensated Emancipation. Speaking of that interview, Lincoln said: "I believed that the indispensable necessity for military Emancipation and arming the blacks would come unless averted by gradual and compensated Emancipation." Again in July, 1862, only two months before he issued the preliminary proclamation, Lincoln summoned the delegates from the Border Slave States to a conference with him, and again most persuasively appealed to them to accept gradual and compensated Emancipation. He said to them: "I do not speak of Emancipation at once, but of a decision at once to emancipate gradually." He also clearly foreshadowed to them that if they refused it, more violent Emancipation must come. He said: "The pressure in this direction is still upon me and is increasing. By conceding what I now ask you can relieve me, and much more can relieve the country, on this important point." He concluded with these eloquent words: "Our common country is in great peril, demanding the loftiest views and boldest action to bring a speedy relief. Once relieved, its form of government is saved to the world; its beloved history and cherished memories are vindicated, and its happy future fully assured and rendered inconceivably grand. To you, more than to any others, the privilege is given to assure that happiness and swell that grandeur, and to link your names therewith for ever."

Strange as it may now seem, in view of the inevitable tendency of events at that time, these appeals of Lincoln were not only treated with contempt by those in rebellion, but the Border State Congressmen, who had everything at stake, and who in the end were compelled to accept forcible Emancipation without compensation, although themselves not directly involved in rebellion, made no substantial response to Lincoln's efforts to save their States and people. Thus did the States in rebellion disregard repeated importunities from Lincoln to accept Emancipation with payment for their slaves. During long weary months he had made temperate utterance on every possible occasion, and by every official act that could direct the attention of the country he sought to attain the least violent solution of the slavery problem, only to learn the bitter lesson that slavery would make no terms with the government, and that it was the inspiration of rebellious armies seeking the destruction of the Republic. Soon after his appeal to the Congressmen of the Border States in July, 1862, Lincoln prepared his Emancipation Proclamation, and quietly and patiently waited the fullness of time for proclaiming it, still hoping that peace might come without resort to the extreme measure of military and uncompensated Emancipation. Seeing that the last hope of any other method of peace had failed, he issued the preliminary proclamation on the 22d of September, 1862, and his final proclamation on the 1st of January following; and there never was a day from that time until Lincoln's death that he ever entertained, even for a moment, the question of receding from the freedom he had proclaimed to the slaves. But while he was compelled to accept the issue of revolutionary Emancipation, he never abandoned the idea of compensated Emancipation until the final overthrow of Lee's army in 1865. He proposed it to his Cabinet in February of that year, only to be unanimously rejected, and I personally know that he would have suggested it to Stephens, Campbell, and Hunter at the Hampton Roads Conference in February, 1865, had not Vice-President Stephens, as the immediate representative of Jefferson Davis, frankly stated at the outset that he was instructed not to entertain or discuss any proposition that did not recognize the perpetuity of the Confederacy. That statement from Stephens precluded the possibility of Lincoln making any proposition, or even suggestion, whatever on the subject. In a personal interview with Jefferson Davis when I was a visitor in his house at Bevoir, Mississippi, fifteen years after the close of the war, I asked him whether he had ever received any intimation about Lincoln's desire to close the war by the payment of $400,000,000 for emancipated slaves. He said that he had not heard of it. I asked him whether he would have given such instructions to Stephens if he had possessed knowledge of the fact. He answered that he could not have given Stephens any other instructions than he did under the circumstances, because as President of the Confederacy he could not entertain any question involving its dissolution, that being a subject entirely for the States themselves.

Lincoln treated the Emancipation question from the beginning as a very grave matter-of-fact problem to be solved for or against the destruction of slavery as the safety of the Union might dictate. He refrained from Emancipation for eighteen months after the war had begun, simply because he believed during that time that he might best save the Union by saving slavery, and had the development of events proved that belief to be correct he would have permitted slavery to live with the Union. When he became fully convinced that the safety of the government demanded the destruction of slavery, he decided, after the most patient and exhaustive consideration of the subject, to proclaim his Emancipation policy. It was not founded solely or even chiefly on the sentiment of hostility to slavery. If it had been, the proclamation would have declared slavery abolished in every State of the Union; but he excluded the slave States of Delaware, Maryland, and Tennessee, and certain parishes in Louisiana, and certain counties in Virginia, from the operation of the proclamation, declaring, in the instrument that has now become immortal, that "which excepted parts are for the present left precisely as if this proclamation were not issued." Thus if only military Emancipation had been achieved by the President's proclamation, it would have presented the singular spectacle of Tennessee in the heart of the South, Maryland and Delaware north of the Potomac, and nearly one-half of Louisiana and one-half of Virginia with slavery protected, while freedom was accorded to the slaves of all the other slaveholding States. Lincoln evidently regarded the Emancipation policy as the most momentous in the history of American statesmanship, and as justified only by the extreme necessity of weakening the rebellion that then threatened the severance of the Union.

From the very day of his inauguration until he issued
his Emancipation Proclamation, Lincoln was constantly
importuned by the more radical element of his supporters
to declare his purpose to abolish slavery. Among them
were a number of the ablest leaders of his party in the
Senate and House, and some of them as impracticable in
their methods as they were imperious in their demands.
That he was glad of the opportunity to destroy slavery
none can doubt who knew him, but he patiently bore the
often irritating complaints of many of his friends until
he saw that slavery and the Union could not survive together, and that the country was at least measurably prepared to accept and support the new policy. He was
many times threatened with open rebellion against his
administration by some of the most potent Republicans
because of his delay in declaring the Emancipation policy, but he waited until the time had come in the fall of
1862, when he felt that it was not only a necessity of war,
but a political necessity as well. Another very grave
consideration that led him to accept Emancipation when
he did was the peril of England and France recognizing
the Confederacy and thereby involving us in war with
two of the greatest powers of Europe. The pretext on
which was based the opposition of England to the Union
cause in the early part of the war was the maintenance
of slavery by the government while prosecuting a war
against a slaveholders' rebellion, and it seemed to be an
absolute necessity that our government should accept the
Emancipation policy to impair the force of the public
sentiment in England that demanded the recognition of
the South as an independent government. These three
weighty considerations, each in itself sufficient to have
decided Lincoln's action, combined to dictate his Emancipation policy in the early fall of 1862. The proclamation did not in itself abolish slavery, but the positive

declaration in the proclamation "that the Executive government of the United States, including the military and naval authorities thereof, will recognize and maintain the freedom of said persons," gave notice to every slaveholder and promise to every slave that every bondman brought within the lines of the Union Army would thereafter be for ever free.

While the Emancipation Proclamation inflicted a mortal wound upon slavery and assured its absolute extinction, sooner or later, throughout the entire country, Lincoln fully appreciated the fact that much was yet to be done, even beyond victories in the field, to efface the blot of slavery from the Republic. As early as the 14th of January, 1863, Representative Wilson of Iowa, then chairman of the Judiciary Committee, and now a United States Senator, reported a proposed amendment to the Constitution declaring slavery "for ever prohibited in the United States." On the 10th of February, 1864, Senator Trumbull reported from the Judiciary Committee of that body a proposed amendment that was finally adopted in 1865, and is now part of the fundamental law of the nation. It was passed in the Senate on the 18th of April by a vote of 38 to 6. It was defeated in the House by a vote of 93 in its favor and 65 against it, lacking the requisite two-thirds. Seeing that the amendment was lost, Ashley of Ohio changed his vote from the affirmative to the negative with a view of entering a motion to reconsider, and the subject went over until the next session. On the 6th of January, 1865, Ashley made his motion to reconsider and called up the proposed amendment for another vote. One of the most interesting and able debates of that time was precipitated by Ashley's motion, and the notable speech of the occasion was made by Mr. Rollins of Missouri, who had been a large slaveholder, and who declared that "the rebellion instigated and carried on by slaveholders has been the death-knell of the institution." Stevens, the great apostle of freedom from Pennsylvania and the Great Commoner of the war, closed the debate, and probably on no other occasion in the history of Congress was such intense anxiety exhibited as when the roll was called on the adoption or rejection of the amendment. The Republicans did not have two-thirds of the House, but several Democrats openly favored the amendment and a number of others were known to be uncertain. The first break in the Democratic line was when the name of Coffroth of Pennsylvania was called, who promptly answered ay, and was greeted with thunders of applause in the House and galleries. He was followed by Ganson, Herrick, Nelson, Odell, Radford, and Steele, Democrats from New York, by English from Connecticut, and by McAlister from Pennsylvania, and when the Speaker declared that the amendment had been adopted by 119 yeas to 56 nays, being more than the requisite constitutional majority, the great battle of Emancipation was substantially won, and Lincoln hailed it with a measure of joy second only to his delight at the announcement of Lee's surrender. Before the members left their seats salvos of artillery announced to the people of the capital that the Constitutional amendment abolishing slavery had been adopted by Congress, and the victorious leaders rushed to the White House to congratulate Lincoln on the final achievement of Emancipation.

The acceptance of the proposed amendment by the requisite number of States was not a matter of doubt, and the absolute overthrow of slavery throughout the entire Republic dates from the adoption of the amendment to the Constitution in the House of Representatives on the 6th of January, 1865. Illinois, the home of Lincoln, fitly led off in ratifying the amendment. Massachusetts and Pennsylvania both ratified on the 8th of February, and one of the most grateful recollections of my life is that as a member of the popular branch of the Pennsylvania Legislature I supported and voted for that measure. Owing to the delay in the meeting of Legislatures in a number of the States the official proclamation of the ratification of the amendment was not made until the 18th of December, 1865, on which day Secretary Seward formally declared to the country and the world that the amendment abolishing slavery had " become to all intents and purposes valid as a part of the Constitution of the United States." Lincoln had thus dealt the deathblow to slavery by his proclamation, but it was not until after he had sealed his devotion to free government by giving his life to the assassin's hate that the great work was consummated and the Republic was entirely free from the stain of human bondage.

The most earnest discussions I ever had with Lincoln were on the subject of his Emancipation Proclamation. I knew the extraordinary pressure that came from the more radical element of the Republican party, embracing a number of its ablest leaders, such as Sumner, Chase, Wade, Chandler, and others, but I did not know, and few were permitted to know, the importance of an Emancipation policy in restraining the recognition of the Confederacy by France and England. I was earnestly opposed to an Emancipation Proclamation by the President. For some weeks before it was issued I saw Lincoln frequently, and in several instances sat with him for hours at a time after the routine business of the day had been disposed of and the doors of the White House were closed. I viewed the issue solely from a political standpoint, and certainly had the best of reasons for the views I pressed upon Lincoln, assuming that political

expediency should control his action. I reminded him
that the proclamation would not liberate a single slave—
that the Southern armies must be overthrown, and that
the territory held by them must be conquered by military
success, before it could be made effective. To this Lincoln answered: "It does seem like the Pope's bull against
the comet;" but that was the most he ever said in any
of his conversations to indicate that he might not issue
it. I appealed to him to issue a military order as Commander-in-chief of the Army and Navy, proclaiming
that every slave of a rebellious owner should be for ever
free when brought within our lines. Looking simply to
practical results, that would have accomplished everything that the Emancipation Proclamation achieved; but
it was evident during all these discussions that Lincoln
viewed the question from a very much higher standpoint
than I did, although, as usual, he said but little and
gave no clue to the bent of his mind on the subject.

I reminded Lincoln that political defeat would be inevitable in the great States of the Union in the elections
soon to follow if he issued the Emancipation Proclamation—that New York, New Jersey, Pennsylvania, Ohio,
Indiana, and Illinois would undoubtedly vote Democratic
and elect Democratic delegations to the next Congress.
He did not dispute my judgment as to the political effect
of the proclamation, but I never left him with any reasonable hope that I had seriously impressed him on the
subject. Every political prediction I made was fearfully
fulfilled in the succeeding October and November elections. New York elected Seymour Governor by 10,700
majority, and chose 17 Democratic and 14 Republican
Congressmen. New Jersey elected a Democratic Governor by 14,500, and 4 Democrats and 1 Republican to
Congress. Pennsylvania elected the Democratic State
ticket by 3500 majority and 13 Democrats and 11 Re-

publicans to Congress, with a Democratic Legislature that chose Buckalew to the United States Senate. Ohio elected the Democratic State ticket by 5500 majority and 14 Democrats and 2 Republicans to Congress, Ashley and Schenck being the only two who escaped in the political Waterloo. Indiana elected the Democratic State ticket by 9500 majority and 7 Democrats and 4 Republicans to Congress, with 30 Democratic majority in the Legislature. Illinois elected the Democratic State ticket by 16,500 majority and 9 Democrats and 5 Republicans to Congress, and 28 Democratic majority in the Legislature. Confidently anticipating these disastrous political results, I could not conceive it possible for Lincoln to successfully administer the government and prosecute the war with the six most important loyal States of the Union declaring against him at the polls; but Lincoln knew that the majority in Congress would be safe, as the rebellious States were excluded, and the far West and New England were ready to sustain the Emancipation policy; and he appreciated, as I did not, that the magnitude of his act cast all mere considerations of expediency into nothingness. He dared to do the right for the sake of the right. I speak of this the more freely because, in the light of events as they appear to-day, he rose to the sublimest duty of his life, while I was pleading the mere expedient of a day against a record for human freedom that must be immortal while liberty has worshipers in any land or clime.

Lincoln issued the Emancipation Proclamation because it was an imperious duty, and because the time had come when any temporizing with the question would have been more fatal than could possibly be any temporary revolt against the manly declaration of right. He felt strong enough to maintain the freedom he proclaimed by the military and naval power of the govern-

8

ment.   He believed it to be the most mortal wound that could be inflicted upon the Confederacy.   He believed that it would disarm the strong anti-Union sentiment that seemed to be fast pressing the English government to the recognition of the South, and he believed that, however public sentiment might falter for a time, like the disturbed and quivering needle it would surely settle to the pole.   He did not issue it for the mere sentiment of unshackling four millions of slaves, nor did he then dream of universal citizenship and suffrage to freedmen. In the last public address that he ever delivered, on the 11th of April, 1865, speaking of negro suffrage, he said: " I would myself prefer that suffrage were now conferred upon the very intelligent and on those who served our cause as soldiers."   He believed it to be simply an act of justice that every colored man who had fought for his freedom and for the maintenance of the Union, and was honorably discharged from the military service, should be clothed with the right of franchise; and he believed that " the very intelligent" should also be enfranchised as exemplars of their race and an inspiration to them for advancement.   He was always stubbornly for justice, stubbornly for the right, and it was his sublime devotion to the right in the face of the most appalling opposition that made the name of Abraham Lincoln immortal as the author of the Emancipation Proclamation, on which he justly invoked " the considerate judgment of mankind and the gracious favor of Almighty God."

LINCOLN AND HAMLIN.

THE fact that Abraham Lincoln conceived and executed the scheme to nominate Andrew Johnson for Vice-President in 1864 has been feebly disputed, but is now accepted as the truth of history. It was not an arbitrary exercise of political power on the part of Lincoln. He had no prejudice against Hannibal Hamlin to inspire him to compass Hamlin's defeat. He had no special love for Andrew Johnson to lead him to overthrow his old associate of 1860 and make the Military Governor of an insurgent State his fellow-candidate for 1864. Hamlin was not in close sympathy with Lincoln; on the contrary, he was known as one who passively rather than actively strengthened a powerful cabal of Republican leaders in their aggressive hostility to Lincoln and his general policy; but Lincoln was incapable of yielding to prejudice, however strong, in planning his great campaign for re-election in 1864. Had Hamlin been ten times more offensive than he was to Lincoln, it would not have halted Lincoln for a moment in favoring Hamlin's renomination if he believed it good politics to do so. He rejected Hamlin not because he hated him; he accepted Johnson not because he loved him. He was guided in what he did, or what he did not, in planning the great campaign of his life, that he believed involved the destiny of the country itself, by the single purpose of making success as nearly certain as possible.

(Photo by Brady, Washington.)

HANNIBAL HAMLIN, 1890.

Hamlin was nominated for the Vice-Presidency in 1860 simply because he was a representative Republican fresh from the Democratic party. Another consideration that favored his selection was the fact that his State had been carried into the Republican party under his leadership, and that its State election in September would be the finger-board of success or defeat in the national contest. His position as Representative, Senator, and Governor, and his admitted ability and high character, fully justified his nomination as the candidate for Vice-President; but when elected there was the usual steadily widening chasm between him and the Executive, and, like nearly or quite all Vice-Presidents, he drifted into the embrace of the opposition to his chief. It was this opposition, led by men of such consummate ability as Wade of Ohio and Henry Winter Davis of Maryland, that admonished Lincoln of the necessity of putting himself in the strongest possible attitude for the then admittedly doubtful battle of 1864. While the defeat of Lee at Gettysburg and the surrender of Vicksburg the year before had done much to inspire faith in the success of the war, the Confederacy was stubbornly maintaining its armies. The opening of the new year of 1864 called for large drafts of men to fill the thinned ranks of the Union forces, and there was a powerful undertow of despondency among the loyal people of the North. The war was costing $3,000,000 a day, and after three years of bloody conflict the end was not in view. The Republican leaders in the early part of 1864 were divided in councils, distracted by the conflicts of ambition, and very many of the ablest of them regarded the defeat of the party as not only possible, but more than probable. The one man who fully understood the peril and who studied carefully how to avert it was Abraham Lincoln.

Lincoln, as was his usual custom, consulted with all

who came within his reach, and developed his views
from time to time with extreme caution. In the early
part of the year he reached the conclusion that it would
be eminently wise to nominate a conspicuous War Democrat for Vice-President along with himself for President.
A number of prominent men who acted with the Democratic party in 1860 against Lincoln's election, but who
patriotically entered the military service and won distinction by their heroism, represented a very large class
of Democratic voters upon whom Lincoln felt he must
rely for his re-election. Hamlin had been a Democrat,
but he did not come under the class of War Democrats,
while Butler, Dix, Dickinson, Johnson, Holt, and others
represented a distinctive and very formidable class of
citizens who, while yet professing to be Democrats, were
ready to support the war under Lincoln until it should
be successfully terminated by the restoration of the Union.
Lincoln's first selection for Vice-President was General
Butler. I believe he reached that conclusion without
specially consulting with any of his friends. As early
as March, 1864, he sent for General Cameron, to whom
he proposed the nomination of Butler, and that, I assume, was his first declaration of his purpose to any one
on the subject. He confided to Cameron the mission to
Fortress Monroe to confer confidentially with Butler.
On that journey Cameron was accompanied by Ex-Con-
gressman William H. Armstrong of Pennsylvania, who
was first informed of the real object of Cameron's visit
when they were returning home, and after Butler had
declined to permit his name to be considered. Butler
was at that time a strong man in the loyal States. He
had not achieved great military success, but his administration in New Orleans had made him universally popular throughout the North, in which the vindictive vituperation of the Southern people heaped upon him was

an important factor. Butler's declination was peremptory, and Cameron returned home without learning in what direction Lincoln would be likely to look for a candidate for Vice-President.

In a later conference with Cameron, in which the names of Johnson, Dickinson, and Dix were seriously discussed, Lincoln expressed his preference for Johnson, to which Cameron, with unconcealed reluctance, finally assented. While Lincoln at that time decided in favor of Johnson, he did not himself regard it as final. His extreme caution and exceptional sagacity made him carefully consider all possible weak points in Johnson's candidacy before he launched the movement for his nomination. He summoned General Sickles to Washington, and sent him to Tennessee on a confidential mission to examine and make report to him of the success of Johnson's administration as Military Governor. That State was in a revolutionary condition; Johnson was charged with violent and despotic official acts, and Lincoln meant to know fully whether Johnson might, by reason of his administration, be vulnerable as a national candidate. Sickles had no knowledge of the real purpose of his mission. The question of nominating Johnson for the Vice-Presidency was never suggested or even intimated to Sickles, and he fulfilled his trust and reported favorably on Johnson's administration, without even a suspicion that he was to determine the destiny of Andrew Johnson, make him Vice-President of the United States, and thus President.

Lincoln's purpose in seeking Johnson as his associate on the national ticket in 1864 was much more far reaching than any but himself at the time supposed. He meant to guard against possible defeat by getting a number of the insurgent States in some sort of line to enable their Electoral votes to be counted if needed.

His most promising experiment was in Tennessee under the guidance of Johnson, but he obviously intended that the States of Louisiana, Arkansas, and West Virginia with Tennessee should be organized with the semblance of full Statehood to make their Electoral votes available should the national contest be close.   Had he developed this policy to his party or to Congress, it would have been met with positive and aggressive opposition, but he developed it in the quietest way possible.   His first movement in that line was to have delegations elected to the National Convention from the Southern States named, and when they appeared at the Baltimore Convention on the 7th of June the battle for their admission was led with consummate skill by the few who understood Lincoln's policy.   Tennessee being in the strongest attitude, the delegation from that State was selected on which to make the fight.   It was desperately contested, because it was then well understood to mean the nomination of Johnson for Vice-President; but the Tennessee delegates were admitted by more than a two-thirds vote.   With Tennessee accepted as entitled to representation, the contest was ended, and Louisiana and Arkansas were given the right of representation without a serious struggle.

When Congress met again after the election in November, and when Lincoln's election by an overwhelming popular as well as Electoral vote was assured, the question of counting the Electoral votes of Louisiana, Tennessee, and Arkansas was raised and elaborately discussed in both branches.   As Lincoln had 212 Electoral votes to 21 for McClellan, exclusive of the votes of the three insurgent States referred to, there was no political necessity to induce Congress to strain a point for the acceptance of these votes; and a joint resolution was finally passed declaring " that no valid election for Electors of

President and Vice-President of the United States" had been held in Louisiana, Tennessee, and Arkansas. Lincoln approved the resolution, but took occasion by special message to disclaim approval of the recital of the preamble. Had the votes of these three States been needed to elect a Republican President, I hazard little in saying that they would have been treated as regular and lawful and counted with the approval of both the Senate and House; as they were not needed and as the development of these States was Lincoln's own conception, those who were not specially friendly scored an empty victory against him.

He moved with masterly sagacity at every step in his efforts to nominate Johnson, and his selection of General Cameron as early as March to be his first ambassador in search of a War Democrat for Vice-President was not one of the least of his many shrewd conceptions. The relations between Lincoln and Cameron had been somewhat strained by Cameron's retirement from the Cabinet in 1862. At least Lincoln assumed that they might be somewhat strained on the part of Cameron, and he took early caution to enlist Cameron in his renomination. He knew the power of Cameron in the manipulation of discordant political elements, and he fully appreciated the fact that Cameron's skill made him a dangerous opponent. He bound Cameron to himself by making him one of his trusted leaders in the selection of a candidate for Vice-President. The man who was probably closest to Lincoln in this movement was Henry J. Raymond, but in this as in all Lincoln's movements his confidence was limited with each of his trusted agents. Raymond was then editor of the only prominent New York journal that heartily supported Lincoln; and he, with the aid of Seward and Weed, who early entered into the movement for the nomination of Johnson, overthrew Dickinson in his own State and was the confessed Lincoln leader in the Baltimore Convention of 1864. With Dickinson beaten in New York and with Hamlin's forces demoralized early in the contest, the nomination of Johnson was easily accomplished, chiefly because it was what Lincoln desired.

Neither Swett nor Lamon had any knowledge of Lincoln's positive movement for the nomination of Johnson until within a day or two of the meeting of the convention. Colonel Lamon has recently given a description of the scene between Lincoln, Swett, and himself a day or two before they went to Baltimore to aid in Lincoln's renomination. Swett earnestly and even passionately protested against the overthrow of Hamlin, but after hearing Lincoln fully on the subject he consented to go to the convention, in which he was a delegate from Illinois, and support the nomination of Johnson; but he wisely declared Holt to be his candidate, as a foil to protect Lincoln. Swett naturally felt uncertain as to how the suggestion of Johnson's name would be received at Baltimore, as he had no knowledge of the extent to which Lincoln had progressed in the Johnson movement. In answer to his inquiry whether he was at liberty to say that Lincoln desired Johnson's nomination, Lincoln answered in the negative, and, as quoted by Colonel Lamon in a recent public letter, said: "No, I will address a letter to Lamon here embodying my views, which you, McClure, and other friends may use if it be found absolutely necessary; otherwise it may be better that I shall not appear actively on the stage of this theatre." The letter was written by Lincoln and delivered to Lamon, who had it with him at Baltimore, but, as there was no occasion for using it, it was never shown to any one and was returned to Lincoln after the convention at his request.

How shrewdly Lincoln moved, and with what extreme caution he guarded his confidence, is well illustrated by the fact that while he consulted Cameron confidentially about the nomination of Johnson some months before the convention, and consulted me on the same subject the day before the convention met, neither of us supposed that the other was acting in the special confidence of Lincoln. On the contrary, I supposed that Cameron was sincerely friendly to Hamlin and would battle for his re-nomination, until he finally proposed to me the night before the convention met that we give a solid compli-mentary vote to Hamlin, and follow it with a solid vote for Johnson. Another evidence of his extreme caution in politics is given by the fact that while he carefully concealed from both Cameron and myself the fact that the other was in his confidence in the same movement, he surprised me a few weeks before the convention by sending for me and requesting me to come to the con-vention as a delegate-at-large. I had already been unani-mously chosen as a delegate from my own Congressional district, and was amazed, when I informed Lincoln of that fact, to find that he still insisted upon me going before the State Convention and having myself elected as a delegate-at-large. To all my explanations that a man in the delegation was good for just what he was worth, whether he represented the district or the State, Lincoln persisted in the request that I should come as a delegate-at-large. When I finally pressed him for an explanation of what seemed to me to be a needless re-quest involving great embarrassment to me, he finally with evident reluctance answered: "General Cameron has assured me that he will be a delegate-at-large from your State, and while I have no reason to question his sincerity as my friend, if he is to be a delegate-at-large from Pennsylvania I would much prefer that you be one

with him." Had he been willing to tell me the whole
truth, he would have informed me that Cameron was enlisted in the Johnson movement, and that he specially
desired at least two of the delegates-at-large, representing
opposing factions, to be active supporters of Johnson's
nomination. There could be no other reasonable explanation of his earnest request to me to accept the embarrassing position of seeking an election from the State
Convention when I was already an elected delegate from
my district. A fortunate combination of circumstances
made it possible for me to be elected without a serious
contest, Cameron and I receiving nearly a unanimous
vote.

Lincoln realized the fact that the chances were greatly
against his re-election unless he should be saved by the
success of the Union army. There was no period from
January, 1864, until the 3d of September of the same
year when McClellan would not have defeated Lincoln
for President. The two speeches of that campaign which
turned the tide and gave Lincoln his overwhelming victory were Sherman's dispatch from Atlanta on the 3d of
September, saying: "Atlanta is ours and fairly won;"
and Sheridan's dispatch of the 19th of September from
the Valley, saying: "We have just sent them (the enemy)
whirling through Winchester, and we are after them to-
morrow." From the opening of the military campaign
in the spring of 1864 until Sherman announced the capture of Atlanta, there was not a single important victory
of the Union army to inspire the loyal people of the
country with confidence in the success of the war.
Grant's campaign from the Rapidan to the James was
the bloodiest in the history of the struggle. He had lost
as many men in killed, wounded, and missing as Lee
ever had in front of him, and there was no substantial
victory in all the sacrifice made by the gallant Army of

the Potomac. Sherman had been fighting continuously for four months without a decisive success. The people of the North had become heartsick at the fearful sacrifices which brought no visible achievement. Democratic sentiment had drifted to McClellan as the opposing candidate, and so profoundly was Lincoln impressed by the gloomy situation that confronted him that on the 23d of August, seven days before the nomination of McClellan and ten days before the capture of Atlanta, he wrote the following memoranda, sealed it in an envelope, and had it endorsed by several members of the Cabinet, including Secretary Welles, with written instructions that it was not to be opened until after the election:

EXECUTIVE MANSION,
WASHINGTON, August 23, 1864.

This morning, as for some days past, it seems exceedingly probable that this administration will not be re-elected. Then it will be my duty to co-operate with the President-elect so as to save the Union between the election and the inauguration, as he will have secured his election on such grounds that he cannot possibly save it afterward.   A. LINCOLN.

Nor was Lincoln alone in his apprehension of defeat. Distrust and disintegration were common throughout the entire Republican organization, and nearly all of the sincere supporters of Lincoln were in next to utter despair of political success. I spent an hour with him in the Executive Chamber some ten days before he wrote the memoranda before given, and I never saw him more dejected in my life. His face, always sad in repose, was then saddened until it became a picture of despair, and he spoke of the want of sincere and earnest support from the Republican leaders with unusual freedom. I distinctly remember his reference to the fact that of all the Republican members of the House he could name but one in whose personal and political friendship he could absolutely confide. That one man was Isaac N. Arnold of Illinois. Stevens, the Great Commoner of the war, while sincerely desiring Lincoln's re-election because he hated McClellan worse than he hated Lincoln, and because he felt that the election of Lincoln was necessary to the safety of the Union, was intensely bitter against Lincoln personally, and rarely missed an opportunity to thrust his keenest invectives upon him. New York had a Democratic Governor of matchless ability, and that great State was regarded as almost hopelessly lost. Pennsylvania was trembling in the balance, as was confirmed by the failure of the Republicans to carry the State at the October election, and Indiana would have been almost in rebellion but for the victories of Sherman and Sheridan during the month of September.

At this interview Lincoln seemed to have but one overmastering desire, and that was to attain peace on the basis of a restored Union. He took from a corner of his desk a paper written out in his own handwriting, proposing to pay to the South $400,000,000 as compensation for their slaves, on condition that the States should return to their allegiance to the government and accept Emancipation. I shall never forget the emotion exhibited by Lincoln when, after reading this paper to me, he said: "If I could only get this proposition before the Southern people, I believe they would accept it, and I have faith that the Northern people, however startled at first, would soon appreciate the wisdom of such a settlement of the war. One hundred days of war would cost us the $400,000,000 I would propose to give for Emancipation and a restored Republic, not to speak of the priceless sacrifice of life and the additional sacrifice of property; but were I to make this offer now it would defeat me inevitably and probably defeat Emancipation." I had seen him many times when army disasters shadowed the land and oppressed him with sorrow, but I never saw him so profoundly moved by grief as he was on that day, when there seemed to be not even a silvery lining to the political cloud that hung over him. Few now recall the grave perils to Lincoln's re-election which thickened almost at every turn in 1864 until the country was electrified by Sherman's inspiring dispatch from Atlanta, followed by Sheridan's brilliant victories in the Valley and Sherman's memorable march to the sea; and it was these grave perils and these supreme necessities, long understood by Lincoln, which made him, in his broad and sagacious way, carefully view the field for the strongest candidate for Vice-President, and finally led him to nominate Andrew Johnson. To Lincoln, and to Lincoln alone, Johnson owed his nomination.

I had no personal knowledge of Lincoln's purpose to nominate Johnson for Vice-President until the day before the Baltimore Convention met. He telegraphed me to visit Washington before attending the convention, and I did so. He opened the conversation by advising me to give my vote and active support to Johnson as his associate on the ticket. It was evident that he confidently relied on my willingness to accept his judgment in the matter. I had expected to support the renomination of Hamlin. I had little respect for Andrew Johnson, and of all the men named for the position he was the last I would have chosen if I had been left to the exercise of my own judgment. It is more than probable that I would have obeyed the wishes of Lincoln even if he had not presented the very strong and, indeed, conclusive reasons for his request; but after hearing the arguments which had led him to the conclusion that Johnson should be nominated as his associate, I was quite as ready to ac-

cept the wisdom of the proposition as to obey the wishes
of the President.

There was not a trace of bitterness, prejudice, or even
unfriendliness toward Hamlin in all that Lincoln said
about the Vice-Presidency, and he was careful to say
that he did not desire the nomination of Johnson to
gratify any personal preference of his own. He naturally preferred a new man, as Hamlin was not in sympathy with Lincoln personally or with the general policy
of his administration, but he preferred Johnson for two
reasons, which he presented with unanswerable clearness: First, he was the most conspicuous, most aggressive, and the most able of all the War Democrats of that
time, and was just in the position to command the largest
measure of sympathy and support from that very important political element. Dix, Dickinson, Butler, and Holt
had made no such impressive exhibition of their loyalty
as had Johnson in Tennessee. He was then just in the
midst of his great work of rehabilitating his rebellious
State and restoring it to the Union, and his loyal achievements were therefore fresh before the people and certain
to continue so during the campaign. There was really
no answer to Lincoln's argument on this point. Second,
the stronger and more imperative reason for Lincoln preferring Johnson was one that I had not appreciated fully
until he had presented it. The great peril of the Union
at that day was the recognition of the Confederacy by
England and France, and every month's delay of the
overthrow of the rebellious armies increased the danger.
Extraordinary efforts had been made by Lincoln to stim-
ulate the Union sentiment, especially in England, but
with only moderate success, and there was no safety
from one day to another against a war with England
and France that would have been fatal to the success of
the Union cause. The only possible way to hinder recog-

nition was to show successful results of the war in restoring the dissevered States to their old allegiance, and Lincoln was firmly convinced that by no other method could the Union sentiment abroad be so greatly inspired and strengthened as by the nomination and election of a representative Southern man to the Vice-Presidency from one of the rebellious States in the very heart of the Confederacy. These reasons decided Lincoln to prefer Johnson for Vice-President, and Lincoln possessed both the power to make the nomination and the wisdom to dictate it without jarring the party organization.

The fact that Lincoln did not make known to Hamlin and his friends his purpose to nominate another for Vice-President in 1864 does not accuse him of deceit or insincerity; and the additional fact that when the Convention was in session and he was asked for a categorical answer as to his position on the Vice-Presidency, he declined to express his wishes or to avow his interference with the action of the party, cannot be justly construed into political double-dealing. It was quite as much a necessity for Lincoln to conceal his movements for the nomination of Johnson as it was, in his judgment, a necessity for him to nominate a Southern man and a War Democrat, and he simply acted with rare sagacity and discretion in his movements and with fidelity to the country, the safety of which was paramount with him. Hamlin was profoundly grieved over his defeat, as were his many friends, and had they seen the hand of Lincoln in it they would have resented it with bitterness; but Hamlin himself was not fully convinced of Lincoln's opposition to his renomination until within two years of his death. I have in my possession an autograph letter from Hamlin to Judge Pettis of Pennsylvania, to whom Lincoln had expressed his desire for Johnson's nomination on the morning of the day the convention met, in which he says that he

9

had seen and heard statements relating to Lincoln's
action in the matter, but he did not believe them until
the evidence had lately been made conclusive to his
mind. In this letter he says: "I was really sorry to be
disabused." And he adds: "Mr. L. [Lincoln] evidently
became some alarmed about his re-election, and changed
his position. That is all I care to say." I have thus the
conclusive evidence from Hamlin himself, that in September, 1889, he had full knowledge of Lincoln's direct
intervention to nominate Johnson for Vice-President in
1864. Hamlin gave an earnest support to the ticket,
believing that the supreme sentiment of Republicanism
had set him aside in the interest of the public welfare.
He maintained his high position in the party for many
years thereafter, filling the office of Collector of Portland
and subsequently returning to the Senate, where he
served until he had passed the patriarchal age, and then
voluntarily retired to enjoy the calm evening of a well-
spent life.

(Photo by Gutekunst, Philadelphia.)

SALMON P. CHASE.

LINCOLN AND CHASE.

SALMON P. CHASE was the most irritating fly in the Lincoln ointment from the inauguration of the new administration in 1861 until the 29th of June, 1864, when his resignation as Secretary of the Treasury was finally accepted. He was an annual resigner in the Cabinet, having petulantly tendered his resignation in 1862, again in 1863, and again in 1864, when he was probably surprised by Mr. Lincoln's acceptance of it. It was soon after Lincoln's unanimous renomination, and when Chase's dream of succeeding Lincoln as President had perished, at least for the time. He was one of the strongest intellectual forces of the entire administration, but in politics he was a theorist and a dreamer and was unbalanced by overmastering ambition. He never forgave Lincoln for the crime of having been preferred for President over him, and while he was a pure and conscientious man, his prejudices and disappointments were vastly stronger than himself, and there never was a day during his continuance in the Cabinet when he was able to approach justice to Lincoln. Like Sumner, he entered public life ten years before the war by election to the Senate through a combination of Democrats and Free-Soilers, and it is worthy of note that these two most brilliant and tireless of the great anti-slavery leaders cast their last votes for Democratic candidates for President.

From the day that Chase entered the Cabinet he seems to have been consumed with the idea that he must be Lincoln's successor in 1864, and to that end he systematically directed his efforts, and often sought, by flagrant abuse of the power of his department, to weaken his chief. He will stand in history as the great financier of the war; as the man who was able to maintain the national credit in the midst of rebellion and disruption, and who gave the country the best banking system the world has ever known. In that one duty he was practical and amenable to wholesome counsel, and his unblemished personal and official integrity gave great weight to his policy as Secretary of the Treasury. With all the vexation he gave Lincoln, and with the many reasons he gave his chief to regard him as perfidious, Lincoln never ceased to appreciate his value as a Cabinet officer. In 1863, when Chase had become an open candidate for the Presidency, and when many of his political movements were personally offensive to the President, Lincoln said of Chase: "I have determined to shut my eyes so far as possible to everything of the sort. Mr. Chase makes a good Secretary, and I shall keep him where he is. If he becomes President, all right. I hope we may never have a worse man. I have observed with regret his plan of strengthening himself." This expression from Lincoln conveys a very mild idea of his real feelings on the subject. In point of fact, Lincoln was not only profoundly grieved at Chase's candidacy, but he was constantly irritated at the methods Chase employed to promote his nomination.

I never saw Lincoln unbalanced except during the fall of 1863, when Chase was making his most earnest efforts to win the Republican nomination. The very widespread distrust toward Lincoln cherished by Republican leaders gave him good reason to apprehend the success of a com-

bination to defeat him.   Scores of national leaders were
at that time disaffected, but when they were compelled
to face the issue of his renomination or Republican defeat, they finally yielded with more or less ill grace, and
supported him.   Lincoln saw that if the disaffected elements of the party should be combined on one strong
candidate, his own success would be greatly endangered.
It was the only subject on which I ever knew Lincoln
to lose his head.   I saw him many times during the summer and fall of 1863, when the Chase boom was at its
height, and he seemed like one who had got into water
far beyond his depth.   I happened at the White House
one night when he was most concerned about the Chase
movement, and he detained me until two o'clock in the
morning.   Occasionally he would speak with great seri-
ousness, and evidently felt very keenly the possibility of
his defeat, while at other times his face would suddenly
brighten up with his never-ending store of humor, and
he would illustrate Chase's attitude by some pertinent
story, at which he would laugh immoderately.   After
reviewing the situation for an hour, during which I assured him that Chase could not be the Republican candidate, whoever might be, and that I regarded his renomination as reasonably certain, I rose at midnight,
shook hands with him, and started to go.   He followed
me to the end of the Cabinet table nearest his desk,
swung one of his long legs over the corner of it, and
stopped me to present some new phase of the Chase battle that had just occurred to him.   After he had gotten
through with that I again bade him good-night and
started to the door.   He followed to the other end of the
Cabinet table, again swung his leg over the corner of it,
and started in afresh to discuss the contest between Chase
and himself.

It was nearly one o'clock when I again bade Lincoln

good-night, and got as far as the door, but when just about to open it he called me and with the merriest twinkling of his eye, he said: "By the way, McClure, how would it do if I were to decline Chase?" I was surprised of course at the novel suggestion, and said to him, "Why, Mr. Lincoln, how could that be done?" He answered, "Well, I don't know exactly how it might be done, but that reminds me of a story of two Democratic candidates for Senator in Egypt, Illinois, in its early political times. That section of Illinois was almost solidly Democratic, as you know, and nobody but Democrats were candidates for office. Two Democratic candidates for Senator met each other in joint debate from day to day, and gradually became more and more exasperated at each other, until their discussions were simply disgraceful wrangles, and they both became ashamed of them. They finally agreed that either should say anything he pleased about the other and it should not be resented as an offense, and from that time on the campaign progressed without any special display of ill temper. On election night the two candidates, who lived in the same town, were receiving their returns together, and the contest was uncomfortably close. A distant precinct, in which one of the candidates confidently expected a large majority, was finally reported with a majority against him. The disappointed candidate expressed great surprise, to which the other candidate answered that he should not be surprised, as he had taken the liberty of declining him in that district the evening before the election. He reminded the defeated candidate that he had agreed that either was free to say anything about the other without offense, and added that under that authority he had gone up into that district and taken the liberty of saying that his opponent had retired from the contest, and therefore the

vote of the district was changed, and the declined candidate was thus defeated. I think,'' added Lincoln,
with one of his heartiest laughs, ''I had better decline
Chase.'' It was evident that the question of inducing
Chase to decline was very seriously considered by Lin·
coln. He did not seem to know just how it could be
done, but it was obvious that he believed it might be
done in one way or another, and what he said in jest he
meant in sober earnest.

Lincoln's anxiety for a renomination was the one
thing ever uppermost in his mind during the third year
of his administration, and, like all men in the struggles
of ambition, he believed that his only motive in his desire for his own re-election was to save the country,
rather than to achieve success for himself. That he
was profoundly sincere and patriotic in his purpose and
efforts to save the Union, and that he would willingly
have given his life as a sacrifice had it been necessary to
accomplish that result, none can doubt who knew him;
but he was only human, after all, and his ambition was
like the ambition of other good men, often stronger than
himself. In this as in all political or administrative
movements Lincoln played the waiting game. When
he did not know what to do, he was the safest man in
the world to trust to do nothing. He carefully veiled
his keen and sometimes bitter resentment against Chase,
and waited the fullness of time when he could by some
fortuitous circumstance remove Chase as a competitor,
or by some shrewd manipulation of politics make him a
hopeless one. His inexperience in the details of politics
made him naturally distrustful and apprehensive as to
his renomination. He could not, at that early day, get
together the political forces necessary to make him feel
safe in the battle, and it was not until about the close of
1863 or early in 1864 that he finally formulated in his

mind his political policy, and began the work of consolidating his forces for action. He did this with a degree of sagacity and method that would have done credit to the ripest politician of the age, but there was no time until the Baltimore Convention met that Lincoln felt secure. Even after an overwhelming majority of the delegates had been instructed in his favor, and when to all but himself it was evident that there could be no effective opposition to him in the convention, he was never entirely free from doubts as to the result. Within a month of his nomination, and when his more violent enemies had abandoned the effort to defeat him, as was evidenced by the Fremont Convention called at Cleveland, he was yet perplexed with anxiety over the possibility of his defeat. In discussing the question as late as May, 1864, I was surprised to find the apprehensions he cherished. I told him that his nomination was a foregone conclusion, and that it was not possible for any combination to be made that could endanger his success. I presented the attitude of the various States, and referred to their delegations to prove to him that his nomination must be made on the first ballot by a two-thirds vote, if not with absolute unity. To this he responded: "Well, McClure, what you say seems to be unanswerable, but I don't quite forget that I was nominated for President in a convention that was two-thirds for the other fellow."

It is needless to say that the official and personal relations between Chase and Lincoln during the latter part of the year 1863 and the early part of 1864 were severely strained. Lincoln felt it deeply, but said little to any one on the subject, and never permitted Chase to know how keenly he grieved him. He knew that Chase sincerely desired to be honest in the performance of his public duty, and he judged his infirmities with generous

charity.   He fully appreciated the fact, so well stated
by Chase's biographer, Judge Warden, that Chase " was
indeed sought less by strong men and by good men than
by weak men and by bad men."   Indeed, Chase, with
all his towering intellect and all his admitted devotion
to the country's cause, was the merest plaything of the
political charlatans who crossed his path, and he was
thus made to do many things which were unworthy of
him, and which, with any other than Lincoln to judge
him, would have brought him to absolute disgrace.   He
wrote many letters to his friends in different parts of
the country habitually complaining of Lincoln's incompetency and of the hopeless condition of the war.   In
none of the many letters which have reached the light
did he give Lincoln credit for capacity or fitness for his
responsible trust.   In disposing of the patronage of his
department he was often fretful and generally ill-advised.

With all these infirmities of temper and of ambition,
Lincoln bore with Chase with marvelous patience until
after Lincoln's unanimous renomination in 1864, when
Chase sent his third resignation to the President.   In
his letter of resignation he said: " My position here is
not altogether agreeable to you, and it is certainly too
full of embarrassment and difficulty and painful responsibility to allow in me the least desire to retain it."
For the first time Lincoln recognized the fact that he
and Chase could not get along together, and he promptly
answered Chase's letter of resignation in the following
terse but expressive note: " Your resignation of the office
of Secretary of the Treasury, sent me yesterday, is accepted.   Of all I have said in commendation of your
ability and fidelity I have nothing to unsay, and yet you
and I have reached a point of mutual embarrassment in
our official relation which it seems cannot be overcome
or long sustained consistently with the public service."

Like all irritable men who are the prey of infirmities, Chase believed, and recorded in his diary, that the embarrassments which arose between him and Lincoln were not of his creation. He thus expresses it in his own language: "I had found a good deal of embarrassment from him, but what he had found from me I cannot imagine, unless it has been caused by my unwillingness to have offices distributed as spoils or benefits." Chase retired from the Cabinet believing that he had severed all political relations with Lincoln for the remainder of his life, and the last thing that he then could have dreamed of was that his name would ever be considered by the President for the office of Chief Justice of the United States.

When Chase retired from the Cabinet, in the latter part of June, he did not expect to support Lincoln for re-election. Within a week thereafter he recorded in his diary the fact that Senator Pomeroy could not support Lincoln, and he added: "I am much of the same sentiment, though not willing now to decide what duty may demand next fall." But he then hoped much from the revolutionary attitude of the supporters of Fremont and the bold assault made upon Lincoln by Senator Wade and Representative Henry Winter Davis. Chase retired to the White Mountains to await events, and it soon became evident that the revolt against Lincoln would not materialize. On the contrary, every week brought wayward stragglers into the Lincoln camp, until at last Fremont himself had to surrender the side-show nomination he had accepted and fall into line in support of the administration, and the manifesto of Wade and Davis had fallen upon listless ears. It soon became evident that the sulking Republican leaders must choose between Lincoln and McClellan—between supporting the war and opposing the war, for the McClellan platform distinctly declared the war a failure and demanded the restoration of the Union by some other method than an appeal to arms. When Chase returned from his rest in the mountains in the latter part of September, he visited Washington, and of course paid his respects to the President. It is evident from Chase's own report of his interview with Lincoln that he was not greatly inspired by Lincoln's professions of devotion. He notes the fact that Lincoln was "not at all demonstrative, either in speech or manner," and he adds, "I feel that I do not know him." It is evident that Chase returned to Washington with the view of getting into some sort of friendly relations with the President. He twice visited Lincoln during his short stay in Washington, and within a week thereafter he publicly declared himself in favor of Lincoln's election at his home in Ohio. He voted the Republican State ticket in October, and sent a congratulatory telegram to Lincoln on the result of the election.

It was known to all about Washington during the fall of 1864 that Chief Justice Taney could not long survive, and after the first of September he was likely to die any day. It would be unjust to Chase to say that he was influenced in his political action by the hope of succeeding Chief Justice Taney, but the fact that his name was pressed upon Lincoln simultaneously by his friends throughout the country, even before the dead Chief Justice had been consigned to the tomb, proves that Chase had cherished the hope of reaching that exalted judicial position. Taney died on the 12th of October, 1864, within two weeks after Chase declared himself in favor of the election of Lincoln, and on the 13th of October Chase's name was on the lips of all his friends as the man for Chief Justice. The movement was dignified by the active and earnest efforts of Senator Sumner, who was in a position to exert considerable influence

9

with the President, although on many questions they had seriously differed. He desired a Chief Justice who could be trusted on the slavery question, and, believing that Chase was the safest of all on that important issue, he made an exhaustive struggle to win the position for Chase. Secretary Stanton, who had been in general harmony with Chase in the Cabinet, was also his earnest friend in the struggle for the Chief Justiceship, but the opposition aroused at the mention of his name came from every part of the country, and from very many of the ablest and most earnest of Lincoln's friends. It was argued against Chase that while his ability was admitted, his practical knowledge of law was limited, and that he was without legal training, because his life had been devoted almost exclusively to politics. He was elected to the Senate a dozen years before the war; he retired from the Senate to become Governor of Ohio, in which position he served two terms, and he was re-elected to the Senate at the close of his gubernatorial service. He gave up the Senatorship to enter the Cabinet in 1861, so that for many years he had given no thought or efforts to the law, and he was regarded by very many as lacking in the special training necessary to the first judicial office of the national government.

Strong as was the hostility to Chase's appointment in every section of the Union, the most intense opposition came from his own State of Ohio. The suggestion that he should become Chief Justice was resented by a large majority of the leading Republicans of the State, and they severely tested Lincoln's philosophy by the violence of their opposition, and especially by the earnestness with which they insisted that it was an insult to Lincoln himself to ask him to appoint Chase. Pennsylvania's most prominent official connected with the administration, and one of her most learned lawyers, Joseph J.

Lewis, then Commissioner of Internal Revenue, reflected the general Republican sentiment of Pennsylvania by his unusual proceeding of sending a formal protest to Lincoln against Chase's appointment. He declared that Chase "was not a man of much legal or financial knowledge; that his selfishness had gradually narrowed and contracted his views of things in general; that he was amazingly ignorant of men; that it was the opinion in the department that he really desired, toward the end of his term of office, to injure, and as far as possible to destroy, the influence and popularity of the administration."

I have, in a previous chapter, related an interview I had with Lincoln a short time before he appointed Chase. It was very evident from Lincoln's manner, rather than from what he said, that he was much perplexed as to his duty in the selection of a Chief Justice. In that conversation he discussed the merits of the half dozen or more prominent men who were suggested for the place. It is hardly proper to say that Lincoln discussed the matter, for the conversation was little else on his part than a succession of searching inquiries to obtain the fullest expression of my views as to the merits and demerits of the men he seemed to have under consideration. As to his own views he was studiously reticent. I tried in various ways to obtain some idea of the leaning of his mind on the subject, but did not succeed. The many inquiries he made about Stanton, and the earnestness he exhibited in discussing, or rather having me discuss, Stanton as the possible Chief Justice, impressed me with the belief that he was entertaining the idea of appointing his Secretary of War; but he gave no expression that could have warranted me in assuming that I could correctly judge the bent of his mind on the subject. The fact that he delayed the appointment for nearly two months after the death of Taney proves that Lincoln gave the subject not only very serious but protracted consideration, and I doubt whether he had fully decided in his own mind whom he would appoint until the 6th of December, the day that he sent the name of Chase to the Senate for Chief Justice.

At no time during Lincoln's administration had he ever submitted to an equal pressure in deciding any public appointment, and, excepting the Emancipation Proclamation, I doubt whether any question of policy was ever so earnestly pressed and opposed by his friends as was the appointment of Chase. Any other President than Lincoln would not have appointed Chase. His personal affronts to Lincoln had been continuous and flagrant from the time he entered the Cabinet until he resigned from it a little more than three years thereafter, and I am quite sure that at no time during that period did Lincoln ever appeal to Chase for advice as his friend. He had many consultations with him, of course, on matters relating to the government, but that Lincoln regarded Chase as his bitter and even malignant enemy during all that period cannot now be doubted. The only pretense of atonement that Chase had ever made was his hesitating and ungracious support of Lincoln's re-election, but only after the brilliant success of the Union armies under Sherman and Sheridan had absolutely settled the contest in Lincoln's favor. Grant overlooked a malignant assault made upon him by Admiral Porter when he promoted him to succeed Farragut; but in that case Porter's record clearly entitled him to the distinction, and Grant simply yielded personal resentment to a public duty. It was not pretended that Chase had any claim to the Chief Justiceship on the ground of eminent legal attainments or of political fidelity, and Lincoln's appointment of Chase was simply one of the many exhibitions of the matchless magnanimity that was one of the greatest attributes of his character. He appointed him not because he desired Chase for Chief Justice so much as because he feared that, in refusing to appoint him, he might permit personal prejudice to do injustice to the nation. *

Of course, Chase promptly and effusively thanked the President when he learned that his name had been sent to the Senate for Chief Justice. In his letter to Lincoln he said: "Before I sleep I must thank you for this mark of your confidence, and especially for the manner in which the nomination was made." But before he was

---

* You give a wrong impression as to Chase's legal training. He was a thorough student of the law, and a careful, painstaking lawyer till he entered the Senate at the age of forty-two. He even was so fond of law as to take up superfluous drudgery, editing with notes and citations the Ohio Statutes. He kept out of politics till he was thirty-three. While in the Senate he argued cases in the Supreme Court—as one involving the title to lands in and about Keokuk.

Now, it is the study and practice a lawyer has before forty which determine his quality and equipment as a jurist. and these are not much affected by diversions afterward. A man culminates professionally by forty : witness B. R. Curtis, Choate, Follett, etc. Edmunds has been in the Senate twenty or twenty-five years, but he has not lost his legal ability acquired before he entered it.

My own impression is, from the conversations with Lincoln which different persons have reported to me and from some manuscript letters of Sumner, that Lincoln intended all along to appoint Chase, though somewhat doubting whether Chase would settle down quietly in his judicial office and let politics alone. That was a sincere apprehension which others shared, but I do not think that Lincoln's mind at all rested on any other person.

I began to write this note only to make the points that Chase had ample legal training, and that his intellect was naturally judicial. See his able argument in the Van Landt case, about 1846.—*Edward L. Pierce to the Author*, December 7, 1891.

three months in the high office conferred upon him by Lincoln he became one of Lincoln's most obtrusive and petulant critics, and his last letter to Lincoln, written on the very day of Lincoln's assassination, was a harsh criticism on the President's action in the Louisiana case. Immediately after the death of Lincoln, writing to an old political associate in Ohio, Chase said: "The schemes of politicians will now adjust themselves to the new conditions; I want no part in them." Indeed, the only specially kind words from Chase to Lincoln that I have been able to discover in all the publications giving Chase's views I find in the one expression of hearty gratitude and friendship, written on the impulse of the moment, when he was first notified of his nomination to the Chief Justiceship. The new conditions of which he spoke after the death of Lincoln, and in which he declared he could have no part, speedily controlled the new Chief Justice in his political actions. The leader of the radical Republicans when he became Chief Justice, he gradually gravitated against his party until he was ready to accept the Democratic nomination for President in 1868, and he never thereafter supported a Republican candidate for President. He hoped to receive the Presidential nomination from the New York Convention of 1868. It had been agreed upon by some who believed that they controlled the convention that Chase should be nominated, and Governor Seymour retired from the chair at the appointed time, as is generally believed, to make the nomination to the convention; but Samuel J. Tilden had no love for Chase, and it was he who inspired the spontaneous movement that forced the nomination of Seymour while he was out of the chair, and carried it like a whirlwind. Tilden did not guide the convention to the nomination of Seymour because he specially desired Seymour's nomination; he did it because he desired

10

to defeat the nomination of Chase.   The result was the
keenest disappointment to the Chief Justice.   He defined
his political position during the contest of 1868 as follows: "The action of the two parties has obliged me to
resume, with my old faith, my old position—that of
Democrat; by the grace of God free and independent."

After 1868, Chase was unknown as a factor in politics.
In June, 1870, he was attacked by paralysis, and from
that time until his death, on the 7th of May, 1873, he
was a hopeless invalid.   His last political deliverance
was a feeble declaration in favor of Greeley's election in
1872, when he was shattered in mind and body.   It may
truthfully be said of him that from 1861 until his death
his public life was one continued and consuming disappointment, and the constant training of his mind to politics doubtless greatly hindered him in winning the distinction as Chief Justice that he might have achieved
had he given up political ambition and devoted himself
to the high judicial duties he had accepted.   While one
of the greatest intellects among all the Republican leaders, he was an absolute failure as a politician, and his
persistence in political effort made him fail to improve
other opportunities.   His life may be summed up in the
single sentence: He was an eminently great, a strangely
unbalanced, and a sadly disappointed man.

LINCOLN AND CAMERON.

ABRAHAM LINCOLN had more varied and complicated relations with Simon Cameron than with any
other Pennsylvanian during his Presidential term. Indeed, Cameron fills more pages in the annals of Pennsylvania politics than any citizen of the State since the
organization of our government. He is the only man
who was four times elected to the United States Senate
by the Pennsylvania Legislature until his son attained
the same distinction as his successor, and he would have
won a fifth election without a serious contest had he not
voluntarily resigned to assure the succession to his son.
Without great popular following, he was the most conspicuous of all our Pennsylvania politicians, measured
by the single standard of success in obtaining political
honors and power. He was first elected to the Senate in
1845 to succeed Buchanan, who had been transferred to
the Polk Cabinet. The tariff of 1842 was then a vital
issue in Pennsylvania, and Cameron was known as a
positive protectionist. The Legislature was Democratic,
and had nominated the late Chief Justice Woodward
with apparent unanimity to succeed Buchanan; but
Cameron organized a bolt from the Democratic party,
commanded the solid Whig vote on the tariff issue, and
was thus elected. The Senate to which he was chosen
was Democratic, and he exhibited his peculiar power
over that body when he served in it by the rejection of

(Photo by Brady, Washington.)

SIMON CAMERON, 1805.

Judge Woodward when nominated by President Polk as Justice of the Supreme Court of the United States. He made a memorable record during his early Senatorial service by his earnest appeal to Vice-President Dallas in favor of protection, when it was known that the repeal of the tariff of 1842 would depend upon the casting vote of the Vice-President. At the expiration of his term, in 1849, Cameron was a candidate for re-election. The balance of power in the Legislature was held by Native American Representatives from Philadelphia, elected on the Fusion ticket. He failed, however, to divert that element from the Whigs, and abandoned the struggle, giving the field to James Cooper, the regular Whig candidate, who was successful.

In 1854 a strange political revolution occurred in Pennsylvania, in which the new American or Know-Nothing party elected the Whig candidate for Governor and the Democratic candidate for Canal Commissioner, and carried an overwhelming majority of the Legislature, embracing nominees of both parties. Cameron supported the Democratic ticket, and made a speech in its favor the night before election, but immediately after the election he associated himself with the Americans and became an aggressive candidate for United States Senator. This was the beginning of the factional conflict between Cameron and Curtin (then Secretary of the Commonwealth) that continued as long as they were in active political life. The new party was without leadership or discipline, and was speedily broken into fragments by a dozen aspirants for the Senatorship, of whom Cameron and Curtin were the leading and apparently only hopeful candidates. The struggle became exceptionally bitter, the joint convention meeting and adjourning from time to time without succeeding in a choice, until finally it became a matter of necessity to elect Cameron or adjourn without an election; and after a protracted contest over that issue the joint convention adjourned *sine die* by one majority. The next Legislature was Democratic, and Governor Bigler was chosen. When the Legislature met in 1857 the Democrats had three majority on joint ballot, and confidently expected to elect a Senator. The late Colonel Forney was made the candidate by the direct intervention of President-elect Buchanan, who was then just on the threshold of the enormous power and patronage of the Presidency. The nomination would naturally have gone to Henry D. Foster, who was a member of the House, but for the attitude assumed by Buchanan. Forney's nomination somewhat weakened the Democratic lines by the general and clamorous discontent of the several candidates who had hoped to win in an open contest. The Republicans were intensely embittered against Forney because they believed that he, as chairman of the Democratic State Committee, had controlled the October election unfairly to defeat the Republican State ticket by a small majority, and thus assured the election of a Democratic President. Cameron had for the first time taken open ground against the Democrats in 1856, when he was one of the Republican candidates for elector at large, and actively supported Fremont's election. But he was not in personal favor with most of the Republicans, and when his name was proposed in the Republican caucus as a candidate for Senator, it was not seriously entertained until Senator Penrose assured the caucus that Cameron could command three Democratic votes if given the solid support of the Republicans. A confidential committee was appointed to ascertain the truth of the statement by personal assurance from the Democratic members, and after a confirmative report, in which the names of the Democratic members were not given, the Republican caucus resolved to cast one vote for Cameron. That resolution was carried out in joint convention, and three Democratic Representatives (Lebo, Maneer, and Wagonseller) voted for Cameron and elected him.

In 1861, Cameron resigned the Senatorship to accept the War portfolio under Lincoln. Early in 1862 he was transferred by Lincoln from the War Department to the Russian Mission, and in 1863 he had resigned his mission and again appeared as a candidate for United States Senator to succeed Wilmot, who had been chosen to fill Cameron's unexpired term. The Legislature contained one Democratic majority on joint ballot. Wilmot would have been unanimously renominated had it been possible to elect him, but Cameron was nominated upon the positive assurance from his friends that he could command one or more Democratic votes and was the only Republican who could be successful. His nomination and the contest that followed led to an eruption that not only prevented any Democratic support, but deprived him of a solid Republican support, and Buckalew was elected. In 1867, Cameron and Curtin again locked horns on the Senatorship, and Cameron was successful after a struggle of unexampled desperation. Cameron served his full term of six years, and was re-elected in 1873 to succeed himself, without a contest. Most of the active opponents within his party had broken to the support of Greeley in 1872, and thereafter Cameron was practically supreme in the direction of the Republican organization. He resigned in 1877, when the Legislature was in session, and after it had been ascertained that his son, the present Senator Cameron, could be elected as his successor. Had Cameron not resigned, he would have been elected to his fifth term in 1879 by the united vote of his party; but from his retirement in 1877 until his death, a dozen years later, he seemed to enjoy freedom from the cares and perplexities of political life, and had the grati- fication of seeing his son thrice elected to the position he had surrendered to him.   He had survived all the many intensified asperities of his long and active political life, and died at the ripe age of fourscore and ten years, with his faculties unabated until the long halt came.   He and his son have each attained the highest Senatorial honors ever awarded by Pennsylvania to any of her citizens by four elections to the Senate—an entirely exceptional rec- ord of political success in the history of all the States of the Union.   It was often complained by his foes that Cameron fought and won unfairly in his political con- tests, but the defeated generals of Europe made the same complaint against Napoleon.

Cameron was a Senator when Lincoln served his single term in Congress, but they did not become even acquaint- ances, and he first became involved in Lincoln's political life in 1860, when both were candidates for the Repub- lican nomination for President.   Cameron's candidacy was not regarded as a serious effort to nominate him, but the peculiar political situation in Pennsylvania greatly favored him in making himself the candidate of the State, and with his sagacity and energy in political affairs he was not slow to avail himself of it.   Curtin was the prominent candidate for Governor, and Cameron led Curtin's opponents.   Curtin commanded the nomina- tion for Governor, and naturally enough desired a united party to assure his election.   Cameron secured a majority of votes in the State Convention for President, and rea- sonably claimed that he was as much entitled to the united support of the party for President as Curtin was entitled to it for Governor.   The conflict between the two elements of the party led to a compromise, by which a nearly united delegation was given to Cameron for a complimentary vote for President. Cameron himself believed, in after years, that he could have been nominated and elected if he had been heartily pressed by Pennsylvania. He many times chided me for refusing to give him an earnest support, saying that he could have been made a successful candidate, and then, to use his own expressive language, "We could all have had everything we wanted." While Cameron had a majority of the delegation, a large minority was more or less bitterly opposed to him, and his name was withdrawn in the convention after the first ballot, because the delegation would have broken. The men who immediately represented Cameron on that occasion were John P. Sanderson, who was subsequently appointed to the regular army, and Alexander Cummings, whose confused use of military authority conferred upon him in the early part of the war led to a vote of censure upon Cameron by Congress. They knew before the convention met that the contest was narrowed down to Seward and Lincoln, and that Cameron, Chase, and Bates were not in the fight. Sanderson and Cummings, with little or no control of the delegation, were early in negotiation with David Davis, who was specially in charge of Lincoln's interest in Chicago, and obtained Davis's positive assurance that if the Pennsylvania delegation would support Lincoln and Lincoln succeeded to the Presidency, Cameron would be appointed Secretary of the Treasury. This agreement was not made known at the time to any in the delegation, nor did it become known to Lincoln, at least as a positive obligation, until after the election.

The success of Lincoln at the November election left the political situation in Pennsylvania without change, except that the war of factions was intensified. Curtin did not give even a perfunctory support to Cameron for the Presidency, and Cameron gave about the same sort

of support to Curtin for Governor; and when it was announced, about the 1st of January, that Cameron had
been to Springfield and had returned with the proffer of
a Cabinet portfolio, it immediately inspired the most aggressive opposition to his appointment. I was not in
sympathy with Cameron, and promptly telegraphed Lincoln, protesting against his appointment, to which Lincoln answered urging me to come immediately to Springfield. When I met Lincoln he frankly informed me that
on the last day of December he had given Cameron a
letter tendering to him a position in the Cabinet, reserv-
ing the right to decide whether it should be that of Secretary of the Treasury or Secretary of War. I explained
to the President, with all the ardor of an intense partisan
in the factional feud, that the appointment of Cameron
would be a misfortune to the party in Pennsylvania, and
a misfortune to the President that he must soon realize
after his inauguration. It is needless now to review the
causes which led to this active and embittered hostility
of the friends of Curtin to Cameron's political advancement. It is sufficient to say that there was persistent
war between these elements, and the usual political demoralization that ever attends such conflicts was pain-
fully visible from the factional battles of that time. I
saw that Lincoln was very much distressed at the situation in which he had become involved, and he discussed
every phase of it with unusual frankness and obviously
with profound feeling. I did not then know that Lincoln had been pledged, without his knowledge, by his
friends at Chicago to the appointment of Cameron, nor
did Lincoln intimate it to me during our conversation.
After an hour or more of discussion on the subject Lincoln dismissed it by saying that he would advise me
further within a very few days.

I left Lincoln conscious that I had seriously impressed

him with my views, but entirely unable to form any
judgment as to what might be his ultimate action. Although I left him as late as eleven o'clock in the evening, he wrote Cameron a private letter dated the same
night, beginning with this sentence: "Since seeing you,
things have developed which make it impossible for me
to take you into the Cabinet." He added: "You will
say this comes from an interview with McClure, and this
is partly but not wholly true; the more potent matter is
wholly outside of Pennsylvania, yet I am not at liberty
to specify. Enough that it appears to me to be sufficient." He followed with the suggestion that Cameron should write him declining the appointment, stating
that if the declination was forwarded he would "not
object to its being known that it was tendered" to him.
He concluded by saying: "No person living knows, or
has an intimation, that I write this letter," and with a
postscript asking Cameron to telegraph the words "All
right." * Lincoln also wrote me a letter of a single sen-

---

* The following is the text of the Lincoln letters to Cameron
on the subject of the Cabinet appointment, as given in Nicolay
and Hay's life of Lincoln, published by the Century Company,
New York:

SPRINGFIELD, ILL., December 31, 1860.

HON. SIMON CAMERON:

MY DEAR SIR: I think fit to notify you now, that by your permission I shall at the proper time nominate you to the U. S. Senate for confirmation as Secretary of the Treasury, or as Secretary
of War—which of the two I have not yet definitely decided.
Please answer at your earliest convenience.

Your obedient servant,
A. LINCOLN.

(*Private.*)

SPRINGFIELD, ILL., Jan. 3, 1861.

HON. SIMON CAMERON:

MY DEAR SIR: Since seeing you things have developed which
make it impossible for me to take you into the Cabinet. You
will say this comes of an interview with McClure; and this is

tence, dated the same night, asking that the accusations against Cameron should be put in tangible shape for his

---

partly, but not wholly, true. The more potent matter is wholly outside of Pennsylvania, and yet I am not at liberty to specify it. Enough that it appears to me to be sufficient. And now I suggest that you write me declining the appointment, in which case I do not object to its being known that it was tendered you. Better do this at once, before things so change that you cannot honorably decline, and I be compelled to openly recall the tender. No person living knows or has an intimation that I write this letter.   Yours truly,

                                                              A. LINCOLN.

P. S. Telegraph me instantly on receipt of this, saying, " All right."—A. L.

                      (*Private and confidential.*)

                                        SPRINGFIELD, ILL., Jan. 13, 1861.
HON. SIMON CAMERON:

MY DEAR SIR: At the suggestion of Mr. Sanderson, and with hearty good-will besides, I herewith send you a letter dated Jan. 3, the same in date as the last you received from me. I thought best to give it that date, as it is in some sort to take the place of that letter. I learn, both by a letter of Mr. Swett and from Mr. Sanderson, that your feelings were wounded by the terms of my letter really of the 3d. I wrote that letter under great anxiety, and perhaps I was not so guarded in its terms as I should have been; but I beg you to be assured I intended no offense. My great object was to have you act quickly, if possible before the matter should be complicated with the Penn. Senatorial election. Destroy the offensive letter or return it to me.

I say to you now I have not doubted that you would perform the duties of a Department ably and faithfully. Nor have I for a moment intended to ostracize your friends. If I should make a Cabinet appointment for Penn. before I reach Washington, I will not do so without consulting you, and giving all the weight to your views and wishes which I consistently can. This I have always intended.   Yours truly,

                                                              A. LINCOLN.

                        (*Inclosure.*)

                                        SPRINGFIELD, ILL., Jan. 3, 1861.
HON. SIMON CAMERON:

MY DEAR SIR: When you were here, about the last of Decem-

consideration. I am unable to quote literally any of the correspondence with Lincoln on this subject, as all of my many letters received from him, and the correspondence relating to the campaign and the organization of the administration, that I had preserved, were destroyed when Chambersburg was burned by McCausland in 1864. I answered Lincoln's very indefinite note by declining to appear as an individual prosecutor of Cameron, and his request for the formulation of Cameron's alleged political and personal delinquencies was not complied with.

Lincoln's letter to Cameron tendering him the Cabinet appointment had been shown to some confidential friends whose enthusiasm outstripped their discretion, and they made public the fact that Cameron was an assured member of the new Cabinet. The second letter from Lincoln to Cameron, recalling the tender of a Cabinet office, was not made public, and doubtless was never seen beyond a very small and trusted circle of Cameron's associates; but it soon became known that Lincoln regarded the question as unsettled, and that led to exhaustive efforts on both sides to hinder and promote Cameron's appointment. Sanderson, who had made the compact at Chi-

---

ber, I handed you a letter saying I should at the proper time nominate you to the Senate for a place in the Cabinet. It is due to you and to truth for me to say you were here by my invitation, and not upon any suggestion of your own. You have not as yet signified to me whether you would accept the appointment, and with much pain I now say to you that you will relieve me from great embarrassment by allowing me to recall the offer. This springs from an unexpected complication, and not from any change of my view as to the ability or faithfulness with which you would discharge the duties of the place.

I now think I will not definitely fix upon any appointment for Pennsylvania until I reach Washington.

Your obedient servant,
A. LINCOLN.

cago with Davis for Cameron's appointment, was sent at
once to Springfield to enforce its fulfillment.   He reasonably complained that Lincoln's letter to Cameron revoking the appointment was offensively blunt and needed
explanation, as it gave no reason whatever for the sudden
change in his judgment.   While Sanderson and other
prominent Pennsylvanians who visited Lincoln about
the same time failed to obtain from him any assurance
of his purpose to appoint Cameron, Lincoln was prevailed upon on the 13th of January, ten days after he
had written the letter revoking the appointment, to
write a confidential letter to Cameron apologizing for
the unguarded terms in which he had expressed himself,
and giving the assurance that he "intended no offense."
He also enclosed to Cameron a new letter, antedated
January   3, which he suggested that Cameron should
accept as the original of that date, and destroy or return the one that had given offense.   In this letter he
said: "You have not as yet signified to me whether you
would accept the appointment, and with much pain I
now say to you that you will relieve me from great embarrassment by allowing me to recall the offer."   The
explanatory letter in which the antedated letter was enclosed gave Cameron only this assurance as to Lincoln's
purpose: "If I should make a Cabinet appointment for
Pennsylvania before I reach Washington, I will not do
so without consulting you and giving all the weight to
your views and wishes which I consistently can."   None
of these letters were made public by Cameron, but it was
well understood that it was an open fight for and against
him, and Pennsylvania was convulsed by that struggle
from the 1st of January until the Cabinet was announced
after the inauguration of the President.

When Lincoln arrived in Washington the five members of the Cabinet who had been positively chosen were

Messrs. Seward, Bates, Chase, Welles, and Smith. The ten days he spent at the Capital before becoming President were given up almost wholly to a battle over the two remaining Cabinet portfolios. The appointment of Cameron and Blair was not finally determined until the day before the inauguration, and then the Cameron issue was decided by the powerful intervention of Seward and Weed. They were greatly disappointed that Cameron had failed to deliver the Pennsylvania delegation to Seward, as they had been led to expect, but they were intensely embittered against Curtin because he and Lane had both openly declared at Chicago that Seward's nomination would mean their inevitable defeat. Looking back upon that contest with the clearer insight that the lapse of thirty years must give, I do not see how Lincoln could have done otherwise than appoint Cameron as a member of his Cabinet, viewed from the standpoint he had assumed. He desired to reconcile party differences by calling his Presidential competitors around him, and that opened the way for Cameron. He acted with entire sincerity, and in addition to the powerful pressure for Cameron's appointment made by many who were entitled to respect, he felt that he was not free from the obligation made in his name by Davis at Chicago to make Cameron a member of his Cabinet. The appointment was not made wholly for that reason, but that pledge probably resolved Lincoln's doubts in Cameron's favor, and he was accepted as Secretary of War. That there was some degree of mutual distrust between Lincoln and Cameron was a necessity from the circumstances surrounding the selection; but as there was no very large measure of mutual trust between Lincoln and any of his Cabinet officers, Cameron's relations with the President were little if any more strained than were the relations of his brother constitutional advisers with their chief;

and Cameron's practical views in the grave emergency
in which the administration was placed were probably
of more value to Lincoln at times than were the counsels of most of the Cabinet. Every member had his
own theory of meeting the appalling crisis, from peaceable dismemberment of the Republic to aggressive war,
while Lincoln had no policy but to await events, and he
counseled with all and trusted none. Cameron entered
the Cabinet, therefore, with about equal opportunity
among his associates to win and hold power with the
President, and his retirement within less than a year was
not due to any prejudices or apprehensions which may
have been created by the bitter struggle against his appointment.

Had the most capable, experienced, and upright man
of the nation been called to the head of the War Department when Lincoln was inaugurated in 1861, it would
have been impossible for him to administer that office
without flagrant abuses. The government was entirely
unprepared for war. It was without armies, without
guns, without munitions of war; indeed, it had to im-
provise everything needed to meet an already well-organ-
ized Confederate army. Contracts had to be made with
such haste as to forbid the exercise of sound discretion
in obtaining what the country needed; and Cameron,
with his peculiar political surroundings, with a horde
of partisans clamoring for spoils, was compelled either
to reject the confident expectation of his friends or to
submit to imminent peril from the grossest abuse of his
delegated authority. He was soon brought under the
severest criticism of leading journals and statesmen of
his own party, and Representative Dawes, now Senator
from Massachusetts, led an investigation of the alleged
abuses of the War Department, which resulted in a
scathing report against Cameron's methods in adminis-

tering the office, and a vote of censure upon Cameron by the House. Lincoln promptly exhibited the generous sense of justice that always characterized him by sending a special message to the House, exculpating Cameron, because the acts for which he was criticised had not been exclusively Cameron's, but were largely acts for which the President and Cabinet were equally responsible. Some ten years later the House expunged the resolution of censure. Notwithstanding the message of Lincoln lessening the burden of reproach cast upon Cameron by the House, popular distrust was very general as to the administration of the War Department, and the demands for Cameron's removal grew in both power and intensity. He was not accused of individual corruption, but the severe strain put upon the national credit led to the severest criticisms of all manner of public profligacy, and it culminated in a formal appeal to the President from leading financial men of the country for an immediate change in the Minister of War.

I have no reason to believe that Lincoln would have appointed a new Secretary of War had not public considerations made it imperative. His personal relations with Cameron were as pleasant as his relations with any other of his Cabinet officers, and in many respects Cameron was doubtless a valuable adviser because of his clear, practical, common-sense views of public affairs. The one vital issue that Cameron very early appreciated was that of slavery. As early as May, 1861, he wrote to General Butler, instructing him to refrain from surrendering to their masters any slaves who came within his lines, and to employ them "in the services to which they may be best adapted." That was the first step taken by the administration toward the overthrow of slavery. In August of the same year General Fremont issued a proclamation in Missouri declaring the slaves

11

of all those in the Confederate service to be for ever free, which was a substantial emancipation of all slaves in Missouri. Lincoln at once revoked the Fremont order, and sent Secretary Cameron and the Adjutant-General to personally examine into the situation in Missouri and report upon it. Cameron obviously sympathized with Fremont's emancipation ideas, and, instead of delivering to Fremont the order for his removal prepared before he left Washington, he finally decided to bring it back with him and to give Fremont an opportunity to retrieve himself. Lincoln, always patient, yielded to Fremont's importunities, and permitted him to remain in command until October, when he sent General Curtis in person to deliver the order of removal, with the single condition that if Fremont "shall then have, in personal command, fought and won a battle, or shall then be actually in battle, or shall then be in the immediate presence of the enemy in expectation of a battle, it is not to be delivered, but held for further orders." As Fremont was not near a battle, he was relieved of his command.

Cameron pressed the slavery issue to the extent of a flagrant outrage upon his chief by recommending the arming of slaves in his first annual report without the knowledge of the President, and sending it out in printed form to the postmasters of the country for delivery to the newspapers after having been presented to Congress. The slavery question had then become an important political theme, and politicians were shaping their lines to get into harmony with it. In this report Cameron declared in unqualified terms in favor of arming the slaves for military service. Lincoln was not only shocked, but greatly grieved when he learned the character of Cameron's recommendation, and he at once ordered that the copies be recalled by telegraph, the report revised, and a new edition printed. Cameron submitted as gracefully as possible, and revised his report, limiting his recommendations about slaves to the suggestion that they should not be returned to their masters.* While this episode did not produce unfriendly personal relations between Lincoln and Cameron, it certainly was a severe strain upon Lincoln's trust in the fidelity of his War

---

* It is as clearly a right of the government to arm slaves when it may become necessary, as it is to use gunpowder taken from the enemy. What to do with that species of property is a question that time and circumstance will solve, and need not be anticipated further than to repeat that they cannot be held by the government as slaves. It would be useless to keep them as prisoners of war; and self-preservation, the highest duty of a government or of individuals, demands that they should be disposed of or employed in the most effective manner that will tend most speedily to suppress the insurrection and restore the authority of the government. If it shall be found that the men who have been held by the rebels as slaves are capable of bearing arms and performing efficient military service, it is the right, and may become the duty, of the government to arm and equip them, and employ their services against the rebels under proper military regulation, discipline, and command.—*Cameron's Original Report, recalled by the President for revision.*

It is already a grave question what shall be done with those slaves who were abandoned by their owners on the advance of our troops into Southern territory, as at Beaufort district in South Carolina. The number left within our control at that point is very considerable, and similar cases will probably occur. What shall be done with them? Can we afford to send them forward to their masters, to be by them armed against us or used in producing supplies to sustain the rebellion? Their labor may be useful to us; withheld from the enemy, it lessens his military resources, and withholding them has no tendency to induce the horrors of insurrection, even in the rebel communities. They constitute a military resource, and, being such, that they should not be turned over to the enemy is too plain to discuss. Why deprive him of supplies by a blockade, and voluntarily give him men to produce them?—*Cameron's Report, as revised by direction of the President.*

Minister; but Lincoln was too wise to put himself in open antagonism to the antislavery sentiment of the country by removing Cameron for his offensive and sur- reptitious antislavery report. The financial pressure for Cameron's removal would probably have accomplished it under any circumstances, and Lincoln waited more than a month after the flurry over Cameron's report.

There have been many and conflicting accounts given to the public of Cameron's retirement from the Lincoln Cabinet, no one of which is wholly correct, and most of them incorrect in vital particulars. Cameron had ver- bally assured the President when censured by Congress, and again when the dispute arose over his annual report, that his resignation was at Lincoln's disposal at any time, but he had no knowledge of Lincoln's purpose to make a change in the War Department until he received Lincoln's letter in January, 1862, informing him of the change. In Nicolay and Hays' life of Lincoln (volume 5, page 128) is given what purports to be the letter de- livered to Cameron notifying him of the change. Lin- coln certainly wrote that letter, as his biographers have published it from his manuscript, but it is not the letter that was delivered to Cameron. Lincoln sent his letter to Cameron by Chase, who met Cameron late in the evening after he had dined with Colonel Forney, and he delivered the letter in entire ignorance of its contents. I happened to be spending the evening with Colonel Thomas A. Scott, then Cameron's Assistant Secretary of War, when Cameron came in near the midnight hour and exhibited an extraordinary degree of emotion. He laid the letter down upon Scott's table, and invited us both to read it, saying that it meant personal as well as political destruction, and was an irretrievable wrong committed upon him by the President. We were not then, and indeed never had been, in political sympathy, but our friendly personal relations had never been interrupted. He appealed to me, saying: "This is not a political affair; it means personal degradation; and while we do not agree politically, you know I would gladly aid you personally if it were in my power." Cameron was affected even to tears, and wept bitterly over what he regarded as a personal affront from Lincoln. I remember not only the substance of Lincoln's letter, but its language, almost, if not quite, literally, as follows: "I have this day nominated Hon. Edwin M. Stanton to be Secretary of War and you to be Minister Plenipotentiary to Russia." Although the message did not go to the Senate that day, it had been prepared and was sent in pursuance of that notice. Colonel Scott, who was a man of great versatility of resources, at once suggested that Lincoln did not intend personal offense to Cameron, and in that I fully agreed; and it was then and there arranged that on the following day Lincoln should be asked to withdraw the offensive letter; to permit Cameron to antedate a letter of resignation, and for Lincoln to write a kind acceptance of the same. The letter delivered by Chase was recalled; a new correspondence was prepared, and a month later given to the public.

Cameron had no knowledge or even suspicion of Stanton succeeding him. Chase and Seward, as well as Cameron, have claimed direct or indirect influence in the selection of Stanton, but there was not a single member of the Cabinet who knew of Stanton's appointment until Lincoln notified Cameron of the change. Stanton had been in open, malignant opposition to the administration only a few months before, but he was then the closest friend and personal counselor of General McClellan; was in hearty sympathy with the war; was resolutely and aggressively honest; and Lincoln chose him without consulting any, as far as I have ever been able to learn, unless it was General McClellan. One of the many good results he expected from Stanton as War Minister was entire harmony between him and the general commanding the armies.

Cameron well concealed his disappointment at the manner of his retirement from the Cabinet; wisely maintained personal relations with Lincoln; and when he returned from Russia, after less than a year of service as minister, he resumed active political life, and was one of the earliest of the political leaders to foresee that the people would force the renomination of Lincoln, regardless of the favor or disfavor of politicians. The early movement in January, 1864, in which Curtin cordially co-operated, by which the unanimous recommendation of the Republican members of the Pennsylvania Legislature was given for Lincoln's renomination, was suggested by Cameron; and Lincoln, with a sagacity that never failed him, took the earliest opportunity to attach Cameron so firmly to his cause that separation would be impossible. His first movement in that line was the Cameron mission to Fortress Monroe to ask Butler to accept the Vice-Presidency. This was in March, 1864, and Cameron was one of the very few whom Lincoln consulted about the Vice-Presidency until he finally settled upon the nomination of Johnson, in which Cameron reluctantly concurred, and he went to the Baltimore Convention as a delegate-at-large to execute Lincoln's wishes. He became chairman of the Republican State Committee in Pennsylvania, and doubtless would have been in very close relations with the President during his second term had Lincoln's life been spared.

I have written of Lincoln and Cameron with some hesitation, because during the thirty years in which Cameron and I were both more or less active in politics we never were in political sympathy. He had retired from his first term of Senatorial service before I had become a voter, and was thirty years my senior. He was then a Democrat and I a Whig, and the political hostility continued when in later years we were of the same political faith. He never was a candidate with my support, nor was I ever a candidate with his support, even when I was the unanimous nominee of our party. We differed radically in political methods, and often in bitterness, but our personal relations were never strained, and on occasions he confided in me and received friendly personal service that he warmly appreciated. We many times had a truce to attain some common end, but it was never misunderstood as anything more than a truce for the special occasion. When he entered the Lincoln Cabinet he knew that I would gladly have aided him to success, and we seldom met without an hour or more of pleasant personal intercourse over a bottle of wine, the only stimulant he ever indulged in. In 1873 he was elected to his fourth term to the Senate and I was a State Senator. An effort was made by legislative mercenaries to call into the field some man of large fortune as his competitor. He called on me, stated the case, and appealed to me to oppose the movement, as it was obviously dishonest. It was expected that my opposition to Cameron would make me willing to join any movement for his defeat; but I at once assured him that, while I would not support his election, I would earnestly oppose any effort to force him into the corrupt conciliation of venal legislators. He thanked me, and added: "I can rely upon you, and I will now dismiss the thieves without ceremony." The movement failed, and he was elected by the united vote of his party, while I voted for the late William D. Kelley. No man has so strongly impressed his personality upon the politics of

Pennsylvania as has Simon Cameron, and the political power he organized is as potent in the State to-day as at any time during his life. He was one of the few men who voluntarily retired from the Senate when he could have continued his service during life. He survived his retirement a full dozen years; his intercourse mellowed into the gentlest relations with old-time friends and foes, and in the ripeness of more than fourscore and ten summers and in peaceful resignation he slept the dreamless sleep of the dead.

(Photo by Brady, Washington.)

EDWIN M. STANTON, 1865.

LINCOLN AND STANTON.

OF all the men intimately connected with Abraham Lincoln during our civil war, Edwin M. Stanton presented the strangest medley of individual attributes. He was a man of whom two histories might be written as widely diverging as night and day, portraying him as worthy of eminent praise and as worthy of scorching censure, and yet both absolutely true. His dominant quality was his heroic mould. He could be heroic to a degree that seemed almost superhuman, and yet at times submissive to the very verge of cowardice. Like Lincoln, he fully trusted no man; but, unlike Lincoln, he distrusted all, and I doubt whether any man prominently connected with the government gave confidence to so few as did Stanton. He in turn trusted and hated nearly every general prominent in the early part of the war. He was McClellan's closest personal friend and counselor when he entered the Lincoln Cabinet, and later became McClellan's most vindictive and vituperative foe. The one general of the war who held his confidence without interruption from the time he became Commander-in-Chief of the armies until the close of the war was General Grant, and he literally commanded it by distinctly defining his independent attitude as General-in-Chief when he accepted his commission as Lieutenant-General. He often spoke of, and to, public men, military and civil, with a withering sneer. I have heard him scores of times thus speak of Lincoln, and several times thus speak to Lincoln. He was a man of extreme moods; often petulant, irritating, and senselessly unjust, and at times one of the most amiable, genial, and delightful conversationalists I have ever met. He loved antagonism, and there was hardly a period during his remarkable service as War Minister in which he was not, on some more or less important point, in positive antagonism with the President. In his antagonisms he was, as a rule, offensively despotic, and often pressed them upon Lincoln to the very utmost point of Lincoln's forbearance; but he knew when to call a halt upon himself, as he well knew that there never was a day or an hour during his service in the Cabinet that Lincoln was not his absolute master. He respected Lincoln's. authority because it was greater than his own, but he had little respect for Lincoln's fitness for the responsible duties of the Presidency. I have seen him at times as tender and gentle as a woman, his heart seeming to agonize over the sorrows of the humblest; and I have seen him many more times turn away with the haughtiest contempt from appeals which should at least have been treated with respect. He had few personal and fewer political friends, and he seemed proud of the fact that he had more personal and political enemies than any prominent officer of the government. Senators, Representatives, and high military commanders were often offended by his wanton arrogance, and again thawed into cordial relations by his effusive kindness. Taken all in all, Edwin M. Stanton was capable of the grandest and the meanest actions of any great man I have ever known, and he has reared imperishable monuments to the opposing qualities he possessed.

Stanton had rendered an incalculable service to the nation by his patriotic efforts in the Cabinet of Bu-

chanan. Cass had resigned from the Premiership because he was much more aggressive in his ideas of meeting rebellion than was the President. Attorney-General
Black was promoted to the head of the Cabinet, and
Stanton was called in as Black's successor. It was Judge
Black who saved Buchanan's administration from sudden and irretrievable wreck at the outset of the issue,
and he doubtless dictated the appointment of Stanton,
who was his close personal friend. From the time that
Stanton entered the Buchanan Cabinet the attitude of
the administration was so pointedly changed that none
could mistake it. He was positively and aggressively
loyal to the government, and as positively and aggressively hated rebellion. While Stanton and Black generally acted in concert during the few remaining months
of the Buchanan administration, they became seriously
estranged before the close of the Lincoln administration
—so much so that Black, in an article published in the
Galaxy of June, 1870, said of Stanton: "Did he accept
the confidence of the President (Buchanan) and the Cabinet with a predetermined intent to betray it?" After
Stanton's retirement from the Buchanan Cabinet when
Lincoln was inaugurated, he maintained the closest confidential relations with Buchanan, and wrote him many
letters expressing the utmost contempt for Lincoln, the
Cabinet, the Republican Congress, and the general policy of the administration. These letters, given to the
public in Curtis's life of Buchanan, speak freely of the
"painful imbecility of Lincoln," of the "venality and
corruption" which ran riot in the government, and expressed the belief that no better condition of things was
possible "until Jeff Davis turns out the whole concern."
He was firmly impressed for some weeks after the battle
of Bull Run that the government was utterly overthrown,
as he repeatedly refers to the coming of Davis into the

National Capital. In one letter he says that "in less than thirty days Davis will be in possession of Washington;" and it is an open secret that Stanton advised the revolutionary overthrow of the Lincoln government, to be replaced by General McClellan as military dictator.

These letters published by Curtis, bad as they are, are not the worst letters written by Stanton to Buchanan. Some of them were so violent in their expressions against Lincoln and the administration that they have been charitably withheld from the public, but they remain in the possession of the surviving relatives of President Buchanan. Of course, Lincoln had no knowledge of the bitterness exhibited by Stanton to himself personally and to his administration, but if he had known the worst that Stanton ever said or wrote about him, I doubt not that he would have called him to the Cabinet in January, 1862. The disasters the army suffered made Lincoln forgetful of everything but the single duty of suppressing the rebellion. From the day that McClellan was called to the command of the Army of the Potomac in place of McDowell, Stanton was in enthusiastic accord with the military policy of the government. The constant irritation between the War Department and military commanders that had vexed Lincoln in the early part of the war made him anxious to obtain a War Minister who was not only resolutely honest, but who was in close touch with the commander of the armies. This necessity, with the patriotic record that Stanton had made during the closing months of the Buchanan administration, obviously dictated the appointment of Stanton. It was Lincoln's own act. Stanton had been discussed as a possible successor to Cameron along with many others in outside circles, but no one had any reason to anticipate Stanton's appointment from any intimation given by the President. Lincoln and Stanton had no personal intercourse whatever from the time of Lincoln's inauguration until Stanton became his War Minister. In a letter to Buchanan, written March 1, 1862, Stanton says: "My accession to my present position was quite as sudden and unexpected as the confidence you bestowed upon me in calling me to your Cabinet." In another letter, written on the 18th of May, 1862, he said: "I hold my present position at the request of the President, who knew me personally, but to whom I had not spoken from the 4th of March, 1861, until the day he handed me my commission." The appointment was made because Lincoln believed that Stanton's loyal record in the Buchanan Cabinet and his prominence as the foe of every form of jobbery would inspire the highest degree of confidence in that department throughout the entire country. In that he judged correctly. From the day that he entered the War Office until the surrender of the Confederate armies, Stanton, with all his vagaries and infirmities, gave constant inspiration to the loyal sentiment of the country, and rendered a service that probably only Edwin M. Stanton could have rendered at the time.

Lincoln was not long in discovering that in his new Secretary of War he had an invaluable but most troublesome Cabinet officer, but he saw only the great and good offices that Stanton was performing for the imperiled Republic. Confidence was restored in financial circles by the appointment of Stanton, and his name as War Minister did more to strengthen the faith of the people in the government credit than would have been probable from the appointment of any other man of that day. He was a terror to all the hordes of jobbers and speculators and camp-followers whose appetites had been whetted by a great war, and he enforced the strictest discipline throughout our armies. He was seldom capable of being civil to any officer away from the army on leave of absence unless he had been summoned by the government for conference or special duty, and he issued the strictest orders from time to time to drive the throng of military idlers from the capital and keep them at their posts. He was stern to savagery in his enforcement of military law. The wearied sentinel who slept at his post found no mercy in the heart of Stanton, and many times did Lincoln's humanity overrule his fiery minister. Any neglect of military duty was sure of the swiftest punishment, and seldom did he make even just allowance for inevitable military disaster. He had profound, unfaltering faith in the Union cause, and, above all, he had unfaltering faith in himself. He believed that he was in all things except in name Commander-in-Chief of the armies and the navy of the nation, and it was with unconcealed reluctance that he at times deferred to the authority of the President. He was a great organizer in theory, and harsh to the utmost in enforcing his theories upon military commanders. He at times conceived impossible things, and peremptorily ordered them executed, and woe to the man who was unfortunate enough to demonstrate that Stanton was wrong. If he escaped without disgrace he was more than fortunate, and many, very many, would have thus fallen unjustly had it not been for Lincoln's cautious and generous interposition to save those who were wantonly censured. He would not throw the blame upon Stanton, but he would save the victim of Stanton's injustice, and he always did it so kindly that even Stanton could not complain beyond a churlish growl.

Stanton understood the magnitude of the rebellion, and he understood also that an army to be effective must be completely organized in all its departments. He had no favorites to promote at the expense of the public service, and his constant and honest aim was to secure the best men for every important position. As I have said, he assumed, in his own mind, that he was Commander-in-Chief, and there was nothing in military movements, or in the quartermaster, commissary, hospital, secret service, or any other department relating to the war, that he did not claim to comprehend and seek to control in his absolute way.* I doubt whether his partiality ever unjustly promoted a military officer, and I wish that I

* Mr. Stanton's theory was that everything concerned his own department. It was he who was carrying on the war. It was he who would be held responsible for the secret machinations of the enemy in the rear as well as the unwarranted success of the enemy in front. Hence he established a system of military censorship which has never, for vastness of scope or completeness of detail, been equaled in any war before or since or in any other country under the sun. The whole telegraphic system of the United States, with its infinite ramifications, centered in his office. There, adjoining his own personal rooms, sat Gen. Eckert, Hymer D. Bates, Albert B. Chandler, and Charles A. Tinker, —all of them young men of brilliant promise and now shining lights in the electrical world. Every hour in the day and night, under all circumstances, in all seasons, there sat at their instruments sundry members of this little group. The passage between their room and the Secretary's was unobstructed. It was an interior communication—they did not have even to go through the corridor to reach him—and every dispatch relating to the war or party politics that passed over the Western Union wires, North or South, they read. Cipher telegrams were considered especially suspicious, so every one of those was reported. The young men I have mentioned were masters of cipher-translation. Every message to or from the President or any member of his household passed under the eye of the Secretary. If one Cabinet Minister communicated with another over the wire by a secret code, Mr. Stanton had the message deciphered and read to him. If Gen. McClellan telegraphed to his wife from the front, Mr. Stanton knew the contents of every dispatch. Hence, as far as the conduct of the war was concerned, Mr. Stanton knew a thousand secrets where Mr. Lincoln knew one; for the Secretary's instructions were that telegrams indiscriminately should not be shown to the President.—*Albert E. H. Johnson*, Stanton's confidential clerk, in *Washington Post*, July 14, 1891.

could say that his prejudices had never hindered the promotion or driven from the service faithful and competent military commanders. His hatreds were intense, implacable, and yielded to the single authority of Lincoln, and that authority he knew would be exercised only in extreme emergencies. The effect of such a War Minister was to enforce devotion to duty throughout the entire army, and it is impossible to measure the beneficent results of Stanton's policy in our vast military campaigns. Great as he was in the practical administration of his office that could be visible to the world, he added immeasurably to his greatness as War Minister by the impress of his wonderful personality upon the whole military and civil service.

Stanton's intense and irrepressible hatreds were his greatest infirmity and did much to deform his brilliant record as War Minister. A pointed illustration of his bitter and unreasonable prejudices was given in the case of Jere McKibben, whom he arbitrarily confined in Old Capitol Prison without even the semblance of a pretext to excuse the act. The Constitution of Pennsylvania had been so amended during the summer of 1864 as to authorize soldiers to vote in the field. The Legislature was called in extra session to provide for holding elections in the army. It was in the heat of the Presidential contest and party bitterness was intensified to the uttermost. Despite the earnest appeals of Governor Curtin and all my personal importunities with prominent legislators of our own party, an election law was passed that was obviously intended to give the minority no rights whatever in holding army elections. The Governor was empowered to appoint State Commissioners, who were authorized to attend the elections without any direct authority in conducting them. As the law was violent in its character and liable to the

12

grossest abuses, without any means to restrain election frauds, the Democrats of the State and country justly complained of it with great earnestness. The Governor decided, as a matter of justice to the Democrats, to appoint several Democratic Commissioners, but it was with difficulty that any could be prevailed upon to accept. He requested me to see several prominent Democrats and obtain their consent to receive his commission and act under it. As McKibben had three brothers in the Army of the Potomac, I supposed it would be pleasant for him to make a visit there in an official way, and I suggested it to him. He promptly answered: "Why, Stanton would put me in Old Capitol Prison before I was there a day. He hates our family for no other reason that I know of than that my father was one of his best friends in Pittsburg when he needed a friend." I assured him that Stanton would not attempt any violence against a man who held the commission of the Governor of our State, and he finally consented to go, having first solemnly pledged me to protect him in case he got into any difficulty.

McKibben and the other Commissioners from Philadelphia were furnished the election papers and started down to the army, then quietly resting on the James River. On the second day after he left I received a telegram from him dated Washington, saying: "Stanton has me in Old Capitol Prison; come at once." I hastened to Washington, having telegraphed to Lincoln to allow me to see him between eleven and twelve o'clock that night, when I should arrive. I went direct to the White House and told the President the exact truth. I explained the character of the law of our State; that I had personally prevailed upon McKibben to go as a Commissioner to give a semblance of decency to its execution; that he was not only guiltless of any offense, as he knew how delicately he was situated, but that he was powerless to do any wrong, and I insisted upon McKibben's immediate discharge from prison. Lincoln knew of Stanton's hatred for the McKibbens, as he had been compelled to protect four of McKibben's brothers to give them the promotion they had earned by most heroic conduct in battle, and he was much distressed at Stanton's act. He sent immediately to the War Department to get the charge against McKibben, and it did not require five minutes of examination to satisfy him that it was utterly groundless and a malicious wrong committed by Stanton. He said it was a "stupid blunder," and at once proposed to discharge McKibben on his parole. I urged that he should be discharged unconditionally, but Lincoln's caution prevented that. He said: "It seems hardly fair to discharge McKibben unconditionally without permitting Stanton to give his explanation;" and he added, "You know, McClure, McKibben is safe, parole or no parole, so go and get him out of prison." I saw that it would be useless to attempt to change Lincoln's purpose, but I asked him to fix an hour the next morning when I could meet Stanton in his presence to have McKibben discharged from his parole. He fixed ten o'clock the next morning for the meeting, and then wrote, in his own hand, the order for McKibben's discharge, which I hurriedly bore to Old Capitol Prison and had him released.

Promptly at ten o'clock the next morning I went to the White House to obtain McKibben's discharge from his parole. Lincoln was alone, but Stanton came in a few minutes later. He was pale with anger and his first expression was: "Well, McClure, what damned rebel are you here to get out of trouble this morning?" I had frequently been to Washington before when arbitrary and entirely unjustifiable arrests of civilians had been made in Pennsylvania, to have the prisoners discharged from military custody; and as I had never applied in such a case without good reason, and never without success even when opposed by Stanton, he evidently meant to square up some old accounts with me over McKibben. I said to him and with some feeling: "Your arrest of McKibben was a cowardly act; you knew McKibben was guiltless of any offense, and you did it to gratify a brutal hatred." I told him also that I had prevailed upon McKibben, against his judgment, to act as a State Commissioner to give a semblance of decency to what would evidently be a farcical and fraudulent election in the army, and that if he had examined the complaint soberly for one minute, he would have seen that it was utterly false. I told him that I had requested his appearance there with the President to have McKibben discharged from his parole, and that I now asked him to assent to it. He turned from me, walked hurriedly back and forth across the room several times before he answered, and then he came up to me and in a voice tremulous with passion said: "I decline to discharge McKibben from his parole. You can make formal application for it if you choose, and I will consider and decide it." His manner was as offensive as it was possible even for Stanton to make it, and I resented it by saying: "I don't know what McKibben will do, but if I were Jere McKibben, as sure as there is a God I would crop your ears before I left Washington." He made no reply, but suddenly whirled around on his heel and walked out of the President's room. Lincoln had said nothing. He was used to such ebullitions from Stanton, and after the Secretary had gone he remarked in a jocular way, "Well, McClure, you didn't get on very far with Stanton, did you? but he'll come all right; let the matter rest." Before leaving the President's room I wrote out a formal application to Stanton for the discharge of McKibben from his parole. Several days after I received a huge official envelope enclosing a letter, all in Stanton's bold scrawl, saying that the request for the discharge of Jere McKibben from his parole had been duly considered, and "the application could not be granted consistently with the interests of the public service." McKibben outlived Stanton, but died a prisoner on parole.

After such a turbulent interview with Stanton it would naturally be supposed that our intercourse thereafter would be severely strained, if not wholly interrupted; but I had occasion to call at the War Department within a few weeks, and never was greeted more cordially in my life than I was by Stanton. The election was over, the military power of the Confederacy was obviously broken, and the Secretary was in the very best of spirits. He promptly granted what I wanted done, which was not a matter of much importance, and it was so cheerfully and generously assented to that I carefully thought of everything that I wanted from his department, all of which was done in a most gracious manner. I puzzled my brain to make sure I should not forget anything, and it finally occurred to me that a friend I much desired to serve had lately appealed to me to aid in obtaining promotion for a young officer in the quartermaster's department whom I did not know personally. It seemed that this was the chance for the young officer. I suggested to Stanton that Quartermaster —— was reputed to be a very faithful and efficient officer, and entitled to higher promotion than he had received. Stanton picked up his pen, saying: "It will give me great pleasure, sir; what is his name?" I had to answer that I could not recall his name in full, but he took down the officer's rank and last name and assured me that he would be promptly pro-

moted. I supposed that a change of mood would make
him forgetful of this promise; but the young quartermaster wore new shoulder-straps within ten days, and
won distinction as the chief of his department in large
independent army movements in Virginia. I never had
the pleasure of meeting the worthy officer who thus unexpectedly secured his promotion, and he is doubtless
ignorant to this day of the peculiar way in which it was
accomplished.

Stanton's hatred for McClellan became a consuming
passion before the close of the Peninsular campaign.
When McClellan was before Yorktown and complaining
of his inadequate forces to march upon Richmond, Stanton summed him up in the following expression: "If he
(McClellan) had a million men, he would swear the enemy had two millions, and then he would sit down in
the mud and yell for three." He was impatient and
often fearfully petulant in his impatience. He was disappointed in McClellan not marching directly upon
Richmond by Manassas, and he was greatly disappointed
again when McClellan laid siege to Yorktown, but he
was ever ready to congratulate, in his blunt way, when
anything was accomplished. When General "Baldy"
Smith made a reconnoissance at Yorktown that produced
the first successful results of that campaign, Stanton answered McClellan's announcement of the movement:
"Good for the first lick; hurrah for Smith and the one-
gun battery!" but from that time until the withdrawal
of the army from the Peninsula, Stanton never found
occasion to commend McClellan, and McClellan was a
constant bone of contention between Stanton and Lincoln. Lincoln's patience and forbearance were marked
in contrast with Stanton's violence of temper and intensity of hatred. McClellan so far forgot himself as to
telegraph to Stanton after the retreat to the James River:

"If I save this army now, I tell you plainly that I owe no thanks to you or to any other person in Washington. You have done your best to sacrifice this army." Any other President than Lincoln would have immediately relieved McClellan of his command, and Stanton not only would have relieved him, but would have dismissed him from the service. Lincoln exhibited no resentment whatever for the ill-advised and insubordinate telegram from McClellan. On the contrary, he seemed inclined to continue McClellan in command, and certainly exhibited every desire to sustain him to the utmost. In a letter addressed to the Secretary of State on the same day that McClellan's telegram was received he expressed his purpose to call for additional troops, and said: "I expect to maintain this contest until successful, or till I die, or I am conquered, or my term expires, or Congress or the country forsakes me."

This was one of the most perplexing situations in which Lincoln was ever placed. The defeat of the army would not, in itself, have been so serious had Lincoln been able to turn to commanders in whom he could implicitly confide. He had abundant resources and could supply all needed additional troops, but where could he turn for safe advice? He had, to a very large extent, lost faith in McClellan. When he counseled with Stanton he encountered insuperable hatreds, and he finally, as was his custom, decided upon his own course of action and hurried off to West Point to confer with General Scott. His visit to West Point startled the country and quite as much startled the Cabinet, as not a single member of it had any intimation of his intended journey. What passed at the interview between Lincoln and Scott was never known to any, so far as I have been able to learn, and I believe that no one has pretended to have had knowledge of it. It is enough to know that Pope was summoned to the command of a new army, called the Army of Virginia, embracing the commands of Fremont, Banks, and McDowell, and that Halleck was made General-in-Chief. The aggressive campaign of Lee, resulting in the second battle of Bull Run and the utter defeat of Pope, brought the army back into the Washington intrenchments in a most demoralized condition. It was here that Lincoln and Stanton came into conflict again on the question of the restoration of McClellan to command. Without consulting either the General-in-Chief or his War Minister, Lincoln assigned McClellan to the command of the defenses of Washington, and as the various commands of Pope's broken and demoralized army came back into the intrenchments in utter confusion they thereby came again under the command of McClellan.

When it was discovered that McClellan was thus practically in command of the Army of the Potomac again, Stanton was aroused to the fiercest hostility. He went so far as to prepare a remonstrance to the President in writing against McClellan's continuance in the command of that army or of any army of the Union. This remonstrance was not only signed by Stanton, but by Chase, Bates, and Smith, with the concurrence of Welles, who thought it indelicate for him to sign it. After the paper had been prepared under Stanton's impetuous lead, some of the more considerate members of the Cabinet who had joined him took pause to reflect that Lincoln was in the habit not only of having his own way, but of having his own way of having his own way, and the protest was never presented. Lincoln knew McClellan's great organizing powers, and he knew the army needed first of all a commander who was capable of restoring it to discipline. To use his own expressive language about the emergency, he believed that "there is no one in the army who can command the fortifications and lick those troops of ours into shape one-half as well as he could." It was this conviction that made Lincoln forget all of McClellan's failings and restore him to command, and Stanton was compelled to submit in sullen silence.

Lincoln's restoration of McClellan to command in disregard of the most violent opposition of Stanton was only one of the many instances in which he and his War Minister came into direct and positive conflict, and always with the same result; but many times as Stanton was vanquished in his conflicts with Lincoln, it was not in his nature to be any the less Edwin M. Stanton. As late as 1864 he had one of his most serious disputes with Lincoln, in which he peremptorily refused to obey an order from the President directing that certain prisoners of war, who expressed a desire to take the oath of allegiance and enter the Union army, should be mustered into the service and credited to the quotas of certain districts. An exact account of this dispute is preserved by Provost-Marshal General Fry, who was charged with the execution of the order, and who was present when Lincoln and Stanton discussed it. Stanton positively refused to obey the order, and said to Lincoln: "You must see that your order cannot be executed." Lincoln answered with an unusually peremptory tone for him: "Mr. Secretary, I reckon you'll have to execute the order." Stanton replied in his imperious way: "Mr. President, I cannot do it; the order is an improper one, and I cannot execute it." To this Lincoln replied in a manner that forbade all further dispute: "Mr. Secretary, it will have to be done." A few minutes thereafter, as stated by Provost-Marshal General Fry in a communication to the New York *Tribune* several years ago, Stanton issued instructions to him for the execution of the President's order.

Notwithstanding the many and often irritating conflicts that Lincoln had with Stanton, there never was an hour during Stanton's term as War Minister that Lincoln thought of removing him. Indeed, I believe that at no period during the war, after Stanton had entered the Cabinet, did Lincoln feel that any other man could fill Stanton's place with equal usefulness to the country. He had the most unbounded faith in Stanton's loyalty and in his public and private integrity. He was in hearty sympathy with Stanton's aggressive earnestness for the prosecution of the war, and at times hesitated, even to the extent of what he feared was individual injustice, to restrain Stanton's violent assaults upon others. It will be regretted by the impartial historian of the future that Stanton was capable of impressing his intense hatred so conspicuously upon the annals of the country, and that Lincoln, in several memorable instances, failed to reverse his War Minister when he had grave doubts as to the wisdom or justice of his methods. It was Stanton's fierce resentment that made just verdicts impossible in some military trials which will ever be historic—notably, the unjust verdict depriving Fitz John Porter at once of his commission and citizenship, and the now admittedly unjust verdict that sent Mrs. Surratt to the gallows. Lincoln long hesitated before giving his assent to the judgment against Porter, as is clearly shown by the fact that, with Pope's accusations against Porter fresh before him, he assented to McClellan's request and assigned Porter to active command in the Antietam campaign, and personally thanked Porter on the Antietam field, after the battle, for his services. Another enduring monument of Stanton's resentment is the Arlington National Cemetery. The home of Lee was taken under the feeblest color of law that Stanton well knew could not be maintained, and the buildings surrounded with graves even to the very door of the venerable mansion, so that it might never be reclaimed as the home of the Confederate chieftain. The government made restitution to the Lees in obedience to the decision of its highest court, but the monument of hate is imperishable.

Soon after the surrender of Lee, Stanton, severely broken in health by the exacting duties he had performed, tendered his resignation, believing that his great work was finished. Lincoln earnestly desired him to remain, and he did so. The assassination of Lincoln called him to even graver duties than had before confronted him. His bitter conflict with Johnson and his violent issue with Sherman stand out as exceptionally interesting chapters of the history of the war. It was President Johnson's attempted removal of Stanton in violation of the Tenure-of-Office Act that led to the President's impeachment, and Stanton persisted in holding his Cabinet office until Johnson was acquitted by the Senate, when he resigned and was succeeded by General Schofield on the 2d of June, 1868. After his retirement Stanton never exhibited any great degree of either physical or mental vigor. I last saw him in Philadelphia in the fall of 1868, where he came in answer to a special invitation from the Union League to deliver a political address in the Academy of Music in favor of Grant's election to the Presidency. I called on him at his hotel and found him very feeble, suffering greatly from asthmatic disorders, and in his public address he was often strangely forgetful of facts and names, and had to be prompted by gentlemen on the stage. It may be said of Stanton that he sacrificed the vigor of his life to the service of his country in the sorest trial of its history, and when President Grant nominated him as Justice of the Supreme Court, on the

20th of December, 1869, all knew that it was an empty honor, as he was both physically and mentally unequal to the new duties assigned to him.   Four days thereafter the inexorable messenger came and Edwin M. Stanton joined the great majority across the dark river.

LINCOLN AND GRANT.

ABRAHAM LINCOLN and Ulysses S. Grant were entire strangers to each other personally until the 9th of March, 1864, when Lincoln handed Grant his commission as Lieutenant-General, which made him three days later Commander-in-Chief of all the armies of the Union. Although Grant entered the army as a citizen of Lincoln's own State, he had resided there only a little more than a year. When he retired from the army by resignation on the 31st of July, 1854, as a captain, he selected Missouri as his home and settled on a farm near St. Louis. He had won promotion at the battles of Molino del Rey and Chapultepec in the Mexican War, and was brevetted for special gallantry. During the nearly seven years between his retirement from the army and re-entering the military service at the beginning of the civil war he had done little or nothing to make himself known to fame. He had moved from Missouri to Galena early in 1860 to improve his worldly condition by accepting a salary of $600 from his two brothers, who were then engaged in the leather business. After remaining with them for a year his salary was advanced to $800, and in a letter to a friend he exhibited his gratification at his business success and expressed the hope of reaching what then seemed to be his highest ambition—a partnership in the firm. His life in Galena was quiet and unobtrusive as was Grant's habit under

(Photo by Gutekunst, Philadelphia.)

GENERAL U. S. GRANT, 1864.

all circumstances; and when the first call for troops was issued and Grant brought a company from Galena to Springfield without any friends to press his promotion, it is not surprising that, while political colonels were turned out with great rapidity, Grant remained without a command. He served on the staff of Governor Yates for several weeks, giving him the benefit of his military experience in organizing new troops, but it does not seem to have occurred to Grant to suggest his own appointment to a command or to Governor Yates to tender him one. He returned to Galena, and on the 24th of May, 1861, sent a formal request to the Adjutant-General of the army at Washington for an assignment to military duty "until the close of the war in such capacity as may be offered." To this no reply was ever received, and a month later he made a personal visit to the headquarters of General McClellan, then in command of the Ohio volunteers at Cincinnati, hoping that McClellan would tender him a position on his staff; but he failed to meet McClellan, and returned home without suggesting to any one a desire to enter the service under the Cincinnati commander.

It was a wayward and insubordinate regiment at Springfield that called Grant back to the military service and started him on his matchless career. The Twenty-first Illinois defied the efforts of Governor Yates to reduce it to discipline, and in despair he telegraphed to the modest Captain Grant at Galena, asking him to come and accept the colonelcy. The prompt answer came: "I accept the regiment and will start immediately." It is needless to say that the appearance of a plain, ununiformed, and modest man like Grant made little impression at first upon his insubordinate command, but in a very short time he made it the best disciplined regiment from the State, and the men as proud

of their commander as he was of them. The story of
Grant's military achievements from Belmont to Shiloh
is familiar to every reader of American history. It was
Grant's capture of Fort Henry, soon followed by the
capture of Fort Donelson and Nashville, that opened
the second year of the war with such brilliant promise
of an early overthrow of the Confederate armies. It was
his sententious answer to General Buckner at Fort Donelson that proclaimed to the nation his heroic qualities
as a military commander. He said: " No terms except
unconditional and immediate surrender can be accepted;
I propose to move immediately upon your works.'' He
soon became popularly known as " Unconditional Surrender Grant,'' and while his superior officers, including
General-in-Chief McClellan and his immediate division
commander Halleck, seemed to agree only in hindering
Grant in his military movements, the country profoundly
appreciated his victories. Soon after the capture of
Nashville he was ordered by Halleck to make a new
military movement that was rendered impossible by immense floods which prevailed in the Western waters.
Halleck reported him to McClellan, complaining that he
had left his post without leave and had failed to make
reports, etc., to which McClellan replied: " Do not hesitate to arrest him at once if the good of the service requires it, and place C. F. Smith in command.'' Halleck
immediately relieved Grant and placed Smith in command of the proposed expedition. Grant gave a temperate explanation of the injustice done to him, but as
the wrong was continued he asked to be relieved from
duty. In the mean time Halleck had discovered his
error, and atoned for it by answering to Grant: " Instead
of relieving you, I wish you, as soon as your new army
is in the field, to assume the immediate command and
lead it on to new victories.''

It was not until after the battle of Shiloh, fought on the 6th and 7th of April, 1862, that Lincoln was placed in a position to exercise a controlling influence in shaping the destiny of Grant. The first day's battle at Shiloh was a serious disaster to the Union army commanded by Grant, who was driven from his position, which seems to have been selected without any special reference to resisting an attack from the enemy, and, although his army fought most gallantly in various separate encounters, the day closed with the field in possession of the enemy and Grant's army driven back to the river. Fortunately, the advance of Buell's army formed a junction with Grant late in the evening, and that night all of Buell's army arrived, consisting of three divisions. The two generals arranged their plans for an offensive movement early the next morning, and, after another stubborn battle, the lost field was regained and the enemy compelled to retreat with the loss of their commander, General Albert Sidney Johnston, who had fallen early in the first day's action, and with a larger aggregate loss of killed, wounded, and missing than Grant suffered. The first reports from the Shiloh battle-field created profound alarm throughout the entire country, and the wildest exaggerations were spread in a floodtide of vituperation against Grant. It was freely charged that he had neglected his command because of dissipation, that his army had been surprised and defeated, and that it was saved from annihilation only by the timely arrival of Buell.

The few of to-day who can recall the inflamed condition of public sentiment against Grant caused by the disastrous first day's battle at Shiloh will remember that he was denounced as incompetent for his command by the public journals of all parties in the North, and with almost entire unanimity by Senators and Congressmen

13

without regard to political faith. Not only in Washington, but throughout the loyal States, public sentiment seemed to crystallize into an earnest demand for Grant's dismissal from the army. His victories of Forts Henry and Donelson, which had thrilled the country a short time before, seemed to have been forgotten, and on every side could be heard the emphatic denunciation of Grant because of his alleged reckless exposure of the army, while Buell was universally credited with having saved it. It is needless to say that owing to the excited condition of the public mind most extravagant reports gained ready credence, and it was not uncommon to hear Grant denounced on the streets and in all circles as unfitted by both habit and temperament for an important military command. The clamor for Grant's removal, and often for his summary dismissal, from the army surged against the President from every side, and he was harshly criticized for not promptly dismissing Grant, or at least relieving him from his command. I can recall but a single Republican member of Congress who boldly defended Grant at that time. Elihu B. Washburne, whose home was in Galena, where Grant had lived before he went into the army, stood nearly or quite alone among the members of the House in wholly justifying Grant at Shiloh, while a large majority of the Republicans of Congress were outspoken and earnest in condemning him.

I did not know Grant at that time; had neither partiality nor prejudice to influence my judgment, nor had I any favorite general who might be benefited by Grant's overthrow, but I shared the almost universal conviction of the President's friends that he could not sustain himself if he attempted to sustain Grant by continuing him in command. Looking solely to the interests of Lincoln, feeling that the tide of popular resentment was so over-

whelming against Grant that Lincoln must yield to it, I
had repeated conferences with some of his closest friends,
including Swett and Lamon, all of whom agreed that
Grant must be removed from his command, and complained of Lincoln for his manifest injustice to himself
by his failure to act promptly in Grant's removal. So
much was I impressed with the importance of prompt
action on the part of the President after spending a day
and evening in Washington that I called on Lincoln at
eleven o'clock at night and sat with him alone until after
one o'clock in the morning. He was, as usual, worn out
with the day's exacting duties, but he did not permit me
to depart until the Grant matter had been gone over and
many other things relating to the war that he wished to
discuss. I pressed upon him with all the earnestness I
could command the immediate removal of Grant as an
imperious necessity to sustain himself. As was his custom, he said but little, only enough to make me continue
the discussion until it was exhausted. He sat before the
open fire in the old Cabinet room, most of the time with
his feet up on the high marble mantel, and exhibited unusual distress at the complicated condition of military
affairs. Nearly every day brought some new and perplexing military complication. He had gone through a
long winter of terrible strain with McClellan and the
Army of the Potomac; and from the day that Grant
started on his Southern expedition until the battle of
Shiloh he had had little else than jarring and confusion
among his generals in the West. He knew that I had
no ends to serve in urging Grant's removal, beyond the
single desire to make him be just to himself, and he listened patiently.

I appealed to Lincoln for his own sake to remove
Grant at once, and in giving my reasons for it I simply
voiced the admittedly overwhelming protest from the

loyal people of the land against Grant's continuance in command. I could form no judgment during the conversation as to what effect my arguments had upon him beyond the fact that he was greatly distressed at this new complication. When I had said everything that could be said from my standpoint, we lapsed into silence. Lincoln remained silent for what seemed a very long time. He then gathered himself up in his chair and said in a tone of earnestness that I shall never forget: *"I can't spare this man; he fights."* That was all he said, but I knew that it was enough, and that Grant was safe in Lincoln's hands against his countless hosts of enemies. The only man in all the nation who had the power to save Grant was Lincoln, and he had decided to do it. He was not influenced by any personal partiality for Grant, for they had never met, but he believed just what he said—"I can't spare this man; he fights." I knew enough of Lincoln to know that his decision was final, and I knew enough of him also to know that he reasoned better on the subject than I did, and that it would be unwise to attempt to unsettle his determination. I did not forget that Lincoln was the one man who never allowed himself to appear as wantonly defying public sentiment. It seemed to me impossible for him to save Grant without taking a crushing load of condemnation upon himself; but Lincoln was wiser than all those around him, and he not only saved Grant, but he saved him by such well-concerted effort that he soon won popular applause from those who were most violent in demanding Grant's dismissal.

The method that Lincoln adopted to rescue Grant from the odium into which he had, to a very large degree, unjustly fallen was one of the bravest and most sagacious acts of his administration. Halleck was commander of the military division consisting of Missouri, Kentucky,

Tennessee, and possibly other States, but he remained at his headquarters in St. Louis until after the battle of Shiloh. Lincoln's first move was to bring Halleck to the field, where he at once superseded Grant as commander of the army. This relieved public apprehension and soon calmed the inflamed public sentiment that was clamoring for Grant's dismissal. Lincoln knew that it would require time for the violent prejudice against Grant to perish, and he calmly waited until it was safe for him to give some indication to the country of his abiding faith in Grant as a military commander. Halleck reached the army at Pittsburg Landing on the 11th of April, four days after the battle had been fought, and of course his presence on the field at once made him the commanding officer. On the 30th of April, when the public mind was reasonably well prepared to do justice to Grant, an order was issued assigning him " as second in command under the major-general commanding the department."

This was an entirely needless order so far as mere military movements were involved, and it is one of the very rare cases in the history of the war in which such an order was issued. Only under very special circumstances could there be any occasion for an order assigning a particular general as second in command of an army. While the army is within reach of orders from the commanding general there can be no second in command. In case of his death or inability to take active command in battle, the military laws wisely regulate the succession, and only in extraordinary cases is it departed from. In this case the purpose of it was obvious. Lincoln had quieted public apprehension by bringing General Halleck to the field and thus relieving Grant of command without the semblance of reproach; but he desired to impress the country with his absolute faith in Grant as a military leader, and it was for that reason that the special order was issued assigning him as second in command of Halleck's army. The effect of that order was precisely what Lincoln anticipated. It made all loyal men take pause and abate or yield their violent hostility to Grant in obedience to the publicly expressed confidence of Lincoln. The country knew that Lincoln best understood Grant, and from the date of Grant's assignment as second in command of the army the prejudice against him rapidly perished. It was thus that Lincoln saved Grant from one of the most violent surges of popular prejudice that was ever created against any of our leading generals, and on the 11th of July, when it was entirely safe to restore Grant to his command for active operations, Halleck was ordered to Washington by Lincoln and assigned as commander-in-chief. Thus was Grant restored to the command of the army that he had lost at the battle of Shiloh, and it was Lincoln, and Lincoln alone, who saved him from disgrace and gave to the country the most lustrous record of all the heroes of the war.

I doubt whether Grant ever understood how Lincoln, single and alone, protected him from dishonor in the tempest of popular passion that came upon him after the disaster at Shiloh. Grant never was in Washington until he was summoned there early in 1864 to be commissioned as Lieutenant-General, and he was entirely without personal acquaintance with Lincoln. After he became Commander-in-Chief he made his headquarters in the field with the Army of the Potomac, and was very rarely in Washington after he crossed the Rapidan and opened the campaign by the battles of the Wilderness. That he frequently saw Lincoln between February and May while perfecting his plans for army movements is well known, but Grant was one of the most silent of

men and most of all reluctant to talk about himself,
while Lincoln was equally reserved in all things pertaining to himself personally. Especially where he had
rendered any service to another he would be quite un-
likely to speak of it himself. Judging the two men from
their chief and very marked characteristics, it is entirely
reasonable to assume that what Lincoln did to save
Grant from disgrace was never discussed or referred to
by them in personal conversation. Grant never, in any
way known to the public, recognized any such obligation
to Lincoln, and no utterance ever came from him indicating anything more than the respect for Lincoln due
from a general to his chief.

I never heard Lincoln allude to the subject but once,
and that was under very painful circumstances and when
the subject was forced upon him by myself. Lincoln
knew that I had personal knowledge of his heroic effort
to rescue Grant from the odium that came upon him
after Shiloh, and an accidental occasion arose in the
latter part of October, 1864, when his relations to Grant
became a proper subject of consideration. The October
elections in 1864, when Lincoln was a candidate for re-
election, resulted favorably for the Republicans in Ohio
and Indiana, but unfavorably for them in Pennsylvania.
There was no State ticket to be elected in Pennsylvania
that year, and the vote for Congress and local officers
gave a small Democratic majority on the home vote in
the State. McClellan, a native of Pennsylvania, was
the Democratic candidate for President, and State pride
naturally added to his strength. General Cameron was
chairman of the Republican State Committee. He was
well equipped for the position, but was so entirely confident of success that he neglected to perfect the organization necessary to gain the victory, and the prestige of
success fell to McClellan. New York was regarded as

extremely doubtful, and there was much concern felt
about the possibility of New York and Pennsylvania
both voting against Lincoln in November. It was not
doubted that the army vote would give Pennsylvania to
Lincoln, but it was of the utmost importance, to give
moral force and effect to the triumph, to give Lincoln a
majority on the home vote. Lincoln was much concerned about the situation, and telegraphed me to come
to Washington the day after the October election. I
went on at once, and after going over the political situation carefully, Lincoln asked me whether I would be
willing to give my personal services to aid the State
Committee during the month intervening between the
October and November elections. I reminded him that
General Cameron and I were not in political sympathy,
and that he would regard it as obtrusive for me to volunteer assistance to him in the management of the campaign. To this Lincoln replied: " Of course, I understand that, but if Cameron shall invite you can you give
your time fully to the contest?" I answered that I
would gladly do so. He did not suggest how he meant
to bring about co-operation between Cameron and myself, but I knew him well enough to know that he would
be very likely to accomplish the desired result. Two
days thereafter I received a cordial letter from General
Cameron inviting me to join him at the headquarters
and assist in the November contest.

I at once went to Philadelphia, and found Wayne
MacVeagh already with General Cameron in obedience
to a like invitation that had been brought about by Lincoln. MacVeagh had been chairman of the State Committee the previous year, when Curtin was re-elected, as
I had been chairman in 1860 when Lincoln was first
elected, and both of us were at the time regarded as
somewhat conspicuous among the opponents of Came-

ron. The failure in Pennsylvania, contrasted with the party successes in Ohio and Indiana, was very mortifying to Cameron, and he was ready to employ every available resource to redeem the State in November. There was the heartiest co-operation by MacVeagh and myself, all being done under the name and immediate direction of Cameron as chairman, and there was not a jar during the month of desperate effort to win the State for Lincoln. I took a private room at another hotel, and never was at headquarters except for confidential conference with Cameron himself; and, as requested by Lincoln, I wrote him fully every night my impressions of the progress we were making. The Democrats were highly elated by their rather unexpected success in October, and they made the most desperate and well-directed battle to gain the State for McClellan. So anxious was Lincoln about the campaign that after I had been a week in co-operation with the State Committee, he sent Postmaster-General Dennison over to Philadelphia specially to talk over the situation more fully than it could be presented in my letters, and to return the same night and make report to him. It was evident that we had gained nothing, and I so informed the Postmaster-General, and expressed great doubts as to our ability to do more than hold our own, considering the advantage the Democrats had in the prestige of their October victory. I told him, however, that in another week the question could be determined whether we were safe on the home vote in Pennsylvania, and that if there was reasonable doubt about it I would notify Lincoln and visit Washington.

A week later, as I had advised Lincoln from day to day, I saw nothing to warrant the belief that we had gained any material advantage in the desperate battle, and I telegraphed Lincoln that I would see him at ten

o'clock that night.   I found him waiting, and he exhibited great solicitude as to the battle in Pennsylvania.
He knew that his election was in no sense doubtful, but
he knew that if he lost New York and with it Pennsylvania on the home vote, the moral effect of his triumph
would be broken and his power to prosecute the war and
make peace would be greatly impaired.   His usually sad
face was deeply shadowed with sorrow when I told him
that I saw no reasonable prospect of carrying Pennsylvania on the home vote, although we had about held our
own in the hand-to-hand conflict through which we were
passing.   "Well, what is to be done?" was Lincoln's
inquiry after the whole situation had been presented to
him.   I answered that the solution of the problem was a
very simple and easy one—that Grant was idle in front
of Petersburg; that Sheridan had won all possible victories in the Valley; and that if 5000 Pennsylvania soldiers could be furloughed home from each army the election could be carried without doubt.   Lincoln's face
brightened instantly at the suggestion, and I saw that
he was quite ready to execute it.   I said to him: "Of
course, you can trust Grant to make the suggestion to
him to furlough 5000 Pennsylvania troops for two
weeks?"   To my surprise, Lincoln made no answer,
and the bright face of a few moments before was instantly shadowed again.   I was much disconcerted, as I
supposed that Grant was the one man to whom Lincoln
could turn with absolute confidence as his friend.   I then
said with some earnestness: "Surely, Mr. President, you
can trust Grant with a confidential suggestion to furlough
Pennsylvania troops?"   Lincoln remained silent and evidently distressed at the proposition I was pressing upon
him.   After a few moments, and speaking with emphasis, I said: "It can't be possible that Grant is not your
friend; he can't be such an ingrate?"   Lincoln hesitated

for some time, and then answered in these words: "Well, McClure, I have no reason to believe that Grant prefers my election to that of McClellan."

I must confess that my response to this to me appalling statement from Lincoln was somewhat violative of the rules of courteous conversation. I reminded Lincoln how, in that room, when I had appealed to him to respect the almost universal demand of the country for Grant's dismissal, he had withstood the shock alone and interposed his omnipotence to save Grant when he was a personal stranger. Lincoln, as usual, answered intemperance of speech by silence. I then said to him: "General Meade is a soldier and a gentleman; he is the commander of the Army of the Potomac; send an order to him from yourself to furlough 5000 Pennsylvania soldiers home for two weeks, and send that order with some trusted friend from the War Department, with the suggestion to Meade that your agent be permitted to bring the order back with him." After a little reflection Lincoln answered: "I reckon that can be done." I then said, "What about Sheridan?" At once his sad face brightened up, like the noonday sun suddenly emerging from a dark cloud, as he answered: "Oh, Phil Sheridan; he's all right." Before I left his room that night he had made his arrangements to send messengers to Meade and Sheridan. The order was sent to Meade, and he permitted it to be returned to the President, but Sheridan needed no order. The 10,000 Pennsylvania soldiers were furloughed during the week, and Lincoln carried Pennsylvania on the home vote by 5712 majority, to which the army vote added 14,363 majority. It was thus that Lincoln made his triumph in Pennsylvania a complete victory without what was then commonly called the "bayonet vote," and Lincoln carried New York by 6749, leaving McClellan the worst defeated candidate

ever nominated by any of the great political parties of
the country.

I left Lincoln fully convinced that Grant was an ingrate, and Lincoln certainly knew that he permitted that
conviction to be formed in my mind. He did not in any
way qualify his remark about Grant, although it was his
custom when he felt compelled to disparage any one to
present some charitable explanation of the conduct complained of. The fact that he refused to send his request
to Grant, while he was willing to send it to Meade,
proved that he was, for some reason, disappointed in
Grant's fidelity to him; and the enthusiasm with which
he spoke of Sheridan proved how highly he valued the
particular quality that he did not credit to Grant. I confess that the conviction formed that day made the name
of Grant leave a bad taste in my mouth for many years.
I heartily supported his nomination for the Presidency in
1868, and was chairman of the Pennsylvania delegation
in the Chicago Convention that nominated him, because
I believed that the chivalrous victor of Appomattox
would command the highest measure of confidence from
the Southern people and hasten the restoration of peace
and business prosperity; but Grant and his immediate
friends knew that while I earnestly supported his nomination and election, I did not have the confidence in him
that he generally commanded. I now believe that Lincoln was mistaken in his distrust of Grant. It was not
until after Grant's retirement from the Presidency that I
ever had an opportunity to hear his explanation. I remembered that on election night, when Grant was advised at his headquarters in front of Petersburg of Lincoln's election, he sent Lincoln a dispatch heartily con-
gratulating him upon his triumph. I never heard Lincoln allude to the subject again, and I am therefore
ignorant as to whether his belief was ever changed.

I never visited the White House during Grant's Presidency, although twice specially invited to do so to consider what I regarded as an impracticable or impossible political suggestion, but I accidentally met him in the Continental Hotel, soon after his retirement, in company with Mr. Childs. Grant came forward in the most cordial manner and thanked me for an editorial that had appeared in *The Times* on the day that ended his Presidential term, in which I had spoken of him and his achievements as history would record them, regardless of the political passions and prejudices of the day. The meeting ended with an invitation to lunch with him that afternoon at Mr. Drexel's office, which I accepted. There were present only Mr. Drexel, Mr. Childs, and one or two others connected with the Drexel house. After luncheon all dispersed but Grant, Childs, and myself, and we had a most delightful conversation with Grant for an hour or more. I was anxious to learn, if possible, what Grant's feelings were in the Presidential battle of 1864. Without intimating to him that Lincoln had doubted his fidelity, I reminded him that he had maintained such a silent attitude that some of Lincoln's closest friends were at a loss to know his preference in the contest. He answered very promptly that he supposed none could have doubted his earnest desire for the re-election of Lincoln, although he studiously avoided any expression, public or private, on the subject. He said: "It would have been obviously unbecoming on my part to have given a public expression against a general whom I had succeeded as Commander-in-Chief of the army." I do not doubt that Grant declared the exact truth in that statement. Naturally silent and averse to any expressions whatever on politics, he felt that he could not with propriety even appear to assail a man who had failed and fallen in the position that he had

won and maintained. Thus for twelve years I cherished
a personal prejudice against Grant because of his supposed want of fidelity to Lincoln that I now believe to
have been wholly unjust. One revelation to me at the
meeting with Grant at the Drexel luncheon was his remarkable and attractive powers as a conversationalist.
He discussed politics during his term and the politics of
the future, public men and public events, with great freedom and in a manner so genial as to amaze me. I had
shared the common impression that Grant was always
reticent, even in the circle of his closest friends, but the
three hours spent with him on that day proved that when
he chose he could be one of the most entertaining of men
in the social circle.

It is evident that from the day that Grant became
Commander-in-Chief, Lincoln had abiding faith in him.
He yielded implicitly to Grant's judgment in all matters
purely military; Grant, like all great soldiers, yielded as
implicitly to Lincoln in all matters relating to civil administration, and the annals of history will testify that
Grant fulfilled every expectation of the government and
of the loyal people of the nation as military chieftain.
Many have criticised some of his military movements,
such as his assaults at Vicksburg and Cold Harbor and
his battles in the Wilderness, but he met the great need
of the country and was as heroic in peace as in war.
When President Johnson attempted to punish Lee for
treason, Grant not only admonished the President, but
notified him that "the officers and men paroled at Appomattox Court-House, and since upon the same terms
given to Lee, cannot be tried for treason so long as they
preserve the terms of their parole;" and he went so far
as to declare that he would resign his commission if the
government violated the faith he had given when Lee
surrendered to him. He fought more battles and won

more victories than any general of any country during his generation, and when on the 23d of July, 1885, Ulysses S. Grant met the inexorable messenger, the Great Captain of the Age passed from time to eternity.

LINCOLN AND McCLELLAN.

NOT until all the lingering personal, political, and military passions of the war shall have perished can the impartial historian tell the true story of Abraham Lincoln's relations to George B.. McClellan, nor will the just estimate of McClellan as a military chieftain be recorded until the future historian comes to his task entirely free from the prejudices of the present. Although more than a quarter of a century has elapsed since the close of the war, and countless contributions have been given to the history of that conflict from every shade of conviction that survived it, McClellan's ability as a military commander, and the correctness of Lincoln's action in calling him to command and in dismissing him from command, are as earnestly disputed to-day as they were in the white heat of the personal and political conflicts of the time. Notwithstanding the bitter partisan assaults which have been made upon McClellan in the violence of party struggles, at times impugning his skill, his courage, and his patriotism, it is safe to say that fair-minded men of every political faith now testify to the absolute purity of his patriotism, to his exceptional skill as a military organizer, and to his courage as a commander. I knew McClellan well, and I believe that no reasonably just man could have known him without yielding to him the highest measure of personal respect. He was one of the most excellent

GENERAL GEORGE B. M'CLELLAN, 1862.

and lovable characters I have ever met, and that he was patriotic in everything that he did, however he may have erred, and that he would have given his life as a sacrifice to his army or his country had duty required it, will not be doubted within the circle of his personal associations. I saw him frequently after he came to Washington heralded as the "Young Napoleon," to perform the herculean task of organizing the best army that ever was organized in any country within the same period of time. I saw him when he started upon his Peninsula campaign with the hope of victory beaming from his bright young face, and I stood close by his side most of the day when he fought his last battle at Antietam. Only a few months thereafter he was finally relieved from his command, and his military career ended on November 5, 1862, when, by order of the President, he transferred his army to General Burnside and went to Trenton, New Jersey, "for further orders." The "further orders" never came until Presidential election day, 1864, when McClellan resigned his commission as major-general in the army and Sheridan was appointed to his place.

Both Lincoln and McClellan now live only in history, and history will judge them by their achievements as it has judged all mankind. Lincoln was a successful President, and, like the great Roman Germanicus, "fortunate in the opportunity of his death." McClellan was an unsuccessful general and a defeated politician. Such will be the imperishable records of history as to these two men; but even the next generation will see continued disputation as to McClellan's capabilities as a commander, and Lincoln will be censured alike for having maintained and supported McClellan as a military leader, and for having failed to appreciate and support him after having called him to responsible command.

None the less, however, will be the irrevocable judgment of history that Lincoln succeeded and that McClellan failed. But why did McClellan fail as a military commander? The answer of his devoted partisans is that he was deliberately hindered and embarrassed in every military movement, and that he would have achieved great success had he been supported as the more successful generals later in the war were supported by the government. To this comes the response from the friends of Lincoln that he earnestly and heartily seconded McClellan to the utmost of his resources; that he long confided in him when the confidence of his friends had been greatly shattered; that he reappointed him to command against his Cabinet and against the general sentiment of his party leaders; and that whatever failures were suffered by McClellan were the result of his own incompetency or of the inability of the government to meet his wants.

It is unjust to McClellan to judge him by the same standard that is applied to the successful generals who succeeded him. I believe that it was McClellan's greatest misfortune that he was suddenly called to the dazzling position of Commander-in-Chief when he was a comparative novice in great war operations and without the experience necessary to make a great commander. I believe that the 23d of April, 1861, was the fateful day that dated the beginning of McClellan's misfortunes. He was then in Cincinnati, in charge of one of the railroads connected with that city. Pennsylvania troops were then being organized by Governor Curtin, and he was in search of a Pennsylvanian of military education and attainments to be placed in command. He first offered the position to McClellan, who promptly arranged his business to go to Harrisburg in person with the view of accepting it. By special request he stopped at Columbus on his way to Harrisburg to confer with Governor Dennison on some military problems which were vexing the Governor of Ohio. He expected to remain at Columbus only a few hours and then proceed to Pennsylvania. While in conference with Governor Dennison he was tendered the commission of major-general commanding the volunteers of Ohio, although ineligible because of his want of residence in that State. The difficulty was obviated by both branches of the Legislature passing, in a few hours, a bill making him eligible, and on the same 23d of April, 1861, he was commissioned as major-general and assigned to the command of the Ohio State troops. This led to his skirmishes in West Virginia, which in that day were magnified into great battles and great victories, and, when it became necessary to select a successor to Scott as Commander-in-Chief, McClellan was the only general whose victories had attracted the attention of the nation. He was thus called to the responsible position of Commander-in-Chief when a little over thirty years of age, with no experience in war beyond a brief campaign in Mexico, and without the training necessary to enable him to comprehend the most colossal war of modern times. Had he accepted the command of the Pennsylvania troops he would doubtless have made them the best disciplined and most effective division of the Army of the Potomac, would have fought them wisely and gallantly in every conflict, and would have won distinction as a commander with the experience that would have enabled him to maintain it. Instead of floundering along in untrodden paths and committing errors for others to profit by, he would have seen others charged with the gravest responsibility that could be assigned to any military man, would have seen them blunder and fall, and would have been ripened, by his own experience and by the misfortunes of his superiors, for the command that he won so suddenly and twice lost by order of a President who sincerely desired to be McClellan's friend and to give him success.

McClellan's fundamental error, and the one that I believe was the fountain of most, if not all, his misfortunes, was in his assumption not only that Lincoln and the government generally were unfriendly to him when he started out on his spring campaign of 1862, but that they deliberately conspired to prevent him from achieving military success.* This was a fatal error, and it was certainly most unjust to Lincoln. If McClellan really believed that the government had predetermined his military failure or if he seriously doubted its fidelity, it exhibited moral cowardice on his part to march an army into hopeless battle. He might have believed the President, the Secretary of War, and the administration generally to have been unfriendly to him, and yet, relying upon his ability to win their confidence by winning victory, he could have retained his command with justice to himself and to the country; but his own statements show that he believed then that he would not be permitted to win a victory or to capture Richmond; and, thus believing, he owed it to himself, to the great army he had organized as none other could have organized it, and to the country to whose cause he was undoubtedly loyal, to resign the command and put the responsibility upon

---

* Don't worry about the wretches in Washington. They have done nearly their worst, and can't do much more. I am sure that I will win in the end, in spite of all their rascality. History will present a sad record of these traitors, who are willing to sacrifice the country and its army for personal spite and personal aims. The people will soon understand the whole matter.—*Gen. McClellan's Letter to his Wife*, dated Yorktown, April 11, 1862, in *McClellan's Own Story*, page 310.

those he believed to be conspirators for the destruction of himself and his army.

McClellan has not left this question open to dispute. In *McClellan's Own Story*, written by himself, on page 150, he says: "They (the President and others) determined to ruin me in any event and by any means. First, by endeavoring to force me into premature movements, knowing that a failure would end my military career; afterward by withholding the means necessary to achieve success." On the same page he says: "They determined that I should not succeed, and carried out their determinations only too well, at a fearful sacrifice of blood, time, and treasure." On page 151 in the same book McClellan says: "From the light that has since been thrown on Stanton's character I am satisfied that from an early day he was in this treasonable conspiracy." * It will thus be seen that McClellan started on

---

* From the light that has since been thrown on Stanton's character I am satisfied that from an early date he was in this treasonable conspiracy, and that his course in ingratiating himself with me, and pretending to be my friend before he was in office, was only a part of his long system of treachery. . . .

I had never seen Mr. Stanton, and probably had not even heard of him, before reaching Washington in 1861. Not many weeks after arriving I was introduced to him as a safe adviser on legal points. From that moment he did his best to ingratiate himself with me, and professed the warmest friendship and devotion. I had no reason to suspect his sincerity, and therefore believed him to be what he professed. The most disagreeable thing about him was the extreme virulence with which he abused the President, the administration, and the Republican party. He carried this to such an extent that I was often shocked by it.

He never spoke of the President in any other way than as the "original gorilla," and often said that Du Chaillu was a fool to wander all the way to Africa in search of what he could so easily have found at Springfield, Illinois. Nothing could be more bitter than his words and manner always were when speaking of the

his Peninsula campaign not merely believing that the President and the administration generally were unfriendly to him, but really believing that they had formed a treasonable conspiracy by which his military movements should be made disastrous and the blood of thousands of brave soldiers sacrificed to accomplish McClellan's overthrow. This is a monstrous accusation against Lincoln, and but for the fact that McClellan presents it so clearly in language from his own pen that none can mistake, it would seem incredible that he could have believed such a conspiracy to exist, and yet led a great army to defeat that treachery on the part of the government would make inevitable. In this I am sure that McClellan does both himself and Lincoln the gravest injustice. Lincoln was the one man of all who was utterly incapable of deliberately hindering military success under any circumstances. There were those who believed it best to protract the war in order to accomplish the overthrow of slavery, but Lincoln was not of that number. On the contrary, he offended many when he distinctly declared in his letter to Greeley, August 22, 1862: "If there be those who would not save the Union unless they could at the same time destroy slavery, I do not agree with them. My paramount object in this struggle is to save the Union, and it is not either to save or to destroy slavery. If I could save the Union without freeing any slave I would do it, and if I could save it by

---

administration and the Republican party. He never gave them credit for honesty or patriotism, and very seldom for any ability.

At some time during the autumn of 1861, Secretary Cameron made quite an abolition speech to some newly-arrived regiment. Next day Stanton urged me to arrest him for inciting to insubordination. He often advocated the propriety of my seizing the government and taking affairs into my own hands.—*Gen. McClellan* in *McClellan's Own Story*, pages 151, 152.

freeing all the slaves I would do it, and if I could save it by freeing some and leaving others alone I would also do that.'' What Lincoln wanted was the speediest overthrow of the rebellion and the restoration of the Union, with or without the destruction of slavery; and the assumption that he could have been capable of such a treasonable conspiracy as to deliberately send a general to the field with a great army solely to have that army sacrificed and its commander dishonored is at war with every attribute of Lincoln's character. There never was the blood of a soldier shed in battle that did not bring grief to the heart of Abraham Lincoln, and there never was a disaster of the Union troops that did not shadow his face with sorrow, no matter whether he loved or distrusted the commander. I am quite sure that the two men of all the nation who most desired McClellan's success in the field were Lincoln and McClellan themselves.

I have said that it is unjust to McClellan to compare his achievements in the first great campaign of the war with the achievements of Grant and Sherman in the later campaigns which culminated in the overthrow of the rebellion. All the generals of the early part of the war were making object-lessons to guide themselves and those who succeeded them in later conflicts. In this work the many failed, and many of the most promising among them. The few succeeded and made their names immortal. One of the greatest wars of history produced but one Grant and one Lee; but one Joe Johnston and one Tecumseh Sherman; but one Phil Sheridan and one Stonewall Jackson. Scores of generals on both sides had opportunities of winning the laurels of these great chieftains, but none was equal to the task. It is no reproach to McClellan to say that Grant fought few battles which McClellan would have fought under precisely similar circumstances. McClellan was an organizer, a disciplinarian, and the best defensive general in all the armies of the late war. He would have made a greater Confederate leader than Lee himself. He would never have made the exhaustive and fruitless campaigns of the second Bull Run and Antietam which cost Lee one-fourth of his army when he had feeble means to replace his losses. He never would have made an aggressive campaign to Gettysburg when the resources of the Confederacy were so nearly exhausted, and Pickett's charge would never have been dreamed of by McClellan. He was the greatest organizer and defensive officer of the age, but the Union cause demanded swift and terrible blows and countless sacrifices. It had to fight on fields chosen by the enemy. It had often to give two men for one in the death-lists of the struggles, but it had boundless resources to fill the shattered ranks. The most aggressive warfare was certain to bring the speediest victory and with the least sacrifice of life and treasure in the end. Grant met this want. He was the great aggressive general of the war. He always fought when he should have fought, and sometimes fought when it would have been wiser to have refrained. Had he been a Southern general, he would have been an utter failure, for the Southern general had to study how to husband his resources; how to protect the life of every soldier; how to fight only when a thousand men could withstand two thousand; and to that system of warfare Grant was an entire stranger. He was the embodiment of aggressive warfare; McClellan was the embodiment of defensive warfare, and McClellan was as great as Grant in his line, and with no greater limitations upon his military genius.

Grant fought one defensive battle at Shiloh and lost it and lost his command. McClellan fought only one pitched battle as the aggressor at Antietam, and then he was strategically defensive, while tactically aggressive, but his military genius shone resplendent in his defensive battles when retreating to the James River.* Thus a condition confronted McClellan to which his great military genius and attainments were not best adapted, and Grant's star rose and brightened as McClellan's faded, because Grant possessed, in the fullest measure, the qualities needed to win peace and restore the Republic.

No man ever commanded the Army of the Potomac for whom the soldiers had so much affection as they had for McClellan. They knew that he was a soldier and a great soldier. They knew that he would never put them into action unless good generalship dictated it. They knew they were safe from wanton sacrifice while under his command. They knew that he valued the life of every man with the tenderness of a parent, and they loved him because they revered and trusted him. Lincoln fully appreciated and greatly valued the devotion of the army to McClellan. He believed that no other general could have so quickly organized and disciplined a great army out of entirely raw materials as McClellan had done, and he never gave up faith in McClellan until he felt that he could no longer trust the destiny of the war to his direction. He was many times

---

* The movement from Washington into Maryland, which culminated in the battles of South Mountain and Antietam, was not a part of an offensive campaign, with the object of the invasion of the enemy's territory and an attack upon his capital, but was defensive in its purposes, although offensive in its character, and would be technically called a "defensive-offensive campaign." It was undertaken at a time when our army had experienced severe defeats, and its object was to preserve the national capital and Baltimore, to protect Pennsylvania from invasion, and to drive the enemy out of Maryland.—*Gen. McClellan* in *McClellan's Own Story*, page 642.

justly fretted at McClellan's complaints about military matters, at his obtrusive criticism about political matters, and especially at his insulting declaration to the Secretary of War, in a letter dated at army headquarters on the Peninsula, June 28, 1862, just after his retreat to the James River, in which he said: "If I save this army now, I tell you plainly that I owe no thanks to you or to any other person in Washington. You have done your best to sacrifice this army." This letter, although addressed to the Secretary of War, distinctly embraced the President in the grave charge of conspiracy to defeat McClellan's army and sacrifice thousands of the lives of his soldiers. None but a man of Lincoln's exceptional forbearance and patience would have tolerated McClellan in command for a day after such a declaration, written from the headquarters of a defeated army, but Lincoln neither dismissed nor reproached him, nor, as far as I can learn, did he ever allude to it.

Ten days after the offensive and insubordinate letter was written Lincoln visited McClellan at his headquarters on the James River. While Lincoln was there McClellan personally handed him a letter dated July 7, 1862, that was a caustic criticism of the political and military policy of the administration, and assumed to define not only the military action of the government, but the civil and political policy of the government on all important questions relating to the war. McClellan himself records the fact that Lincoln read the letter in McClellan's presence without comment, and that he never alluded to the subject again. McClellan vigorously protested against the withdrawal of the army from the Peninsula, but the order was peremptory, and he obeyed it with obvious reluctance. His personal feeling toward Lincoln and the administration is clearly exhibited in a letter to his wife written on the 31st of August and published in *McClellan's Own Story*, p. 532. Speaking of Washington, he says: "As a matter of self-respect I cannot go there." On the 1st of September, however, he was called to Washington and given a verbal order by General Halleck, then Commander-in-Chief, to take charge of the defenses of Washington. On the following morning Lincoln and Halleck called on General McClellan at his house and asked him to take command. McClellan states that Lincoln asked him as a favor to the President to "resume command and do the best that could be done." The same day an order was issued from the War Department by Halleck stating that "Major-General McClellan will have command of the fortifications of Washington and all the troops for the defense of the capital." The manner of the restoration of McClellan to command has given rise to latitudinous dispute, but the short story is that most of the Army of the Potomac had been put under command of General Pope in his disastrous battles of the second Bull Run campaign, and both the armies of McClellan and Pope were compelled to retreat into the Washington defenses in a very demoralized condition.

No man better understood McClellan's value as an organizer and as a defensive commander than Lincoln, and he solved the problem himself by calling McClellan to the new command because he believed the capital to be in danger and McClellan the best man to protect it. If he ever consulted any one on the subject, the fact has never been given to the public in any authentic form. Had he consulted his Cabinet, it would have been next to unanimous against giving McClellan any command whatever, and the administration leaders in both branches of Congress would also have been nearly unanimous in demanding McClellan's dismissal from command. Lincoln acted in this case, as was his custom in all severe trials, on his own personal responsibility, and Lincoln, and Lincoln alone, is responsible for calling McClellan to command the defenses of Washington and for permitting McClellan, under that assignment, to take the field for the Antietam campaign without any special orders from the government. The assumption that Lincoln simply consulted his fears in restoring McClellan to command is an absurdity. There were twenty generals in the Army of the Potomac and in Pope's army who could have taken command of the complete defenses of Washington, constructed under McClellan's faultless engineering skill, and protected the capital against double the number of men Lee had in his entire army. That McClellan handled the demoralized army better than any other could have done I do not doubt, but that he was a necessity to save the capital is not to be considered for a moment. It is obvious also that Lincoln believed McClellan to be the best man to command the army in the campaign in pursuit of Lee, but he was prudent enough to avoid any specific order to McClellan assigning him to the command. He put McClellan in position to take the command to move against Lee, and McClellan, always obedient to what he believed to be his duty, availed himself of it and fought the battle of Antietam.

So far from Lincoln being unfriendly to McClellan when he started on his spring campaign of 1862, there is the strongest evidence in support of the belief that Lincoln hoped for McClellan's success and earnestly desired him to win his way back as Commander-in-Chief of the armies. It was on March 11, 1862, that Lincoln relieved McClellan from his position of Commander-in-Chief and limited him to the command of his own immediate army, but no Commander-in-Chief was appointed until July 11, 1862. Had Lincoln intended that McClellan should never return to the command of all the

armies, he certainly would have appointed Halleck Commander-in-Chief before the 11th of July. It is known
that General Scott, when he retired from the command,
desired the appointment of Halleck as his successor, and
McClellan himself was in doubt for some weeks whether
he or Halleck would be called to the supreme command.
After McClellan, Halleck was the one man to whom Lincoln turned as the most competent for Commander-in-
Chief, but he delayed filling the position not only until
after the disastrous close of the Peninsula campaign, but
for two weeks after McClellan's insulting letter to Stanton and four days after McClellan's offensive political
letter handed to the President at Harrison's Landing. It
was not until McClellan had proclaimed himself a political as well as a military general on the 7th of July,
1862, that Lincoln abandoned all hope of McClellan ever
regaining the position of Commander-in-Chief, and four
days thereafter he called Halleck to that task. I many
times heard Lincoln discuss McClellan. I do not mean
that he usually or even at any time expressed fully his
views as to McClellan, but I have reason to know that
with all the troubles he had with him about moving in
the early part of 1862 and about the Peninsula campaign,
he sincerely and earnestly hoped that McClellan would
capture Richmond and thus reinstate himself as Commander-in-Chief of the armies, with his laurels fairly
won and his ability to maintain them clearly demonstrated.

If Lincoln had been capable of resentment against
McClellan or against any of his military leaders, many
heads would have fallen that were saved by Lincoln's
patience and generosity. He knew that McClellan and
more than one other general had at times listened to the
whispers of a military dictatorship. McClellan states,
on page 152 of his own book, that Stanton once urged

him to arrest Secretary Cameron for inciting to insubordination by making an Abolition speech to a newly-arrived regiment, and he adds: "He (Stanton) often advocated the propriety of my seizing the government and taking affairs in my own hands." In a letter to his wife, dated August 9, 1861, also published in his own volume, page 85, McClellan refers to the fact that he is earnestly pressed by letter after letter and conversation after conversation to save the nation by assuming the powers of the President as dictator. Writing in the free confidence of a devoted husband to a devoted wife, he said: "As I hope one day to be united with you for ever in heaven I have no such aspiration. I would cheerfully take the dictatorship and agree to lay down my life when the country is saved." Had Lincoln been jealous of McClellan's power, he had ample opportunity to relieve him from command long before he did, but he never feared those who prattled about the dictatorship, although well informed of the many, including some prominent generals, who had advised it. His generosity to military men who committed such follies is clearly exhibited in his letter of January 26, 1863, to General Hooker, notifying him of his assignment to the command of the Army of the Potomac. Hooker was one of those who had believed in a military dictatorship, and Lincoln believed that Hooker had not given cordial support to General Burnside when he was in command of the army. To use Lincoln's own plain language, he told Hooker that he had done "a great wrong to the country and to a most meritorious and honorable brother-officer." He then said to Hooker: "I have heard, in such a way as to believe it, of your recently saying that both the army and the government needed a dictator. Of course it was not for this, but in spite of it, that I have given you the command. Only those generals who gain success can be dictators. What I now ask of you is military success, and I will risk the dictatorship.'' Thus did Lincoln assign Hooker to the command of the Army of the Potomac when he knew that Hooker had been guilty of the failure to support his commanding officer in important military movements, and that he had advised a dictator to usurp the prerogatives of the President. He believed McClellan to be in political sympathy with the men who were most implacably hostile to his administration, but he was sagacious enough to know that military success under any general of his appointment would give political success to the administration; and I am certain that he would have preferred McClellan as the conqueror of Richmond in 1862, and would gladly have restored him to the command of all the armies, knowing that the victory would have been as much the victory of Lincoln as the victory of McClellan.

I saw Lincoln many times during the campaign of 1864, when McClellan was his competitor for the Presidency. I never heard him speak of McClellan in any other than terms of the highest personal respect and kindness. He never doubted McClellan's loyalty to the government or to the cause that called him to high military command. But he did believe, until after the capture of Atlanta by Sherman and Sheridan's victories in the Valley, which settled the political campaign in favor of Lincoln, that McClellan was quite likely to be elected over him, and that if elected, with all his patriotism and loyalty to the Union, he would be powerless to prevent the dissolution of the Republic. The convention that nominated McClellan for President met only a few days before Sherman captured Atlanta. There had been no important victories for any of the Union armies until that time during the year 1864, and there had been great sacrifice of life in both Sherman's and Grant's campaigns.

The convention that nominated McClellan voiced the sentiment that regarded the war as a failure, and it was so declared in the platform in the clearest terms, with the call for a suspension of hostilities because of the failure to obtain peace by force of arms. Lincoln believed that McClellan, if elected, would be coerced into a policy of humiliating peace and the loss of all the great issues for which so much blood and treasure had been sacrified. But that he ever cherished the semblance of resentment against McClellan, even when McClellan was offensively insubordinate as a military man and equally offensive in assuming to define the political policy of the administration, I do not for a moment believe. Had McClellan understood Lincoln half as well as Lincoln understood McClellan, there never would have been serious discord between them. It was the creation of what I believe to be McClellan's entirely unwarranted distrust of Lincoln's personal and official fidelity to him as a military commander, and that single error became a seething cauldron of woe to both of them and a consuming misfortune to McClellan.

Lincoln's position in history is secure, but it is doubtful whether the impartial historian of the future will give McClellan his full measure of justice. History records results—only achievements and failures. It will tell of McClellan that he was an unsuccessful military chieftain, and that on his own record in an appeal to the country he was the most overwhelmingly defeated candidate for President in the history of the present great parties of the nation; but no truthful historian can fail to say of him that he was one of the great military geniuses of his day, one of the purest of patriots, and one of the most loyal of men in the great battle for the preservation of the Union.

15

(Photo by Sarony, New York.)

GENERAL WILLIAM T. SHERMÁN, 1890.

LINCOLN AND SHERMAN.

ABRAHAM LINCOLN and William T. Sherman had never met until Sherman came to Washington to visit his brother, the present Senator Sherman, ten days after Lincoln's inauguration. Sherman's mission to the capital was not to obtain a command. He had resigned as president of a military institute in Louisiana, because, as he frankly said to the State officials who controlled the institution, he could not remain and owe allegiance to a State that had withdrawn from the Union. In his letter of resignation, dated January 18, 1861, he said: "Should Louisiana withdraw from the Federal Union, I prefer to maintain my allegiance to the Constitution as long as a fragment of it survives, and my longer stay here would be a wrong in every sense of the word." He left New Orleans about the 1st of March to make his home in the North. Like Grant, he tendered his services to the government, but, again like Grant, his offer was not answered. His first meeting with Lincoln was in company with his Senator brother to pay a brief visit of courtesy to the President. After the Senator had transacted some political business with Lincoln, he turned to his brother and said: "Mr. President, this is my brother, Colonel Sherman, who is just up from Louisiana; he may give you some information you want." To this Lincoln replied, as reported by Sherman himself: "Ah! How are they getting along down there?"

Sherman answered: "They think they are getting along swimmingly; they are prepared for war." To which Lincoln responded: "Oh, well, I guess we'll manage to keep house." Sherman records in his *Memoirs* that he was "sadly disappointed," and that he "broke out on John, damning the politicians generally," saying: "You have got things in a hell of a fix; you may get them out as best you can." Sherman then, as ever, was ruggedly honest and patriotic, and often more impressive than elegant in his manner of speech. Some old St. Louis friends had obtained for him the presidency of a street-railway of that city at a salary of $2500. Speaking of this position, he says: "This suited me exactly, and I answered Turner that I would accept with thanks."

Before Sherman was comfortably installed in his position as street-railway president, Postmaster-General Blair telegraphed him, on the 6th of April, asking him to accept a chief clerkship in the War Department, with the assurance that he would be made Assistant Secretary of War when Congress met. Sherman answered with the laconic dispatch: "I cannot accept." In a letter written at the same time to Blair he says that after his visit to Washington, where he saw no chance of employment, he had gone to St. Louis, accepted an official position and established his home, and that he was not at liberty to change. He added that he was thankful for the compliment, and that he wished "the administration all success in its almost impossible task of governing this distracted and anarchical people." A few days thereafter General Frank Blair called on Sherman and said that he was authorized to select a brigadier-general to command the Department of Missouri, and he tendered the position to Sherman, who declined it, and General Lyon was then appointed. Feeling, however, as the clouds of war darkened upon the country, that his services might be needed, on the 8th of May Sherman addressed a formal letter to the Secretary of War, again tendering his services to the government, and on the 14th of the same month he was appointed colonel of the Thirteenth regiment of regulars. On the 20th of June he reported at Washington in obedience to orders from General Scott, who assigned him to inspection duty; and before the movement was made to Manassas, Sherman was ordered to the command of a brigade of Hunter's division, and in that position was in the first battle of the war.

Sherman was one of the very few generals who seldom grieved Lincoln. While he was one of the most voluminous of writers on every phase of the war and every question arising from it, he never assumed to be wiser than the government, and he never committed a serious blunder. He had the most profound contempt for politicians in and out of the army, and for political methods generally, and his bluntness of both manner and expression emphasized his views and purposes so that none could misunderstand them. Naturally impulsive, he often felt keenly the many complications which surrounded all great generals, and he spoke and wrote with unusual freedom, but always within the clearest lines of military subordination. He was an earnest, ardent, outspoken patriot, and had more controversy than any other general with the single exception of McClellan; but I doubt whether there is a single important utterance of Sherman's during the four long years of war, when new and grave problems had to be met and solved from time to time, that he would have recalled in the later years of his life. He had learned to cherish the most profound respect for Lincoln, although they never met after his first introduction to the President during the early period of the war, until the spring of 1865 at City Point, after Sherman had made his march to the sea and his great campaign had practically ended at Raleigh, North Carolina.

There is no doubt that Lincoln's earliest impressions of Sherman were quite as unfavorable to Sherman as were Sherman's early impressions of Lincoln. It was not until Sherman had been assigned to Kentucky, along with General Anderson, that he attracted the attention of the country. Along with a number of others he had won his star at Bull Run, and on the 24th of August he was sent with Anderson to Louisville. Anderson's feeble health soon demanded that he should be relieved, and Sherman was thus left in command. The position of Kentucky was a most delicate and important one. Sherman succeeded to the command on the 8th of October, and within a few weeks thereafter it was whispered throughout Washington that he was a lunatic. This belief was accepted in most if not all military circles at the capital, and was doubtless shared by Lincoln himself, as in little more than two months after Sherman had assumed command in Kentucky he was ordered to report at Benton Barracks, St. Louis, and General Buell was assigned as his successor. The attitude of Kentucky attracted very general interest throughout the country, and the repeated changes of commanders caused great solicitude. I remember calling on Colonel Scott, Assistant Secretary of War, on the day that the announcement was made of Sherman's transfer to Missouri and Buell's appointment to Kentucky, and asking him what it meant. Scott answered: "Sherman's gone in the head;" and upon inquiry I found that Scott simply voiced the general belief of those who should have been best informed on the subject. Reports were published in all the leading newspapers of the country speaking of Sherman as mentally unbalanced, and it naturally mortified the blunt, straightforward soldier to the last degree. General Halleck, in a letter to McClellan asking for more officers, said: "I am satisfied that General Sherman's physical and mental system is so completely broken by labor and care as to render him, for the present, unfit for duty. Perhaps a few weeks' rest may restore him." But it is only just to Sherman to say that the chief reason for the military authorities in Washington assuming that he was a lunatic was his report soon after assuming command in Kentucky, stating that it would require an army of 60,000 men to hold Kentucky and 200,000 men to open the Mississippi and conquer the rebellion in the South-west. This was at that time regarded as conclusive evidence of his insanity, and his mental condition was a matter of almost daily discussion in the public journals, with Halstead's Cincinnati *Commercial*, published in Sherman's own State, leading the attack against his mental capacity.

When Secretary Cameron and Adjutant-General Thomas were returning from their investigation of General Fremont's department, soon after Sherman had assumed command of Kentucky, Sherman took special measures to prevail upon Cameron to stop over in Louisville and personally inquire into the condition of that State. Cameron did so, and had a confidential conference with Sherman at the Galt House, in which Sherman said to Cameron that for the purpose of defense in Kentucky he should have 60,000 men, and for offensive movements 200,000 would be necessary. Cameron's answer, as reported by Sherman himself, was: "Great God! where are they to come from?" That demand of Sherman's convinced Cameron that Sherman was mentally unbalanced, and on his return to Washington he united with all the military authorities of that day in ridiculing Sherman's demand. Those who have distinct recollections of the war, as well as every intelligent reader of its history, need not now be reminded that Sherman was the only military man of that day who thoroughly and accurately appreciated the situation in the South-west, and that his original estimate of the forces necessary to overthrow the rebellion in that section of the country is proved to have been substantially correct. Buell, who succeeded Sherman in command of Kentucky, had nearly 60,000 men when he was ordered to Grant at Shiloh, and fully 200,000 men were reapers in the harvest of death before the rebellion was conquered in the South-west and the Father of Waters again "went unvexed to the sea."

Sherman was not permitted to take the field until after the capture of Forts Henry and Donelson and the city of Nashville. From December 23, 1861, to the 13th of February, 1862, he was in charge of the St. Louis barracks as military instructor. He was first ordered from St. Louis to take command of the post at Paducah, Kentucky, where he remained until the 10th of March, when he was placed in command of a division and ordered to join Grant for the Shiloh campaign. It will be remembered that he exhibited great skill and courage as a general during the disastrous first day at Shiloh. That was the first action in which Sherman had an opportunity to prove his ability as a military commander, and it is safe to say that from that day until the close of the war Grant regarded him as the best lieutenant in his entire army. He was with Grant at Vicksburg, shared Grant's victory at Missionary Ridge, and when the Atlanta campaign was determined upon in the spring of 1864 there was no question in military circles as to the pre-eminent fitness of Sherman to take the command. His campaign from Chattanooga to Atlanta was one of the most brilliant of all the campaigns of the war. It exhibited the most accomplished military strategy coupled with the wisest direction of an army that had to contend with an enemy always intrenched and to fight every battle under the greatest disadvantages. Many even of our successful military campaigns have been severely criticised, but I doubt whether any intelligent military man at home or abroad has ever found fault with Sherman's generalship in his Atlanta campaign. With all his natural impetuosity of temper, he was always clear-headed and abundant in caution when charged with the command of an army. In his march to Atlanta he was passing through a country that was, to use his own language, "one vast fort," and with "at least fifty miles of connected trenches with abatis and finished batteries." With the single exception of his assault upon Johnston's lines at Kenesaw he did not meet with a serious reverse until he entered Atlanta, and it was his dispatch to Lincoln, announcing the capture of that city, that reversed the political tide of the country and assured Lincoln's re-election.

Sherman's march to the sea, that furnished the most romantic story of the civil war, was really a holiday picnic as compared with the march from Chattanooga to Atlanta. On the 12th of November, 1864, Sherman severed communications with the North, and started for Savannah with a picked army full 60,000 strong, and on the 10th of December he was in front of the Confederate defenses of Savannah. On the 13th, after the capture of Fort McAllister, he had opened communications with the Union squadron and was enabled to obtain the supplies his army so much needed. Thus for more than one entire month the country had no word whatever from General Sherman except in the vague and often greatly exaggerated reports which came from the Southern newspapers. I saw Lincoln several times during Sherman's march, and while he did not conceal his anxiety concerning him, he always frankly expressed his unbounded confidence in Sherman's ability to execute what he had undertaken. He had the strongest faith in Sherman as a military commander. On one occasion during Sherman's march, when he had been out for two or three weeks, I called at the War Department and ascertained that no word had been received from him, and that none need be expected for some days to come. I went from the War Department to the White House, and after a brief conference with Lincoln, in which Sherman was not alluded to at all, I bade him good-day and started to leave the room. Just as I reached the door he turned round and with a merry twinkling of the eye he said: "McClure, wouldn't you like to hear something from Sherman?" The inquiry electrified me at the instant, as it seemed to imply that Lincoln had some information on the subject. I immediately answered: "Yes, most of all I should like to hear from Sherman." To this Lincoln answered with a hearty laugh: "Well, I'll be hanged if I wouldn't myself." When Sherman reached Savannah, Lincoln overflowed with gratitude to him and his army. He then felt fully assured that the military power of the rebellion was hopelessly broken.

The names of Lincoln and Sherman are indissolubly linked together in the yet continued dispute over Lincoln's original views on reconstruction, as Sherman claimed to represent them in the terms of the first surrender of Johnston to Sherman at Durham Station, North Carolina. On the 18th of April, 1865, Sherman and Johnston met at the house of Mr. Bennet to agree upon the terms for the surrender of Johnston's army. On the 12th of April Sherman had announced to his army the surrender of Lee. Two days later a flag of truce was received from Johnston proposing "to stop the further effusion of blood and devastation of property," and suggesting that the civil authorities of the States be permitted " to enter into the needful arrangements to terminate the existing war." Sherman's answer of the same date said: " I am fully empowered to arrange with you any terms for the suspension of further hostilities between the armies commanded by you and those commanded by myself." An interview with Johnston having been arranged by a staff officer, Sherman started from Raleigh on the 17th to fill the appointment with Johnston. When he was about to enter the car he was stopped by a telegraph-operator, who gave him the startling information of the assassination of Lincoln on the 14th. He gave orders that no publicity should be given to the death of Lincoln, and he did not even inform the staff officers accompanying him. As soon as he was alone with Johnston he communicated to him the fact of Lincoln's assassination, and he adds that " the perspiration came out in large drops on his (Johnston's) forehead, and he did not attempt to conceal his distress." This conference with Johnston did not result in formulating the terms of surrender. Johnston did not assume to possess authority to surrender all the various armies yet in the field, but as Jefferson Davis, with Breckenridge, his Secretary of War, and Reagan, his Postmaster-General, was within reach of Johnston, he proposed to meet Sherman on the following day, when he hoped to have authority to surrender the entire Confederate armies remaining in the service. When they met again Breckenridge was with Johnston without assuming to act in any official capacity, and the terms of surrender were formulated and signed by Sherman and Johnston. So far as the purely military terms were involved, they were practically the same as those agreed to by Grant and Lee at Appomattox. The third article of the basis of agreement provided for " the recognition by the Executive of the United States of the several State governments on their officers and legislatures taking the oath prescribed by the Constitution of the United States.'' The fifth article provided for substantial amnesty, so far as in the power of the President, to all who accepted the terms of surrender, who should be protected in ''their political rights and franchise as well as their rights of person and property.'' It was provided also that the armies of Sherman and Johnston should refrain from all warlike movements until the terms of surrender were finally accepted, and in the event of failure forty-eight hours' notice should be given by either side for the resumption of hostilities. Sherman transmitted the agreement to the government through Grant, and Stanton published the disapproval by the administration with most offensive reflections upon Sherman.

But for the dispute that arose over Sherman's original terms of surrender with Johnston, Lincoln's views as to reconstruction would never have been crystallized in history. The fact that Sherman claimed to act under the direct authority of Lincoln in the terms he gave to Johnston and to the civil governments of the insurgent States brings up the question directly as to Lincoln's contemplated method of closing the war; and it is notable that many of Lincoln's biographers have injected partisan prejudice into history and have studiously attempted to conceal Lincoln's ideas as to the restoration of the Union. Whether he was right or wrong, it is due to the truth of history that his convictions be honestly presented. The plain question to be considered is this: Did or did not Lincoln expressly suggest to Sherman the terms he gave to Johnston in his original agreement of surrender? If he did, it clearly portrays Lincoln's purposes as to reconstruction and fully vindicates Sherman. If he did not thus suggest and instruct Sherman, then Sherman is a deliberate falsifier; and who is prepared to doubt the integrity of any positive statement made by William T. Sherman? There were four persons present at the conference held at City Point on the 28th of March, 1865. They were Lincoln, Grant, Sherman, and Admiral Porter. It was before these men that Lincoln freely discussed the question of ending the war, and in Sherman's *Memoirs* he says: "Mr. Lincoln was full and frank in his conversation, assuring me that in his mind he was all ready for the civil reorganization of affairs at the South as soon as the war was over." Had Lincoln stopped with the general assurance of his purpose to restore the South to civil government, it might be plausible to assume that Sherman misinterpreted his expressions, but Sherman adds the following positive statement: "He (Lincoln) distinctly authorized me to assure Governor Vance and the people of North Carolina that as soon as the rebel armies laid down their arms and resumed their civil pursuits they would at once be guaranteed all their rights as citizens of a common country; and that to avoid anarchy the State governments then in existence, with their civil functionaries, would be recognized by him as the governments de facto till Congress could provide others." * There was no possibility for Sherman to

---

* Your note of the 26th inst., enclosing proof sheet of your article on Lincoln and Sherman, has been received and very carefully read. I have no criticisms to make, for I think it is a just and fair delineation, well stated, of the character of these two conspicuous actors in the war of the Rebellion. I remember very well the interview with Mr. Lincoln in March, 1861. A good deal more was said than you have noted. Among other things, I remember that Lincoln said to Sherman: "I guess we will get along without you fellows," or some such remark, meaning that he thought there would be no war. This was the remark that made the most impression upon Captain Sherman, as he was then called, and led him to a want of confidence in Lincoln, who

mistake this expression of Lincoln. He was distinctly instructed to assure the Governor of North Carolina, the State in which Sherman's army was then operating, that upon the surrender of the insurgent forces all would be guaranteed their rights as citizens, and the civil governments then in existence would be recognized by Lincoln. There was no chance for misunderstanding on this point.

---

did not seem to appreciate the condition of the South and the peril in which the whole country was then involved. During General Sherman's march to the sea I went to Lincoln as you did. I was somewhat troubled by the reports from rebel sources that General Sherman had been flanked and that this wing or that wing had been driven back, etc., and went to Lincoln for encouragement, and asked him if he knew anything about the correctness of these reports. Lincoln said, "Oh no. I know what hole he went in at, but I can't tell what hole he will come out of," but seemed to be entirely confident that he would come out safely.

In respect to the conditional arrangement made between General Sherman and General Johnston for the surrender of Johnston's army your statement agrees entirely with what I understood from General Sherman a few days after the surrender. I went with General Sherman on his return from the interview with Lincoln to Goldsborough, N. C., where the army was encamped, and was fully advised by General Sherman of the conference between Lincoln, Grant, Porter, and himself at Hampton Roads. I did not at the time agree with the generous policy proposed by Mr. Lincoln, but at the meeting with Johnston General Sherman acted upon it in exact accordance with what he understood were the instructions of Mr. Lincoln, and afterward complained bitterly at the injustice done him for obeying what he regarded as the orders of the President. Immediately after Stanton's cruel statement of his reasons for setting aside the agreement between Sherman and Johnston, I wrote a reply which was published in Washington, stating my view of this agreement at that time. I have not seen it since, but I have no doubt if you have access to it you will find it supports the statements you now make. You are at liberty to use the contents of this letter or any part of it at your discretion.—*Senator John Sherman* to the Author, January 29, 1892.

Either Lincoln thus instructed Sherman or Sherman states what is deliberately untrue.

These were the last instructions that Sherman received from Lincoln or from the government until the surrender of Johnston. In a little more than two weeks thereafter Lincoln was assassinated, and the only event that could have been regarded as an additional guide for Sherman was the surrender of Lee, in which all the rights that Sherman accorded to Johnston's army were given to Lee's army by Grant. The testimony of Lincoln could not be had after the issue was raised with Sherman, as Lincoln was then dead; but Sherman knew that on the 6th of April, Lincoln had authorized the reconvening of the Virginia Legislature, and thus felt sure that Lincoln was doing in Virginia precisely what he had instructed Sherman to do in North Carolina. Grant, always reticent in matters of dispute except when testimony was a necessity, was not called upon to express any opinion as to the correctness of Sherman's understanding of Lincoln's instructions. General Badeau, who was with Grant at the time he received Stanton's offensive revocation of the agreement between Sherman and Johnston, says that Grant pronounced Stanton's ten reasons for rejecting the terms of surrender to be "infamous." An entirely new condition had been produced by the murder of Lincoln and the succession of Johnson, and had Sherman been advised of the frenzy of public sentiment that followed the assassination of the President, he probably would not have obeyed Lincoln's instructions by giving the promise that the government would recognize the Confederate civil authorities of the States.

The tragic death of Lincoln aroused public sentiment to the highest point of resentment. The new President was ostentatious in his demand for vengeance upon the

Southern leaders.   Stanton was most violent in his cry
for the swiftest retribution, and it was in this changed
condition of sentiment and of authority that Sherman's
terms, accorded to Johnston in obedience to the peaceful
purposes of Lincoln, were sent to the government for
approval or rejection.   Stanton immediately proclaimed
the rejection of the terms of surrender in a dispatch given
to the public press, in which he denounced Sherman with
unmingled ferocity as having acted without authority and
surrendered almost every issue for which the war had been
fought.   So violent was this assault upon Sherman from
Stanton that soon after, when Sherman's victorious army
was reviewed in Washington by the President and Secretary of War, Sherman refused the proffered hand of
Stanton before the multitude.   President Johnson subsequently assured Sherman that Stanton's public reflection
upon him had not been seen by the President nor any
of Stanton's associates of the Cabinet until it had been
published.   Admiral Porter, who was the remaining witness to the instructions received by Sherman, took down
notes immediately after the conference ended, and within
a year thereafter he furnished Sherman a statement of
what had occurred, in which he fully and broadly sustained Sherman as to Lincoln's instructions.   I assume,
therefore, that it is true beyond all reasonable dispute
that Sherman in his original terms of Johnston's surrender in North Carolina implicitly obeyed the directions of Lincoln, and was therefore not only fully justified in what he did, but would have been false to his
trust had he insisted upon any other terms than those he
accepted.

This issue made with General Sherman and feebly
sustained by a few partisan historians of the time has
led intelligent students to study carefully Lincoln's ideas
of reconstruction, and they should be correctly under-

stood to correctly estimate Lincoln's character. I frequently saw Lincoln during the summer and fall of 1864 and winter of 1865. Some time in August, 1864, I spent several hours with him alone in the White House, when he spoke most earnestly about the closing of the war. He had but a single purpose, and that was the speedy and cordial restoration of the dissevered States. He cherished no resentment against the South, and every theory of reconstruction that he ever conceived or presented was eminently peaceful and looking solely to re-attaching the estranged people to the government. I was startled when he first suggested that it would be wise to pay the South $400,000,000 as compensation for the abolition of slavery, but he had reasoned well on the subject, and none could answer the arguments he advanced in favor of such a settlement of the war. He knew that he could not then propose it to Congress or to the country, but he clung to it until the very last. He repeatedly renewed the subject in conversations when I was present, and on the 5th of February, 1865, he went so far as to formulate a message to Congress, proposing the payment of $400,000,000 for emancipation, and submitted it to his Cabinet, only to be unanimously rejected. Lincoln sadly accepted the decision of his Cabinet, and filed away the manuscript message with this indorsement thereon, to which his signature was added: "February 5, 1865. To-day these papers, which explain themselves, were drawn up and submitted to the Cabinet and unanimously disapproved by them." When the proposed message was disapproved Lincoln soberly asked: "How long will the war last?" To this none could make answer, and he added: "We are spending now in carrying on the war $3,000,000 a day, which will amount to all this money, besides all the lives."

At Lincoln's conference with Sherman and Grant at

16

City Point on the 28th of March he exhibited profound sorrow at the statement of these generals that another great battle would probably have to be fought before closing the war.   Sherman says that "Lincoln exclaimed more than once that there had been blood enough shed, and asked us if another battle could not be avoided."   His great desire was to attain peace without the sacrifice of a single life that could be saved, and he certainly desired that there should be no policy of retribution upon the Southern people.   He intimated to Sherman very broadly that he desired Jefferson Davis to escape from the country.   Sherman in his *Memoirs* repeats a story told by Lincoln to him illustrative of his wish that Davis should escape "unbeknown to him;" and in discussing the same subject in the White House in the presence of Governor Curtin, Colonel Forney, several others, and myself, he told the same story to illustrate the same point, obviously intending to convey very clearly his wish that the Southern leaders should escape from the land and save him the grave complications which must follow their arrest.   Secretary Welles, in an article in the *Galaxy*, quotes Lincoln as saying on this subject: "No one need expect he would take any part in hanging or killing these men, even the worst of them. Frighten them out of the country; open the gates; let down the bars, scare them off.   Enough lives have been sacrificed; we must extinguish our resentments if we expect harmony and union."

Lincoln's greatest apprehension during the last six months of the war was that the South would not return to the Union and recognize the authority of the government.   He knew that the military power of the rebellion was broken, but he knew that the bitterness that prevailed among the Southern people would be an almost insuperable barrier to anything like cordial reconstruction. He knew that they were impoverished, and he feared almost universal anarchy in the South when the shattered armies of the Confederacy should be broken up, and, instead of a restoration of peace and industry or anything approaching friendly relations between the Southern people and the government, he anticipated guerilla warfare, general disorder, and utter hopelessness of tranquility throughout the rebellious States. It was this grave apprehension that made Lincoln desire to close the war upon such terms as would make the Southern people and Southern soldiers think somewhat kindly of the Union to which they were brought back by force of arms. It was this apprehension that made him instruct Sherman to recognize the civil governments of the South until Congress should take action on the subject, and that made him personally authorize General Weitzel to permit the Virginia State government to reconvene, as he himself stated it, to "take measures to withdraw the Virginia troops and their support from resistance to the general government." He meant to do precisely what Sherman agreed to do in his terms with Johnston. On Lincoln's return to Washington from Weitzel's head-quarters in Richmond he was surprised to find that his consent to the reassembling of the Virginia State government, like his proposed message offering $400,000,000 as compensation for slavery, was disapproved by the Cabinet, and that it was likely to be disapproved by the country. He was greatly distressed, and hesitated some time before he attempted to extricate himself from the complication. Secretary Welles, in the *Galaxy* of April, 1872, page 524, speaking of the question in the Cabinet, says: "The subject had caused general surprise, and on the part of some dissatisfaction and irritation." Stanton and Speed were especially disturbed about it, and Secretary Welles quotes Lincoln as finally saying that he "was surprised that his object and the movement had been so generally misconstrued, and under the circumstances perhaps it was best the proceeding should be abandoned."

In the mean time Lee's army had surrendered, and Lincoln was given a reasonable opportunity to stop the proposed meeting of the Virginia Legislature; and on the 12th of April he wrote to General Weitzel that as the proposed meeting had been misconstrued, and that as Grant had since captured the Virginia troops, so that they could not be withdrawn by the Virginia Legislature, his letter to Judge Campbell should be recalled and the legislature not allowed to assemble; but if any had come in pursuance of the order to allow them a safe return to their homes. In his interview with Judge Campbell and others in relation to the proposed assembling of the Virginia Legislature, Lincoln had distinctly agreed that if Virginia could be peaceably restored to the Union, confiscation should be remitted to the people. The evidence is multiplied on every side that Lincoln intended to give the Virginians exemption from all the retributory laws of war, including amnesty to all who obeyed the government, just as Sherman provided in his terms of surrender with Johnston; but he was halted in his purpose, as he was halted in his proposed compensated emancipation, by the bitter resentments of the time, which prevailed not only in his Cabinet, but throughout the country. Had he been able to see Sherman after he had revoked the authority for the Virginia Legislature to assemble, he would doubtless have modified his instructions to him, but Lincoln never again communicated with Sherman. Two days after his revocation of the Weitzel order he was assassinated, and four days after Lincoln's assassination Sherman made his terms of surrender with Johnston. Had Lincoln been alive when Sherman's first report of Johnston's surrender was received in Washington, his experience in assenting to the reassembling of the Virginia State government would doubtless have made him disapprove the terms given to Johnston in obedience to Lincoln's instructions to Sherman; but he would have cast no reproach upon the heroic victor of Atlanta and Savannah, and would have manfully assumed his full share of responsibility for Sherman's action.* What policy of reconstruction Lincoln would

---

* In a recent publication which I understand to be a fragment of a forthcoming book from your pen you referred to the terms of surrender which Gen. Sherman agreed to with Gen. Jo Johnston at the close of the civil war. You express the opinion that had Mr. Lincoln been alive he would have rejected these terms, but you censure Mr. Stanton very emphatically for publishing the reasons for their disapproval. You seem to think that Mr. Stanton in stating these reasons to Gen. John A. Dix, and permitting their publication, was guilty of a wanton and unnecessary assault on Gen. Sherman. In reply to your criticism I beg leave to submit to you the opposite view from yours expressed in a letter written at the time by a statesman of calm temper and good judgment. The letter is as follows:

WOODSTOCK, VT., June 14th, 1865.
DEAR SIR:

Gen. Sherman promulgated to his army and the world his arrangements with Johnston. Indeed, the armistice could be in no other way accounted for, and the army were gratified with the expectation of an immediate return home.

To reject that arrangement was clearly necessary, and to do it without stating any reason for it would have been a very dangerous experiment, both to the public and the army. Indeed, many had serious apprehensions of its effect on the army even with the conclusive reasons which were given. Should not this view be presented in any and every true manifesto of the case?

Yours respectfully,

J. COLLAMER.

HON. E. M. STANTON:

There is no ground for the belief that Mr. Stanton had any other motive in the action he took than to guard against the

have adopted had he lived to complete his great work cannot now be known; but it is entirely safe to assume that, while he would have yielded to the mandatory sentiment of the nation, he would in the end have taught the country that " with malice toward none, with charity for all," he could assure the world that " government of the people by the people and for the people shall not perish from the earth."

---

danger of disturbances in the army and throughout the country, which might have resulted had the inadmissible terms been rejected without explanation.—*Hon. George C. Gorham* to the Author, February 16, 1892.

(From Sypher's Pennsylvania Reserves.)

ANDREW G. CURTIN, 1860.

LINCOLN AND CURTIN.

ANDREW G. CURTIN has written the most brilliant chapters in the annals of our great civil conflict by his official record as Governor of Pennsylvania. I am not unmindful, in paying this high tribute to the great War Governor of the Union, that there are many Pennsylvania names that have become memorable for their heroism in the struggle for the preservation of our free institutions. Nor am I unmindful that Pennsylvania has within her borders the great battle-field of the war, and that the names of such Pennsylvania heroes as Meade, Reynolds, and Hancock are inseparably linked with the decisive victory that gave assured safety and unsullied freedom to the Union. While Pennsylvania heroism was making itself immortal on every battle-field of the war, the civil administration of the State was more intimately involved with every issue growing out of the war than that of any other State of the Republic. Pennsylvania was second only to New York in population and physical power, and first of all in the importance of her position and in moulding the policy of the States and their relations to the parent government. Bordered by slave commonwealths from her eastern to her western lines, and more exposed to the perils of war than any of the other loyal States, her people were conservative to the utmost limits of positive loyalty to the Union. In January, 1861, when Curtin was inaugurated as Governor, not a single Northern State had officially defined its relations to the Union or its attitude as to the threatened civil war, and any utterance from a State of such pre-eminent physical and political power could not but make its impression on every State of the Union, North and South.

Few of the present day can have any just appreciation of the exceptional delicacy and grave responsibility of the position of the new Governor of Pennsylvania. An ill-advised utterance from him might have wantonly inflamed the war spirit of the South or chilled the loyal devotion of the North. He was called upon to define, in advance of all the other States, the position of the North when confronted by armed treason, and there were no precedents in our history to guide him. His inaugural address was prepared entirely by himself before he came to the capital to assume his most responsible trust. Before he delivered it he summoned to his council a number of the most intelligent and considerate men of both parties in the State, but after careful and dispassionate reflection upon every sentence of the document it was not substantially changed in any particular, and the highest tribute that history could pay to his statesmanship is in the fact that the position of his great State, and its relations with the general government as defined in that address, were accepted by every loyal State and vindicated alike by the loyal judgment of the nation and by the arbitrament of the sword.

Curtin stood single among the public men of Pennsylvania in 1860 as a popular leader. His strength was with the people rather than in political invention. He had made himself conspicuously known by his services as Secretary of the Commonwealth when that officer was charged with the control of the school system. It was he who first organized a distinct department to extend and elevate our schools, and he succeeded in greatly liberalizing our educational system and starting it on the high way to its present matchless advancement. As early as 1844 he had made himself known as one of the most eloquent stump-speakers of the State, and from that time until his nomination for Governor in 1860 he was in the forefront of every political contest, and was greeted with boundless enthusiasm by his political followers wherever he appeared. When the great battle of 1860 was to be fought Pennsylvania was accepted by all as a doubtful State, and as her vote in October would be the unerring finger-board of national victory or defeat in November, it became not only a State but a national necessity for the Republicans to nominate their most available candidate to lead in that pivotal contest. The Republican people, almost as with one voice, demanded the nomination of Curtin, and there would have been no other name presented to the convention but for the peculiar political complications arising from General Cameron being a candidate for President before the same convention, and bitterly hostile to Curtin. But despite the peculiar power of Cameron as an organizer and manager of political conventions, he was finally compelled to assent to Curtin's nomination without being able to obtain an earnestly united delegation in his favor for President. When Curtin was called before the convention to accept the leadership conferred upon him, he aroused the enthusiasm of that body and of his party friends throughout the State by declaring that he accepted the flag of the convention and would carry it in the front of battle from Lake Erie to the Delaware; and he grandly fulfilled his promise. He was one of the most magnetic popular speakers Pennsylvania has ever known, combining matchless wit, keen invective, and persuasive argument with singular felicity, and his tow-

ering and symmetrical form and his genial face and
manner made him the most effective of all our men on
the hustings. He was aggressive from the day he entered
the battle until it closed with his magnificent victory that
declared him Governor. by a majority of over thirty-two
thousand.

Many circumstances combined to bring Lincoln and
Curtin into the closest official and personal relations
from Lincoln's nomination until his death. As I have
shown in a previous chapter, the nomination of Lincoln
was made possible by two men—Henry S. Lane of Indiana and Curtin of Pennsylvania. Both would have been
defeated had Seward been nominated, and Curtin's first
great struggle to give himself even a winning chance in
Pennsylvania was his effort to defeat the nomination of
Seward at Chicago. After that had been accomplished
he united with Lane to nominate Lincoln. He and Lincoln never met until Curtin received the President-elect
on his way to Washington on the 22d of February, 1861,
and it was at the dinner given to Lincoln by Curtin on
the evening of that day that Lincoln's route was changed
and he suddenly started on his memorable midnight journey to the national capital. The appointment of Cameron to the Lincoln Cabinet was regarded by Curtin as
unfortunate, and would have made very strained relations between Lincoln and Curtin had not both been
singularly generous in all their impulses and actions.
Notwithstanding the frequent irritating complications
which arose between the Secretary of War and the Governor in the organization of troops in the early part of
the war, there never was a shadow upon the relations
of these two men. Curtin was profoundly loyal and an
enthusiast in everything pertaining to the war. He was
proud of his great State, and especially of the hundreds
of thousands of heroes she sent to the field, and so tire-

less in his great work that he always commanded the sincerest affection and confidence of the President. Although often disappointed in the political action of the national administration, and at times keenly grieved personally because of political honors unworthily conferred, or withheld from those he deemed most worthy of them, he never for a moment lost sight of his paramount duty to give unfaltering support to the government in the great struggle for the maintenance of the Union.

The two men of the country who are distinctly upon record as having appreciated the magnitude of the war when it first began are General Sherman and Governor Curtin. Sherman was judged a lunatic and relieved of his command in Kentucky because he told the government the exact truth as to the magnitude of the rebellion in the South-west and the forces necessary to overthrow it. In a little time the country began to appreciate Sherman's military intelligence. He was finally permitted to go to the front in command of a division, and in his first battle he proved himself to be one of the most skillful and courageous of our generals. Curtin proved his appreciation of the necessities of our imperiled government by issuing his proclamation on the 25th of April, 1861, calling for twenty-five additional regiments of infantry and one of cavalry to serve for three years or during the war, in addition to the quota furnished by Pennsylvania under the President's call of April 15, 1861, summoning 75,000 three months' men to the field. This call of Curtin was made without the authority of the general government, and entirely without the knowledge of the President or Secretary of War. Pennsylvania and the whole loyal North had been cut off from all communication with the national capital for several days by treasonable rioters in Baltimore, who burned the railroad bridges and prevented all railroad or even telegraphic communication with Washington. In this grave emergency, although Pennsylvania had furnished every man called for by the government, and had offered many more than the quota, after the most careful study of the situation with General Robert Patterson and Colonel Fitz John Porter, then serving as Assistant Adjutant-General, and a number of civilians who were heartily sustaining Curtin in his arduous labors, it was decided to assume the responsibility of calling out twenty-six additional regiments for service under the general government, because it was believed by all that they would be needed as speedily as they could be obtained.*

The requisition for troops made by Pennsylvania was in pursuance of the unanimous judgment of the military and civil authorities then at Harrisburg, and it was not doubted that the government would gratefully accept them. The response to Curtin's proclamation for vol-

---

* HEADQUARTERS
MILITARY DEPARTMENT OF WASHINGTON,
PHILADELPHIA, April 25th, 1861.

SIR :

I feel it my duty to express to you my clear and decided opinion that the force at the disposal of this department should be increased without delay.

I therefore have to request Your Excellency to direct that twenty-five additional regiments of infantry and one regiment of cavalry be called for forthwith, to be mustered into the service of the United States.

Officers will be detailed to inspect and muster the men into service as soon as I am informed of the points of rendezvous which may be designated by Your Excellency.

I have the honor to be, with great respect,

Your obedient servant,

R. PATTERSON,
Major-General.

His Excellency ANDREW G. CURTIN,
Governor of Pennsylvania.

unteers was unexampled, and in the few days during
which Harrisburg was without communication with
Washington thousands of patriotic men were crowding
the trains for the capital from every part of the State
to enter the military service. To the utter surprise of
the Governor and the commander of the department,
the first communication received from Washington after
notice of this requisition for additional troops had been
forwarded was a blunt refusal to receive any of the regiments under the new call; and to emphasize the attitude
of the government and its appreciation of the magnitude
of the war, Secretary Cameron stated in a dispatch to the
Governor not only that the troops could not be received,
but "that it was more important to reduce than enlarge
the number." Earnest appeals were made to the President and the War Department from the Governor and
General Patterson to have these troops, or at least part
of them, accepted, but every such appeal was met with
a positive refusal. John Sherman, then as now Senator
from Ohio, was a volunteer aide on General Patterson's
staff, and he fully agreed with the authorities at Harrisburg that it was of the utmost importance to the government that the additional Pennsylvania troops be accepted.
In view of his important political position and presumed
influence with the President and Secretary of War, he
was hurried to Washington as soon as communications
were opened to make a personal appeal for the acceptance of the troops. On the 30th of May, five days after
the requisition had been made, he wrote General Patterson from Washington, stating that he had entirely failed
to persuade the government to accept any part of these
new regiments. It was not within the power of the government to depose Governor Curtin and order him to
some military barracks as a lunatic, but it could rebuke
him for proposing to furnish a large number of addi-

tional troops, when, as subsequent events proved, the government had the most pressing need for them. Fortunately for the government and for the complete vindication of the broad sagacity and heroic fidelity of Curtin, he resolved to perform his duty to his State and nation regardless of the Washington authorities.

After a bitter contest, in which some prominent Republicans opposed the Governor's recommendations, a bill had been passed by the Legislature some weeks before appropriating half a million of dollars to provide for the defense of the State, and he had issued his call for an extraordinary session of the Legislature as early as the 20th of April to meet the great issue of civil war. He revoked his proclamation for additional regiments called for by General Patterson's requisition, but much more than one-half the number called for had already volunteered, and were practically in charge of the State for organization. When the special session of the Legislature met on the 30th of April he sent an earnest message calling for the organization of the volunteers then in camp into fifteen regiments as a State corps, but to be subject to the call of the United States in any emergency. It was this brave action of Curtin that gave us the Pennsylvania Reserve Corps, whose heroism crimsoned nearly every battle-field of the Army of the Potomac. These troops were organized not only without the aid of the national government, but in defiance of its refusal to accept them and of its positive declarations that they could not and would not be needed. It was a most heroic policy on the part of Curtin. It involved a loan of $3,000,000 when the credit of the State was severely strained, and every partisan or factional foe was inspired to opposition by the known fact that the national government declared additional troops to be entirely unnecessary. The Legislature and the people had faith in Curtin, had faith in his integrity, his patriotism, and his judgment of the nation's peril, and the bill creating a loan and organizing fifteen regiments of the Reserve Corps was passed by an overwhelming majority in both branches of the Legislature. He had around him a number of leading men of both parties who cheerfully gave their time and ceaseless labor to assist him. Among those I recall who sat in his councils by day and night to strengthen his hands by voluntary service on his staff were such men as the late Thomas A. Scott, John A. Wright, R. Biddle Roberts, Reuben C. Hale, and John B. Parker, and Craig Biddle and Joseph E. Potts, who yet survive. These men, as well as the military officers on duty in Pennsylvania with General Patterson, all heartily concurred in the policy of the Governor and shared his vindication at an early day.

Even before the disastrous battle of Bull Run was fought on the 21st of July, two of the Reserve regiments were called for by the government to march to Cumberland to the relief of Colonel Wallace, and the regiments commanded by Colonel Charles J. Biddle and Colonel Simmons and a battery of artillery were on the march the same day the order was received, and soon thereafter the Tenth regiment followed. Notwithstanding the refusal to entertain the question of accepting these troops, Curtin again tendered the Reserve Corps to the government on the 18th of July, just before the battle of Bull Run, and the same day brought orders from the War Department that four regiments should be sent to Hagerstown and the remaining, exclusive of those in West Virginia, should be sent to Baltimore. These regiments were encamped at Pittsburg, Easton, West Chester, and Harrisburg, and the Governor at once ordered them to march as requested by the Washington authorities. His answer to the request to forward the troops was in these

words: "All the regiments have been ordered to Harrisburg in obedience to your dispatch just received, and on
arrival will be immediately forwarded to the seat of war,
as previously ordered. If there is not time to muster
them in at this place, mustering officers can follow them
into the field." Had these troops been on the battle-
field of Bull Run, as they could have been had not the
government persistently refused to accept them, it would
have given an overwhelming preponderance of numbers
to the Union forces, and doubtless reversed the disaster
of that day. On the night of July 21st, when the government learned that the army had been routed at Bull
Run, most frantic appeals were made to Curtin from the
Washington authorities to hasten his troops to the front
to save the National Capital, and within twenty-four
hours after the retreat of McDowell's army into the
Washington fortifications the welcome tread of the Pennsylvania Reserves was heard on Pennsylvania Avenue,
and the panic was allayed and confidence restored by
regiment after regiment of the once-rejected troops
hurrying to Washington. One dispatch from the War
Department thus appeals to Curtin: "Get your regiments
at Harrisburg, Easton, and other points ready for immediate shipment. Lose no time in preparing. Make
things move to the utmost." Another dispatch said:
"To-morrow won't do for your regiments; you must
have them to-night. Send them to-night. It is of the
utmost importance." Another appeal to him said: "Stop
the regiment at Greencastle, and send it to Washington
to-night. Do not fail." Thus the war authorities that
had treated with contempt the appeals of Curtin to accept
the troops he had called for when cut off from the national capital, in a few months thereafter sent the most
earnest appeals to him to save them from their own folly

17

by forwarding the troops he had organized in defiance of their protest.

I speak advisedly when I say that there was not a single new phase of the war at any time that did not summon Curtin to the councils of Lincoln. He was the first man called to Washington after the surrender of Sumter, and I accompanied him in obedience to a like summons to me as chairman of the Military Committee of the Senate. Pennsylvania was to sound the keynote for all the loyal States of the North in the utterance of her loyal Governor, and her action was to be the example for every other State of the Union. How grandly Curtin performed that duty is proved by the fact that he organized and furnished to the national government during the war 367,482 soldiers, and organized, in addition to that number, 87,000 for domestic defense during the same period. New duties and grave responsibilities were multiplied upon him every week, but he was always equal to them, and was a tireless enthusiast in the performance of his labors. Three times during the war was his State invaded by the enemy, and at one time 90,000 of Lee's army, with Lee himself at their head, were within the borders of our State on their way to their Waterloo at Gettysburg. While responding with the utmost promptness to every call of the national government, whether for troops or for moral or political support, he was most zealous in making provision for the defense of his exposed people in the border counties. He had an ample force within the State to protect the border against raids by the enemy, and would have saved Chambersburg from destruction by the vandal torch, had not his own State troops been ordered away from him to save General Hunter after his disgraceful and disastrous raid into Virginia in 1864. Hunter's vandalism had justly inflamed the South, and when he was driven across the Potomac the Pennsylvania regiments organized for the special defense of the State, being subject to orders from Washington because mustered into the United States service, passed through Chambersburg, within forty-eight hours of the period of its destruction, to join Hunter in Maryland and save him from the retribution his folly had invited. Had these Pennsylvania troops remained subject to the orders of the State authorities, they could have been in Chambersburg before McCausland reached there, and would have outnumbered him nearly three to one. Chambersburg was thus destroyed solely because of the grave emergency that called the State troops to the support of Hunter, and they were almost within sound of McCausland's guns when he opened on the defenseless people of Chambersburg at daylight on the 30th of July, 1864, before he entered the town to destroy it.

Curtin's relations with Stanton were never entirely cordial and at times embarrassing; but Lincoln always interposed when necessary, and almost invariably sustained Curtin when a vital issue was raised between them. The fact that Lincoln supported Curtin against Stanton many times greatly irritated the Secretary of War, and doubtless intensified his bitterness against the Pennsylvania War Governor. In one notable instance only, in which Curtin and Stanton were in bitter conflict, did Lincoln hesitate to sustain Curtin, but Lincoln was overruled by his military commanders and bowed to their exactions with profound reluctance. In the winter or early spring of 1864, Curtin, always alive to the interests of humanity, and feeling keenly the sorrows of the Pennsylvania soldiers who were in Southern prison-pens suffering from disease and starvation, went to Washington on three different occasions and appealed to both Stanton and Lincoln for the exchange of prisoners as the Southern commissioners proposed. We then held about 30,000 Southern prisoners, and the South held as many or more of Union soldiers, and General Grant, looking solely to military success, peremptorily refused to permit the exchange of these men, because Lee would gain nearly 30,000 effective soldiers, while most of the 30,000 Union prisoners would be unfit for service because of illness. On Curtin's third visit to Washington on that subject he was accompanied by Attorney-General William M. Meredith, and they both earnestly pressed upon the government the prompt exchange of prisoners. Stanton grew impatient and even insolent, retorting to the Governor's appeal: "Do you come here in support of the government and ask me to exchange 30,000 skeletons for 30,000 well-fed men?" To which Curtin replied with all the earnestness of his humane impulses: "Do you dare to depart from the laws of humane warfare in this enlightened age of Christian civilization?" Curtin and Meredith carried their appeal to Lincoln, who shared all of Curtin's sympathies for our suffering prisoners, and who exerted himself to the utmost, only to effect a partial exchange. In 1863, when Curtin was a candidate for re-election, Stanton gave most earnest support to his cause, notwithstanding he rarely spoke of Curtin personally except with bitterness. Curtin keenly appreciated what Stanton had done, and went to Washington soon after his election with the purpose of paying his respects to Stanton and thanking him for the hearty support he had given him. A mutual acquaintance, who knew that Curtin was in Washington to pay his respects to Stanton, happened to meet Stanton during the evening and spoke with much enthusiasm of Curtin's victory, and of his presence there to visit and thank the Secretary of War. Stanton replied in his cynical way: "Yes, Pennsylvania must be a damned loyal State to give such a victory to

Curtin.'' This was repeated to Curtin the same evening, and the result was that Curtin's visit to the War Office was indefinitely postponed, and Stanton died without having received the thanks that Curtin had intended for him. Soon after the war was over, however, Stanton seemed to have justly appreciated Curtin, as he wrote him a voluntary and most affectionate letter, reviewing the great work he had done as Governor of Pennsylvania, thanking him for his patriotism and fidelity, and offering a full apology for anything that he might have done to give him unpleasant recollections.

Lincoln played a most conspicuous part in Curtin's second nomination and re-election. So profoundly was Curtin impressed with the necessity of uniting all parties in the support of the war for the suppression of the rebellion that he was the first man to suggest his own retirement from the office of Governor if the Democrats would present the name of General William B. Franklin, a gallant Pennsylvania Democratic soldier. I was present when Curtin first made this suggestion to a number of his friends, and he made it with a degree of earnestness that impressed every one. He said that it was vastly more important to thus unite the whole Democratic party with the Republicans on an honest war platform than that any party or any individual should win political success. So earnestly did he press the matter that communication was opened with a number of leading Democrats of the State, many of whom regarded the suggestion with favor and sought to accomplish it. Unfortunately for the Democracy, the more Bourbon element controlled its councils and a Supreme Judge who had declared the national conscription act unconstitutional, thereby depriving the government of the power to fill its wasted armies, was nominated for Governor when the thunders of Lee's guns were heard in the Cumberland Valley and almost within hearing of the capital where the convention sat. Had Franklin been nominated by the Democrats, Curtin would have publicly declared for him, and the Republican Convention would have welcomed him as their candidate, regardless of his political faith. Failing in that movement, there seemed to be but one hopeful loyal candidate for Governor—Curtin himself. He was broken in health and entirely unequal to the strain of a desperate battle. In political contests he was expected to be leader of leaders in Pennsylvania. In addition to his shattered health, there were over 70,000 of his soldiers in the field who had not then the constitutional right to vote in their camps, while the bitter factional feud between the Curtin and Cameron wings of the party seriously threatened his defeat. Curtin's greatest desire, next to the faithful fulfillment of the high responsibilities cast upon him, was to retire from public office and recover his physical vigor. It was believed in his own household that he could not survive another political campaign in which he was compelled to take the lead. His devoted and estimable wife, who brightened every public honor he attained, appealed to me with tears in her eyes to take absolute measures to retire him from the field, and the Governor heartily assented if he could be permitted to retire in any way honorable to himself.

Of Curtin's renomination there was no doubt whatever if he permitted his name to be used, and it became merely a question how he could retire gracefully. Entrusted with this matter, acting entirely upon my own judgment, I went to Washington, called upon Colonel Forney and told him my mission. I said: "Senator Cameron will desire the retirement of Curtin because he is his enemy; I desire it because I am his friend; may we not co-operate in bringing it about?'' Cameron was sent for; the matter was presented to him, and he at once said, with some asperity, that "Curtin should be got rid of." I suggested that if Lincoln would tender to Curtin a foreign mission in view of his broken health, it would solve the difficulty and enable Curtin to retire. To this Cameron agreed, and within half an hour thereafter we startled Lincoln by appearing before him together, accompanied by Forney. It was the first time Cameron and I had appeared before Lincoln to unite in asking him to perform any public act. I stated the case briefly but frankly, and he promptly responded that Curtin was entitled to the honor suggested, and that it would be a great pleasure to him to tender him the place. "But," said he, "I'm in the position of young Sheridan when old Sheridan called him to task for his rakish conduct, and said to him that he must take a wife; to which young Sheridan replied: 'Very well, father, but whose wife shall I take?' It's all very well," he added, "to say that I will give Curtin a mission, but whose mission am I to take? I would not offer him anything but a first-class one." To this Cameron replied that a second-class mission would answer the purpose, but Forney and I resented that, and said that if a second-class mission was to be discussed we had nothing further to say. Lincoln closed the conference by suggesting that as it seemed to be my affair I should call to see him in the morning. I did so, when Lincoln handed me the following autograph letter, tendering Curtin a first-class mission, to be accepted at the close of his gubernatorial term:

EXECUTIVE MANSION,
WASHINGTON, April 13, 1863.

HONORABLE ANDREW G. CURTIN.

MY DEAR SIR : If, after the expiration of your present term as Governor of Pennsylvania I shall continue in office here, and you

Executive Mansion,

Washington, April 13——, 1863.

Hon. Andrew G. Curtin

My dear Sir

If, after the expiration of your present term as Governor of Pennsylvania, I shall continue in office here, and you shall then desire to go abroad, you can do so with one of the first. class missions.

Yours truly

A. Lincoln

FAC-SIMILE OF LINCOLN'S LETTER TO CURTIN.

shall desire to go abroad, you can do so with one of the first-class missions. Yours truly,

ABRAHAM LINCOLN.

This letter I delivered to Curtin. The announcement was at once made to the Associated Press that a foreign mission had been tendered to Curtin, that he had signified his acceptance of it, and that he would not be a candidate for renomination for Governor. The popular demand for Curtin's renomination came with such emphasis from every section of the State that within a few weeks after his declination he was compelled to accept the candidacy, and he was nominated in Pittsburg by an overwhelming majority on the first ballot, and after one of the most desperate contests ever known in the State was re-elected by over 15,000 majority, even with his soldiers disfranchised. Lincoln exhibited unusual interest in that struggle, and his congratulations to Curtin upon his re-election were repeated for several days, and were often as quaint as they were sincere.

The secret of Curtin's re-election in 1863 was the devotion of the Pennsylvania soldiers to him and his cause. He was the earliest of all the Governors in the States to devise and put into practical execution every measure that could lessen the sorrows of war to his people. After every battle in which Pennsylvania troops were engaged Curtin was always among the first visitors to camp and hospital, and his sympathetic hand was felt and his voice heard by the sick and wounded. He had his official commissioners to visit every part of the country in search of Pennsylvania troops needing kind ministrations, and early in the war he obtained legislative authority to bring the body of every soldier who was killed or died in the service home for burial at the cost of the State. Every Pennsylvania soldier in the army felt that he had

one friend upon whom he could always rely in the War
Governor of his State, and many hundreds of letters
poured in upon Curtin at the Capitol every day appealing to him for redress from real or imaginary grievances,
every one of which was promptly answered.   If injustice
was done to any Pennsylvania officer or any hindrance
of gallant men in the ranks from just promotion, an early
appeal to Curtin invariably brought him to the front to
correct it.   It is not surprising, therefore, that when he
became a candidate for re-election and was assailed on
every side with bitterness, nearly every soldier in the
army, whether Democrat or Republican, appealed to his
people at home to support and vote for Curtin.   While
the soldiers were themselves unable to testify their appreciation of their patriotic Governor at the polls, every
soldier at home on leave, however unskilled in rhetoric,
was a most eloquent advocate of Curtin's re-election, and
there was hardly a home in the State that had a soldier
in the field to which did not come earnest appeals by
letters to fathers and brothers to vote for the Soldier's
Friend.   Thus was Curtin re-elected by a large majority,
and by the votes of Democrats who were influenced solely
by their sympathy with their sons and brothers in the
field whose gratitude to Curtin was reflected in almost
every family circle.

It was on Thanksgiving Day of 1863 that Curtin first
conceived the idea of State provision for the care and
education of the orphans of our fallen soldiers.   While
on his way in Harrisburg to hear Dr. Robinson's Thanksgiving sermon, he was met by two shivering and starving
children, who piteously appealed to him to relieve them
of their distress, saying that their father had been killed
on the Peninsula and that their mother was broken in
health by her efforts to provide for them.   He was so
deeply impressed and his sympathies so keenly aroused

by the children that he heard little of the eloquent sermon. He remembered that all over Pennsylvania there were such orphans without home or bread, and he resolved from that day that some provision should be made for the care of these helpless little ones. Soon after he presided at a meeting at which Henry Ward Beecher was ·the speaker. Beecher had just returned from England, where he had been most eloquent in his defense of the Union cause, and he was welcomed in Pennsylvania with enthusiasm by the loyal people. In Curtin's introductory speech he, for the first time, made public allusion to the duty of the State to provide for the orphans of our soldiers who had fallen in battle, and the suggestion was greeted with round after round of applause. Some time before that period the Pennsylvania Railroad had placed at the disposal of the State $50,000 to equip troops. The money was received by Curtin, but he had no need to use it for the equipment of troops, and if he had covered it into the treasury, it would have merged into the general fund. This money lay idle on special deposit for some months, and Curtin conceived the plan of making it the basis of a fund for the care of our soldiers' orphans. To this President Thomson assented, and with $50,000 already assured, the Governor presented the subject to the Legislature in his annual message, and earnestly urged early action. There was much hesitation to support such a bill, and no progress was made in it until near the close of the session. The bill was finally defeated, and when the next Legislature met Curtin arranged with President Thomson for the transportation of a large number of our soldiers' orphans to visit Harrisburg. They were sent free of cost for transportation, and were received into the homes of generous people, ten of them being guests of Curtin in the Executive Mansion. They came bearing the flag under which their fathers had fallen, and the House received them at three o'clock, when patriotic speeches were made, the little orphans sang patriotic songs, and Curtin made a most eloquent appeal to the Legislature to make these children the wards of the commonwealth. The Legislature speedily retraced its steps, passed the bill, and the Governor had the gratification of signing it the next morning. Such was the beginning of the Soldiers' Orphans' Schools which have lasted now for nearly thirty years, which have educated thousands and thousands of the war orphans of the State, and are still performing that humane mission to the few yet in our midst. In this sublime beneficence to the helpless children of our heroes Pennsylvania stands single and alone among the loyal States, and there has not been a class of orphans in any school in Pennsylvania that has not lisped the name of Curtin with affectionate reverence.

Some of the most momentous official acts of Curtin's public career have almost passed from the recollection of the men of the present who lived at that day, yet they rendered the greatest service to the national government when it was in the gravest peril. After the disastrous Peninsula campaign it became a necessity to summon a large additional force to the field, and it was regarded as a dangerous experiment in view of the despairing condition of public sentiment in the North. Volunteering had entirely ceased; there was at that time no national conscription act; the appeal had to be made directly to the States to raise their respective quotas of troops. As was common in every serious emergency, Curtin was called into the councils of Lincoln, and the subject discussed with a full appreciation of the solemn responsibilities that devolved upon both of them. It was Curtin's suggestion that the Governors of the loyal States should be conferred with and got to unite in a formal demand upon the President to call out a large additional force. Eighteen loyal Governors responded, and on the 28th of June, 1862, they aroused every loyal heart in the country by their bold demand for the promptest measures to fill up our armies and for the most vigorous prosecution of the war. The address concludes with this patriotic sentence: "All believe that the decisive moment is near at hand, and to that end the people of the United States are desirous to aid promptly in furnishing all reinforcements that you may deem necessary to sustain our government." This address was delivered in person by a number of the Governors themselves, and Lincoln replied: "Gentlemen: Fully concurring in the wisdom of the views expressed to me in so patriotic a manner by you in the communication of the 28th of June, I have decided to call into the service an additional force of 300,000 men." The Altoona conference of the loyal Governors was originally proposed by Curtin to Lincoln and cordially approved by the President before the call was issued. It was a supreme necessity to crystallize the loyal sentiment of the country in support of the coming and then clearly foreshadowed Emancipation policy. Curtin telegraphed Governor Andrew of Massachusetts: "In the present emergency would it not be well that the loyal Governors should meet at some point in the Border States to take measures for the more active support of the government?" The Governors of Massachusetts, Ohio, and West Virginia responded promptly, and the call was issued on the 14th of September, and the Altoona conference met on the 24th, the day after the Emancipation Proclamation had been published to the world. There were seventeen Governors in attendance, and after a full interchange of views, Curtin and Andrew were charged with the duty of preparing an address to the President and the country. That address, coming as the united voice of the loyal States through their Governors, was regarded by Lincoln as of inestimable service to the cause of the Union. It not only gave the keynote for every loyal man to support the Emancipation policy, but it suggested to the President to call out additional troops to keep a reserve of 100,000 men for any emergency of the war. *

---

* In 1862, after the disaster on the Peninsula, and when I was in New York under medical treatment and not able to receive my personal friends, I sent for a newspaper and read of the defeat of McClellan's army. Soon after a messenger came to see me from Mr. Seward, who was at the Astor House, inviting me to meet Mr. Seward, saying that he would come to see me if I could not go to see him. With much risk and suffering I went at once to the Astor House, where I found Mr. Seward with the Mayor of New York and the Mayor of Philadelphia, who were then considering the question of going to Boston. Mr. Seward gave me all the telegrams from the front, which I read carefully, and found that of McClellan's army there were not over 80,000 effectives left. I suggested to Mr. Seward that it might be better to ask the Governors of the loyal States than the Mayors of our cities to unite in an address to the President, asking for a more vigorous prosecution of the war and an immediate call for additional troops. He asked me to put it in writing. I did so, and he immediately telegraphed it to the President, who promptly answered that it was just what he wanted done. I at once prepared a telegram to the other Governors, and Colonel Scott, who happened to be there, hurried it off to all the Governors of the loyal States. Approving answers were received from all but Governor Andrew, who made the objection that a public policy should be declared, which of course meant Emancipation. The names of the Governors were appended to the paper, and it was immediately returned to Lincoln. Governor Andrew afterward acquiesced, and I then wrote him asking his views as to the propriety of calling the loyal Governors to meet at Altoona for the purpose of declaring a policy and demanding a more vigorous prosecution of the war. He agreed to it at once, and we commenced writing and telegraphing to the Governors, and I had favorable answers to all excepting Governor Morgan of New York, whose relations with me were not friendly. Governor Andrew, Governor Todd,

(Photo by Brady, Washington.)

ANDREW G. CURTIN, 1892.

Thus, from the day that Curtin welcomed Lincoln in the Hall of the House of Representatives at Harrisburg when on his way to be inaugurated, until their last meeting in the same hall when it was the chamber of death, and sorrowing patriots passed silently through it to take their last look upon the face of the martyred President, he was side by side with Lincoln in every trial; and, backed by his great State, he was enabled to render a service to the President and to the country unapproached by any other Governor of the Union. How gratefully his public record was appreciated by the people of Pennsylvania of that day is clearly shown by reference to the journals of our Legislature of April 12, 1866, when a resolution was passed, by unanimous vote in both branches, thanking him, in the name of Pennsylvania, "for the fidelity with which, during the four years of war by which our country was ravaged and its free institutions threatened, he stood by the national government and cast into the scales of loyalty and the Union the honor, the wealth, and the strength of the State." These resolutions were offered in the House by Repre-

---

and myself consulted Mr. Lincoln, and he highly approved of our purpose. In that interview he did not attempt to conceal the fact that we were upon the eve of an Emancipation policy, and he had from us the assurance that the Altoona conference would cordially endorse such a policy. All that was done at the Altoona conference had the positive approval of President Lincoln in advance, and he well understood that the whole purpose of the movement was to strengthen his hands and support the bolder policy that all then knew was inevitable. The address presented to Mr. Lincoln from the Altoona conference was prepared by Governor Andrew and myself. I did not then doubt that it would lose us the coming election in Pennsylvania, and so said to Mr. Lincoln, but I believed that the country then knew what the war was about, and that it was time to bring slavery to the front as the great issue.—*Ex-Governor Curtin's Letter to the Author*, Feb. 16, 1892.

sentative Ruddiman, the Republican leader of that body, and were passed by a vote of 97 ayes and no nays, being within 3 of the entire membership of the body.* On the same day the resolutions were called up in the Senate by Senator Wallace, the Democratic leader of that body, and on the call of the ayes and nays received the vote of every Senator. No Governor of any State ever received such a tribute as this from all parties when about to retire from his high office after six years of service during the most heated partisan and factional strife

* *Whereas*, The term of His Excellency Andrew G. Curtin as Governor of the Commonwealth of Pennsylvania will expire with the present year, and the Legislature of the State will not stand toward him in the relation of official courtesy and personal regard which they have heretofore sustained;

And whereas, This House cannot contemplate his course during the recent struggle of our country without admiration of the patriotism which made him one of the earliest, foremost, and most constant of the supporters of the government, and without commendation of the spirit which has prompted him with untiring energy and at the sacrifice of personal repose and health to give to the soldier in the field and in the hospital, and to the cause for which the soldier fell and died, fullest sympathy and aid; be it

Resolved, That in the name of the Commonwealth of Pennsylvania we tender to Governor Curtin our thanks for the fidelity with which, during the four years of war by which our country was ravaged and its free institutions threatened, he stood by the national government and cast into the scale of loyalty and the Union the honor, the wealth, and strength of the State.

Resolved, That by his devotion to his country, from the dark hour in which he pledged to the late lamented President of the United States the faith and steadfast support of our people, he has gained for his name an historical place and character, and while rendering himself deserving of the nation's gratitude he has added lustre to the fame and glory to the name of the Commonwealth over which he has presided during two terms of office with so much ability, and in which he has tempered dignity with kindness and won the high respect and confidence of the people.

18

ever known in our political history. Again on the 6th
of April, 1869, when he had been a private citizen for
several years, the Legislature passed joint resolutions of
thanks to President Grant for his appointment of Curtin
as Minister to Russia, and they received the vote of every
member present of both branches, and were approved by
Governor Geary on the following day.*   In 1868 the
Republican State Convention proclaimed Curtin with
almost entire unanimity for the Vice-Presidency of the
United States on the ticket with Grant, who was then
the accepted candidate of the party for President, and I
went to Chicago as chairman of the Pennsylvania delegation to present his name and cast the vote of the State
for her honored War Governor.

Political necessities rather than individual merit controlled the National Convention, and Schuyler Colfax

---

* *Joint Resolutions* relative to the appointment of Andrew
Gregg Curtin Minister to Russia:

Whereas, His Excellency the President of the United States
has appointed Andrew Gregg Curtin, the former Chief Magistrate of this Commonwealth, to a high and responsible position
in the representation at the Court of the ruler of the European
nation whose boast is that he has always been a friend of the
United States of America;

Be it resolved, by the Senate and House of Representatives of
the Commonwealth of Pennsylvania in General Assembly met,
That the *best wishes* of the members of this Assembly be con-
veyed to His Excellency Andrew G. Curtin, Minister Plenipotentiary and Envoy Extraordinary of the United States at St.
Petersburg, Russia, for *his restoration to health*, so much impaired
by *his heroic and constant labors* in behalf of this Commonwealth,
and that he has and always will receive the *grateful assurance* of
the *high regard and esteem* in which he is held by his fellow-citi-
zens, *without regard* to partisan views, on account of the *noble
and self-sacrificing spirit* displayed by him alike in the hours of
victory and defeat, and the *fidelity* with which he executed the
solemn and responsible trusts committed to his hands by his fel-
low-citizens.

was taken to turn the scale in doubtful Indiana; but Curtin was, as ever, in the front of the battle, as Grant gratefully acknowledged by nominating him as Minister to Russia a few days after the inauguration. He had been offered the same mission by President Johnson several years earlier, but his fidelity to the cause that had enlisted the best efforts of his life forbade his even considering it. In the Republican revolt against the despotic political and sectional policy of Grant in 1872, Curtin sincerely sympathized with the Liberals, and he resigned his mission to obtain freedom in political action. When on his way home he was met in both Paris and London by authorized offers of either of those missions if he would remain abroad, but he declined. On his return home he was nominated by the Liberal Republicans for delegate-at-large to the Constitutional Convention, and Ex-Governor Bigler voluntarily retired from the Democratic ticket to enable that party to tender Curtin an unanimous nomination, resulting in his election. His exceptional experience in State government made him one of the most practical and useful members of the body, and many of the most beneficent reforms of the new fundamental law are of his creation. In 1880, and again in 1882 and 1884, he was elected to Congress, and during his six years of service in the House he was the favorite of every social and political circle. Since then he has enjoyed the mellow evening of his life in his mountain-home, where every face brightens at his coming, and on every hillside and valley of the State there are grizzled veterans and their children and their children's children whose hearts throb with grateful emotion as they speak of the Soldier's Friend.

(Photo by Brady, Washington.)

THADDEUS STEVENS, 1866.

LINCOLN AND STEVENS.

ABRAHAM LINCOLN and Thaddeus Stevens were strangely mated. Lincoln as President and Stevens as Commoner of the nation during the entire period of our sectional war assumed the highest civil responsibilities in the administrative and legislative departments of the government. While Lincoln was President of the whole people, Stevens, as Commoner, was their immediate representative and oracle in the popular branch of Congress when the most momentous legislative measures of our history were conceived and enacted. No two men were so much alike in all the sympathy of greatness for the friendless and the lowly, and yet no two men could have been more unlike in the methods by which they sought to obtain the same great end. Lincoln's humanity was one of the master attributes of his character, and it was next to impossible for him to punish even those most deserving of it. In Stevens humanity and justice were singularly blended, and while his heart was ever ready to respond to the appeal of sorrow, he was one of the sternest of men in the administration of justice upon those who had oppressed the helpless. No man pleaded so eloquently in Congress for the deliverance of the bondmen of the South as did Stevens, and he made ceaseless battle for every measure needed by ignorant freedmen for the enjoyment of their rights obtained through the madness of Southern rebellion; and there was no man of all our statesmen whose voice was so eloquent for the swift punishment of the authors of the war.   He declared on the floor of Congress that if he had the power he would summon a military commission to try, convict, and execute Jefferson Davis and other leaders of the rebellion "for the murders at Andersonville, the murders at Salisbury, and the shooting down of prisoners-of-war in cold blood;" and when the whole world was shocked by the relentless vengeance of Juarez in the summary execution of Maximilian, he was the one man of Congress who rose and boldly defended the Mexican President; and his ground of defence was that Maximilian had sought to usurp power from the weak.   Lincoln's humanity was always predominant in his nature and always reflected itself in his public and private acts.   He never signed a death-warrant unless it was absolutely unavoidable, and then always with a degree of sorrow that could not be concealed.   He earnestly desired that Davis and all Southern leaders who might be called to account after the war for precipitating the nation into fraternal strife should safely escape from the country; and Maximilian could not have appealed in vain to Lincoln for his life had it been within his power to save him.   Such were the conflicting attributes of the two great civil leaders of the country during the war.   Each filled his great trust with masterly fidelity, and the opposing qualities of each were potent upon the other.

The country has almost forgotten the exceptionally responsible position of Stevens as the Great Commoner of our civil war.   It is the one high trust of a free government that must be won solely by ability and merit.   The Commoner of a republic is the organ of the people, and he can hold his place only when all confess his pre-eminent qualities for the discharge of his duties.   Presidents, Cabinets, Senators, and Representatives may be

accidents. Fortuitous circumstances or sudden muta-
tions in politics may create any of these civil functionaries in a popular government to serve their brief terms
and pass away into forgetfulness, but the Commoner of
the nation must be the confessed "leader of leaders."
Mere popular attributes are valueless in struggling for
such a place. Only he who can come to the front whenever occasion calls, lead discordant elements to a common
end, and maintain his position in all the sudden changes
of a mercurial body can go into history as an American
Commoner; and Stevens grandly, undisputedly, met these
high requirements. There were those around him in
Congress much riper in experience in national legis-
lation, for he had served but six years in the House
when the war began, and four of those were nearly a
decade before the rebellion; but when the great conflict
came before which all but the bravest-hearted quailed,
Stevens' supreme ability and dauntless courage made
him speedily accepted by all as the leader of the popular
branch of Congress. In all the conflicts of opinion and
grave doubts among even the sincerest of men as to the
true policy of the government in meeting armed rebellion, Stevens was the one man who never faltered, who
never hesitated, who never temporized, but who was ready
to meet aggressive treason with the most aggressive assaults. He and Lincoln worked substantially on the
same lines, earnestly striving to attain the same ends,
but Stevens was always in advance of public sentiment,
while Lincoln ever halted until assured that the considerate judgment of the nation would sustain him.
Stevens was the pioneer who was ever in advance of the
government in every movement for the suppression of
the rebellion, whether by military or civil measures. He
always wanted great armies, heroic chieftains, and relentless blows, and he was ready to follow the overthrow of

rebellion with the sternest retributive policy.   He had
faith that the people would sustain the war—that they
would patriotically submit to any sacrifice of blood and
treasure necessary to preserve the Union and overthrow
slavery that was the cause of fraternal conflict, and he
was always in the lead in pressing every measure that
promised to weaken the slave power in any part of the
Union.

Lincoln was inspired by the same patriotic purpose
and sympathies with Stevens in everything but his policy of vengeance. Lincoln possessed the sagacity to
await the fullness of time for all things, and thus he
failed in nothing.   These two great civil leaders were
not in close personal relations.   Stevens was ever impatient of Lincoln's tardiness, and Lincoln was always
patient with Stevens' advanced and often impracticable
methods.   Stevens was a born dictator in politics; Lincoln a born follower of the people, but always wisely aiding them to the safest judgment that was to be his guide.
When Stevens proposed the abolition of slavery in the
District of Columbia, and followed it with the extension
of the elective franchise to the liberated slaves, very
many of his party followers in the House faltered and
threatened revolt, and only a man of Stevens' iron will
and relentless mastery could have commanded a solid
party vote for the measures which were regarded by
many as political suicide.   I sat by him one morning
in the House before the session had opened when the
question of negro suffrage in the District of Columbia
was about to be considered, and I heard a leading Pennsylvania Republican approach him to protest against
committing the party to that policy.   Stevens' grim face
and cold gray eye gave answer to the man before his bitter words were uttered.   He waved his hand to the trembling suppliant and bade him go to his seat and vote for

the measure or confess himself a coward to the world. The Commoner was obeyed, for had disobedience followed the offender would have been proclaimed to his constituents, over the name of Stevens, as a coward, and that would have doomed him to defeat.

The relations between Lincoln and Stevens were always friendly, but seldom cordial. Stevens did not favor the nomination of Lincoln in 1860, although he voted for him as a second choice in preference to Seward. He was the champion of John McLean for President, and presented the anomaly of the most radical Republican leader of the country, Giddings excepted, supporting the most conservative candidate for the Presidency. He was politician enough to understand that there was a large conservative element, especially in Pennsylvania and Indiana, that had to be conciliated to elect a Republican President, and he loved McLean chiefly because McLean had dared to disobey the commands of Jackson when in his Cabinet. He was again a delegate when Lincoln was renominated in 1864, and he voted for Lincoln simply because it was not possible to nominate any other man more in accord with his convictions; but in neither of these conventions, in both of which he voted for Lincoln, was he enthusiastic in Lincoln's cause. He had faith in Lincoln's patriotism and integrity, but he believed him weak because he kept far behind Stevens in his war measures, and he was especially bitter against the nomination of Johnson for Vice-President instead of Hamlin, but he permitted his vote to be recorded for Johnson in obedience to the obvious purpose of his own delegation and of the convention to nominate him. I sat close by him in the first informal meeting of the Pennsylvania delegation in Baltimore in 1864, and, being a delegate-at-large, I was one of the first four who voted on the choice for Vice-President. When I voted for

Johnson, Stevens was startled, and turning to me he said in a tone of evident bitterness, "Can't you find a candidate for Vice-President in the United States, without going down to one of those damned rebel provinces to pick one up?" I gave a kind answer and evaded discussion of the subject. He had no personal love for either of the candidates for whom his own vote had been finally cast, but his hatred of McClellan called out his fiercest invective and made him ready to do tireless battle for his defeat. He harshly judged all men who pretended to prosecute the war while protecting slavery, and he believed that McClellan was a traitor to the cause for which he was leading his armies, and, believing it, he declared it.

Stevens never saw Lincoln during the war except when necessity required it. It was not his custom to fawn upon power or flatter authority, and his free and incisive criticism of public men generally prevented him from being in sympathetic touch with most of the officials connected with the administration. He was one of the earliest of the party leaders to demand the unconditional and universal freedom of the slaves, and he often grieved Lincoln sorely by his mandatory appeals for an Emancipation Proclamation, and by the keen satire that only he could employ against those who differed from him. It was known to but few that he suffered a serious disappointment from Lincoln when Cameron was appointed to the Cabinet. Stevens took no part in the contest for a Pennsylvania Cabinet officer until after it became known that Lincoln had revoked his offer of a Cabinet portfolio to Cameron about the 1st of January. Stevens then entered the field with great earnestness as a candidate for the Cabinet himself, and the position he desired was that of Secretary of the Treasury. In obedience to his invitation I met him at Harrisburg, and found him more interested in reaching the Cabinet than I had ever known him in any of his political aspirations. Later, when Cameron became again prominent as a Cabinet expectant, Stevens bitterly protested, and when Cameron's appointment was announced he felt personally aggrieved, although few even of his most intimate acquaintances had any knowledge of it. It was his second disappointment in his efforts to reach Cabinet honors. In December, 1839, when the Whig National Convention was about to meet at Harrisburg to decide whether Clay, Harrison, or Scott should be honored with the candidacy, Harrison sent to Stevens by Mr. Purdy an autograph letter voluntarily proposing that if Harrison should be nominated and elected President, Stevens would be made a member of his Cabinet. Stevens was one of the most potent of the political leaders in that convention, and he finally controlled the nomination for Harrison. He never saw or heard from Harrison from that time until he was inaugurated as President, and he was astounded when the Cabinet was nominated to the Senate to find his name omitted. So reticent was he as to Harrison's previous proffer of the position that Mr. Burroughs, who was at the head of the Pennsylvanians in Washington urging Stevens' appointment, was never advised of the promise he held from Harrison for the place. Harrison died too early to feel the retribution that would surely have come from Stevens, but in his second disappointment Stevens was face to face with Lincoln and side by side with him until death divided them. Only once during Lincoln's administration can I recall Stevens' positive and enthusiastic commendation of Lincoln, and that was when he issued his Emancipation Proclamation in 1862. He then believed in Lincoln, and expected a rapid advance in every line of aggression against slavery and rebellion, but soon new causes of dissent arose between them, as Stevens called for the speedy confiscation of property of those in rebellion and for the punishment of all who were responsible for the civil war. Thus they continued during the whole period of Lincoln's administration, both earnestly working to solve the same great problems in the interest of free government, and yet seldom in actual harmony in their methods and policies.

I am quite sure that Stevens respected Lincoln much more than he would have respected any other man in the same position with Lincoln's convictions of duty. He could not but appreciate Lincoln's generous forbearance even with all of Stevens' irritating conflicts, and Lincoln profoundly appreciated Stevens as one of his most valued and useful co-workers, and never cherished resentment even when Stevens indulged in his bitterest sallies of wit or sarcasm at Lincoln's tardiness. Strange as it may seem, these two great characters, ever in conflict and yet ever battling for the same great cause, rendered invaluable service to each other, and unitedly rendered incalculable service in saving the Republic. Had Stevens not declared for the abolition of slavery as soon as the war began, and pressed it in and out of season, Lincoln could not have issued his Emancipation Proclamation as early as September, 1862. Stevens was ever clearing the underbrush and preparing the soil, while Lincoln followed to sow the seeds that were to ripen in a regenerated Union; and while Stevens was ever hastening the opportunity for Lincoln to consummate great achievements in the steady advance made for the over-throw of slavery, Lincoln wisely conserved the utterances and efforts of Stevens until the time became fully ripe when the harvest could be gathered. I doubt not that Stevens, had he been in Lincoln's position, would have been greatly sobered by the responsibility that the President must accept for himself alone, and I doubt not that if Lincoln had been a Senator or Representative in Congress, he would have declared in favor of Emancipation long before he did it as President. Stevens as Commoner could afford to be defeated, to have his aggressive measures postponed, and to take up the battle for them afresh as often as he was repulsed; but the President could proclaim no policy in the name of the Republic without absolute assurance of its success. Each in his great trust attained the highest possible measure of success, and the two men who more than all others blended the varied currents of their efforts and crystallized them in the unchangeable policy of the goverment were Abraham Lincoln and Thaddeus Stevens.

After the death of Lincoln, Stevens was one of the earliest of the Republican leaders to place himself in an aggressively hostile attitude to Johnson, and he persisted in it with tireless energy until he performed his last great task in his plea before the Senate for the conviction of the President under articles of impeachment preferred by the House. He was then greatly enfeebled by broken health, but his mental powers were unabated. I remember meeting him one morning in acting Vice-President Wade's room of the Capitol, before the meeting of the Senate, when the impeachment trial was in progress. Chase had just startled some of the Republican leaders by rulings which foreshadowed the probable acquittal of Johnson. Stevens came limping into Wade's room, dropped into an easy-chair, and at once opened his invective upon Chase. He ended his criticism of the trial with these words: "It is the meanest case, before the meanest tribunal, and on the meanest subject of human history." After the acquittal of Johnson he seemed almost entirely hopeless of preserving the fruits of the victory won by our armies in the overthrow of the rebellion. I remember meeting him at his house some three weeks before his death. He spoke of the perfidy of Johnson with great bitterness, and seemed clouded with gloom as to the achievements of his own life. He then hoped to go to Bedford Springs to recover sufficient vigor to be able to resume his seat at the next session, but he saw little of the future that promised restoration of the Union with justice to the liberated slaves. Although he was the acknowledged Commoner of the war, and the acknowledged leader of the House as long as he was able to retain his seat after the war had closed, he said, "My life has been a failure. With all this great struggle of years in Washington, and the fearful sacrifice of life and treasure, I see little hope for the Republic." After a moment's pause his face suddenly brightened, and he said, "After all, I may say that my life has not been entirely vain. When I remember that I gave free schools to Pennsylvania, my adopted State, I think my life may have been worth the living." He had lately reprinted his speech delivered in the Pennsylvania House in 1835 that changed the body from its purpose to repeal the free-school law, and he handed me a copy of it, saying, "That was the proudest effort of my life. It gave schools to the poor and helpless children of the State." Thus did the Great Commoner of the nation, crowned with the greenest laurels of our statesmanship, turn back more than a generation from his greatest achievements because they were incomplete, although fully assured, to find the silver lining to the many disappointments of his life.

Stevens, like Lincoln, had few intimate acquaintances, and no one in whom he implicitly confided. That he had had some untold sorrow was accepted by all who knew him well, but none could venture to invade the sacred portals of his inner life. He seldom spoke of himself, but his grim, cynical smile and his pungent invective against the social customs of the times proclaimed his love of solitude, except when his lot could be cast with the very few congenial spirits he found around him. One name alone ever brightened his stern face and kindled the gray eye that was so often lustreless, and that name was "mother." He loved to speak of her, and when he did so all the harsh lines of his countenance disappeared to give place to the tenderness of a child. That one devotion was like an oasis in the desert of his affections, and, regardless of his individual convictions, he reverenced everything taught him by his mother. In his will he provided that the sexton of her little churchyard in the bleak hills of Vermont should ever keep her grave green, "and plant roses and other cheerful flowers at each of the four corners of said grave every spring." He also made a devise of $1000 to aid in the building of a Baptist church in Lancaster, giving in the will this reason for it: "I do this out of respect to the memory of my mother, to whom I owe what little prosperity I have had on earth, which, small as it is, I desire emphatically to acknowledge."

I need hardly say that a man of Stevens' positive and aggressive qualities left an enduring record of his greatness in both the statutes and the fundamental law of the nation. Unlike his distinguished fellow-townsman, President Buchanan, who with all his long experience in both branches of Congress never formulated a great measure to stand as a monument of his statesmanship, Stevens was the master-spirit of every aggressive movement in Congress to overthrow the rebellion and slavery. His views of the civil war and of reconstruction were pointedly presented in the Confiscation Act of July 17, 1862. It was a radical measure, and clearly foreshadowed the employment of freedmen in the military service of the Union. It was practically the abolition of slavery by

Congress under the war powers of the government. Lincoln saw that the passage of the bill was inevitable, and he took occasion to make known the fact that it could not meet with his approval, because it assumed that Congress had the power to abolish slavery within a State. He went so far as to prepare a veto, but Stevens wisely obviated the necessity of a veto by consenting to an explanatory joint resolution of Congress relieving the bill of its acutely offensive features, and Lincoln signed the bill and the explanatory resolutions together. Stevens was the author of the Fourteenth Amendment to the national Constitution, although it was not accepted as he would have preferred it. This new article of the fundamental law, next to the Thirteenth Article abolishing slavery, is the most important of all the actions of Congress relating to reconstruction. It conferred unchangeably upon the liberated slaves the high right of American citizenship, and made it impossible for any State to abridge the privileges of any race. It also limited representation to the enfranchised voters of the States; it made the validity of the public debt absolutely sacred; prohibited the assumption or payment of Confederate debt by any State; and it disqualified most of the Southern leaders from ever again enjoying citizenship unless their disability were relieved by a two-thirds vote of Congress. Stevens was bitterly opposed to the provision allowing restoration to citizenship of any who had taken the oath of office, military or civil, to support the government and afterward engaged in the rebellion, but, being unable to obtain the absolute disqualification of those men, he accepted the gravest obstacles that he could interpose against the restoration of civil rights. His policy of reconstruction, exclusive of his fierce confiscation and retributive purposes, would have been a priceless blessing to the South, although at the time it would have been accepted as ex-

tremely vindictive. He would have held the rebellious
States as provinces and governed them as Territories, to
await the period when they might with safety be restored
to the Union. Had that policy been adopted the desola-
tion almost worse than war would have been averted in
the Southern States. Sadly as the people of the South
were impoverished by war, the greatest humiliation they
ever suffered was in the rule of the carpet-bagger and
the adventurer who despoiled them of safety and credit
and ran riot in every channel of State authority. Had
they been held as provinces there would have been peace,
their industries would have been speedily revived, mutual confidence between the North and South would have
rapidly strengthed, and in a very few years at the most
they would have resumed their position in the galaxy of
States; and universal negro suffrage would not have been
in the cup of bitterness they had to drain. Stevens was
bitterly denounced by many for his vindictive reconstruction policy; but, stripped of its utterly impracticable and impossible confiscation and retributive features, it would have been the wisest policy for both
North and South that could have been adopted.

It is a common belief that on the question of reconstruction and on many other questions relating to the
war Stevens planted himself entirely above the Constitution and acted in utter contempt of the supreme law.
I have heard thoughtless and malicious people many
times quote him as having said "Damn the Constitution!" but Stevens never uttered or cherished such a
sentiment. He defined his views on the subject so
clearly that none could mistake them in his speech giving his reasons for voting for the admission of West
Virginia as a State. He quoted the requirements of the
Constitution, and said that it was a mockery to assume
that the provisions of the Constitution had been com-

19

plied with. He did not justify or excuse his vote in favor of the creation of a new State because of his disregard of, or contempt for, the Constitution. On the contrary, he presented the unanswerable argument that Virginia was in rebellion against the government and the Constitution, and had been conceded belligerent rights by our government and by the governments of Europe, thus making her subject to the rules of war governing a public enemy, whereby she placed herself beyond the pale of the Constitution and had no claim upon its protecting attributes. He said, "We may admit West Virginia as a new State, not by virtue of any provision in the Constitution, but under the absolute power which the laws of war give us under the circumstances in which we are placed. I shall vote for this bill upon that theory, and upon that alone, for I will not stultify myself by supposing that we have any warrant in the Constitution for this proceeding." The logic that a belligerent power, recognized by ourselves and by the world, was entirely beyond the protecting power of our Constitution was indisputable, and in that case, as in all cases, he always maintained the sanctity of the Constitution to all who had not become public enemies with conceded belligerent rights.

Being outside the pale of the Constitution in war, he held that the insurgent States occupied the legal status of conquered enemies when the war closed, and upon that theory was based his whole policy of reconstruction, including the confiscation of property and the punishment of the leaders of the rebellion. That he was abstractly right in his interpretation of the laws of war cannot be questioned, however widely others may differ from him in the expediency or justice of the measures he proposed. He was one of the first to appreciate the truth that President Johnson had adopted a policy of re-

Washington Dec 16. 1865

Dear Sir

I thank you
write this over to me
personally in your
letter. But I am more
particularly thank
you for the grand
argument in favor
of the right policy —
You ought
to speak from this
in a daily of 100,000
circulation — Why
cannot you get
up such a paper?

Thaddeus Stevens

Col. McClure Esq

FAC-SIMILE OF LETTER FROM STEVENS.

construction that the Republican party could not sustain. In this I heartily agreed with him, and one of my most valued mementos of the men of war-times is an autograph letter received from Mr. Stevens warmly commending an editorial on the subject published in the Chambersburg *Repository*, which I then edited, in which he expressed the hope, since proved gratefully prophetic, that I should one day conduct a daily newspaper in Philadelphia with a hundred thousand readers.* I had voted for Johnson's nomination for Vice-President in disregard of Stevens' bitter complaint, but when Johnson had disgraced himself before the nation and the world by his exhibition of inebriety at his inauguration, I had denounced him and demanded his resignation. He never was permitted to return to the Senate as Vice-President, but a little more than a month thereafter the assassination of Lincoln made him President. Assuming that my free criticism and demand for his resignation would preclude cordial relations between us, I did not visit him in the White House until he had twice requested me to do so through Governor Curtin, and my first and only interview with him convinced me that his policy of reconstruction could not be sustained by the North.

My relations with Stevens for a dozen years before his death were peculiarly pleasant, and as intimate perhaps as was common between him and those in the narrow circle of his close acquaintances. He spent his summers

---

* WASHINGTON, Dec. 16, 1865.

DEAR SIR : I thank you for the kindness to me personally in your letter; but I more particularly thank you for the grand argument in favor of the right policy.

You ought to speak from Philadelphia in a daily of 100,000 circulation. Why cannot you get up such a paper?

THADDEUS STEVENS.

COL. A. K. MCCLURE.

at his quiet mountain-furnace home in Franklin county, where I resided, and during the few years that I was in active practice at the bar in Chambersburg he attended our courts and tried one side of nearly every important cause. In all my acquaintance with the lawyers of Pennsylvania I regard Stevens as having more nearly completed the circle of a great lawyer than any other member of the Pennsylvania bar. He was perfect in practice, a master of the law, exceptionally skillful in eliciting testimony from witnesses, a most sagacious, eloquent, and persuasive advocate, and one of the strongest men before a law court that I have ever heard. He was thoroughly master of himself in his profession, and his withering invective and crushing wit, so often employed in conversation and in political speeches, were never displayed in the trial of a cause unless it was eminently wise to do so; and he was one of the most courteous of men at the bar whether associate or opponent. He was especially generous in his kindness to young members of the bar unless they undertook to unduly flap their fledgling wings, when they were certain to suffer speedy and humiliating discomfiture. His trial of the Hanway treason case before Judge Greer in the United States Court at Philadelphia exhibited his matchless skill in the best use of his matchless powers. While he conceived and directed every feature of the defence, he was the silent man of the trial. He knew the political prejudices which were attached to his then odious attitude on the slavery question, and he put upon the late Chief Justice, John M. Read, the laboring oars of the trial, as Read was a Democrat of State and even national fame. It was a trial that attracted the attention not only of the nation, but of the civilized world, and was the first case adjudicated in Pennsylvania in our higher courts under the Fugitive Slave Law of 1850. Mr. Gorsuch, a Virginia minister, pursuing his slave into Chester county, was killed in an altercation at Christiana by the friends of the hunted bondman, and Hanway and others were indicted for treason in inciting to rebellion and murder. Hanway was acquitted, and he owed his deliverance to the legal acumen and skill of Thaddeus Stevens.

The highest tribute ever paid to an American statesman since the foundation of the Republic was paid to Thaddeus Stevens by his bereaved constituents of Lancaster county when his dead body lay in state at his home. He died on Thursday, the 11th of August, 1868, and his body was brought from Washington to his home on the following day, and on Saturday it was viewed by thousands of sorrowing friends. The Republican primary elections had been called for that day, and, although Stevens had died three days before and a nomination was to be made for his successor, no one of the several candidates in the county dared to whisper his name as an aspirant while Stevens' body was untombed. Acting under a common inspiration, the people of the county who were entitled to participate in the primary elections cast a unanimous vote for Stevens' renomination as their candidate for Congress when they knew that he had passed away and his body was in state in his humble house in Lancaster. There is nothing in Grecian or Roman story of such a tribute to a dead leader. Monuments were erected in those days to greatness which have crumbled away under the gnawing tooth of time, but the dust of Thaddeus Stevens reposes under an humble monument suggested by himself, located in an humble "City of the Silent," chosen by him because it recognized "equality of man before his Creator," and admitted any of every race and color to sleep the sleep that knows no waking. The inscription on his monument, dictated by himself, is in these words:

THADDEUS STEVENS,
Born at Danville, Caledonia Co., Vermont,
April 4, 1792.
Died at Washington, D. C.,
August 11, 1868.

I repose in this quiet and secluded spot,
Not from any natural preference for solitude,
But, finding other Cemeteries limited as to Race
By Charter Rules,
I have chosen this that I might illustrate
In my death
The Principles which I advocated
Through a long life:

EQUALITY OF MAN BEFORE HIS CREATOR.

Thus passed away the Great Commoner of the war; the friend of the lowly, the oppressed, and the friendless; the author of our free-school system of Pennsylvania that now gives education to the humblest of every township; and I can fitly quote the eloquent tribute of Charles Sumner: "I see him now as I have so often seen him during life; his venerable form moves slowly with uncertain steps, but the gathered strength of years in his countenance and the light of victory on his path. Politician, calculator, time-server, stand aside; a Hero Statesman passes to his reward."

(Photo by Saylor, Lancaster, Pa.)

JAMES BUCHANAN, 1865.

LINCOLN AND BUCHANAN.

IT is now more than thirty years since James Buchanan retired from the office of President of the United States, but I doubt whether there is any one of our great national characters whose relations to our civil war are so widely and so flagrantly misunderstood. It will surprise many at this day when I say that Abraham Lincoln took up the reins of government just where James Buchanan left them, and continued precisely the same policy toward the South that Buchanan had inaugurated, until the Southern leaders committed the suicidal act of firing upon Fort Sumter. From the time that Buchanan's original Cabinet was disrupted on the sectional issues that culminated in armed rebellion, the administration of Buchanan was not only thoroughly loyal to the preservation of the Union, but it fixed the policy that Lincoln accepted, and from which he took no marked departure until actual war came upon him. This is not the common appreciation of Buchanan among the American people, but it is the truth of history. He retired from his high office in the very flood-tide of sectional and partisan passion. The loyal people were frenzied to madness by what was regarded as the perfidy of Buchanan's War Minister, Mr. Floyd, in shipping valuable arms and munitions to the South; by the insolent treason of his Secretary of the Treasury, Mr. Cobb; by the boldly-asserted and generally-believed treachery of his Secretary of the Navy, Mr. Toucey, in scattering our navy throughout the world; and it is now accepted by many, amongst even intelligent people of this country, that Buchanan was faithless to his duty in failing to reinforce Major Anderson at Sumter.   In addition to these deeply-seated unjust convictions in regard to Buchanan, he is commonly believed to have been in hostility to the Lincoln administration and to the war, and his sympathies to have been with the South in the bloody struggle for the preservation of the Union.   It is certainly time that these utterly erroneous and most unjust impressions as to Buchanan should be dissipated; and, fortunately for his own good name, he has left on record the most positive evidence of his devotion to the Union and his earnest support of the government in the most vigorous prosecution of the war that had been, as he always held, wantonly precipitated upon the nation by the South.   I never was in political sympathy with Buchanan while he was in public life, excepting the few closing months of his administration, when, as I then knew, both he and his Cabinet were estranged from their ultra-Democratic friends North and South, and were in daily intercourse with the leading friends of Lincoln as the incoming President.   My personal acquaintance with him was of the most casual character, and I have therefore neither lingering personal nor political affection to inspire me to any strained attempt to vindicate his memory.

Buchanan as President should be judged by the circumstances under which he reached that position, by his long-cherished and conscientious convictions, and by his peculiar political environment, that led him into the most sympathetic relations with the South.   It should be remembered that he was elected President over General Fremont, a distinctly sectional candidate who was not thought of with any degree of favor in any State south of Mason and Dixon's line. It was an earnest battle against what was assailed as the ultra-sectionalism of the North, and it consolidated the South in support of Buchanan. It naturally intensified the sober judgment of his life against political Abolitionism, and he entered the Presidency owing his election to the solid vote of the Slave States. To these facts, which could not fail to profoundly impress Buchanan, it should be added that he was naturally a most conservative and strict-constructionist statesman. Born and reared in the Federal school, acting with the Federal party until he had become noted as a leader in Congress, and gravitating thence into the Democratic school when strict constructionists had settled upon State rights as the jewel of their faith, it is not surprising that Buchanan sympathized with the South in all the preliminary disputes which finally ended in sanguinary war. That he was radically wrong on the fundamental issues relating to the war when he entered the Presidency cannot be doubted. He foreshadowed the Dred Scott decision in his inaugural address, and evidently believed that it was to come as a final solution of the slavery dispute, as it greatly enlarged the constitutional protection of slave-holders; and his support of the lawless and revolutionary Lecompton policy, into which he and his party were dragooned by the Southern leaders, engulfed him and his administration in the maëlstrom of secession. Thus was he drifting, step by step, insensibly into the hands of those who, however fair in declaration or promise, were treasonable in purpose, and sought through him to wield the power of the government to aid rather than hinder the disruption of the Republic. It is only just to Buchanan, however, to say that whenever he was brought face to face with the true purposes of the Southern leaders he reversed his own policy, revised his Cabinet, and made his administration quite as aggressive as was wise under the circumstances in asserting the paramount authority of the Union.

The crisis that changed Buchanan's whole policy on the question of Secession was initiated on the 12th of December, 1860, when General Cass resigned his position as Secretary of State because he could not harmonize with Buchanan's views in meeting the question. Cass was greatly enfeebled by age, and Buchanan left a private record on Cass' resignation in which he stated that until that time the only difference between them that he had knowledge of was on the ground that Buchanan had failed to assert with sufficient clearness that there was no power in Congress or the government to make war upon a State to hinder it in separating from the Union. The retirement of Cass was speedily followed by the enforced resignations of Floyd from the War Department and Cobb from the Treasury. Philip Thomas of Maryland succeeded Cobb; Joseph Holt of Kentucky succeeded Floyd; Attorney-General Black was promoted to Secretary of State; and Edwin M. Stanton made his successor as Attorney-General. Thomas remained in office only a month, when he was succeeded by General Dix, an aggressive loyalist. Stanton, Dix, and Holt were aggressively against every form of treasonable rebellion, and they gave a visibly altered tone to everything about the administration in the preliminary disputes with the leading Secessionists. One of the first acts of South Carolina after her formal withdrawal from the Union was to appoint Commissioners to proceed to Washington to treat with the government of the United States for peaceable separation and the recognition of the independence of the Palmetto State. These Commissioners proceeded to Washington, and were courteously received by Buchanan as citizens of South Carolina, without any recognition of their official capacity, and several misunderstandings arose between them as to what was accepted or agreed upon in relation to the military status in Charleston.

It finally became necessary for Buchanan to give a formal answer to the South Carolina Commissioners as to the attitude of the government and his purposes as its Executive. He prepared an answer without consulting any of the members of his Cabinet, in which he said: "I have declined for the present to reinforce these forts (in Charleston harbor), relying upon the honor of South Carolinians that they will not be assaulted while they remain in their present condition, but that Commissioners will be sent by the convention to treat with Congress on the subject." In this paper Buchanan assumed that he had no power to take any action as President— that the whole dispute was one to be submitted to Congress. He added, however, that "if South Carolina should take any of these forts, she will then become the assailant in a war against the United States." In the many interesting conversations I had with the late Judge Black on the subject of the difficulties in Buchanan's Cabinet, I received from his own lips detailed accounts of almost every incident of importance that occurred, and what I state in regard to the answer of Buchanan to the South Carolina Commissioners I give from distinct recollection on his authority. On the 29th of December, soon after Buchanan had written the original draft of his answer to the Commissioners, he submitted it to his Cabinet. It was little criticised at the Cabinet meeting by any of the President's constitutional advisers, and Black was ominously silent. He was profoundly grieved at the attitude the President had assumed, and his strong personal devotion to Buchanan made his position one of extreme delicacy.   He was the one man of the Cabinet whom Buchanan regarded as his close personal and political friend.   He did not express his views to any of his Cabinet associates until he had spent an entire night in anxious reflection as to his duty.   On the following day he called upon Buchanan and told him frankly that if he sent the answer to the South Carolina Commissioners as originally prepared he (Black) must resign from the Cabinet, because he could not assent to the government being placed in such an attitude.   It was seldom that Buchanan ever betrayed emotion, but when Black informed him that they must separate Buchanan was moved even to tears.   Few words passed between them, and Buchanan handed Black the original paper with the request to modify it in accordance with his own views, and return it as speedily as possible.   Black then wrote the paper that went into history as the answer of Buchanan to the Commissioners.   Before he presented it to the President it was carefully considered and revised by Black, Holt, and Stanton, who then were, and thereafter continued to be, with Dix, the aggressively loyal members of the Buchanan Cabinet; and in their actions they had the hearty sympathy and support of the President.

One of the common accusations against Buchanan is that he failed to reinforce the garrisons in the Southern forts and protect them from capture by the Secessionists. A careful study of the facts, however, shows that Buchanan was utterly without an army to protect these forts.   He and General Scott had a somewhat bitter dispute on this point after Buchanan's retirement from office, but Scott's own statement proves that he had no intelligent knowledge of the ability of the government to reinforce the forts, or that he, as commander-in-chief of the army, made an official suggestion to the President that was impossible of execution. On the 29th of October, 1860, Scott addressed Buchanan on the subject of these Southern forts, and he enumerated nine of them that would be exposed to easy capture unless speedily reinforced. On the day after thus addressing the President, Scott pointedly illustrated the absurdity of his recommendation by saying to the President, "There is one regular company at Boston, one here at the Narrows, one at Portsmouth, one at Augusta, Georgia, and one at Baton Rouge." According to Scott's own statement, there were but five companies of the army then within the reach of the government to garrison or reinforce the threatened forts. These five companies did not aggregate four hundred men, and these four hundred men, scattered from Boston to Baton Rouge, were presented by Scott himself as the resources of the government for the protection of nine forts in six Southern States.

Our little army of that day was all needed on our then remote frontiers to protect settlers and emigrants from the savages who ruled in those regions, and it would have required weeks, and in some cases months, to bring them to the East for the protection of the endangered forts. Even when war came and the frontiers had to be stripped of their military protection wherever it was possible, there were but few regular troops at the battle of Bull Run. Scott and Buchanan both agreed that there was danger of turbulence at the inauguration of Lincoln, and they cordially co-operated with each other to take the most effective measures to preserve peace on that occasion. After gathering all the troops that could be marshaled from every part of the country to serve at the inauguration, they finally got together six hundred and thirty, and they made their arrangements for the inauguration with that small military display because the commander-in-chief of the army could not summon a larger force. It was simply impossible, therefore, for President Buchanan to garrison or reinforce the Southern forts, for the reason that he had not the men with which to do it. There was but one way to save the Southern forts, and that was to garrison them so strongly, with ample provisions and munitions of war, that they would be invulnerable to assault. To have sent inadequate reinforcements to any of these forts in the then inflamed condition of the public mind in the South would have been to wantonly provoke attack upon forces that could not protect themselves. Had Lincoln been President he could not have done more without doing what would have been accepted as an open declaration of war against the South, and Lincoln would no more have committed that folly than did Buchanan. It would have been a wise thing to do if we had had an army of thirty or forty thousand men. Then all the forts could have been garrisoned and reinforced, and they could have had the support necessary in case of threatened assault; but our government was entirely unprepared for defence, and when we were compelled to face the peril of war the army could not be increased without making the North either measurably or wholly responsible for precipitating a civil conflict. The intelligent and dispassionate American citizen, who carefully reads the whole story of the action of Buchanan and his Cabinet in co-operation with Scott, must reach the conclusion that Buchanan was not in any degree at fault for the failure to garrison or reinforce the forts in the Southern States.

On the important question of Buchanan's support of the government after war had been commenced by the assault on Sumter, he has fortunately left the most positive and multiplied evidence of his patriotic loyalty to the Union. He was singularly reticent during the war, and his silence was misconstrued into a lack of sympathy with the government. After his retirement from the Presidency he was most mercilessly vilified, brutally misrepresented as deliberately disloyal, and he seems to have abandoned the hope of correcting public sentiment and doing himself justice until the flood-tide of passion had run its course. He was, however, in constant communication with his leading friends throughout the country, and to every one of them, from the beginning of the war until its close, he expressed the most patriotic convictions, and uniformly urged the earnest support of the war and its most vigorous prosecution. In September, 1861, he was invited by an intimate friend to deliver a public address on the condition of the country and the attitude of the government. In his answer he said, writing in the frankness of sacred friendship, "Every person who has conference with me knows that I am in favor of sustaining the government in the vigorous prosecution of the war for the restoration of the Union. But occasion may offer when it may be proper for me authoritatively to express this opinion to the public. Until that time shall arrive I desire to avoid any public exhibition." In a private letter to James Buchanan Henry, his nephew, immediately after he had heard of the firing upon Sumter, he said: "The Confederate States have deliberately commenced a civil war, and God knows where it may end. They were repeatedly warned by my administration that an assault on Fort Sumter would be civil war and they would be responsible for the consequences."

On the 19th of April, 1861, soon after the bombardment of Sumter, he wrote to General Dix, who had then been announced as the president of a great Union meeting soon to be held, at which he advised him to repeat the admonitions the administration had given to South

20

Carolina against precipitating war. He referred to the fact that as Dix had been a member of the Cabinet at the time he could speak with great propriety of the utter want of excuse on the part of South Carolina for firing upon Sumter. In this letter he said: "The present administration had no alternative but to accept the war initiated by South Carolina or the Southern Confederacy. The North will sustain the administration to a man, and it ought to be sustained at all hazards." Again, on the 26th of April, writing to Mr. Baker, he said: "The attack on Fort Sumter was an outrageous act. The authorities at Charleston were several times warned by my administration that such an attack would be civil war, and would be treated as such. If it had been made in my time it should have been treated as such." In a letter to Mr. Stanton, May 6, when Stanton was writing to Buchanan fiercely criticising Lincoln and every act of the administration, Buchanan said: "The first gun fired by Beauregard aroused the indignant spirit of the North as nothing else could have done, and made us an unanimous people. I repeatedly warned them that this would be the result." In a letter to Mr. King, July 13, he said: "The assault upon Fort Sumter was the commencement of war by the Confederate States, and no alternative was left but to prosecute it with vigor on our part. Up until all social and political relations ceased between the Secession leaders and myself I had often warned them that the North would rise to a man against them if such an assault was made. . . . I am glad that General Scott does not underrate the strength of his enemy, which would be a great fault in a commander. With all my heart and soul I wish him success." In a letter to Mr. Leiper, August 31, he said: "I agree with you that nothing but a vigorous prosecution of the war can now determine the question between the North and the South. It is vain to think of peace at the present moment.''

In a letter to Dr. Blake, September 12, he said: ''We must prosecute the war with the utmost vigor. May God grant us a safe deliverance and a restoration of the Union!'' In a letter to Mr. King, September 18, he said: ''I think I can perceive in the public mind a more fixed, resolute, and determined purpose than ever to prosecute the war to a successful termination with all the men and means in our power. Enlistments are now proceeding much more rapidly than a few weeks ago, and I am truly glad of it. The time has passed for offering compromises and terms of peace to the seceded States. . . . There is a time for all things under the sun, but surely this is not the moment for paralyzing the arm of the national administration by a suicidal conflict among ourselves, but for bold, energetic, and united action.'' On the 28th of September, Buchanan addressed a letter to a committee of the citizens of Chester and Lancaster counties who had invited him to address a Union meeting at Hagersville. He declined because ''advancing years in the present state of my health render it impossible.'' He said: ''Were it possible for me to address your meeting, waiving all other topics, I should confine myself to a solemn and earnest appeal to my countrymen, and especially those without families, to volunteer for the war and join the many thousands of brave and patriotic volunteers who are already in the field. This is the moment for action—for prompt, energetic, and united action—and not for discussion of peace propositions.'' In closing the letter he said that until the South shall voluntarily return to the Union ''it will be our duty to support the President with all the men and means at the command of the country in a vigorous and successful prosecution of the war.''

In a letter to Mr. King, January 28, 1862, he said: "I
do most earnestly hope that our army may be able to do
something before the first of April.   If not, there is
great danger not merely of British, but of European,
interference."   In a letter to Mrs. Boyd, February 16,
he said: "The Confederate States commenced this un-
happy war for the destruction of the Union, and until
they shall be willing to consent to its restoration there
can be no hopes of peace."   On the 4th of March he
wrote Judge Black: "They (the South) chose to com-
mence civil war, and Mr. Lincoln had no alternative but
to defend the country against dismemberment.   I certainly should have done the same thing had they begun
the war in my time, and this they well knew."   In a
letter to Dr. Blake, July 12, he speaks of the deep anxiety he felt about the safety of McClellan's army, with a
heavy pressure removed from his heart when he learned
that it was safe, and he then adds: "Without doubt his
change of position in the face of a superior army evinced
great skill in strategy; but why was the wrong position
originally selected?   I still feel great confidence in
McClellan, and with all my heart wish him success.
Still, there is a mystery in the whole affair which time
alone can unravel."   On February 14, 1863, in a letter
to Mr. Roosevelt, he expressed his great disappointment
that a country so great as ours "has not yet produced
one great general."   In a letter to Mr. Leiper, March
19, he said: "I cannot entertain the idea of a division
of the Union; may God in His good providence restore
it!"   In a letter to Mr. Schell, July 25, he expresses his
profound regret at Governor Seymour's hostility to the
national conscription law, and said: "The conscription
law, though unwise and unjust in many of its provisions,
is not in my opinion unconstitutional."   So earnest was
Buchanan in his efforts to have the Democracy of Penn-

sylvania give the most cordial support to Lincoln and to the war that he even trangressed the lines of delicacy in a letter addressed to Judge Woodward, then a Supreme Justice and candidate for Governor of Pennsylvania, earnestly appealing to him to sustain the national conscription law by a judicial decision. This he did as early as July, 1863, when the question was first raised in our courts. In a letter of September 5, also addressed to Judge Woodward, he offered an apology for having advised him as to his judicial duties, and his apology was, as stated by himself, "I perceived that in New York the party was fast making the unconstitutionality of the conscription law the leading prominent point in the canvass."

On January 27, 1864, he wrote Mr. Capen, expressing his regret that "the Democrats have made no issue on which to fight the Presidential battle," and on the 14th of March he wrote to the same friend, expressing the belief that it would be best if the Democrats would fail to succeed to power at the Presidential election of that year. On the 25th of August he wrote to the same friend, assuming that McClellan would be nominated, in which he said: "A general proposition for peace and an armistice without reference to the restoration of the Union would be, in fact, a recognition of their independence. For this I confess I am far from being prepared." On the 22d of September, writing to his nephew, Mr. Henry, he said: "Peace would be a very great blessing, but it would be purchased at too high a price at the expense of the Union." In a letter to Mr. Capen of October 5 he declares his purpose to support McClellan for President, and he denounces the Chicago peace platform, and specially commends McClellan for having patriotically dissented from it. In the same letter he expresses some hope of McClellan's election, and frankly says that "the recent victories of Grant, Sherman, and Farragut have helped the Republicans," but he rejoiced at the victories of our armies and the prospect of the South submitting to a restoration of the Union. In a letter to Mr. Capen, December 28, he says: "I agree in opinion with General McClellan that it is fortunate both for himself and the Democratic party that he was not elected." In a letter to Mr. Flinn, April, 1865, he speaks most feelingly of the assassination of Lincoln, and says: "I deeply mourn his loss from private feelings, and still more deeply for the sake of the country. Heaven, I trust, will not suffer the perpetrators of the deed and their guilty accomplices to escape just punishment, but we must not despair of the Republic." In a letter to Mr. Capen, October 19, 1867, he says: "Negro emancipation is a fixed fact, and so let it remain for ever; but the high privilege of voting can only be constitutionally granted by the legislatures of the respective States." He heartily accepted emancipation, but he felt that the Democracy had an issue on which it could stand in a patriotic attitude opposing universal negro suffrage.

Thus from the day that civil war was precipitated upon the country by the madness of secession until the last insurgent gun was fired there was not an utterance from James Buchanan that did not exhibit the most patriotic devotion to the cause of the Union.

In the flood of light thrown upon the actions of Buchanan and Lincoln as nearly a generation has come and passed away, the intelligent and unbiased reader of the truth of history will be amazed to learn how closely the policy of Lincoln adhered to the policy inaugurated by Buchanan after he had been compelled to face the issue of actual secession and armed rebellion. From the day that Judge Black revised the answer of Buchanan to the South Carolina Commissioners the aims and efforts of Buchanan were uniformly and earnestly in the line of the most patriotic devotion to his responsible duties; and when he had such men as Black, Dix, Stanton, and Holt by his side, the majority, and the absolutely dominant element, of his Cabinet were aggressively loyal to the government, and made heroic effort to exercise every power they possessed to maintain the integrity of the Union. Whatever may have been Buchanan's political errors during the greater part of his administration, and however those errors may have strengthened the arms of secession, it is only simple justice to one of the most conscientious and patriotic of all our Presidents to say that when Buchanan was brought face to face with the fruits of his policy he severed all political and social intercourse with the leaders who had controlled his election, and cast his lot and all the power of the government on the side of unqualified loyalty. Not only did the call of Lincoln for troops to prosecute the war after the firing upon Sumter command the uniform and earnest support of Buchanan, but he heartily sustained the government in every war measure, even to the extent of assenting to emancipation. Such a record demands the commendation rather than the censure of our only Pennsylvania President; and I have performed the task of attempting to present him justly to the American people all the more gratefully because there are no lingering bonds of special personal or political sympathy between us. He is entitled to justice from every honest American citizen, and I have sought to give him justice—nothing more, nothing less.

LINCOLN AND GREELEY.

HORACE GREELEY was one of the earliest and most fretting of the many thorns in the political pathway of Abraham Lincoln. They served together in Congress in the winter of 1848–49, when Greeley was chosen to a short term to fill a vacancy. Speaking of Lincoln some years after his death, Greeley, referring to his association with him in Congress, said that Lincoln was "personally a favorite on our side," and adds: "He seemed a quiet, good-natured man; did not aspire to leadership, and seldom claimed the floor." For ten years after these two memorable characters separated as members of Congress Lincoln was little known or heard of outside of his State of Illinois, and when his great contest with Douglas for the Senate attracted the attention of the whole country in 1858, Greeley, with his powerful Republican organ, vastly the most potent political journal in the country, took positive grounds in favor of the return of Douglas to the Senate by the Republicans of Illinois, because of Douglas' open hostility to the Lecompton policy of the Buchanan administration. This attitude of Greeley's *Tribune* was one of the most serious obstacles that confronted Lincoln in his great campaign against Douglas, and it is possible that the influence of the *Tribune* may have lost Lincoln the legislature. He carried the popular vote and elected the Republican State ticket, but Douglas won the legislature

HORACE GREELY, 1872.

and was re-elected to the Senate. Thus did Greeley antagonize Lincoln in the first great battle he made for national leadership in politics, and with the exception of a single act of Greeley's, in which he served Lincoln to an extent that can hardly be measured, when in the early part of 1860 he opened the broadsides of the *Tribune* against Seward's nomination for President, he was a perpetual thorn in Lincoln's side, seldom agreeing with him on any important measure, and almost constantly criticising him boldly and often bitterly.

The first assault made on the Seward lines that attracted any attention from the country was the unexpected and aggressive revolt of Greeley's *Tribune* against Seward some months before the meeting of the Chicago Convention that nominated Lincoln. It attracted special attention from considerate Republicans throughout the country, because this assault came from the ablest Republican editor of the nation, from Seward's own State, and from one who was presumed to be Seward's personal and political friend. It was not then known to the public that on the 11th of November, 1854, he had written a pungent letter to Seward and formally severed all political association with him, to take effect in the following February, when Seward was re-elected to the United States Senate. The letter was written in strict confidence, but in 1860, when the friends of Seward keenly felt Greeley's criticisms on Seward's availability as a Presidential candidate, and especially in the bitter disappointment of Seward's friends after his defeat at Chicago, such free allusions were made to the contents of this letter and to Greeley's personal animosity that at Greeley's request the letter was made public. Until Greeley had thus thrown his great *Tribune* into the contest against Seward's nomination Seward was the generally-accepted Republican candidate for President in

1860, and, notwithstanding the ability and influence exerted by Greeley and his newspaper, the Republicans of the country elected a convention overwhelmingly in favor of Seward. It was Greeley, however, who drove the entering wedge that made it possible to break the Seward column, and I shall never forget the smile that played upon his countenance as he sat at the head of the Oregon delegation in the Wigwam at Chicago and heard the announcement that Abraham Lincoln had been nominated as the candidate of the convention for President. He had made no battle for Lincoln. His candidate was Edward Bates of Missouri, whose cause he championed with all his fervency and power; but it is evident that in selecting Bates as his favorite he had been influenced solely to choose the most available candidate to contest the honor with Seward. After Bates, he was for any one to beat Seward, and when Lincoln became the chief competitor of Seward he was more than willing to accept him. After the nomination of Lincoln, Greeley's *Tribune* was leader of leaders among the Republican journals of the land in the great struggle that elected Lincoln President. But his rejoicing over the success of Lincoln was speedily chilled by the announcement that Seward would be called as premier of the new administration. The appointment of Seward as Secretary of State meant the mastery of Thurlow Weed in wielding the patronage and power of the administration in New York, and it meant much more than that to Greeley. It meant that all the power that Seward and Weed could exercise would be wielded relentlessly to punish Greeley for his revolt against Seward. On the very day that Lincoln entered the Presidency, therefore, Greeley was hopelessly embittered against him, and while no man in the whole land was more conscientious than Greeley in the performance of every patriotic and per-

sonal duty, he was also human, and with all his boundless generosity and philanthropy he was one of the best
haters I have ever known.

Soon after Lincoln's election Greeley put himself in
an attitude that he must have known at the time was an
utterly impossible one for Lincoln to accept. That he
was influenced in any degree by a desire to embarrass
Lincoln I do not for a moment believe, but it is none
the less the truth of history that, after having done
much to make Lincoln's nomination possible, he did
more perhaps than any one man in the country to assure
his election, and then he publicly demanded that Lincoln should be so far forgetful of his oath to maintain the
Constitution as to permit the Southern States to secede
in peace. Only three days after Lincoln's election Greeley published an editorial in the *Tribune* in which he
said: "If the Cotton States shall become satisfied that
they can do better out of the Union than in it, we insist
on letting them go in peace. . . . The right to secede
may be a revolutionary one, but it exists nevertheless.
We must ever resist the right of any State to remain in
the Union and nullify or defy the laws thereof. To
withdraw from the Union is quite another matter, and
whenever a considerable section of our Union shall deliberately resolve to get out we shall resist all coercive
measures designed to keep it in. We hope never to live
in a republic whereof one section is pinned to another
by bayonets." Again, on the 17th of December, 1860,
just after the secession of South Carolina, a leading editorial in the *Tribune*, speaking of the Declaration of
Independence, said: "If it justified the secession from
the British empire of three million of colonists in 1776,
we do not see why it would not justify the secession of
five million of Southerners from the Federal Union in
1861. . . . If seven or eight contiguous States shall pre-

sent themselves at Washington saying, 'We hate the Federal Union; we have withdrawn from it; we give you the choice between acquiescing in our secession and arranging amicably all incidental questions on the one hand, and attempting to subdue us on the other,' we would not stand up for coercion, for subjugation, for we do not think it would be just. We hold to the right of self-government even when invoked in behalf of those who deny it to others." Less than two weeks before the inauguration of Lincoln, on the 23d of February, 1861, and the same day on which his paper announced Lincoln's midnight journey from Harrisburg to Washington, Greeley said in a leading editorial: "We have repeatedly said, and we once more insist, that the great principle embodied by Jefferson in the Declaration of American Independence, that governments derive their just powers from the consent of the governed, is sound and just, and that if the Slave States, the Cotton States, or the Gulf States only choose to form an independent nation, they have a clear moral right to do so. Whenever it shall be clear that the great body of Southern people have become conclusively alienated from the Union and anxious to escape from it, we will do our best to forward their views."

Such were the pointed and earnest utterances of Greeley between the period of Lincoln's election and of his inauguration, and it is needless to say that these utterances not only grieved but embarrassed Lincoln to an extent that can hardly be appreciated at this time. Had Greeley stood alone in these utterances, even then his position and power would have made his attitude one of peculiar trouble to Lincoln, but he did not stand alone. Not only the entire Democratic party, with few exceptions, but a very large proportion of the Republican party, including some of its ablest and most trusted leaders, believed that peaceable secession, that might reasonably result in early reconstruction, was preferable to civil war. The constitutional right of coercion by the government upon a seceded State was gravely disputed by most Democratic statesmen and by many Republican statesmen; and it is worthy of note that Lincoln, like Buchanan, studiously avoided any attempt at coercion until the South wantonly precipitated war by firing upon the starving garrison in Fort Sumter. The first gun fired upon Sumter solved the problem of coercion. Coercion at once ceased to be an issue. The South had coerced the government into war by causelessly firing upon the flag of the nation and upon a garrison that had committed no overt act of war; and from that day until the surrender of the Southern armies to Grant and Sherman the overwhelming sentiment of every Northern State demanded the prosecution of the war to conquer Secession. Had Buchanan or Lincoln fired a single gun solely to coerce the Southern States to remain in the Union, the North would have been hopelessly divided, and the administration would surely have been overthrown in any attempt to prosecute the war. Greeley recognized the fact that the firing upon Sumter ended the issue of coercion as understood and discussed until that time, and from the day that Lincoln issued his call for seventy-five thousand troops to engage in the war that had been so insanely precipitated against the government he heartily sustained the President and his policy; but he added new grief and fresh embarrassments to Lincoln by his fretful impatience and his repeated and emphatic demands that the army should be hurled against the Confederates as soon as it was organized. "On to Richmond!" was his almost daily battle-cry, and Greeley was overwhelmed with sorrow and humiliation when at last his impetuous orders were obeyed and McDowell's army was defeated and hurled back into the intrenchments of Washington.

When war was accepted as a necessity no man in the country was more earnest in his support of a most vigorous and comprehensive war policy than was Greeley. After the lesson of the first Bull Run he appreciated the fact that a great war was upon us, and every measure looking to the increase of our armies and the maintenance of our severely strained credit was supported by the *Tribune* with all of Greeley's matchless ability and vigor; but he was never without some disturbing issue with Lincoln and the policy of the administration. Sincerely patriotic himself, he was as sincere in his convictions on all questions of public policy, and he seldom took pause to consider the claims of expediency when he saw what he believed to be the way dictated by the right. He believed Lincoln equally patriotic with himself, and equally sincere in every conviction and public act, but no two men were more unlike in their mental organization. Greeley was honest, aggressive, impulsive, and often ill advised in attempting to do the right thing in the wrong way. Lincoln was honest, patient, considerate beyond any man of his day, and calmly awaited the fullness of time for accomplishing the great achievements he hoped for. Writing of Lincoln some time after his death, Greeley said that after the war began "Lincoln's tenacity of purpose paralleled his former immobility; I believe he would have been nearly the last, if not the very last, man in America to recognize the Southern Confederacy had its armies been triumphant. He would have preferred death." That two such men should differ, and widely differ, and that Greeley should often differ in bitterness from Lincoln's apparent tardiness, was most natural; and with a great war constantly creating new issues of the gravest magnitude

Greeley was kept in constant conflict with Lincoln on some great question while honestly and patriotically supporting the government in the prosecution of the war.

The question of destroying slavery enlisted Greeley's most earnest efforts when it became evident that a great civil war must be fought for the preservation of the Union, and on that issue he fretted Lincoln more than any other one man in the United States, because he had greater ability and greater power than any whose criticisms could reach either Lincoln or the public. While the Cabinet had as much discord as there was between Lincoln and Greeley, and while even great Senators and Representatives of the same political faith with the President had serious dispute with him on the subject, Greeley was the most vexatious of all, for he was tireless in effort and reached the very heart of the Republican party in every State in the Union with his great newspaper. Notwithstanding the loyal support given to Lincoln by the Republicans throughout the country, Greeley was in closer touch with the active loyal sentiment of the people than even the President himself, and his journal constantly inspired not only those who sincerely believed in early Emancipation, but all who were inclined to factious hostility to Lincoln, to most aggressive efforts to embarrass the administration by untimely forcing the Emancipation policy. Finally, Greeley's patience became exhausted over what he regarded as the inexcusable inaction of Lincoln on the subject of Emancipation, and on the 20th of August, 1862, he published in his own newspaper an open letter to Lincoln denouncing him for his failure to execute the Confiscation Act in "mistaken deference to rebel slavery," for bowing to the influence of what he called "certain fossil politicians hailing from the Border States," and because our army officers "evinced far more solicitude to uphold slavery than to put down the rebellion." Thus plainly accused by one whose patriotism Lincoln did not question and whose honesty of purpose he could not doubt, Lincoln felt that he could no longer be silent, and on the 22d of August he addressed a letter to Greeley that did more to steady the loyal sentiment of the country in a very grave emergency than anything that ever came from Lincoln's pen. It is one of Lincoln's clearest and most incisive presentations of any question. Greeley, with all his exceptional tact and ability in controversy, was unable successfully to answer it. It was in that letter that Lincoln said: "I would save the Union; I would save it the shortest way under the Constitution;" and he followed these terse utterances with the statement, several times referred to in these articles, that he would save the Union either by the destruction or the maintenance of slavery as might best serve the great end he had in view. It should be remembered that at the time this letter was written by Lincoln to Greeley his draft of the Emancipation Proclamation had been prepared nearly one month, and precisely one month after he wrote the letter he issued his preliminary proclamation; but the letter gives no indication whatever as to his action on the issue beyond his concluding sentence, in which he says: "I intend no modification of my often expressed personal wish that all men for ever could be free."

This constant friction between Greeley and Lincoln logically led Greeley into the ranks of the opposition to Lincoln's renomination in 1864, and he labored most diligently to accomplish Lincoln's overthrow. His ripe experience in politics prevented him from falling in with the few disappointed Republican leaders who nominated Fremont at Cleveland before the Baltimore Convention met. He would gladly have joined in that effort had he not fully appreciated the fact that the occasion was too

21

momentous to organize a faction on personal or political grievances; but, while he kept aloof from the Fremont movement, he aggressively resisted the nomination of Lincoln, and on the day the convention met he published an earnest protest and indicated very clearly that Lincoln's nomination meant Republican defeat. He had long been in intercourse with the friends of Chase, and he would gladly have accepted Chase or Grant, or, indeed, almost any other Republican in the country whose name had been mentioned for the Presidency, in preference to Lincoln. When Lincoln was renominated by practically an unanimous vote, Greeley avoided direct antagonism to the party, but earnestly co-operated with Senator Wade and Representative Davis in their open rebellion against Lincoln. Wade and Davis issued an address to the people of the United States that appeared in Greeley's journal on the 5th of August, in which Lincoln was severely arraigned for usurping the authority of Congress and for withholding his approval to a bill presented to him just on the eve of adjournment, for the purpose, as they assumed, of holding "the Electoral votes of the rebel States at the dictation of his personal ambition." Such an appeal, coming from two of the ablest of the Republican leaders, cast a dark gloom over the prospects of the Republican party, and to the support of this revolt Greeley added an ostentatious and ill-advised effort to negotiate a peace through a plausible adventurer commonly known as "Colorado" Jewett. The effusive and irrepressible George N. Sanders was involved in it, and through Greeley they communicated to Lincoln a basis of peace that Greeley was led to believe the South would accept.

The terms suggested were the restoration of the Union, the abolition of slavery, universal amnesty, payment of $400,000,000 for the slaves, full representation to be given to the Southern States in Congress, and a National Convention to be called at once to engraft the new policy on the Constitution. Instead of maintaining the secresy necessary to the success of an adjustment of the difficulty between the sections then at war, the Greeley-Jewett negotiations soon became public, and Lincoln was earnestly importuned by Greeley to meet the emergency by opening the doors widely to the consideration of any proposition of peace. Lincoln, in his abundant caution, although entirely without hope of accomplishing anything by the Greeley negotiations, transmitted a paper to be delivered to the Confederates who were assuming to act for the South—a statement over his signature—saying that any proposition for "the restoration of peace, the integrity of the whole Union, and the abandonment of slavery, and which comes by and with an authority that can control the armies now at war against the United States, will be received and considered by the executive government of the United States, and will be met by liberal terms on other substantial and collateral points, and the bearer or bearers thereof shall have safe-conduct both ways." Greeley had become enthusiastic in his efforts to accomplish peace. He was a lover of peace, an earnest and inherent foe of the arbitrament of the sword under all circumstances, and when he found that the whole effort made to arrest fraternal war brought only a contemptuous rejection of Lincoln's proposition from those who assumed to represent the Confederate government, he was profoundly humiliated. It is fortunate for both Greeley and the country that Messrs. Clay and Holcombe, who assumed to speak for the Confederate government, refused even to consider the question of peace on the basis of a restored Union and the abandonment of slavery. Had they entertained the proposition, or even pretended to entertain it, they would have misled

Greeley into a violent crusade against the further prosecution of the war and into as violent hostility to the
re-election of Lincoln.

The pronounced anti-war platform of the Democratic
Convention that nominated McClellan against Lincoln
was even less to Greeley's liking than the attitude of the
Republicans, and finally, as the Wade and Davis manifesto seemed to have fallen stillborn upon the country,
and Greeley's negotiations for peace had ended disas-
trously, without credit to any, Greeley had no choice but
to fall in with the Lincoln procession and advocate the
success of the Republican ticket. Sherman's capture
of Atlanta and Sheridan's victories in the Valley started
the tidal wave in favor of Lincoln, and Greeley was quite
prepared, through his sad experiences in his hostility to
the administration, to fall in with the tide and share the
victory his party was then certain to win. After Lincoln's re-election there was little opportunity for Greeley
to take issue with Lincoln. During the winter of 1865
he earnestly favored every suggestion looking to the termination of the war upon some basis that would bring
the South back into cordial relations with the Union.
The failure of the Hampton Roads conference between
Lincoln and the Confederate Commissioners was regretted
by Greeley, but he no longer criticised Lincoln with his
old-time severity; and when, after Lee's surrender and
the final triumph of the Union cause, Lincoln's life was
taken by the assassin's bullet, Greeley and Lincoln were
more nearly in harmonious relations than they had ever
been at any time from the day of Lincoln's inauguration.
When the war ended Greeley was the first prominent
man of the country to demand universal amnesty and
impartial suffrage. A leading editorial in the *Tribune*
demanding the forgiveness of the insurgents as the price
of universal suffrage to the freedmen startled the coun-

try, and cost Greeley the Senatorial honors he much coveted.

While Greeley was one of the founders of the Republican party, and certainly did more to make it successful than any other one man of the nation, he gathered few of its honors and was seldom in harmony with Republican authority in State or nation. His rebellion against Seward in 1860 cost him an election to the United States Senate in 1861. His universal amnesty and suffrage policy, proclaimed immediately after the war, again defeated him as a Senatorial candidate in 1865, and while he accepted Grant for President in 1868 and supported his election with apparent cordiality, he very soon drifted into a hostile attitude toward the administration. Grant had none of Lincoln's patience and knew little of Lincoln's conciliatory methods; and when Greeley rebelled Grant allowed him to indulge his rebellious ideas to his heart's content. Long before the close of Grant's first administration Greeley was ripe for revolution, and was one of the earliest of those who inaugurated the Liberal Republican movement of 1872 that nominated Greeley as its candidate for President. I cordially sympathized with the revolt against Grant in 1872, and was chairman of the delegation from Pennsylvania in the Cincinnati Convention. My relations with Greeley had been of the most friendly character from the time I first met him when a boy-journalist at the Whig Convention in Philadelphia in 1848, and I not only profoundly respected his sincerity, his philanthropy, and his masterly ability, but I cherished an affection for him that I felt but for few, if any, of our public men. He was surprised when he learned from me, after the delegation to the Liberal Convention had been selected in Pennsylvania, that I was not urging his nomination for President. He believed that all my personal inclinations would make me favor him at any time that it might be in my power to do so, and he made an appointment by telegraph to meet me at the Colonnade Hotel in Philadelphia to discuss the question of the Presidency. We met at the appointed time, and I greatly pained Greeley when I told him that I did not believe his nomination would be a wise one, because I saw no possible chance for his election. He believed me when I assured him that I had no candidate whom I preferred to him, and that I was influenced solely by my desire to protect him from a great personal disaster and the country from a failure in the then promising effort to overthrow the despotic political rule that had obtained under Grant. I told him that I did not believe it possible for the Democrats to support him, and without their support his election would be utterly hopeless. After hearing me very fully, and evidently in great sorrow because of the attitude I assumed, he finally made this significant remark: "Well, perhaps the Democrats wouldn't take me head foremost, but they might take me boots foremost." I well understood that Greeley meant that while he might not be an available candidate for President, he might be an acceptable candidate for the second place on the ticket. I at once answered: "Yes, Mr. Greeley, with a conservative Republican for President you can easily be nominated for Vice-President and add great strength to the ticket." I said: "There are two names which seem to me to be the strongest—David Davis and Charles Francis Adams: which would you prefer?" Greeley answered: "The name of Adams leaves a bad taste in my mouth; I would prefer Davis;" and we finally agreed that I should go to the Cincinnati Convention and support the nomination of Davis for President and Greeley for Vice-President.

While I knew that Greeley most reluctantly gave up the idea of being nominated for President, I did not doubt that his candidacy for that office was practically ended by our conference. When I went to Cincinnati, I there met Leonard Swett, John D. Defrees, Senator Fenton, and others, and we started out to accomplish the nomination of Davis and Greeley. Some fifteen or twenty of us met at ten o'clock in the evening and decided on a programme by which we confidently expected to nominate Davis and Greeley on the first ballot. But while we were thus conferring General Frank P. Blair had gotten together a conference between some of the more radical supporters of Greeley and the supporters of B. Gratz Brown, and their conference ended by deciding to nominate Greeley for President and Brown for Vice-President. By this new combination we were deprived of the support of the important State of New York, and also lost a large support in the West. While many of the New York delegates would have preferred the nomination of Davis and Greeley, when Greeley was presented as a hopeful candidate for President the delegation naturally united in his support, and Brown brought into the combination a large number of Western delegates who would have preferred Davis had they been free to exercise their own judgment in selecting a candidate. Davis was thus practically out of the race, and after giving a complimentary vote to Curtin a large majority of the Pennsylvania delegation united with me in supporting the nomination of Adams. I did not regard Adams as possessing the qualities of availability presented in Davis, but Adams seemed to be the only man who had a reasonable prospect of winning the nomination over Greeley. I was placed in the most unpleasant attitude of supporting a man for President to whom I was almost an entire stranger, and for whom I had little personal sympathy, against Greeley, for whom I cherished the 'profoundest respect and affection.

On the first ballot Adams led Greeley by a vote of 203 to 147, with a large scattering vote between Trumbull, Brown, Davis, Curtin, and Chase. On the second ballot Adams rose to 243 and Greeley to 239, with Trumbull to 148. On the third ballot Adams had 264, Greeley 258, and Trumbull 156. On the fourth ballot Adams increased to 279, and Greeley fell off to 251, with Trumbull still holding 141. On the fifth ballot Adams had 309 and Greeley 258; and on the sixth and final ballot, as first reported, Greeley led Adams 8 votes, having 332 to Adams 324. This was the first ballot on which Greeley led Adams, and it clearly indicated that the convention was resistlessly drifting to Greeley as its candidate. There was at once a rush from different delegations to change votes from Adams to Greeley. I did not participate in it, and only when a majority of votes had been cast and recorded for him did I announce the change of the Pennsylvania delegation to Greeley. The ballot as finally announced was 482 for Greeley and 187 for Adams. While the balloting was in progress Greeley was sitting in his editorial room in the *Tribune* office along with one of his editorial assistants, who informed me that Greeley became intensely agitated as the sixth ballot developed his growing strength; and when the. telegrams announced that he led Adams on that vote, he excitedly exclaimed: "Why don't McClure change the vote of Pennsylvania?" The next bulletin he received announced his nomination, and he promptly telegraphed to Whitelaw Reid, then his chief editorial associate, who was in attendance at the convention: "Tender my grateful acknowledgments to the members of the convention for the generous confidence they have shown me, and assure them that I shall endeavor to deserve it."

I was greatly disappointed at the result of the convention, and was deeply grieved at what I regarded as a cruel sacrifice of one of the men I most loved and the surrender of a great opportunity to win a national victory in the interest of better government and sectional tranquility. The nomination of Greeley carried with it the nomination of B. Gratz Brown for Vice-President, and when the convention adjourned I returned to my room at the hotel feeling that our work was farcical, because I did not regard it as possible for the Democrats to accept Greeley. Before midnight, however, a number of leading Democrats from different parts of the country who were in constant touch with the convention pulled themselves together, and their utterances given to the world the next morning foreshadowed the possibility that the Democrats would accept Greeley and Brown; but even when the Democratic National Convention with substantial unanimity accepted both the candidates and the platform of the Liberal Republicans, I saw little hope for Greeley's election, as I feared that the Democratic rank and file could not be brought to his support. For some time after both conventions had nominated Greeley we had a Greeley tidal-wave that seemed likely to sweep the country. In Pennsylvania, as chairman of the Liberal State Committee, I had voluntary letters from hundreds of leading Republicans in every section of the State indicating their purpose to fall in with the Greeley current, but the loss of North Carolina early in August not only halted the Greeley tide, but made its returning ebb swift and destructive. With this obvious revulsion in the political current the great business interests of the country were speedily consolidated in opposition to any change in the national administration, and there never was a day after the North Carolina defeat when Greeley's election seemed to be within the range of possibility.

The September elections proved that Greeley's nomi-

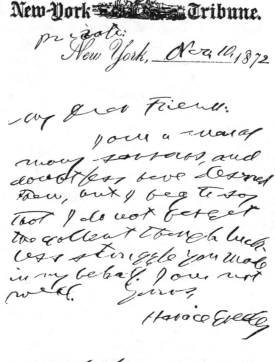

GREELEY'S LAST LETTER.

nation made no impression upon the Republicans in New England, including his native State of Vermont, where it was hoped he would have thousands of Republican followers, and the October elections came like an avalanche against the Liberal movement. Greeley delivered campaign speeches in New England and in the Middle States which were models of statesmanlike ability, but he was fighting a hopeless battle; and when the October elections cast their gloom upon his political hopes he was called to nurse a dying wife, where for nearly a month he passed sleepless nights, and closed her eyes in death only a week before his overwhelming defeat in November. Thus at once broken in heart and hope, the most brilliant and forceful editor the country has ever produced, and one of the sincerest and most tireless of American philanthropists, pined away in the starless midnight of an unsettled mind until the 29th of November, 1872, when he passed to his final account. Immediately after the election I had written him a personal letter expressing my sincere sympathy with him in his multiplied misfortunes. One of the most valued of my mementos of the men of the past is his reply, dated November 10th, the last day on which he ever wrote anything, as follows:

(*Private.*)

NEW YORK, November 10, 1872.

MY DEAR FRIEND :

I am a man of many sorrows, and doubtless have deserved them, but I beg to say that I do not forget the gallant though luckless struggle you made in my behalf. I am not well.

Yours truly,

HORACE GREELEY.

COL. A. K. MCCLURE,
144 So. Sixth St., Philada.

Thus ended one of the most useful and one of the saddest lives of the last generation. He was of heroic

mould in his matchless battles for the lowly and helpless, and was always invincible in political controversy,
because his integrity was ever as conspicuous as his ability; but he was as impatient as he was philanthropic,
and he most longed for what was so pointedly denied
him—the generous approval of his countrymen.   He
was made heart-sore when he saw the colored voters,
whose cause he had championed when no political party
had the courage to espouse it, almost unitedly oppose his
election to the Presidency; and finally, smitten in his
home, in his ambition, and in his great newspaper, Horace Greeley, broken in heart and hopelessly clouded in
intellect, gave up the battle of life, and slept with his
loved ones who had gone before.

(Photo by Gutekunst, Philadelphia.)

JOHN BROWN.

AN EPISODE OF JOHN BROWN'S RAID.

FAR down in the beautiful Cumberland Valley, the old-time heartsome village of Chambersburg was one of the chief attractions a generation ago. It was founded by the sturdy Scotch-Irish pioneers, who carried their severe religion and not less severe detestation of despotism with them, and mingled their prayers with their warfare against the savage and the soldiers of King George. The memorable pioneer whose name the village bears chose a lovely spot as his home and the heritage of his children, where the soft murmurs of the crystal waters of Falling Spring are lost in the Conococheague, and the united waters course through the centre of the town on their journey to the sea. Here more than a century had been devoted to the genial civilization that made Chambersburg first in the affections of its people; and its homes, palatial for that day; its grand elms and lindens which arched the walks with their shades; its cultured people, with just pride of ancestry and equal pride of present character and usefulness,—made it one of the most delightful of Pennsylvania towns for citizen or visitor. It had none of the paralysis that comes when "wealth accumulates and men decay;" large fortunes were unknown, but plenty, thrift, and comfort stamped their impress upon the community.

In the summer of 1859 a man of rather rude aspect, but of grave and quiet demeanor, was noticed by the

334

village crowd that usually gathered in social converse about the post-office while the evening mail was being distributed. He attracted little attention, as he seldom spoke save when spoken to, and then only in the briefest way. He was known as "Dr. Smith," and was reputed to be engaged in the development of iron-mines on the Potomac, some twenty-five miles distant. He lodged at a private boarding-house off from the centre of the town, and there was nothing in his sayings or doings to excite any apprehension that his mission was anything else than a peaceful one. This man was John Brown, then of Kansas fame, and later immortalized in song and story throughout every civilized land. The supposed mining-implements which he was storing in Chambersburg were the rude pikes with which the negroes of Virginia were to be armed in their expected insurrection against their masters. There was not a man, woman, or child in Chambersburg who then dreamed that "Dr. Smith" was John Brown—not one who knew or suspected his real purpose. None of the many who then saw him casually from day to day could have dreamed that the harmless-looking and acting "Dr. Smith" was engaged in a drama the sequel of which would be enacted when the vandals' torch left the beautiful old village in ashes only five years later. The South ever believed that John Brown made Chambersburg the base for his mad raid on Harper's Ferry because he had many sympathizing confidants and abetters there; and that unjust prejudice resolved all doubts as to dooming the town when McCausland rioted in its destruction on the 30th of July, 1864.

In the early part of October, 1859, two men, unknown to me, entered my office and asked to submit some legal matters in private. We retired to the private office, when the younger of the two, an intelligent and evidently positive man, gave his name as Francis Jackson

Meriam of Boston, and his companion gave his name as John Henry.   Meriam said that he was göing on a journey South; that he had some property at home; that accidents often happened to travelers; and that he desired me to draw his will.   I did so, and was not surprised that a young Boston traveler, after making a few special bequests, gave his property to the Abolition Society of his native State.   There was nothing in his appearance, manner, or conversation to attract any special attention to his proceeding, and his will was duly executed, witnessed, and, in obedience to his orders, mailed to the executor in Boston.   When I asked Meriam's companion to witness the will, he declined, saying that he was a traveler also, and that both the witnesses had better be in the same town.   His real reasons for declining to witness the will of his friend were—first, that "John Henry" was none other than John Henry Kagi, and, second, because he presumed his life to be as much in peril as was that of his friend.   The sequel proved that he judged well, for Kagi was killed in the attack on Harper's Ferry, while Meriam escaped.   When the two visitors left they were no more thought of in the village lawyer's office until the startling news came of Brown's attempt to capture Harper's Ferry and to arm the slaves of Virginia in general insurrection.   Then, to my surprise, I read the name of the testator in the will I had written a short time before, and the name and description of another assured me that his fellow-visitor in my office was the then fallen John Henry Kagi.

It may be remembered that of the twenty-one who composed John Brown's army of invasion, Watson Brown, Oliver Brown, John Henry Kagi, Adolphus Thompson, and Stewart Taylor, whites, and Sherrard Lewis Leary, Dangerfield Newby, and Jeremiah Anderson, colored, were killed in the battle, and that William

H. Leeman and William Thompson were killed in attempting to retreat. Owen Brown, Barclay Coppoch, Charles P. Tidd, and Francis Jackson Meriam, whites, and Osborne P. Anderson, colored, escaped. They made their way through the forests of the South Mountain to Chambersburg, traveling only by night; were concealed in a retired grove near Chambersburg for several days to enable the wounded men of the party to recruit their strength, and then went on by short night-marches across the North Mountain to the Juniata Valley, near Bell's Mills, where they were taken in charge by a prominent citizen of Harrisburg, whose dust has long mouldered with that of John Brown. Meriam left the party at Chambersburg, took the cars, and went through to Boston without detection. Only two residents of Chambersburg knew of the presence of the fugitives, and they are no longer numbered among the citizens of the town whose history forms such an important chapter in the annals of our terrible civil war. John E. Cook, Edwin Coppoch, Aaron Dwight Stevens, and Albert Hazlitt, whites, and John Copeland and Shields Green, colored, were captured, and, with John Brown their leader, convicted of murder at Charlestown, Virginia, and executed in December, 1859. Hazlitt was the first of the fugitives captured in Pennsylvania. He was arrested while walking along the Cumberland Valley Railroad near Shippensburg, and lodged in the jail at Carlisle. His captors supposed him to be Captain Cook, and that error cost Cook his life on the gibbet. A requisition was quietly obtained from Richmond for the rendition of Cook. When it arrived the identity of Hazlitt had been established, but the requisition remained within thirty miles of Chambersburg, to surprise Cook and return him to Virginia just when he had perfected his plans for escape. Cook was the last of the fugitives to be cap-

22

tured, and the circumstances and manner of his arrest, the strange miscarriage of his apparently certain opportunities of escape, and his heroism in the lawless cause that so blindly misguided him make a truthful story before which the fascinating inventions of romance pale.

I was the counsel of John E. Cook in Chambersburg, and the only person entirely familiar with the inner history of his capture and the plans of escape. The community of which Chambersburg was the centre of business and sentiment was nearly equally divided on the political issues of that day; but the undertow of anti-slavery conviction was stronger than the partisan dogmas which made one-half the people declare slavery a lawful and therefore a defensible institution. Fervent and eloquent speeches would be made on the stump in every campaign against interference with slavery and in favor of the faithful observance of the mandates of the Constitution, and glittering resolves would emanate from party conventions in favor of the Union, the Constitution, and the laws; but the practical division of the community on the issues of obedience to the Constitution and the laws which commanded the rendition of fugitive slaves left here and there a despised negro-catcher on the one side and all the people on the other side. There was no Democrat in Franklin County to accept a commissionership under the Fugitive Slave Law. I have seen two Democratic president judges administer the laws with a singleness of purpose to hold the scales of justice in even balance; and I have known a prominent Democratic candidate for the same position, once a member of Congress, who publicly demanded justice to the South by the rendition of slaves; but all of them would feed the trembling sable fugitive, hide him from his pursuers, and bid him God-speed on his journey toward the North Star. The Democratic president judge who personally remanded Captain

Cook to the custody of the Virginia authorities for execution would have assented to and aided his escape had
they met simply as man and man outside the sacred obli-
gations of the law. There was no sentiment in Franklin County or elsewhere in the North to give any practical
enforcement to the Fugitive Slave Law; and in every
contest between slave and master and in every issue relating to slavery the people were profoundly anti-slavery,
however they resolved in convention or spoke in the
forum or voted at the polls. This statement of the public sentiment that prevailed a quarter of a century ago
in Southern Pennsylvania, hard by the slave border, and
which was but a reflex of the sentiment of the North
that gave practical effect to its teachings, will make the
story of Captain Cook's apparently certain but singularly-
defeated opportunities of escape better understood.

It had been known for some days after the Brown raid
on Harper's Ferry that Captain Cook was at large, and,
as a liberal reward for his capture had been offered by
Governor Wise of Virginia, and a minute description of
his person published throughout the country, the whole
skilled and amateur detective force of the land was
watching every promising point to effect his capture.
The Northern cities, East and West, were on the watch
to discover his hiding-place, but the forest-schooled and
nature-taught detective of the South Mountain knew
that some of its fastnesses must be his retreat. The
broken ranges of the mountain on the southern border
of Franklin embraced the line between Pennsylvania
and Maryland, between the free and the slave States.
It was the favorite retreat of the fugitive slave, and its
nearness to Harper's Ferry, and its sacred temples of
solitude where only the hunter or the chopper wandered,
made it the most inviting refuge for the fleeing insurrec-
tionist. Cook was known as a man of desperate courage,

as a rare expert in the use of pistol and rifle, as a reckless desperado in the anti-slavery crusade; and his capture alive was not expected. He had braved assassination in Kansas, and all believed that he would resist to the death any attempt to capture him for Virginia vengeance on the gallows. He had been concealed in the mountain-recesses for some days with his companions, who subsequently escaped through Chambersburg to the North, when he decided to seek out some woodman's home and obtain provisions. They were afraid to shoot game, lest the reports of their guns might indicate their retreat and lead to their capture. Cook was of a nervous, restless, reckless disposition, and he started out alone, going he knew not whither, to obtain food. He reasoned plausibly that he could not be captured by any one or two men, as he was well armed and thoroughly skilled in the use of his weapons. He took no thought of arrest, as, had a score of armed men confronted him, he would have sold his life as dearly as possible and died in the battle for his liberty. He understood that he might die any day or hour, but to be made a prisoner and be rendered up to Virginia justice to die on the gibbet was the one doom that he meant to escape. He felt safe, therefore, in his venture out in the pathless mountains to claim the hospitality of some humble home in the wilderness. And his judgment would have been justified had he not walked into the hands of the only man in Franklin County who combined with the courage and the skill the purpose to capture him.

Among the sturdy population of the mountaineers on the southern Pennsylvania border was a family of Logans. There were two brothers, both shrewd, quiet, resolute men, both strongly Southern in their sympathies, both natural detectives, and both trained in the summary rendition of fugitive slaves without process of law. It

was common for slaves to escape from Maryland and
Virginia into the South Mountain, whose broken spurs
and extended wings of dense forest gave them reasonably
safe retreat. Their escape would be followed by hand-
bills describing the fugitives and offering rewards for
their capture and return. These offers of rewards always
found their way into the hands of Daniel and Hugh
Logan, and many fleeing sons of bondage were arrested
by them and quietly returned to their masters. Hugh
followed his natural bent and went South as soon as the
war began. He at once enlisted in the Confederate service, rose to the rank of captain, and was the guide in
General Stuart's raid to Chambersburg in October, 1862.
He then saved me from identification and capture, although my arrest was specially ordered, with that of a
dozen others, in retaliation of Pope's arrest of Virginia
citizens; and I was glad at a later period of the war to
save him from summary execution as a supposed bush-
whacker by General Kelley. Whatever may be said or
thought of his convictions and actions, he sealed them
with his life, as he fell mortally wounded in one of the
last skirmishes of the war. His brother Daniel was less
impulsive, and he did not believe that either slavery or
freedom was worth dying for. He was then just in the
early vigor of manhood and a man of rare qualities.
He possessed the highest measure of courage, but never
sought and seldom shared in a quarrel. He was a complete picture of physical strength, compactly and sym-
metrically formed, and with a face whose clear-cut features unmistakably indicated his positive qualities. He
was a born detective. Silent, cunning, tireless, and resolute, he ever exhausted strategy in his many campaigns
against fugitives, and he seldom failed. Had he been
city-born, with opportunities for culture in the profession, Logan would have made one of the best chiefs

of a detective bureau to be found in the country. But, mountain-born, unschooled save by himself, and trained only in the rude contests with fugitive slaves and an occasional criminal in the border wilderness, he finally wearied of his trade, and his arrest of Captain Cook was his last exploit in the detective line. He subsequently removed to Lancaster, where a very quiet, well-to-do, well behaved, and respected dealer in horses answers to the name of Daniel Logan.

In a mountain-ravine near Mont Alto Furnace, Cleggett Fitzhugh, manager of the works, and a man of Southern birth and strong Southern sympathies, was overseeing a number of men at work, and Daniel Logan had happened to come that way and was engaged in casual conversation with him. The ravine is so hidden by the surrounding forest that one unacquainted with the locality would not know of its existence until he entered it. Captain Cook, in his wanderings in search of food, was surprised to find himself suddenly emerge from the mountain-thicket into an open space and within less than fifty yards of a number of workmen. He was clad and armed as a hunter, and he at once decided to evade suspicion by boldly meeting the men he could not hope to escape by flight. The moment he appeared the keen eye of Logan scanned him, and, without betraying his discovery in any way, he quietly said to Fitzhugh, "That's Captain Cook; we must arrest him; the reward is one thousand dollars." Fitzhugh heartily sympathized with Logan alike in hatred of the John Brown raiders and in desire for the reward, and he knew enough about Logan to say nothing and obey. Cook advanced in a careless manner to Logan and Fitzhugh, and told them that he was hunting on the mountains and wanted to replenish his stock of bread and bacon. Logan at once disarmed suspicion on the part of Cook by his well-affected hospitality, as he proposed to go at once with Cook to Logan's store—which had no existence, by the way—and supply the hunter's wants. Cook was so completely thrown off guard by the kind professions of Logan and Fitzhugh that he fell in between them without noticing how he was being flanked. His gun rested carelessly on his shoulder, and the hand that could grasp his pistol and fire with unerring aim in the twinkling of an eye was loosely swinging by his side. None but a Daniel Logan could have thus deceived John E. Cook, who had studied men of every grade in many perils; but there was not the trace of excitement or the faintest betrayal of his desperate purpose on the face of Logan. Thus completely disarmed by strategy, the little blue-eyed blonde, the most sympathetic and the fiercest of all John Brown's lieutenants, was instantly made powerless, as two rugged mountaineers, at a signal from Logan, grasped his arms and held him as in a vice. Cook was bewildered for a moment, and when the truth flashed upon him he struggled desperately; but it was one small, starved man against two strong mountaineers, and he soon discovered that resistance was vain.

"Why do you arrest me?" was his inquiry, when he perceived that violence was useless.

"Because you are Captain Cook," was the cool reply of Logan.

Cook neither affirmed nor denied the impeachment, and the speedy search of his person settled the question, as his captain's commission in John Brown's army was found in an inner pocket. Cook was taken to Fitzhugh's house and stripped of his weapons, consisting of gun, revolver, and knife. He was allowed to eat a hasty meal, and was then placed, unbound, in an open buggy with Logan, to be taken to Chambersburg. He was informed that if he attempted to escape he would be shot; and it did not need an extended acquaintance with his captor to assure him that what he threatened he would certainly perform. He then gave up all hope of escape by either fight or flight. As they were journeying along the eighteen miles Cook found that his captor was less bloodthirsty than mercenary; and the following conversation, subsequently repeated to me by both parties, passed substantially between them:

"You will get a reward of one thousand dollars for me, you say?" queried Cook.

"Yes, a thousand dollars," answered the sententious Logan.

"They will hang me in Virginia, won't they?" was Cook's next inquiry.

"Yes, they will hang you," was the chilling answer.

"Do you want to have me hung?" was Cook's first venture upon the humane side of his captor.

"No," was the prompt but unimpassioned answer of Logan.

"Then you want only the reward?" was Cook's half-hopeful appeal to Logan.

"Yes; that's all," was Logan's reply.

Cook's naturally bright face beamed at once with hope as he enthusiastically entered into various plans for the payment of the sum that would ransom his life. He told Logan how a thousand dollars, or five times that sum, would not be a matter of a moment's consideration to his brother-in-law, Governor Willard of Indiana, or his other brother-in-law, a man of large fortune residing in Brooklyn; but Logan distrusted this story of high dignitaries and large fortunes, and no practical way seemed open to make Cook's credit good enough to assure his discharge. Finally, he inquired of Logan whether there was no one in Chambersburg who would be likely to take an interest in him, and who could act as his counsel and

assure Logan of the payment of the reward. Logan
named me as a Republican Senator just elected, who
might agree to act as his counsel. He proposed to take
Cook to my office without revealing his identity to any
others, and if I assured him of the payment of the reward he would walk away and leave Cook with me.
With this truce between captor and captive they arrived
in Chambersburg a little before sunset, put up at a hotel,
and Logan sent for me. I had walked out to the southern suburbs of the town that evening after tea to look at
some lots, and on my way back had stopped with a circle
of men gathered about a small outskirt store. We had
just closed one of the most desperate local contests of
the State, and only those who know the sunny side of
village politics can appreciate how an evening hour or
more could thus be pleasantly spent. It was an out-of-
the-way place, and among the last that would be thought
of in deciding to look for me. Meantime, Logan had
me searched for in every place where I was accustomed
to stroll in the evening, until, as it grew late, his evident
concern attracted attention, and he feared the discovery
or suspicion of the identity of his prisoner. When darkness began to gather and all efforts to find me had been
unsuccessful, he sent for an officer and started with his
prisoner for the office of Justice Reisher, to deliver Cook
to the custody of the law. The office of the justice was
on the main street, about midway between the hotel and
the suburban store where I had tarried, and as I walked
leisurely homeward I noticed a crowd about the door of
the little temple of justice. As I came up to the door
Logan first noticed me from the inside, and hurried out
to meet me, exclaiming in a whisper, with a betrayal of
excitement that I had never before seen in him, "My
God, Colonel McClure! where have you been? I have
been hunting you for more than an hour. That's Cap-

tain Cook, and I had agreed to bring him to you. Can't you get him yet?"

I was greatly surprised, of course, and equally perplexed at the grave results likely to follow. I quietly pressed my way into the office until the justice noticed me, and he at once addressed Cook, saying, "Here's your counsel now."

Cook beckoned me to his side in the corner, and said, in a tone of visible despair, "I had expected to meet you at your office and escape this misfortune." He added, "I am Cook: there's no use in denying it. What's to be done?"

I turned to the justice, and said, "There is no dispute as to the identity of the prisoner: a hearing is needless. Let him be committed to await the demand for his rendition."

The justice would have been quite content had Cook been able to bounce through a window and escape, but that was not possible, and Cook was committed to prison. Logan repented of his work when he saw that he had surrendered a life for a price, and his last direction to me as we passed out of the office was, "Get Cook away, reward or no reward."

Cook was conducted to the old jail, accompanied by the officer and myself; and I shall never forget the tremulous voice in which the sheriff inquired of me what precautions he should take to secure the prisoner. I was in the doubly unpleasant position of being counsel for a prisoner whose life depended upon his escape from prison, and also counsel for the sheriff, who was more than ready to obey any instructions I might give him to facilitate Cook's escape without legal responsibility for the act. The sheriff was one of a class of simple countrymen who are as rugged in their political convictions and prejudices as in their physical organization. He ill concealed his willingness to let Cook get away if it could be done without official responsibility for the escape; and this he was more than willing to leave me to decide. I told him to take Cook and myself to a cell, leave us together, and admit no others. When the lawless little captive had got comfortably seated in his cell, I had my first opportunity to note his appearance and qualities. His long, silken, blonde hair curled carelessly about his neck; his deep-blue eyes were gentle in expression as a woman's; and his slightly bronzed complexion did not conceal the soft, effeminate skin that would have well befitted the gentler sex. He was small in stature, barely five feet five, and his active life on the Western theatre of war had left him without superfluous flesh. He was nervous and impatient; he spoke in quick, impulsive sentences, but with little directness, save in repeating that he must escape from prison. I reminded him that he could not walk out of jail, and that his escape that night, under any circumstances, would be specially dangerous to himself and dangerous to the sheriff. My presence with him in the jail until a late hour and my professional relations as counsel of the sheriff forbade any needless haste. We carefully considered every possible method of getting a requisition for him from Richmond; and, assuming that Cook's arrest was telegraphed to Richmond that evening, a requisition by mail or special messenger could not possibly reach Chambersburg the next day or night. It was decided, therefore, that he should not attempt to escape that night, but that the next night he should have the necessary instructions and facilities to regain his liberty. How or by whom he was to be aided need not be told. The two men who took upon themselves the work of ascertaining just where and by what means Cook could best break out of the old jail were never known or suspected as actively aiding the prisoner. One is now dead and the other is largely interested in Southern enterprises. They did their part well, and, had Cook remained in Chambersburg over the next day, he would have been following the North Star before the midnight hour.

I had spent half an hour with Cook when he first entered the prison, and then left him for an hour to confer with my law-partner about the possibility of a legal contest to delay or defeat the requisition in case it should be necessary. I returned to the jail about ten o'clock, and had my last interview with Cook. As he never dreamed of a requisition reaching him before the second day, and as he was entirely confident of his escape the following night, he threw off the cloud of despair that shadowed him in the early part of the evening, and startled me with the eloquence and elegance of his conversation. His familiar discussion of poetry, painting, and everything pertaining to the beautiful would have made any one forget that he was in a chilly prison-cell, and imgine that he was in the library of some romantic lover of literature and the fine arts. I became strangely interested in the culture that was blended with the mad desperation of the Virginia insurgent. He was evidently a man of much more than common intellectual qualities and thoroughly poetic in taste and temperament, with a jarring mixture of wild, romantic love of the heroic. He told me of his hairbreadth escapes in Kansas, of the price set upon his head; and his whole soul seemed to be absorbed in avenging the Kansas slavery crusades by revolutionary emancipation in the Slave States. When I asked him whether he would not abandon his lawless and hopeless scheme when he escaped, his large, soft eyes flashed with the fire of defiance as he answered, with an emphasis that unstrung every nerve in his body: "No!

the battle must be fought to the bitter end; and we must triumph, or God is not just.''

It was vain to argue with him the utter madness of attempting such a revolution, and its absolute lawlessness: he rejected all law and logic and believed in his cause. And more: he fully, fanatically, believed in its justice: he believed in it as a duty—as the rule of patriotism that had the sanction of a higher law than that of man. In short, John E. Cook was a wild fanatic on the slavery question, and he regarded any and every means to precipitate emancipation as justified by the end. He did not want to kill or to desolate homes with worse than death by the brutal fury of slave insurrection; but if such appalling evils attended the struggle for the sudden and absolute overthrow of slavery, he was ready to accept the responsibility and believe that he was simply performing his duty. I do not thus present Cook in apology for his crime; I present him as he was—a sincere fanatic, with mingled humanity and atrocity strangely unbalancing each other, and his mad purposes intensified by the barbarities which crimsoned the early history of Kansas.

After half an hour thus spent almost wholly as a listener to the always brilliant and often erratic conversation of the prisoner, I rose to leave him. He bade me good-night with hope beaming in every feature of his attractive face. I engaged to call again the next afternoon, and left him to meet nevermore. He could have made his escape in thirty minutes that night, but it would have compromised both the sheriff and myself, and the second opportunity for his flight was lost. I reached my home before eleven o'clock, and was surprised to find Mrs. McClure and her devoted companion, Miss Virginia Reilly, awaiting me in the library, dressed to face the storm that had begun to rage without. They stated that they were about to proceed to the jail, ask to see Cook—which they knew would not be refused them by the sheriff—dress him in the extra female apparel they had in a bundle, and one of them walk out with him while the other remained in the cell. It was entirely practicable, and it required more than mere protestation on my part to prevent it. Even when assured that Cook would certainly escape the following night without embarrassment to the sheriff or any one else, the woman's intuition rejected the reason it could not answer, and only when it was peremptorily forbidden as foolish and needless did they reluctantly consent to abandon the last chance Cook could then have to escape. They were both strongly anti-slavery by conviction, and their lives were lustrous in the offices of kindness. Miss Reilly, better known in Philadelphia as the late accomplished wife of Rev. Thomas X. Orr, was the daughter of a Democratic member of Congress, and was positive in her party faith in all save slavery; and both women were of heroic mould. They many times reproached themselves for not acting upon their woman's intuition without waiting to reason with man on the subject. Had they done so, Cook would have been out of prison, fleetly mounted, and the morning sun would have greeted him in the northern mountains. Their mission failed because forbidden when the escape of the prisoner by other means seemed as certain as anything could be in the future, and the ill-fated Cook lost his third chance for liberty. Both his fair would-be rescuers sleep the dreamless sleep of the dead, and the winds of the same autumn sang their requiem and strewed their fresh graves with Nature's withered emblems of death.

About noon on the following day the sheriff rushed into my office, wild with excitement and his eyes dimmed by tears, and exclaimed, "Cook's taken away!" A thunderbolt from a cloudless sky could not have startled me more, but the painful distress of the sheriff left no doubt in my mind that he had stated the truth. He soon calmed down sufficiently to tell me how a requisition for Cook had been lying in Carlisle, only thirty miles distant by railroad, where it had been brought some days before when Hazlitt had been arrested and was believed to be Cook. The error had been corrected when the identity of Hazlitt had been discovered, and another requisition forwarded, on which he had been returned to Virginia; but the Cook requisition remained with the sheriff of Cumberland. When Cook's arrest was announced the requisition was brought on to Chambersburg in the morning train, and the officer, fearing delay by the sheriff sending for his counsel, called on the president judge, who happened to be in the town, and demanded his approval of the regularity of his papers and his command for the prompt rendition of the prisoner. The judge repaired to the prison with the officer, and performed his plain duty under the law by declaring the officer entitled to the custody of Cook. The noon train bore the strangely ill-served prisoner on his way to Virginia and to death. No man in like peril ever seemed to have had so many entirely practicable opportunities for escape; but all failed, even with the exercise of what would be judged as the soundest discretion for his safety.

His return to the Charlestown jail, his memorable trial, his inevitable conviction, hsi only cowardly act of submitting to recapture when he had broken out of his cell a few hours before his execution, and his final execution with his captive comrades,—are familiar to all. His trial attracted more attention than that of any of the others, because of the prominent men enlisted in his cause and of the special interest felt in him by the community in and about Harper's Ferry. He had taught

school there some years before, had married there, and
his return as one of John Brown's raiders to kindle the
flame of slave insurrection intensified the bitterness of
the people against him.   From the 28th day of October,
1859, when he was lodged in the Charlestown jail, until
the last act of the tragedy, when he was executed, Cook
attracted the larger share of public interest in Harper's
Ferry, much as Brown outstripped him in national or
worldwide fame.   Governor Willard, the Democratic
executive of Indiana, appeared in person on the scene,
and made exhaustive efforts to save his wayward but beloved brother-in-law.   Daniel W. Voorhees, now United
States Senator from Indiana, was then United States District Attorney of his State, and his devotion to his party
chief made him excel every previous or later effort of his
life in pleading the utterly hopeless cause of the brilliant
little Virginia insurgent.   It was a grand legal and for-
ensic battle, but there was not an atom of law to aid the
defense, and public sentiment was vehement for the
atonement.

Viewed in the clearer light and calmer judgment of
the experience of more than thirty years, it would have
been wiser and better had Virginia treated John Brown
and his corporal's guard of madmen as hopeless lunatics
by imprisonment for life, as was strongly advised by confidential counsels from some prominent men of the land
whose judgment was entitled to respect; but Governor
Wise, always a lover of the theatrical, made a dress-
parade burlesque of justice, and on the 16th day of December, 1859, amidst the pomp and show of the concentrated power of the Mother of Presidents, John E. Cook
paid the penalty of his crime on the gallows.   No demand
was ever made for the rendition of Cook's companions
who had escaped from Harper's Ferry into the South
Mountain with him.   Some of them lived in Northern

Pennsylvania without concealment, but no one thought of arresting them. A few months thereafter the long-threatening clouds of fraternal war broke in fury upon the country; the song of John Brown inspired great armies as they swept through the terrible flame of battle from the Father of Waters to the Southern Sea, and the inspiration that made lawless madmen of Brown and Cook at Harper's Ferry crowned the Republic with universal freedom at Appomattox.

23

OUR UNREWARDED HEROES.

OUR UNREWARDED HEROES.

ALL great wars produce great victors, and they are crowned with the greenest laurels of the people for whose cause they have achieved success. These chieftains live in history and their memory is gratefully cherished long after they have passed away ; but every great war has also its unrewarded heroes, whose merits are often equal to, sometimes even greater than, those who attained the highest measure of distinction. In war and politics nothing is successful but success, and the unsuccessful military commander and the unsuccessful politician are forgotten, whatever may be their personal merits, while those who win victories win the applause of the world. Accident, fortuitous circumstance, and personal or political influence aid largely in winning promotion in both peace and war, and a lost battle, however bravely and skillfully fought, often deposes a commander, while a victory won, even in spite of the absence of the elements of greatness, may make a name immortal. The rewarded heroes of our late civil war are well known to the country and to the world, but that great conflict left unrewarded heroes whose names and merits should be crystallized in the history of the Republic. Prominent among these are General George G. Meade, General George H. Thomas, General Fitz John Porter, General G. K. Warren, and General D. C. Buell.

The country has never done justice to General Meade

as a military commander, and our varied histories, as a rule, have grudgingly conceded to him only what could not be withheld from him. The man who fought and won the battle of Gettysburg should have been the commander-in-chief of the armies of the Union and held that position during life. It was the great battle of the war; it was the Waterloo of the Confederacy, and the victory there achieved was won by the skill of the commanding general and the heroism of his army. No man ever accepted a command under circumstances as embarrassing and in every way discouraging as those which confronted General Meade when he succeeded Hooker as commander of the Army of the Potomac. That superb army had never up to that time won a decisive victory in a great battle. It had been defeated in 1861 under McDowell, in the spring of 1862 under McClellan on the Peninsula, again under Pope on the second Bull Run field, next under Burnside at Fredericksburg in the fall of 1862, and in 1863 under Hooker at Chancellorsville; and the only success it had achieved in pitched battle was the victory of Antietam. That was a victory only because Lee left the field unassailed after the battle had been fought. Meade was called to the command within three days of the battle of Gettysburg, and was compelled to advance to meet the strongest and most defiant army that ever marched under the Confederate flag, and one that fully equaled his in numbers and that was flushed with repeated triumphs. His army was fresh from the humiliating discomfiture of Chancellorsville, distrustful of its own ability because of distrust in its commanders, and it had to be concentrated by forced marches to meet the shock of battle on Cemetery Hill.

The Gettysburg campaign was in all material respects defensive. The government had little hope of anything more than repelling Lee's advance upon the national capital or upon Baltimore or Philadelphia. The destruction of Lee's army was not to be thought of, for it was equal in numbers, equipment, and prowess to the ever-gallant though often-defeated Army of the Potomac. It was the single hope of the nation, for had it been defeated in a great battle Washington and the wealth of our Eastern cities would have been at the mercy of the insurgents. It was an occasion for the most skillful and prudent generalship, united with the great courage essential to command successfully in such an emergency. All these high requirements General Meade fully met, and the most critical examination of the records he made in the Gettysburg campaign develops nothing but what heightens his qualities for the peculiarly grave emergency that confronted him. He has been thoughtlessly or maliciously criticised because he took the wise precaution to provide for his retreat from Gettysburg had the chances of war made it necessary, and also because he failed to pursue Lee more vigorously on the retreat, and decided not to assault him at Williamsport.

When General Meade arrived at Gettysburg, which he did at the earliest hour possible, he knew how desperate the battle must be and how the advantage was with the enemy, as Lee had largely superior numbers on the first day, and should have had largely superior numbers on the second day. Not until the morning of the third day was Meade's army all upon the field, and then one corps had made a forced march of nearly thirty miles. He had expected to fight a defensive battle east of Gettysburg, and his topographical examinations had been carefully made and his lines fully formulated. He thus acted as a wise and skillful general in making the earliest preparations for the retirement of his army to another position in case he should be assaulted or flanked from his lines on Cemetery Hill. He was thus prepared to retire his army at any moment in perfect order, with every corps advised precisely where to form its new lines; but he proved by the dauntless courage with which he held his position at Gettysburg that he did not contemplate retreat until retreat became an absolute necessity. So far from being complained of for having looked beyond Gettysburg for a position in which to fight the decisive battle with Lee, he is entitled to the highest commendation as a most skillful, brave, and considerate soldier.

When Lee was defeated and retired from the field, the Army of the Potomac was worn by forced marches and fighting for more than a week, and more than twenty thousand of its gallant warriors were killed or wounded, and when the two armies were brought face to face again at Williamsport, they were yet equal in numbers, equal in prowess, and presumably equal in equipment, and Lee had the advantage of a chosen position for repelling assaults upon his lines. Meade might have won another victory, but it would have been at such fearful sacrifice that no wise soldier would have attempted it. After Gettysburg, General Meade had but a single opportunity of displaying his generalship in handling the Army of the Potomac, and that was in the fruitless movement upon Mine Run, where by disobedience of his orders, owing to a mistake of one of his corps commanders, Lee was enabled to unite his forces in an impregnable position before the Army of the Potomac was ready for assault. He might have done at Mine Run as Grant did at Vicksburg and Cold Harbor, and as Burnside did at Fredericksburg, and sacrificed ten thousand men with only defeat as his reward; but General Meade was too great a soldier to sacrifice an army to conceal failures in generalship. General Grant, the victor of Vicksburg on the same day that Meade was victor at Gettysburg, added fresh laurels to his crown at Missionary Ridge, where he had overwhelming numbers to assure success. That achievement made him Lieutenant-General, as Meade would have been made had he succeeded at Mine Run and Grant failed at Missionary Ridge, and thenceforth Grant was the only chieftain the nation could know until his final victory at Appomattox.

I first saw General Meade on the day that he reported for duty at Tenleytown, wearing his new brigadier's uniform, to take command of a brigade of the Pennsylvania Reserves. He impressed me then, as he ever impressed those who came in close contact with him, as a thorough gentleman and soldier, quiet, unobtrusive, intelligent, and heroic, and in every battle in which he led his brigade or his division or his corps he was ever first in the fight and last to leave it. He would have won Fredericksburg had he been half supported, as his movement in the early part of the day was the only success achieved by any effort of the army in that disastrous battle; and when he was called to the command of the Army of the Potomac he hesitated long before accepting it, and finally accepted it only when it was pressed upon him as an imperious duty that he could not evade.

I have reason to believe that Meade lost the Lieutenant-Generalship that was conferred upon Sheridan in 1869 because of the disappointment in Washington at his failure to deliver battle to Lee at Williamsport. I saw Lincoln within a week after Lee's retreat from Pennsylvania, and he inquired most anxiously and in great detail as to all the roads and mountain-passes from Gettysburg to the Potomac. I was entirely familiar with them, and gave him minute information on the subject. After a somewhat protracted inquiry into the topography of the country, I asked Lincoln whether he was not satisfied with what Meade had accomplished. He answered with the caution that always characterized Lincoln in

speaking of those who were struggling for the preservation of the government.   I remember his exact language
as well to-day as if it had been spoken but yesterday.
He said. "Now, don't misunderstand me about General
Meade.   I am profoundly grateful down to the bottom of
my boots for what he did at Gettysburg, but I think that
if I had been General Meade I would have fought another battle."   The atmosphere about Washington was
not friendly to Meade.   He was all soldier, and would
have died unpromoted had he been compelled to seek
or conciliate political power to attain it.   Stanton raved
against him because he did not do the impossible thing
of capturing Lee and his army, and political sentiment
in and around the administration and in Congress settled
down in the conviction that Meade had lost a great opportunity.   They would have deified Meade, when terror-
stricken as Lee was marching upon Gettysburg, had he
given them the assurance that he could drive Lee's army
back defeated and broken upon its desolated Virginia
homes; but when their fears were quieted by Meade's
hard-fought battle and decisive victory, they forgot the
grandeur of his achievement and accused him of incompetency for failing to fight at Williamsport.   Had he
fought there and been repulsed, as he had every reason
to believe was more than probable had he attacked, he
would have been denounced as rash and unfitted for command; but he was censured for his wisdom; multiplied
censure fell upon him for his wisdom at Mine Run; and
thus the man who should have been the Great Captain
of the war was subordinated, but performed his duty with
matchless fidelity until the last insurgent flag was furled.

That Meade was sore at heart because he felt that his
best efforts as a soldier were not fully appreciated is
known to all his personal associates.   One month before
General Grant was inaugurated as President, I met him

on a railway-train going to Washington. He and his
family were in a private car at the rear of the train.
When I learned that he was there, along with others I
called to pay my respects. After a very brief conversation I was about to leave him when he asked me to
remain for a moment, as he wished to speak to me about
the proposed abolishment of the rank of General, which
he was soon to vacate when he became President, and to
which Sherman was fairly entitled by regular promotion.
He asked me to take some interest in the matter at Washington and urge some of our prominent Pennsylvania
Representatives to defeat the passage of the bill. I fully
agreed with him, and in leaving him said, "The country well understands who should succeed you as General
in the army, but there is dispute as to who should succeed Sherman as Lieutenant-General." I did not expect
any intimation from Grant as to his choice for Lieutenant-General, but to my surprise he answered, "Oh, that
is not a matter of doubt; Sheridan is fully entitled to it."
The remark was not made in confidence, although none
heard it but his family and myself. The names of Meade
and Thomas were both freely discussed at that time as
likely to reach the Lieutenant-Generalship, while few,
if any, expected Sheridan, a junior major-general, to
attain it. On my return from Washington I happened
to meet General Meade in Col. Scott's room of the Pennsylvania Railroad office, and without intimating that I
had any information on the subject I inquired of him
whether the Lieutenant-Generalship, soon to be vacant,
would not, of right, go to the senior major-general of the
army. General Meade answered very promptly and with
great emphasis: "Of course, it can go only to the senior
major-general; I could not with self-respect remain in
the army for a day if any other should be appointed over
me." I need hardly say that I did not venture to inform

General Meade of the positive views expressed by General Grant on the subject, as it would have wounded him beyond expression. A few weeks thereafter Grant was inaugurated and Sheridan promptly appointed to the Lieutenant-Generalship. I saw Meade many times thereafter, but always wearing the deep lines of sad disappointment in his finely-chiseled face. The Lieutenant-Generalship was obviously a forbidden topic with him, and he went down to his grave one of the sorrowing and unrewarded heroes of the war.

GEORGE H. THOMAS was another of the unrewarded heroes of the war. He was the same type of soldier as General Meade, cautious in movement and heroic in action, and both were modest and gentle as a woman in their private lives. No two men in the army more perfectly completed the circle of soldier and gentleman, and either was equal to the highest requirements of even the exceptional duties imposed upon a great commander by our civil war. Either would have taken Richmond with Grant's army, and saved tens of thousands of gallant men from untimely death. Both of these men fought one great battle when in supreme command, Meade at Gettysburg and Thomas at Nashville, and they stand out single and alone in history as the two most decisive battles of the war. Meade dealt the deathblow to the Confederacy from Cemetery Hill; Thomas annihilated the army of Hood from the heights of Nashville, and thenceforth Hood's army is unknown in the history of the conflict. In all the many other achievements of these men they fought as subordinate commanders, and their records are unsurpassed by any of the many heroic records made by our military commanders. Both were considered as hopeful candidates for the Lieutenant-Generalship to which Grant appointed Sheridan. I remember a conversation with Senator John Sherman soon after the election of Grant to the Presidency in 1868, in which he expressed the opinion that either Thomas or Meade would certainly be promoted when Grant became President; and at that time he certainly reflected the belief of his brother, then Lieutenant-General, who was soon to be promoted to the highest rank of the army.

General Thomas's military record is one of the most remarkable to be found in the history of our civil conflict. He is one of the very few commanders who never committed a serious military error, who never sacrificed a command, and who never lost a battle. He was probably more cautious than Meade, but I doubt whether any man of all the generals of the war was better equipped for the supreme command of all our armies than George H. Thomas. He lacked Grant's persistent aggression, but Grant never lost a battle that Thomas would have fought, and never failed in an assault that Thomas would have ordered. His battle at Mill Spring, fought on the 19th of January, 1862, with an army of entirely raw troops, was one of the first important victories of the war, and it directed the attention of the country to the great skill and energy of Thomas as a military commander. Soon after he was called to the command of one of the three wings of the army of Rosecrans, and in the bloody battle of Stone River his command played a most conspicuous part and contributed more than any other to the victory that was finally wrested from Bragg on that memorable field. Again his name called out the homage of every loyal heart as he and his brave warriors stood alone to resist the successful enemy on the sanguinary battle-field of Chickamauga. He, and he alone, saved the army from utter rout in that disastrous battle, and it led to his promotion to the command of the army as the successor of Rosecrans. In Sherman's great campaign from Chattanooga to Atlanta, Thomas was one of his most efficient lieutenants. So highly was he appreciated by Sherman that he was chosen from all of Sherman's subordinates to protect Sherman's rear by confronting Hood in Tennessee when Sherman started on his march to Savannah. When Sherman cut loose from his base of supplies and started on his romantic march through the heart of the rebellion, he left Thomas to give battle to Hood, knowing that Thomas would be outnumbered by the enemy, but entirely confident in Thomas's ability to maintain his position.

The duty assigned to Thomas was one that required exceptional discretion and courage, and he was doubtless chosen because he possessed those qualities in a preeminent degree. Had he given battle to Hood before he was entirely prepared to fight, even under the most favorable circumstances, he could have been easily overwhelmed, but Sherman confidently trusted Thomas, knowing that if any man could save an army Thomas was the man. Because of the inadequacy of his force to make an aggressive movement against Hood, Thomas was compelled to fall back upon Nashville, where he could best concentrate his army for the decisive conflict. He reached Nashville on the 3d of October, 1864, where he summoned scattered commands with all possible speed until he had gathered 25,000 infantry and 8000 cavalry to resist Hood's advance with 40,000 infantry and over 10,000 cavalry.

Sherman did not start upon his march to the sea until a month or more after Thomas had begun the concentration of his army at Nashville, and until Hood had moved far enough against Thomas to make it impossible for him to pursue Sherman. So rapidly did Hood march northward that General Schofield was compelled to fight a desperate battle at Franklin before he was able to join Thomas at Nashville, where he arrived on the 1st of December. On the next day after Schofield's arrival the authorities at Washington became most importunate to have Thomas deliver battle at once. Stanton telegraphed Grant on the 2d of December, complaining of the "disposition of Thomas to lay in fortifications for an indefinite period. . . . This looks like the McClellan and Rosecrans strategy of do nothing and let the enemy raid the country." On the same day Grant telegraphed Thomas urging him to make an early attack upon Hood. On the same day he telegraphed him again, complaining that he had not moved out from Nashville to Franklin and taken the offensive against the enemy. To these complaints General Thomas replied on the same day that had he joined Schofield at Franklin he could have had no more than 25,000 men to take the offensive against nearly 50,000. Again, on the 5th of December, Grant telegraphed Thomas complaining of his delay in attacking Hood, and again Thomas answered that he could not take the aggressive for want of sufficient cavalry force that he was rapidly increasing and equipping. On the 6th of December, Grant telegraphed Thomas a peremptory order in these words: "Attack Hood at once, and wait no longer for a remount for your cavalry." This dispatch was dated 4 P. M., and at 9 P. M. of the same evening Thomas replied: "I will make the necessary disposition and attack Hood at once, agreeably to your orders, though I believe it will be hazardous with the small force of cavalry now at my service." On the next day Stanton telegraphed Grant: "Thomas seems unwilling to attack because it is hazardous, as if all war was any but hazardous. If he waits for Wilson to get ready, Gabriel will be blowing his last horn." On the 8th of

December, Grant telegraphed Halleck: "If Thomas has not struck yet, he ought to be ordered to hand over his command to Schofield. There is no better man to repel an attack than Thomas, but I fear he is too cautious to take the initiative." Halleck replied: "If you wish General Thomas relieved, give the order. No one here will, I think, interfere. The responsibility, however, will be yours, as no one here, so far as I am informed, wishes General Thomas removed." On the same day Grant telegraphed Thomas: "Why not attack at once? By all means avoid the contingency of a foot-race to see which, you or Hood, can beat to the Ohio." On the same day, in answer to Halleck's inquiry about removing Thomas, Grant said: "I would not say relieve him until I hear further from him." At 11.30 P. M. of the same day Thomas telegraphed Grant: "I can only say, in further extenuation why I have not attacked Hood, that I could not concentrate my troops and get their transportation in order in shorter time than it has been done, and am satisfied I have made every effort that was possible to complete the task." On the 9th of December, Halleck telegraphed Thomas: "Lieutenant-General Grant expresses much dissatisfaction at your delay in attacking the enemy;" and on the same day Grant telegraphed to Halleck: "Please telegraph orders relieving him (Thomas) and placing Schofield in command." In obedience to this request of Grant, the War Department issued a general order reciting Grant's request to have Thomas relieved by Schofield, and assigning Schofield to the command of the Department and Army of the Cumberland. On the afternoon of December 9th, Thomas telegraphed Halleck, expressing his regret at Grant's dissatisfaction at his delay in attacking the enemy, and saying that "a terrible storm of freezing rain has come on since daylight, which will render an attack impossible till it breaks." On the same day he telegraphs Grant that if Grant should deem it necessary to relieve him, "I will submit without a murmur." At 5.30 P. M. of the same day Grant thought better of his purpose to relieve Thomas, and telegraphed to Halleck: "I am very unwilling to do injustice to an officer who has done so much good service as General Thomas has, however, and will therefore suspend the order relieving him until it is seen whether he will do anything." Two hours later he telegraphed to General Thomas, earnestly pressing him to give early battle. The severe freeze that had covered the ground with ice, so that troops could not be manœuvred at all, contined for several days, and on the 11th Grant again telegraphed Thomas: "Delay no longer for weather or reinforcements." To this dispatch Thomas answered: "The whole country is now covered with a sheet of ice so hard and slippery it is utterly impossible for troops to ascend the slopes, or even move on level ground in anything like order. . . . Under these circumstances I believe that an attack at this time would only result in a useless sacrifice of life." On the following day, December 13th, Grant issued special orders No. 149, as follows: "Major-General John A. Logan, United States Volunteers, will proceed immediately to Nashville, Tennessee, report by telegraph to the Lieutenant-General his arrival at Louisville, Kentucky, and also his arrival at Nashville, Tennessee."

General Logan started immediately upon his mission with an order in his pocket requiring General Thomas to transfer to him the command of the army. When he reached Louisville he learned that the battle was in progress, and he wisely halted and returned without visiting Nashville. On the evening of the 14th, Thomas telegraphed Halleck: "The ice having melted away to-day, the enemy will be attacked to-morrow morning."

In the mean time Grant had become alarmed at the possible consequences of his own order in transferring the command from Thomas to Logan, and on the 14th he started for Nashville himself to take personal command. When he reached Washington he received the first information of Thomas's attack, and later in the evening a report of the great victory achieved, to which Grant responded by the following dispatch to Thomas: "Your dispatch of this evening just received. I congratulate you and the army under your command for to-day's operations, and feel a conviction that to-morrow will add more fruits to your victory." Stanton also telegraphed Thomas: "We shall give you a hundred guns in the morning." Two days later, when Grant learned how complete were Thomas's methods and his victory, he telegraphed Thomas: "The armies operating against Richmond have fired two hundred guns in honor of your great victory."

I give the substance of these dispatches because it is necessary to convey to the public the peculiar attitude in which Thomas was placed before he fought the battle at Nashville. He was soldier enough to disobey the peremptory order of the commander-in-chief when he knew that his commander could not know or appreciate the peril of an attempt to obey his orders, and he exhibited the most sublime qualities of a great soldier when, even in the face of his threatened removal from his command, he peremptorily refused to fight a battle that he was convinced could result only in disaster and in the needless sacrifice of life. The result so fully vindicated General Thomas that none have since questioned the wisdom of the position he assumed and maintained so heroically; but the fact that the battle of Nashville proved that Thomas was entirely right, and that Grant, Halleck, and Stanton were entirely wrong, doomed Thomas to disfavor with the government; and while he never could be censured by those who so severely criticised him, I fear that even Grant, with all his greatness, never fully forgave Thomas for the wrong that Grant had done him in regard to the battle of Nashville. It was the one battle of the war that was planned on the most thorough principles of military science and executed in its entirety with masterly skill; and it is the only great battle of our civil war that is studied in the military schools of the world because of the completeness of the military strategy exhibited by Thomas. There were no more battles to be fought in the South-west after the battle of Nashville, as Thomas had left no enemy to confront him.

I first met George H. Thomas in May, 1861, when he dined at my home in Chambersburg along with Generals Patterson, Cadwalader, Doubleday, and Keim, and Colonels Fitz John Porter and John Sherman, who were serving as staff officers. Thomas was then a colonel, and commanded the regulars in Patterson's movement into the Shenandoah Valley. The war was freely discussed by this circle of military men, and I well remember that all those present, with the exception of Doubleday and Thomas, freely predicted that it would not last over three months, and that no more than one or two battles would be fought. Doubleday aggressively disputed the theory generally advanced of an early peace, and Thomas, with that modesty that always characterized him, was silent. Doubleday had met the Southerners in battle at Sumter, and he knew how desperately earnest they were; and Thomas was a son of Virginia, and knew that the Southern people were as heroic as any in the North. I saw him several times during that campaign, and much enjoyed visits to his camp; but even in the privacy of personal conversation he was most reluctant to discuss the situation, evidently because

24

he knew that the North did not understand, and could not be made to understand, the determined purpose of the Southern people to win independence. Our acquaintance that began at Chambersburg was maintained until his death, and whenever opportunity presented I always sought his companionship. He was one of the most lovable characters I have ever known, but it required exhaustive ingenuity to induce him to speak about any military movements in which he was a prominent participant. Any one might have been in daily intercourse with him for years and never learned from him that he had won great victories in the field.

After the war Thomas suffered in silence the disfavor of those in authority. It was doubtless the more distressing to one of his sensitive temperament from the fact that there was no visible evidence of the injustice that was studiedly done him. Politicians tempted him to enter the field as a candidate for President, but he wisely declined, and on no occasion did he so grandly exhibit the higher qualities of the soldier and gentleman as when President Johnson, having quarrelled with Grant, decided to supersede Grant as commander-in-chief of the army by nominating Thomas to the same brevet rank held by Grant. The President went so far as to send his name to the Senate for confirmation as General by brevet, which would have enabled Johnson to assign Thomas to the command of the army. The President acted without conference with or the knowledge of Thomas, and as soon as Thomas learned of it he promptly telegraphed to Senator Chandler and others peremptorily refusing to accept the proffered promotion. After having served as commander of the third military district in the South and of his old Department of the Cumberland, he was finally assigned to the Military Division of the Pacific, and he arrived in San Francisco to assume his last command in June, 1869. My last meeting with him was some time during the winter of 1870, when he made his last visit to Washington. We spent the evening together at the opera, and afterward sat until late in the night conversing on topics of general interest. I doubt whether any one ever heard him utter a single complaint, but it was obvious to those who knew him well that he felt humiliated and heart-sore at the treatment he had received from the military power of the government. Within a few weeks thereafter the lightning flashed from the Western coast the sad news that the great warrior's head had fallen upon his breast while sitting in his office, and on the evening of the same day one of the noblest but unrewarded heroes of the war passed away.

GENERAL FITZ JOHN PORTER was the most conspicuous victim of military injustice in the history of our civil war. I doubt whether the military records of modern times in any civilized country present such a flagrant instance of the overthrow of one of the bravest and most skillful of officers by a deliberate conspiracy of military incompetents and maddened political partisans. He was the only one of McClellan's lieutenants who had proved his ability to exercise supreme command in fighting great battles, and I doubt whether there was then in the entire Army of the Potomac a more competent man for the supreme command than Fitz John Porter; and certainly no one was more patriotic in his devotion to the cause of the Union. I first met him in the dark days of April, 1861, when he was sent to Harrisburg to represent General Scott in organizing and forwarding troops to the national capital. When communication between Washington and the North had been severed by the treasonable revolution in Baltimore, it became a grave question what action should be taken in Pennsylvania in the absence of orders from the national authorities. I shall never forget the last council held in the Executive Chamber at Harrisburg when General Patterson, Governor Curtin, and their advisers were compelled to act upon their own responsibility. Each in turn advised caution, as revolution was in the air and it was impossible to devise a plan of operations with any assurance of safety. After all had spoken Fitz John Porter, the youngest of the party, who had won his promotion on the battle-fields of Mexico, spoke with an earnestness that inspired every one present. With his handsome face brightened by the enthusiasm of his patriotism, and his keen eye flashing the fire of his courage, he said to General Patterson and Governor Curtin: "I would march the troops through Baltimore or over its ashes to the defence of the capital of the nation." He was a thorough soldier and an earnest patriot, and had his counsels prevailed it would not have been left for General Butler to command obedience to the laws in Baltimore by his shotted guns on Federal Hill, nor would the government have been compelled to confess its weakness by shipping troops surreptitiously by Annapolis to Washington.

Colonel Porter had been among the first of our soldiers called to active duty when the madness of Secession took shape by the capture of forts in the Secession States. He was ordered by General Scott to Texas, where he made earnest effort to save Albert Sydney Johnson from being engulfed in the maelstrom of rebellion. By his skill and energy the garrisons at Key West and Tortugas were reinforced and saved from capture, and when at Harrisburg, unable to reach his commander-in-chief or the War Department because of the interruption of communications, he took the responsibility of telegraphing to General Frank P. Blair of Missouri authority to muster in troops for the protection of that State, whereby, as General Blair subsequently stated, Missouri was saved to the Union. Before the close of the first year of the war he had organized a division that attained the highest reputation as a model of discipline, and early in 1862 he went to the Peninsula with McClellan as a division commander. Immediately after the capture of Yorktown he was assigned to the command of the Fifth Army Corps, and with that corps he fought the battles of Mechanicsville and Gaines' Mill, and won the highest encomiums from both General McClellan and the government for the ability he exhibited. After the failure of the Peninsula campaign, and when Pope was playing the braggart and sacrificing his army to his incompetency in the second Bull Run campaign, Porter was ordered to the relief of Pope, and, learning that Lee was rapidly advancing upon Pope's defeated army, Porter disobeyed orders to stop at Williamsburg, and assumed the responsibility whereby he was enabled to join Pope several days earlier. He participated in the second Bull Run battle, and was finally compelled with the rest of the army to retreat into the defences of Washington.

Pope was smarting under the disgraceful failure he had made as a military commander, and his cause was taken up by the embittered partisans who then sought the overthrow of McClellan and all who were supposed to be in friendly relations with him. General Porter was singled out for sacrifice, although so fully did General-in-chief Halleck and Secretary-of-War Stanton confide in Porter's ability as a military commander that when the movement was made against Lee in the Antietam campaign, Porter was directed to select a division of 12,000 from among several divisions and a commander among twenty general officers, and add them to his corps. With this command he held the centre of the line of battle at Antietam, and was one of the first to pursue Lee in his retreat, and with his single corps fought the battle of Shepherdstown. Early in November, General McClellan was removed from the command of the Army of the Potomac, and one week later General Porter was relieved of the command of his corps. Pope preferred charges against him, and on the 25th of November, Porter was placed under arrest. The substance of the charges against him was that he had failed to obey an order from General Pope requiring him to start with his division to General Pope in the field. The court was chosen by Secretary Stanton, who had become so intensely inflamed against McClellan and all who were supposed to be in sympathy with him that he had determined to eliminate them from the army, and he could dispense with so skillful and heroic a soldier as Porter, after Lee had been driven back to Virginia, only by disgracing him. The court was organized to convict. By the verdict of the court-martial he was not only dismissed from the army, but he was made a stranger to the country for which he had so gallantly fought, by depriving him of his citizenship and making him ineligible to any public position under the government.

For fifteen years General Porter was compelled to bear the fearful stigma that had been put upon him by a court that simply obeyed the vindictive orders of its master. Many applications had been made from time to time to have his case reopened, and fully ten years before the effort was successful men like Governor Curtin, Senator Wilson of Massachusetts, and others had made earnest efforts to have a review of Porter's case. During the eight years in which Grant was President he had been earnestly urged to open the door for justice to a fellow-soldier, but he stubbornly refused; and it was not until after he had retired from the Presidency, and had **care-**

fully studied the whole question from the accurate history of both sections, that he became fully convinced of his error, and manfully declared, in an article published in the *North American Review*, that Porter had not only not failed to perform his duty as a soldier, but that he was entitled to the highest measure of credit for having performed his duty to the uttermost. In 1878, President Hayes authorized a military commission to review the judgment in Porter's case, and three of the most experienced and respected generals of the army, Schofield, Terry, and Getty, were assigned to that duty. Two of these generals entered upon that duty inclined to the belief that Porter deserved censure if not dismissal, and it is not known that any one of the three was specially friendly to his cause. They heard all the evidence in the case, and they not only reversed the judgment of the partisan court that had condemned Porter by relieving him of all accusations of failing to perform his duty, but they declared: " Porter's faithful, subordinate, and intelligent conduct that afternoon (August 29th) saved the Union army from the defeat which would otherwise have resulted that day in the enemy's more speedy concentration. . . . Porter had understood and appreciated the military situation, and so far as he had acted upon his own judgment his action had been wise and judicious." Such was the unanimous judgment of three of the ablest and confessedly among the most fair-minded generals of the army, but it was not until 1885 that a bill was finally passed authorizing General Porter's restoration to the army roll, upon which he had shed such conspicuous lustre in the early part of the war, and that bill was vetoed by President Arthur. General Porter was restored to the army on the 7th of August, 1886, by a subsequent act of Congress, and was permitted to exercise his own discretion as to active service or retiring with his original rank.   In obedience to his own request he was placed upon the retired list.

A memorable incident, not generally known in history, occurred about this time, arising from the retirement of General Pope from the major-generalship to which he had been so unjustly promoted.   General Terry, who was one of the members of the military commission that had heard and decided the Porter case, was entitled by rank to succeed Pope as major-general, but he was as chivalrous in peace as he was in war, and so keenly did he feel the injustice under which General Porter had suffered that he not only proposed, but insisted, that General Porter should be promoted to the major-generalship in preference to himself as the only possible atonement the government could make for the unspeakable wrong it had perpetrated.   General Porter gratefully appreciated this manly action of General Terry, and, in the face of General Terry's appeal to him to accept the promotion, he resolutely declined to be considered for the place, because it would have hindered the promotion of the equally gallant soldier who had vindicated the majesty of justice. General Grant, in a letter written December 30, 1881, speaking of Porter's case, said: "I have done him an injustice, and have so written to the President;" and from that time until the verdict of the military commission was rendered Grant left no opportunity unemployed to aid in the restoration of Porter to the position and respect to which he was justly entitled.

In 1869, General Porter was tendered by the Khedive of Egypt the position of commander-in-chief of his army, but he declined it, and recommended General Stone, who accepted it.   Since then he has made his home in New York, where he has filled most important public and private positions, having served as Commissioner of Public Works, Assistant Receiver of the Central Railroad of New Jersey, as Police Commissioner, and later as Fire Commissioner of that city. He retired in 1889, since when he has been engaged in private business pursuits. Despite the fearful flood-tide of injustice that was flung upon him, General Porter has survived nearly all his assailants, and the few who survive with him are now ashamed to whisper even an accusation against his heroism or his honor as a soldier. He is yet in the full vigor of life, and while his accusers have been forgotten where the names of men are cherished with respect, he lives beloved by all who know him and honored by every soldier of the land. Many of the heroes of the war failed to meet just reward for the devotion they gave to the country, but Fitz John Porter stands out single from all as the one man who suffered a judgment of infamy, formally declared by a military court, for the single offence of having been one of the wisest, noblest, and bravest of our army's commanders.

THE record of GENERAL G. K. WARREN is the story of a brilliant military career touched with every hue of promise cut short by the unjust exercise of that power that resides in military rank, used upon impulse and in ignorance of actual existing conditions, without hesitation and without reference to inquiry or investigation. It was the 1st of April, 1865; the war was yet in progress, and the two armies still faced each other at Petersburg. Our lines had been extended to the left, which brought them in immediate contact with the enemy. On the 31st of March, Sheridan with his cavalry had struck the enemy's combined force of infantry and cavalry at Dinwiddie Courthouse under Pickett, and had been roughly handled. Warren with the Fifth Corps had come to his support; upon the next day a battle was fought at Five

Forks, wholly decisive, far-reaching in its results, and ending in the rout of the enemy's forces. The whole nation was exulting, when suddenly the news was flashed over the land that Major-General Warren, the commander of the Fifth Corps, had been relieved of his command, by order of General Sheridan, on the field of battle.

It is with a recognition of what Warren, in long and faithful service, in character and achievement, brought to the discharge of his duties as a corps commander in this battle that I am to deal with him. Just before the Wilderness campaign, when Sykes had been relieved as commander of the Fifth Corps, Warren was at once named as its commandant. He brought to the command of the Fifth Corps a reputation for ability and energy and brilliant service that had won for him steady and well-deserved promotion. With a courage that never quailed he had fought his way from the command of a regiment to that of an army corps. There was no military reputation more promising than his when at the head of one of the army's best corps of veteran soldiers he crossed the Rapidan and became at once involved in the battles of the Wilderness. Initiating almost every flank movement after the investment of Petersburg, his corps participated prominently in all the battles of the army, his restless spirit knowing no repose. He was beloved by his men, who trusted him, and who testified to their affection when, on the return march of the corps through Petersburg, recognizing him as he stood among the crowd, they rent the air with shouts of recognition.

On the 1st of April, 1865, after some preliminary fighting in front of Dinwiddie Courthouse on the 31st, in which he had been unsuccessful, Sheridan applied to Grant for infantry support. He wanted the Sixth Corps, which had been with him in the Valley of the Shenandoah. He objected to Warren, and only took him and

his corps when Grant had authorized him to relieve Warren upon any occasion justifying that action. Warren
moved his corps to Gravelly Run Church. Pickett had
fallen back to the White Oak road and intrenched.
Warren with his corps was to move upon the left intrenched flank of Pickett's works. A faulty reconnaissance had been made, and when the Fifth Corps moved
at noon of the 1st the intrenchments of the enemy were
found to be three-quarters of a mile to the left of the
position supposed by Sheridan. To meet this unexpected
fire upon his flank Ayres broke away from Crawford and
Griffin. Warren went at once to these flanking divisions,
where he remained in person, directing their movements,
changing their direction to meet the force on Ayres's
flank as well as their own front, getting into the enemy's
rear with Crawford's division, capturing guns and thirteen hundred prisoners, and compelling the retreat of the
enemy.

The battle as it was fought was a series of flank movements, and was, as such, wholly unanticipated by Sheridan. Warren had just reached a point directly in rear
of the enemy at the Forks, and was pursuing his success
when he sent his adjutant-general to Sheridan to report
that he was in the enemy's rear, had taken a large number of prisoners, and was pursuing his advantages, when
the stroke fell, in the midst of the victory he had done
so much to secure. "Tell General Warren," said Sheridan, "that, by God! he was not at the front: this is all
I've got to say to him." He had already replaced him
without any attempt to communicate with him, and
this with the victory won, the enemy in retreat, and the
evacuation of Richmond and Petersburg made inevitable. Conscious of his innocence and knowing what he
had accomplished, Warren went in person to Sheridan
and asked him to reconsider his action. "Hell!" said

Sheridan; "I don't reconsider my determinations." Nor did he.

Warren at once sought an investigation, which was then refused him, and fifteen years of incessant application and pleading were to pass before it was secured; but at last the long-hoped-for investigation came, an inquiry where the keenest legal acumen was instrumental in bringing facts to light, wholly regardless of that pedantry that belongs to military life—a search for truth, unawed by the glitter of the uniform or the prestige of rank, no matter how high, and with a result so wholly different from that which had been assumed and acted upon as to seem almost romance. And what was gained by this investigation, to which were summoned witnesses from every quarter, and where the Confederate testimony established the facts of the battle beyond controversy? This, that but for the movement of Crawford's division under Warren's immediate orders the enemy's lines would have been held, and were held until the movement of Crawford, and that the results of Ayres's attack were rendered possible by that movement. What, then, could excuse the action of General Sheridan in view of the victory secured to him? Nothing but that he was ignorant of what was done, as he himself testifies, and that he knew nothing of the Confederate Mumford's engagement with Crawford's division, nor of the fighting of that division, nor of the cavalry. He knew that in relieving Warren he was pleasing General Grant, and he ignored then and subsequently anything presented to him that might in any way question his action. Warren made every effort to carry out the order and execute the plan of this battle; and when asked by his own counsel if he had or had not done this, his reply was noble. Asking that the question be withdrawn, he said, "I do it on the ground that I am willing to be judged by my deeds.'' Sheridan, with a magnetism second to none, a fighter beyond all other qualities, was deficient in strong mental or moral sense.

When the battle of Five Forks had been fought and won he did not know what had been accomplished nor by whom. His testimony distinctly shows this: he made his official report without that knowledge, and, although the commanding general upon the field, he saw but one of the many movements which contributed to the victory, and ignored the rest; nor would he give any account of his own personal movements after Ayres's assault; and yet he committed an act of despotic power so uncalled for, unjust, and cruel as to wellnigh constitute a crime. The record of Warren's court of inquiry will remain for ever an enduring stain upon an otherwise great reputation. Warren, after long and patient waiting, at last began to despond and to doubt as to the final result. His health was breaking. He lost the fiery spirit that had animated him. Grant and Sheridan were omnipotent, the heroes of the hour, and unassailable. And so the end came at last before the decision of his court was known, and they buried him in that sunny city by the sea where he was known and loved and where he worked in peace. His last request was that there should be no military display, no emblems of his profession upon his coffin, and no uniform upon his person. Devoted friends followed him to his last resting-place, and as they turned homeward the conviction came to each of them that the earth with which they had filled his grave gave rest to a generous and broken heart.

GENERAL DON CARLOS BUELL very clearly demonstrated in the early part of the war that he was one of the most accomplished soldiers of our army. While he was not dishonored, as were General Porter and General Warren, he was displaced from command in obedience to partisan clamor. He was a thorough soldier, brave, intelligent, skillful, and equal to every emergency in which he was placed; but he was not a politician. He believed that war was war; he believed that armies were organized to fight battles, and to fight them, according to the established rules of military science, to accomplish the speediest and most substantial results. During the period that he was in command in Kentucky he accomplished more in the same length of time than any other general in the Western army. When he assumed command at Louisville on the 15th of November, 1861, his entire effective Union force was less than 30,000 men, and they largely without organization, arms, equipment, or transportation. During the seven months he remained there he organized one of the best disciplined armies that ever marched on the continent. He defeated the enemy at Middle Creek and Mills Springs in January, aided in the capture of Fort Donelson, occupied Middle Tennessee and the northern part of Alabama, and moved with the main body of his army by a forced march to the rescue of Grant at Shiloh. All this was accomplished between the 15th of November, 1861, and the 10th of January, 1862. He committed no military mistakes, met with no military disasters, and he strengthened the Union cause unspeakably in Kentucky by the strict discipline he enforced in his command.

The temptation was great to Union troops in Kentucky to demoralize themselves by pillage and plunder, as one-half the people of the State were earnestly disloyal and very many of them in the Confederate service; but Buell was placed in command in Kentucky to save it to the Union, and he performed that duty most conscientiously and patriotically. But the most effective means he employed to save Kentucky were seized upon by the politicians of the times, and he was denounced from one end of the country to the other as a semi-rebel because he strictly restrained his troops from the plundering of private property of either friend or foe. He was not only a soldier himself, but he made a soldier of every man in his command as far as he could be obeyed. But for his timely arrival at Pittsburgh Landing on the evening of the first day's battle, when Grant's army had been literally routed and driven to the river, the army of Grant would have ceased to exist in history at the close of the following day. It was Buell whose energy and skill as a soldier brought relief to Grant, and it was his courage and skill on the battle-field, co-operating with Grant on the second day, that gave the victory to the Union armies at Shiloh. Both were as generous as they were brave, and Buell never claimed the victory as his, and Grant proved his appreciation of Buell by asking his assignment to an important command when he was commander-in-chief of the army. Stanton was implacable in his hatred of Buell, as he was in his hatred against all who incurred his displeasure, and Buell was left without a command, although his services were called for by the one who certainly best understood his value as a soldier.

On the 10th of June, Buell was assigned to make a campaign for the capture of Chattanooga. It was ordered by General Halleck, who was then in personal command at Corinth. This movement was regarded by the authorities at Washington as the most important of all our army operations, with the single exception of the campaign against Richmond. Stanton, in a dispatch to Halleck, declared that the capture of Chattanooga " would be equal to the capture of Richmond," but soon after Buell was assigned to this task the disasters on the Peninsula and the second Bull Run campaign brought importunate calls from Washington for troops from Halleck's army to strengthen the Army of the Potomac. On the 4th of July, Lincoln telegraphed Halleck: "You do not know how much you would oblige us if, without abandoning any of your positions or plans, you could promptly send us 10,000 infantry. Can you not?" On receipt of this dispatch Halleck called a council of war, and sent a dispatch saying that no troops could be sent to the East without abandoning the Chattanooga expedition, and Halleck himself became alarmed at his position at Corinth, as, after having detached Buell to the Chattanooga campaign, he had sent reinforcements to General Curtis in Arkansas. After having started Buell on his Chattanooga campaign, in which he was to confront Bragg with his 75,000 men and maintain a long line of communication, Buell was notified by Halleck that Thomas's division must be withdrawn from him, and perhaps other portions of his command would be called away. Thus, after starting Buell with an inferior force to fight his way to Chattanooga and maintain hundreds of miles of communication in an enemy's country, his force was depleted, his plan of campaign was overruled, and because he failed to march with a rapidity that Halleck had never approached he was censured from day to day by both Halleck and the War Department for his failure to accomplish the impossible. Halleck had required two months to remove his army from Shiloh to Corinth, a distance of twenty miles, and soon thereafter he telegraphed Buell complaining of his slow movement, when he had marched with four times the rapidity that Halleck had himself.

When it is remembered that Buell was compelled to fortify every bridge for more than three hundred miles of road in his rear, the depletion of his forces and the necessity for caution may be intelligently understood. Especially did Halleck become mandatory about rapid movements on the part of Buell after he became commander-in-chief and had been transferred to Washington. On the 13th of August he telegraphed Buell that he had been notified to have him removed, but intimating that he interposed to save him. To this Buell replied on the same day: "I beg that you will not interpose in my behalf. On the contrary, if the dissatisfaction cannot cease on grounds which I think may be supposed if not apparent, I respectfully request that I may be relieved. My position is far too important to be occupied by any officer on sufferance. I have no desire to stand in the way of what may be deemed for the public good." Buell was not then relieved from command, but the clamor for his removal grew more imperious, and all the partisan rancor of that time was thrown into the scale against Buell as a military commander. His command was composed largely of Illinois and Indiana troops, and Governors Morton and Yates pursued him with intense ferocity because he enforced discipline in his army and would not permit his soldiers to plunder private homes. It was political clamor and not military necessity, nor even military expediency, that made the War Department issue an order on the 27th of September relieving Buell of his position and ordering him to Louisville, limiting his authority to the command of the troops in that city, and directing him to transfer the army to the direction of General Thomas. Buell promptly called General Thomas to this place, but Thomas was one of the bravest and noblest of our soldiers, and he at once telegraphed to Secretary Stanton: "General Buell's preparations have been complete to move against the enemy, and I therefore respectfully ask that he may be retained in command." In obedience to

25

Thomas's request the order relieving Buell was revoked, only to be met by a fiercer clamor from the political passions of the day for his sacrifice. On the 8th of October he fought and won the battle of Perrysville, after a sanguinary conflict in which he lost over four thousand men. Even when Buell had won a decisive victory, instead of being complimented by the authorities at Washington, he was daily criticised for his failure to pursue and destroy Bragg's army that largely outnumbered him. On the 19th of October he was notified by Halleck that the capture of East Tennessee should be the main object of his campaign, and saying, "Buell and his army must enter East Tennessee this fall." Four days later, on the 23d of October, Buell was removed from his command and General Rosecrans assigned to it. General Buell in his modest but soldierlike farewell to his army, after referring to its heroic achievements, broadly took upon himself all responsibility for any failures it might be charged with. He said: "If anything has not been accomplished which was practicable within the sphere of its duty, the general cheerfully holds himself responsible for the failure."

Strange as it may seem, while the Secretary of War notified Halleck in the early part of the Tennessee campaign that the capture of Chattanooga was second only in importance to that of Richmond, and while only ten days before Buell was relieved of command General Halleck notified him that he "must enter East Tennessee this fall," Rosecrans immediately abandoned the East Tennessee movement and pushed his army as directly as possible to Nashville. To show how promptly Buell had moved in comparison with others, it may be stated that General Rosecrans, although only thirty-two miles away from Bragg, permitted two months to elapse before he delivered battle at Stone River; and he did not march his army a mile for six months thereafter. The same army under Buell in about the same period of eight months marched across the State of Kentucky, 185 miles; thence across Tennessee, 217 miles; thence across the State of Alabama to East Tennessee, 217 miles; thence across Tennessee and Kentucky to Louisville, 336 miles; thence through Central and Eastern Kentucky in pursuit of Bragg and back to Nashville, 485 miles—making nearly fifteen hundred miles of march and several hard-fought battles.

Thus ended the military career of one who could and should have been one of the great military leaders of our civil war. He was retired from command solely because of the intense partisan hatred that had pursued him for no other reason than being a true, faithful, and skillful soldier. When Grant asked for his restoration to command on the 19th of April, 1864, Halleck replied: "I would like very much to see Buell restored to command, and have several times pressed him at the War Department, but there has been such a pressure against him from the West that I do not think the Secretary will give him any at present." In obedience to Buell's request for an official investigation of the operations of the armies under his command, a military commission was appointed for the purpose on the 20th of November, 1862, and its labors continued until May 10, 1863. The record and opinion of the commission were received at the War Department, but were never published, and after they had been suppressed for nearly ten years the House of Representatives, by resolution passed March 1, 1872, called for a copy of the proceedings, which brought the astounding answer from the Secretary of War that "a careful and exhaustive search among all the records and files of the Department fails to discover what disposition was made of the proceedings of the commission and the papers enclosed.'' It is obvious that the evidence and the finding of the commission were not in accord with the violent passions which had forced the removal of one of the most gallant soldiers of our army, and the proceedings were deliberately suppressed and justice withheld from General Buell. The Governors of the Western States who had so boldly assailed Buell were called upon to confront him and testify before the commission, but all refused. His accusers dared not meet him, and when a packed commission, chosen and manipulated by the filling of vacancies to hinder justice, had failed to convict him, the proceedings were deliberately suppressed for ten years, and General Buell permitted to live under the false and malicious charges made against him by reckless politicians who did not even venture to testify against him.

That Stanton himself felt that his injustice to Buell was so flagrant as to call for some atonement is evident by the fact that in the spring of 1864 he invited Buell to a personal interview, received him most cordially, and asked him which one of several important commands he would prefer to receive. Buell's only answer was that it was first a necessity to dispose of the proceedings of the military commission that inquired into his case. Buell's self-respect as a soldier forbade his acceptance of a command when his fidelity and ability as a commander had been inquired into by a military commission whose judgment was withheld not only from the accused, but from the public. This was a degree of manliness that Stanton was unprepared for, and they parted for the last time, as Stanton never again conferred with Buell. Subsequently, Stanton twice voluntarily offered Buell important commands, but he very properly declined both, as the verdict of the commission was denied publicity, and in both cases he would have been compelled to serve under officers whom he outranked.

Thus the war closed with· one of its ablest and most patriotic chieftains not only refused the right to give the gallant service he offered, but he was assailed by partisan passion for having faithfully performed his duty as a soldier, and he was finally tried by a military commission whose testimony and judgment were stolen from the archives of the Department to give license to his malicious slanderers. His chief accusers have all passed away, but General Buell yet lives, honored and respected by the country as one of the noble but unrewarded Heroes of the War.

BORDER-LIFE IN WAR-TIMES.

WHILE all sections of the country keenly felt the sad bereavements and sacrifices of the civil war, only those who lived on the border between the two contending sections involved in bloody fraternal strife, with all the fierce passions it inspires, can have any just conception of the severe trials and constant strain which fell upon the border people. My home was then in Chambersburg, in one of the most beautiful valleys of the country, and among a people exceptionally comfortable and forming one of the most delightful communities of the State. The first distant murmurs of the coming war were heard in Chambersburg in October, 1859, when John Brown and his few insane followers attempted the conquest of Virginia by assaulting Harper's Ferry. Although Brown had made Chambersburg his base of operations for some weeks before he moved upon Harper's Ferry, freely mingling with the citizens of the town and known only as "Dr. Smith," who was ostensibly engaged in mining pursuits in Maryland, there was not a single resident of Chambersburg who had any conception or suspicion of his purpose; but when the startling news came that actual conflict had been precipitated at Harper's Ferry by the stubborn fanatic fresh from the Kansas battles, it appalled the community, as it seemed to be the precursor of civil war. In little more than a year thereafter the people of the town were again startled

(Photo by Brady, Washington.)

GENERAL ROBERT E. LEE, 1865.

by Lieutenant Jones and straggling members of his command reaching there, exhausted and footsore, to announce that he had been compelled to abandon Harper's Ferry, where he was in command, and had blown up the works as far as he was able to accomplish it. This was one of the first of the many thrilling events of the great war that was soon to burst upon us. From that time, through four long years of bloody battle until the end came at Appomattox, there was not a day nor an hour of absolute peace in the border counties.

Chambersburg was within a night's ride of the Confederate lines during the whole war, and not only the repeated raids made into that community by the Confederate commanders, but the constant sense of insecurity and the multiplied reports of incursions from the enemy, made tranquility impossible. Not only did these people suffer their full share of the exactions of war which fell upon every community, but they were subject to constant convulsions by actual or threatened raids of the enemy, and often by destructive incursions of militia defenders; and they suffered unspeakable loss of property from both armies. Finally, upon Chambersburg fell the avenging blow for Hunter's vandalism in Virginia, and the beautiful old town was left in its ashes and its people largely impoverished. On the 12th of April, 1861, the brief telegraphic bulletins which were then obtainable in country districts announced the bombardment of Sumter. Business was practically suspended, public meetings were held in support of the government at which the leading men of every political faith were orators, the Stars and Stripes were displayed from every house, and patriotic badges and shields graced almost every person. Volunteering was so rapid that companies could not even be organized to keep pace with them. The first call for troops was responded to more generously in that section than from any other in the State. Its very nearness to the seat of war and the exceptional dangers which fell upon it seemed to call out the highest measure of patriotic purpose and action. Party differences were obliterated in the common effort to maintain the cause of the Union. It is only in times of great danger that the greatest qualities of both men and women are developed, and the border people, of whom Chambersburg was the central altar, grandly illustrated the truth of the adage.

On the 28th of May the advance of General Patterson's army reached Chambersburg, and from that day until the war closed Chambersburg was the military headquarters for all movements on the border. Even with a great army in our midst, it was impossible for the people to appreciate what war really meant. I well remember that when two officers of General Patterson's command had crossed the Potomac as scouts, and had been captured by the Confederates, it was spoken of by all in bated breath as if some unspeakable calamity had befallen them. Both the North and the South seemed to believe that they were about to engage in war with a barbarous enemy, and all expectations of humane and civilized warfare appeared to have perished in the minds of the people. For two months General Patterson's army kept the border people in a state of restless suspense. He crossed the Potomac to Falling Waters, then fell back upon Maryland, and then renewed his march into the enemy's country. The wildest excitement prevailed in every circle: a great battle was expected every day, as Patterson was threatening Johnson at Winchester and McDowell marched against Beauregard at Manassas. Finally, on Monday, July 22d, the news of a great triumph won by McDowell was posted on the bulletin-boards, and all business was forgotten as the people rejoiced over the victory, but before the sun had set on the same day the reports from Manassas told the sad story that McDowell was not only defeated, but that his army was routed and retreating into the defences of Washington, with little hope that the capital would be saved from the enemy.

The call for additional troops was responded to by a regiment of volunteers made up almost entirely of the sturdy young men of Franklin and Fulton counties. When the regiment started for Harrisburg the people turned out almost *en masse* to inspire them in their patriotic work. Speeches were made, flags were waved, tears shed, sorrowing hearts were left behind as the brave men went to their great task, and many to death. In May, 1862, the border people were thrown into convulsion by the retreat of Banks from Strasburg to Winchester, thence to Martinsburg, and finally to the north side of the Potomac. This was assumed to mean the invasion of Pennsylvania. Stock and valuables, including the goods of merchants and money of banks, were all hurried away to places of safety. This was only the first of many like disturbances that came during every year of the war. General Ewell, who had driven Banks to the north side of the Potomac, did not pursue his victory upon Northern soil, but in August of the same year, when Pope was defeated in the second Bull Run campaign and Lee crossed the Potomac into Maryland, war was brought to the very doors of the people of the border. As Lee's army moved westward from Frederick, a portion of it extended northward as far as Hagerstown, while Jackson hastened to Williamsport, thence to Martinsburg and Harper's Ferry, where he captured 10,000 men and 60 guns, and was back on the Antietam battle-ground in time to fight McClellan.

An interesting story may here be told of the methods

·by which information was obtained to guide the actions of great armies. I was then Assistant Adjutant-General of the United States, assigned to duty at Harrisburg to make a draft under the State laws of Pennsylvania. There was no military force on the border, and not even an officer of the army who had exercised any command of troops. I was compelled, therefore, to exercise what little military authority could be enforced under the circumstances, and Governor Curtin ordered a half-organized company of cavalry, that Captain W. J. Palmer was recruiting at Carlisle, to report to me at Chambersburg for duty as scouts. I thus became commander of an army of nearly one hundred men, or about one man to each mile of border I had to guard, but Captain Palmer proved to be a host within himself, as he entered the Confederate lines every night for nearly a week under various disguises, obtained all information possible as to the movements of Lee's command, and with the aid of William B. Wilson, an expert telegrapher, who was co-operating with him, attached his instrument to the first telegraph-wire he struck and communicated to me all movements of the enemy, present and prospective, as far as he had been able to ascertain them. As rapidly as these telegrams reached me they were sent to Governor Curtin, who promptly forwarded them to the War Department, whence they were hastened to General McClellan's headquarters, who was then moving through Maryland against Lee; and all the important information that McClellan received from the front of Lee's army until their lines faced each other at Antietam came from Captain Palmer's nightly visits within the enemy's lines and his prompt reports to me in the morning. Howell Cobb's division finally reached as far north as Hagerstown, and Captain Palmer spent most of the night within Cobb's camp, and learned from leading subordinate officers that the destination of Lee's army was Pennsylvania, and that Cobb's command would lead the movement probably the next day.

I need hardly say that I hastened the information to Curtin, who hurried it through to Washington, whence McClellan received it within a few hours. McClellan was then ignorant of the exact movements of General Reynolds, whom he had sent to Pennsylvania to organize a force of "emergency-men" and bring them to the aid of McClellan in Western Maryland. He did not know, therefore, who was in command at Chambersburg or what force was there, but doubtless supposed that either Reynolds or some part of his command was already there on its way to join him. General McClellan, on receipt of the news that Lee was likely to advance into Pennsylvania, sent substantially this telegram to the commander at Chambersburg, without naming him: "I am advised that Lee's probable destination is Pennsylvania, and if he shall advance in that direction, concentrate all your forces and obstruct his march until I can overtake him and give battle. The occasion calls for prompt action." As I was the commander and had less than one hundred men, all told, and not twenty of them within fifteen miles of me, the prospect of concentrating my forces and marching out to meet one of Lee's army corps was not specially enticing. I promptly advised Curtin of the situation and of the orders I had received from McClellan. Thaddeus Stevens happened to be in the Executive Chamber when the message was received, and McClellan's order to me to confront one of Lee's army corps with my force, which did not amount to a corporal's guard within reach, caused considerable merriment. Stevens, who at that time never lost an opportunity to slur McClellan, said: "Well, McClure will do something. If he can't do better, he'll instruct the tollgate keeper not to permit Lee's army to pass through; but as to McClellan, God only knows what he'll do."

Thus one bold, heroic, and adventurous young captain, aided by an equally heroic young telegrapher, furnished McClellan all the reliable information he received about Lee's movements from the time McClellan left Rockville in the Antietam campaign until the shock of battle came ten days later. I met Captain Palmer at Antietam when the battle was in progress, and, after complimenting him as he so well deserved for the great work he had done, I earnestly cautioned him against attempting to repeat his experiments if Lee should be driven into Virginia. He was a young man of very few words, and made no response to my admonition beyond thanking me for my kind expressions of confidence. When Lee retreated across the Potomac, Captain Palmer followed him the next night, entered his lines again, and brought important reports which, as I believe, led to the battle of Shepherdstown that was successfully fought by General Fitz John Porter. He then passed beyond my jurisdiction, and became known to some of the leading officers of McClellan's army as the scout or spy who had given McClellan most reliable and important information. For several nights he entered Lee's lines and reported in the morning. Finally, he was missed at the usual time his report was expected. When the second day passed without any word from him, great anxiety was felt for his safety, and every effort was made that could be made without exposing him to the discovery of his identity to learn of his whereabouts, but without success. When he had been missing a week it was evident that he had been captured, and, upon being advised of it from the headquarters of McClellan's army, I hastened to Philadelphia to confer with President J. Edgar Thompson of the Pennsylvania Railroad Company, whose secretary Captain Palmer had been until he entered the service, and who was greatly interested in him personally.

A conference with President Thompson and Vice-President Scott resulted in the purpose to endeavor to save Palmer from being identified by his captors, and it was finally decided that I should go to the offices of the *North American*, the *Press*, and the *Inquirer*, the leading morning journals of the city, and write up for publication the next morning displayed dispatches announcing the arrival in Washington of Captain W. J. Palmer, who had been scouting in Virginia for some days, and who had brought most important information of the movements and purposes of the enemy. Some details of his reported facts were given to make the story plausible, to which was added the statement that he had brought momentous information that could not be given to the public, but that would doubtless lead to early military movements against the enemy. The dispatches were all accepted by the publishers, as all felt a special interest in Captain Palmer's fate, and that publication doubtless saved him from being gibbeted as a spy. He had been arrested by the enemy, tried, and convicted as a spy, but he had managed to maintain doubt as to his identity. His execution was delayed from time to time to ascertain who he was. The dispatches published in the Philadelphia papers, all of which reached the enemy's lines within forty-eight hours, if not sooner, entirely misled the Confederates as to Captain Palmer, and the failure to identify him saved him, until he finally effected his own exchange by quietly taking the place of a dead prisoner in the ranks and responding to his name when the roll was called for the men who were to be sent to the North. He is better known to the world of to-day as President Palmer of New York, lately of the Denver and Rio Grande Railway, and one of the fortunate and potential railroad magnates of the land.

After the battle of Antietam and the retreat of Lee beyond the Potomac the border people began to breathe freely again, and felt that they were reasonably safe at least for a season, but twenty days after the retreat of Lee they were thrown into panic again, as General Stuart made the first great raid of the war clear around McClellan's army, crossing the Potomac near Hancock, swinging through Mercersburg and Chambersburg, and getting safely back to Lee again. It was on Friday evening, October 10, 1862, and I had gone home from Harrisburg after weeks of almost ceaseless labor night and day, expecting a quiet rest until Monday morning. When I landed on the dépôt platform at Chambersburg, Mr. Gilmore, the telegraph-operator, called me into his private office and exhibited to me several dispatches he had just received from Mercersburg, stating that a strong Confederate force of cavalry was just entering that town, and other dispatches stating that they were moving from Mercersburg toward St. Thomas, which was on the direct line toward Chambersburg. I could not believe it possible that Stuart would venture to Chambersburg, when he must have known that part of McClellan's force was at Hagerstown, within one hour of us by railway, and that troops could be brought there to overwhelm him by the exercise of any reasonable military skill. I at once telegraphed to the commander at Hagerstown, who turned out to be General Wood, telling him that Stuart was approaching Chambersburg, to which I received an impertinent reply, saying in substance that Stuart was no such fool, and not to bother myself about it. I remained at the telegraph-office for two hours without communicating the information to any one, as I hoped that Stuart would not get so far from his base as Chambers-

(Photo by Brady, Washington.)

GENERAL J. E. B. STUART, 1862.

burg, and that our people could be spared the panic that must follow the announcement of his coming. I soon learned that Stuart's force had reached the turnpike six or eight miles west of Chambersburg, and was moving toward us, and I urgently appealed to General Wood to throw a force into Chambersburg to protect the town. Even then he had ample time to do so, as the railway facilities were at his command, but the only answer I received was a repetition of the assumption that Stuart would not dare to venture into Chambersburg, and broadly intimating to me not to annoy him any further.

Finding that nothing could be done to protect Chambersburg, I quietly went to my home, took tea, and returned to my office to await events. A cold, drizzling rain had been falling during the day, and between the clouds and fog darkness came unusually early. Some of the prominent citizens of the town had been advised of the approach of Stuart, but all agreed that it could do no good to make an alarm or to attempt defence. About seven o'clock in the evening there was a knock at my office-door, which I promptly opened, and in came three Confederate soldiers with a dirty rag tied to a stick which they called a flag of truce. Judge Kimmell and Colonel Thomas B. Kennedy were present. The Confederate officer said he had been sent in advance to demand the surrender of Chambersburg. We told him that there were no troops in the town and nobody to oppose the entrance of the insurgents. I asked who was in command of the Confederate forces, but they refused to answer. I then asked where the forces were, which they also refused to answer. I then asked them whether they would take us to the commanding general and give us safe-conduct back. They assured us that they would do so, and we three mounted horses and rode out on the western turnpike for nearly a mile, and were there brought

26

up before a solid column of soldiers. General Wade
Hampton came to the front and announced his name.
He said he desired to take peaceful possession of the
town, and in answer to our inquiries assured us that private citizens and private property would be respected,
excepting such property as might be needed for the purposes of the army. Remembering that I was a commissioned officer, I said to General Hampton: "There are
several military officers in the town in charge of hospitals, recruiting service, etc.; what will be done with
them?" He promptly answered: "They will be paroled,
unless there are special reasons for not doing so, but you
must not give information to any of them, so that they
may escape." As we were not in a position to quibble
about the terms of surrender, and as General Hampton's
proposition seemed reasonably fair, we decided to give
him a town that he could take without opposition, and
rode back into Chambersburg, with Hampton's command
immediately following.

In a short time the large square in the centre of the
town was filled with soldiers in gray, the first our people
had ever seen in fighting force. In crossing the square
to my office through a crowd of the enemy, I was tapped
on the shoulder, and, turning round, I recognized Hugh
Logan, who was a Franklin county man, and to whom I
had rendered some professional service when he was a
resident of the county. His exclamation was: "Why,
colonel, what are you doing here? Don't you know that
Stuart has orders to arrest a number of civilians, and you
among them, and that we have half a dozen with us now,
including Mr. Rice of Mercersburg?" I answered that
I had not been informed of that interesting fact. He
advised me quietly to get out of the way, and I reminded
him that I was a commissioned officer, and that under
my agreement with General Hampton I assumed that I

would be entitled to parole if arrested. His answer was unpleasantly significant. He said: "If you are arrested and can reach Hampton he will parole you, for he's a gentleman; but Jeb Stuart wants you, and I am not certain that he would release you on parole." As I lived a mile out of the centre of the town, I decided that I would return home and await events, rather than leave my family alone. When I reached there, I found that a detachment of Stuart's troops had been in advance of me and relieved me of the possession of ten fine horses. My house stood back from the highway some fifty yards and was largely hidden by shade trees, and I closed up the house, so as to leave no lights visible, and sat on the porch awaiting visitors, whom I sincerely hoped would not come. Shortly after midnight I heard the clatter of hoofs and the jingle of sabres coming down the road toward the town. Soon they arrived in front of my house. They saw corn-shocks on one side of the road, a large barn and water on the other side, and a paling fence that promised a quick fire. They halted, apparently about one hundred and fifty in number, and immediately proceeded to tumble the corn-shocks over to the horses and tear down the palings to start the fire.

Seeing that their acquaintance was inevitable, I walked down to the gate and kindly said to them that if they wanted to make a fire they would find wood just a few feet from them, and showed them a short way to water. The commander of the detachment stepped up to me and very courteously inquired whether I resided there, without asking my name, and said he would be greatly obliged if he and some of his officers could get a cup of coffee. I told them that I had plenty of coffee, but that my servants were colored and had hidden. He assured me that they were not after negroes, whether slave or free, and that if I could find the servants and get them some coffee I could promise them absolute safety. My servants were hidden in the thicket but a little distance from the house, and I soon found some twenty negroes, who swarmed back and speedily had hot coffee and tea for the officers of the command. It was evident they had no idea at whose place they were stopping, but they were thinly clad, without their overcoats and blankets, in order to be in the lightest trim for rapid marching, and they were suffering from the cold rain of the entire day. They gladly accepted my invitation to come into the house and warm themselves, and they were not five minutes in the library, where the New York and Philadelphia papers lay on my table with my name on them, before they all intuitively comprehended the fact that they had asked hospitality and were about to receive it in the house of a man whom they were ordered to take as a prisoner to the South. They were all Virginians and gentlemen of unusual intelligence and culture, as the young bloods of that State with fine horses filled up the ranks of the cavalry in the early part of the war. I watched with unusual interest to see what the effect would be when they discovered in whose house they were as guests, but they did not long leave me in doubt as to their appreciation of the peculiar condition in which they were placed. They at once took in the situation without opportunity to confer on the subject. It was soon evident that they had decided that, having asked and accepted hospitality, they would not permit themselves to know that they were in the house of a host whom it was their duty to arrest as a prisoner. We sat at tea and over our pipes and cigars until at daylight the bugle called them to the march. Every phase of the war was discussed with the utmost freedom, but no one of them spoke the name of himself or any of his fellows, and not one assumed to know my identity. It was to me one of the most interesting events of the war, and I doubt whether the war itself was ever discussed with equal candor on both sides without a single exhibition of prejudice or passion. When the bugle sounded they arose and bade me good-bye, thanking me for my hospitality and earnestly expressing the hope that we should some time meet again under more pleasant auspices. Soon after I followed them into the town, and stood in the crowd close beside Jeb Stuart for some time before he started on his homeward march. He did not doubt that I was one of his prisoners, and it was not until he had crossed the Potomac that he learned that I was not among his captives, when, as I have since been told by officers who were present, he made the atmosphere blue with his profane lamentations.

I much regretted that I had no clue whatever to the identity of any of the Virginia officers who had spent the night with me, and after the war had closed, and President Johnson was breathing the fiercest vengeance against the South, I felt that I might be of some service to these men if I could discover who they were. I wrote to a newspaper in Winchester and also to the Richmond *Whig*, stating the facts and asking for information as to these officers, but there was then universal distrust in the South, and, as my property had been burned with Chambersburg but a year before, I infer that my suggestions were regarded as insincere, and no answers were received to either of my letters. It was not until ten years after the war that I accidentally learned the names of some of the officers who were with me. On a visit to Washington I was in conversation with the late Heister Clymer on the floor of the House just before the meeting of the body, when he remarked to me that a Virginia member desired to renew his acquaintance with me, and asked permission to bring him and introduce him. I of course

assented, and he brought up Colonel Whitehead, then a
Congressman from the Lynchburg district, who informed
me that he had spent a night with me at my house during
Stuart's raid, and that he desired to renew his acquaintance of that evening under the more pleasant circumstances which then surrounded us, and to thank me for
the kindness they had all received. From him I learned
that Lieutenant-Colonel James W. Watts commanded the
detachment, and that Captain W. W. Tebbs, Captain
Thomas W. Whitehead (himself), Lieutenant Kelso, and
two others, whose names he did not then recall, constituted the unique tea-party at Norland on the night of
October 10, 1862. John Paxton of Adams County, who
was on the list with myself from that town, was taken
by Stuart's command, but released soon after he had
reached Richmond. Perry A. Rice of Mercersburg, a
prominent member of the bar, was held in Libbey Prison
for some months, and died there. It was thus that I escaped being Jeb Stuart's captive in the first and one of
the most brilliant cavalry raids of the war. It is but just
to Captain Hugh Logan, however, to state that he advised me, when telling me of my danger, that if captured and refused parole I should quietly submit and join
the procession, and he would put me out of the ranks the
first night. That he would have done so, even at the
peril of his life, I do not doubt, and I am as grateful to
him as if he had had occasion to perform that act of
kindness to me.

The Stuart raid of October, 1862, was the first actual
experience of the border people of Pennsylvania with a
Confederate force in their midst, but beyond the general
panic and disturbance it produced, the loss of some twelve
hundred horses by our farmers and the destruction of railroad property, we felt none of the serious results of war.
The Pennsylvania "emergency-men" followed to give

protection when it was no longer needed, as they did again in 1863, after Lee had retreated, and again in 1864, after McCausland had burned Chambersburg. These suddenly-organized and undisciplined commands were inspired by patriotic purpose, but they really never rendered any service in protecting the people of the border, and at times were very destructive because of their want of discipline and properly-organized supplies.

After the militia had been quietly disposed of, there was comparative peace along the border until after the defeat of Hooker at Chancellorsville and Lee commenced his movement northward. The first sullen murmurs of invasion came, as usual, from the Shenandoah Valley, as General Milroy was routed at Winchester and his stampeded army scattered in fragments over the border region. With them came fleeing loyal fugitives from Virginia and swarms of negroes, creating panic in every direction, and on the evening of the 15th of June positive information was received that General Jenkins, commanding the cavalry advance of Lee's army, was approaching. They took possession of Chambersburg the same night, and General Jenkins exhibited the good taste of all commanders of both armies by camping on my farm, and he further honored me by taking possession of my house as his headquarters.

A short time before this advance of Lee a prominent citizen who lived just south of the Pennsylvania line in Maryland, who was a client and friend of mine, and whose release I had obtained after he had been condemned by General Schenck and banished into the Southern lines, rode nearly all night from his home to Chambersburg to advise me that an invasion was inevitable, and that I must not permit myself to be captured. He had spent some weeks within the Confederate lines after he had been banished by court-martial, and he felt

it to be his duty to inform me of the excessive estimate
the Southern leaders put upon me as a prisoner, as they
supposed that with me as captive they could make unusually good terms with Governor Curtin and President
Lincoln. I heeded his advice, and thereafter did not
remain in Chambersburg to extend hospitality to the
sons of the South. General Jenkins was hospitably
treated by my family, and his sick soldiers, for whom
my barn had been improvised as hospital, were kindly
ministered to by Mrs. McClure. It was this same command that one year later, under General McCausland,
burned Chambersburg and went a mile out of its way to
burn my house and barn. Of course all stock and valuables that could be shipped away had been sent to Harrisburg or points beyond, and our people were living
under many discomforts. Jenkins remained only a few
days in Chambersburg, when he suddenly fell back toward
the Potomac between Greencastle and Hagerstown, and
from there sent out marauding parties to capture horses
and supplies. The whole southern portion of Franklin
county was mercilessly plundered while Jenkins was
waiting the arrival of Lee's infantry. General Rhodes'
division was the first to reach Pennsylvania, and with
that command Jenkins again advanced and took possession of Chambersburg.

The history of the great Gettysburg campaign and
battle is so familiar to all that I need not dwell on details. Lee then commanded the largest and the most
defiant army the Confederates ever had during the war.
General Ewell's corps, over twenty thousand strong, encamped on my farm, and thence Generals Rhodes and
Early made their movements against York and Harrisburg. On the 26th of June, General Lee entered Chambersburg with his staff, and it is needless to say that his
movements were watched with intense interest by all in-

telligent citizens. Early and Rhodes were already operating on the lines of the Susquehanna, and Lee's army
was so disposed that it could be rapidly concentrated for
operations in the Cumberland Valley and against Philadelphia or thrown south of the South Mountain to ope-
rate against Washington. Lee held a brief council in
the centre square of Chambersburg with General A. P.
Hill and several other officers, and when he left them
intense anxiety was exhibited by every one who observed
them to ascertain whether his movements would indicate
the concentration of his army in the Cumberland Valley
or for operations against Washington. When he came
to the street where the Gettysburg turnpike enters the
square, he turned to the right, went out a mile along
that road, and fixed his headquarters in a little grove
close by the roadside then known as Shetters' Woods.
When Lee turned in that direction, Benjamin S. Huber,
a country lad, happened to be present, and, as he had
already exhibited some fitness for such work, he was
started immediately overland for Harrisburg to communicate to Governor Curtin the fact that Lee's movement
indicated Gettysburg as his objective point. Lee was
fated to lose three days of invaluable time at his headquarters in the quiet grove near Chambersburg, as his
cavalry had been cut off from him by encountering our
cavalry forces in Eastern Maryland, and he could get no
information whatever of the movements of the Union
army.

It was not until the 29th of June that he received information from one of Longstreet's scouts of the position
of the Army of the Potomac, and he immediately decided to cross South Mountain and accept battle on the
line to Baltimore and Washington. On the night of
Monday, June 29th, General Ewell's wagon-trains passed
through Chambersburg and turned eastward on the Get-

tysburg turnpike. This movement was carefully watched, and it soon became evident to intelligent observers that Lee's army was moving rapidly to concentrate south of the South Mountain. I was then at Harrisburg with Governor Curtin, and the only news we received of Lee's movement, and the only reliable news received at Meade's headquarters for some days, came from the several energetic young men who performed scout-duty between Chambersburg and Harrisburg by traversing the mountains north of the Cumberland Valley. It was known to us that Lee was in the Cumberland Valley with the largest Southern army ever organized, and the gravest apprehensions were felt by all as to the ability of the Army of the Potomac to meet it in battle. There was no sleep for the weary men at Harrisburg who were compelled to watch and to await events.

The first intimation received of Lee's movement toward Gettysburg came from John A. Seiders of Chambersburg, who had entered the enemy's lines in Confederate uniform and saw General Rhodes begin the movement from Carlisle in the direction of Gettysburg; but as Rhodes and Early were both moving from point to point, the fact that Rhodes was apparently retiring from Carlisle was no indication of Lee's movements in Chambersburg.

I shall never forget the first dispatch received at the Executive Mansion at Harrisburg giving the information that Lee had moved toward Gettysburg. It was some time between midnight and morning on the 1st of July, while a dozen or more were waiting with the intensest interest for news, that an unsigned dispatch was received by Governor Curtin from Port Royal in Juniata county, stating that the writer had left Chambersburg the day before at the request of Judge Kimmell to convey the information to the Governor that Lee was marching

Lexington Va
21 Decr 1866

My dear Sir

In reply to your letter
of the 15th Inst: I have to state,
that should I Complete the
history I Contemplate, the arrangements for its publication
are made

Very respy
R E Lee

Mr Alexr K McClure

FAC-SIMILE OF LETTER FROM GENERAL LEE.

toward Gettysburg. The fact that the dispatch was un-signed threw doubt upon the value of the information, but as it described minutely the route the scout had trav-eled through Franklin and Juniata counties, with which I was personally quite familiar, I was able to give reason-able assurance that the dispatch was genuine. The tele-graph-office at Port Royal had been opened to send the dispatch, and was closed immediately after, so that no details could be obtained. General Couch, then in com-mand of the Union force at Harrisburg, was present in the Governor's room, and he immediately communicated with General "Baldy" Smith, giving the information received and asking him to see whether the enemy had retired from his front. Before noon the next day the correctness of the statement given by the unknown scout was fully verified; and it is a most remarkable fact that the identity of this man was never discovered by Gov-ernor Curtin until twenty years thereafter.

This scout was Stephen W. Pomeroy, whose father had sat on the bench as associate with Judge Kimmell, and Kimmell, knowing the trustworthiness of the young man, wrote the dispatch for Governor Curtin, cut a hole in the buckle-strap of Pomeroy's pantaloons, and hid the telegram therein. Information came from so many quar-ters during the next day that the message of the young scout was almost forgotten, and the thrilling events that followed and the many conspicuous feats performed by the young men of the Cumberland Valley in scouting service prevented minute inquiry into the source of the important dispatch of the early morning. Twenty years later the Presbyterian Synod of that section met in Belle-fonte, and several ministers in attendance were guests of Governor Curtin. In the course of his reminiscent con-versations about the war he happened to mention the receipt of this important dispatch, and the fact that he had never been advised as to the author of it. To his surprise, Rev. S. W. Pomeroy, then his own guest, told him that he was the man, and at Curtin's request he wrote a letter that was given to the public stating the full particulars of his marvelous journey.* It was upon

---

* MOUNT UNION, PA., Nov. 13, 1883.

HON. A. G. CURTIN—DEAR SIR : In compliance with your request, I send you the account of how I came to send you the telegram of the concentration of the Confederate army at Gettysburg during the war. After being discharged from the nine months' service of the Pennsylvania volunteers, I happened to be home, at my father's—Judge Pomeroy of Roxbury, Franklin county—when the enemy were marching down the Cumberland Valley. There was, of course, great excitement, for the enemy were at our doors and taking what they would. Farmers hid their horses and other stock in the mountains as far as possible. One day three hundred cavalry marched into Roxbury. When we learned of their coming, ten of the men who had been out in the nine months' service armed ourselves as best we could and went out to intercept them; but the odds were too great, so we retired. Anxious to hear the news and render what service we might to our country, a number of us walked to Chambersburg, a distance of fourteen miles, reaching there in the afternoon. That night the rebels were concentrated at Gettysburg. Next morning Judge F. M. Kimmell, with whom my father sat as associate judge, learned that a son of Thomas Pomeroy was in town. He sent for me to come to him at once. I found the judge on the street that leads to McConnellsburg, a short distance from the Franklin Hotel, where the Central Presbyterian Church now stands. As the town was full of rebels and a rebel had his beat near us, the judge asked me in a low tone if I was a son of Judge Pomeroy. I replied in the affirmative. With apparent unconcern he asked me to follow him. I did so, and he led me into a little dark back room and told me that the rebels were concentrating at Gettysburg and Governor Curtin did not know it. He said it was of the utmost importance that the Governor should know at the earliest possible moment, and asked me if I would take a telegram to the nearest point on the Pennsylvania Railroad and send it to him. He added: "It is of infinite importance to him and to our country." I replied that I would try it. The telegram

this information that General Meade, then just placed in
the command of the Army of the Potomac, hastened to

---

was already written, so he cut a hole in the buckle-strap of my
pantaloons and deposited there the telegram to be sent, and
said: "Get this safely and in the shortest time possible to the
Governor." Assuming indifference, I came to the street and met
the rebel guard, who did not disturb me. Some of those who
came with me wishing to return to Roxbury, we set out together.
We met many at the edge of the town returning who could not
get through the guards, who were stationed around the town.

Coming to the forks of the Strasburg and Roxbury roads, we
found both cavalry and infantry. On the left there was a slight
hollow, also several wheat-fields, and beyond these there were
woods. This was the only way to hope for escape. At my proposal we crept along this hollow, at the end of which there were
some wheat-fields; we kept these between us and the guard till
we reached the woods. When getting over the fence into the
woods we were seen by the enemy. They called, rode after us,
and leveled their muskets at us, but we ran on, and, as they did
not fire or follow far, we escaped. Still fearing capture, we kept
to the fields. Before we reached Strasburg all had fallen behind
but one. We must have walked about seventeen miles before we
got to Roxbury. As the horses were hid in the mountains, I was
in dread lest I should not get a horse; but I met Mr. L. S. Sent-
man riding into town to get feed for his horses in the mountains.
Telling him of the message I was carrying, he gave me his horse.
Informing my father of my errand, I set out on my trip at once.
It was about noon. The mountain-road to Amberson Valley
was, I knew, blockaded with trees to prevent the marauders from
entering the valley to steal horses. The Barrens below Concord
were blockaded by citizens of Tuscarora Valley, many of whom
knew me. The report having reached them that I was killed
while trying to hinder the rebels from entering Roxbury, the obstacles and excitement of my friends at finding me alive hindered
me about ten minutes. Free from them, I hastened down the
Tuscarora Valley as fast as my horse could carry me. At Beal-
town, Mr. Beal (now the Rev. D. J. Beal) speedily got me a fresh
horse. When I reached Silas E. Smith's I did these two things:
got lunch and proved to the future Mrs. Pomeroy that I was not
dead, as she supposed, but good for many years to come. From
thence I rode to my uncle's, Joseph Pomeroy, at Academia, found

concentrate his army, and he ordered General Reynolds to make a recognizance in force at Gettysburg to ascertain the position of the enemy. The young men who performed the most important duty of maintaining communications between Harrisburg and Chambersburg by circuitous journeys through the mountains were Stephen W. Pomeroy, Thomas J. Grimison, Sellers Montgomery, J. Porter Brown, Anthony Holler, Shearer Houser, Benjamin S. Huber, and probably others whose names I cannot recall.

When Lee had passed the South Mountain and the battle at Gettysburg had begun it was impossible to obtain any news from Lee's rear as to important movements between the two armies, and thenceforth until Lee's retreat the only information received at Harrisburg and Chambersburg came from General Meade through Washington. On the evening of the first day's battle we learned the sad news that Reynolds had fallen and that

them likewise mourning my supposed death, and he supplied another horse, the fastest he had. That carried me to within a mile of my destination, when a soldier on guard called, "Halt!" I told the sergeant on guard my mission, and requested one of the guard to go with me, that I might get the telegram off to Harrisburg in the shortest time possible.

Getting on the horse behind me, we rode in a few minutes to the office. Finding the operator, he cut the telegram out of the strap of my pantaloons and sent it at once to you. The excitement and journey being over and the telegram being off to you, I began to look at the time and found it about midnight. I had walked that day about seventeen miles and ridden about forty-one miles. Anxious as I was about the critical state of the country, I was so tired I had to seek the house of my kinsman, Major J. M. Pomeroy, in Perryville (now Port Royal), for rest.

The above is the history of that telegram that, I believe, first gave you notice of the concentration of the rebel troops at Gettysburg just before the famous battle in that place.

Respectfully yours,

STEPHEN W. POMEROY.

the Union troops had been badly defeated. On the second day no material news came, and for two days the government at Harrisburg and the people in the Valley were agonized by fearful suspense as to the issue of the conflict. Late in the evening of July 3d, Wayne Mac-Veagh, who had been with the Governor during the whole period of trial, and whose anxiety kept him close beside the telegraph-operator, rushed into the Executive Chamber with Meade's report of the repulse of Pickett on Cemetery Hill. It was the first silver lining of the dark cloud flung upon us by the Gettysburg invasion, and when the next morning it was known that Lee had retreated, while every loyal heart of the land was gladdened, the border people felt a relief that was unknown in any other part of the country.

One of the incidents of Lee's retreat I do not recall with pleasure, but it is due to the truth of history to tell the story of the fierce passions which ran riot in our civil war. Lee left thousands of his wounded scattered along the line of his retreat, and a number of them were gathered into a hospital in Chambersburg. Little attention was paid to the fact that there was a Confederate hospital in our midst, as "uncommon things make common things forgot." Some ten days after Lee's retreat, Dr. A. H. Senseny, my own family physician, came to me and informed me that he was attending the Confederate wounded in the hospital, and that they were in great need of some things which were not supplied by army regulations. He appealed to me to go in person and see them and take the lead to have them properly supplied, as he believed I could do it without suspicion of disloyalty. I visited the hospital with him and found a number of severely-wounded men who had great need of some delicacies necessary to their recovery or comfort. Mrs. McClure immediately took charge of the effort, and was heartily seconded by a number of estimable ladies. I became specially interested in a young Confederate, Colonel Carter, who resided in Texas, but who was a native of Tennessee. It was evident that his wound was mortal, and he fully understood it. When he was informed by the doctor that I had come to perform some kind offices for the wounded in that hospital, he thanked me effusively, and made a piteous appeal to me to assure him decent Christian burial after his death. I gave him the promise, little dreaming of the angry passions it would arouse in a Christian community. He died a few days thereafter, and I applied to the trustees of the Presbyterian church I attended for permission to bury him in the graveyard attached to it. To my surprise it was refused. I made like application to the several other churches in the town which had cemeteries, and was refused in every instance. I then applied to a company that had recently started a new cemetery near the town, and proposed to purchase a lot for the burial of the dead Confederate colonel, but that was refused, and indignation was expressed on almost every side because of my effort to give a Confederate soldier decent burial. I then announced that I would set apart a small lot in the corner of the field in front of my house to bury him there and dedicate it as his resting-place. Finally Mr. Burnett, an estimable Christian character, gave Colonel Carter's remains a resting-place in his own lot in the Methodist burial-ground. Such were the fierce passions of civil war in one of the most intelligent, generous, and Christian communities of the North, and I recall it often as one of the saddest memories of our fraternal conflict.

After the battle of Gettysburg the border people had seen war in its most horrible aspect. The constant peril from incursions of the enemy, and the possibility of other great battles being fought upon the border or north of

27

the Potomac, destroyed all hope of tranquility in that region until the war closed. There was comparative peace and quiet during the winter of 1863–64, but when the spring of 1864 opened the border counties were almost constantly threatened by cavalry raids or hostile armies. Governor Curtin had taken the precaution to organize an ample force to protect the border from raids, but as these troops were mustered into the service of the national government, and thereby subject to the call of the War Department, they were ordered from the State to rein-force Hunter on the north side of the Potomac after his disastrous advance into Virginia. While Hunter was thus endeavoring to reorganize his demoralized forces and the border was threatened in the direction of Hagers-town, the startling news came to General Couch's head-quarters on the evening of July 29, 1864, that a Confed-erate force had entered Mercersburg and was marching toward Chambersburg. General Couch, although com-manding a department with headquarters at Chambers-burg, had but one hundred and fourteen men under his command, and they were scattered over half as many miles as scouts on the border. The troops that he could have summoned to repel invasion under ordinary circum-stances had passed through Chambersburg within twenty-four hours to join Hunter, in command of another de-partment, and were beyond his control.

I remained with Couch the night of the 29th until three o'clock the next morning. He received frequent reports from the heroic Lieutenant McLean, who had just thirteen men with him, but who in the darkness of the night confronted McCausland at every cross-roads in his advance upon Chambersburg, and so hindered him that he did not arrive in front of the town until daylight. McCausland in his official report states that he was con-fronted by a regiment that fought him most gallantly and greatly delayed his advance, but I happened to know that the entire force opposed to him was the lieutenant and his thirteen men. It was evident at three o'clock in the morning that the Confederate force would reach the town before daylight, and, as General Couch had no means whatever for defending the place, he ordered a special train to be in readiness to take himself, staff, and official records away when it became necessary. He urged me to go with him, believing that it was unsafe for me to remain at home, but I decided that I would not leave my family, perilous though it seemed to be, and left him to go to my own house. When I reached there and gave the condition of affairs, Mrs. McClure most earnestly urged me to go with General Couch, and while I was hesitating he sent a staff-officer to my house, saying that he felt it his duty to command me to accompany him out of the town, and to come at once and leave with him on the train. I still hesitated and sent his staff-officer away, but soon after Mr. Taylor, an old friend, drove up in his buggy and proposed to take me with him, and I accompanied him to Shippensburg.

Telegraphic communication was of course cut off, but the next morning I took the cars for Harrisburg, where I was greeted with the information that McCausland had burned the town and had sent a special detachment, commanded by a son of Ex-Governor Smith of Virginia, to burn my house and barn, after having burned my printing-office and law-office in the town. Rev. Samuel J. Niccolls, now of St. Louis, was my immediate neighbor, and he came to my house when he found that a detachment of the enemy had entered it. Mrs. McClure was ill, confined to her room, but Captain Smith entered it and notified her to leave immediately, as he was going to burn the house in retaliation for the destruction of private property by Hunter in Virginia, and forbade her to

take anything with her.   Mr. Niccolls attempted to take
some of my clothing on his arms, but it was grasped
from him and cast into the flames.   The only thing
saved from the house was a portrait that Miss Virginia
Riley seized, and with it ran out of the house through a
back door, and the family Bible was taken charge of by
Mrs. Gray, the mother of my wife.   When Captain Smith
was about to fire the room in which Mrs. McClure was
an invalid, she opened a drawer in her bureau and handed
him a letter she had received but a few days before and
requested him to read it.   It was from one of the same
command who had been there under Jenkins the year
before, and who had been ill and received generous ministrations from her.   It was a letter of thanks from one of
Captain Smith's own associates for the kind offices she
had given to an enemy when in distress, but it did not
stop the vandal's work, and everything perished by the
vandal's torch.

I need not describe the brutality that is inevitable
when a military command is ordered to play the barba-
rian.   Many of the men became intoxicated, and there
were numerous records of barbarity which all would be
glad to forget.   A large brick house on another part of
my farm was fortunately occupied by the family of Colonel Boyd, one of our most gallant troopers and successful scouts.   Learning that that property belonged to me,
Colonel Harry Gilmore led a detachment to burn it.
Colonel Boyd was absent on duty, but his wife was an
heroic woman, and, when Colonel Gilmore entered the
house and informed her of their purpose, she amazed
them by her coolness of manner and much more by her
defiance.   She said: "Do you know whose home this
is?"   The answer was: "Yes, we know that this belongs
to Colonel McClure, and we are ordered to burn it."
Her answer was: "This is the home of Colonel Boyd,

of whom you have some knowledge. I am now ready to walk out of it, and you can burn it if you choose, but don't forget that it is the home of Colonel Boyd." They knew of Colonel Boyd, and they knew also that if his home was burned it would make a hundred Virginians homeless before another month, as he would have given fearful retribution. Colonel Gilmore bowed to Mrs. Boyd, saying: "We will not burn the home of so gallant a soldier;" and thus the property was saved. He gives a different account of the incident in his book, but all who remember Mrs. Boyd well know that she was not the whimpering dame he represents her.

I need not describe the burning of Chambersburg. It was ordered by General Early upon the failure of the people to pay a tribute of $500,000, which was an impossible demand, and the order was executed in unexampled barbarity. It accomplished nothing in the war beyond making hundreds of homeless families in the South, and especially in Columbia, South Carolina, when Sherman was marching north, where the people learned to associate the cry of Chambersburg with sweeping destruction. Every drunken Union soldier in Southern cities applied the torch as did the drunken soldiers of McCausland in Chambersburg, always preceding it with the cry of "Remember Chambersburg!" The fact remains that one of the most beautiful towns of the State had been ruthlessly destroyed by war; that the people of Chambersburg and of the border regions had suffered spoliation to the extent of not less than $4,000,000; and that the burning of Chambersburg was the direct result of the general government calling away the troops organized for State service that would have been ample to defend the town. It was not the accident of a lost battle; it was the result of the extreme necessities of the national government that deprived Pennsylvania of her own rightful defenders, and it is a blistering stain upon the government that it has not made reasonable restitution for the loss which resulted from the action of the government itself. The people of Chambersburg heroically struggled to rebuild their homes and revive their business, but soon after the war closed there was a general paralysis and depression of values, and many were hopelessly bankrupted, while others struggled on for years in the vain effort to retrieve their fortunes.

This fearful strain upon the people of the border continued for four long years. Finally, on the night of April 9, 1865, when the long-suffering residents of Chambersburg were at rest in the homes they had improvised in their ashes, they were suddenly startled by the ringing of the courthouse bell, in which the chimes of several church bells were soon mingled. There had been no rumors of a raid, but the people hurried from their beds to inquire what new peril confronted them or what great victory had been achieved. In a very short time the streets resounded with the shouts: "Lee has surrendered!" Soon the people of the town, young and old, were upon the streets, many of them weeping with joy, and all mingling in congratulations; and thus the fearful strain upon them was ended. To them it meant more than peace between the North and the South; it meant much more than a restored nation: it meant the ending of the strife that entered their own homes and desolated the places where their affections centered, and it meant that at last, after the bloodiest war of modern history, they had—rest.

THE PENNSYLVANIA RESERVE CORPS.

WHILE none will claim that the soldiers of the Pennsylvania Reserve Corps were more heroic than other scores of thousands of Pennsylvania soldiers who volunteered for the defence of the Union, it is none the less true that this organization, alike by reason of the peculiar circumstances under which it was created and because of its opportunities for the most heroic service in nearly every battle of the Army of the Potomac, occupies a distinctive place in the history of Pennsylvania heroism. How it was organized has already been stated in these articles. How it was summoned by the patriotism and sagacity of Governor Curtin when the national government had not only not called for it, but refused to accept it; how the legislature was appealed to by the Governor, and a State organization effected alike for the protection of the State and the general government; how it was frantically called for by the same authorities who had rejected it when disaster fell upon the Union forces at Bull Run; how it promptly marched to Washington and ended panic by assuring the safety of the capital,—are matters of history known to all; and when it is remembered that it had such commanders as McCall, Meade, Reynolds, Ord, and Crawford, and brigade commanders who have shed lustre upon the skill and heroism of Pennsylvania soldiers, and that more than one-half of its entire force fell wounded or dead

(Photo by Gutekunst, Philadelphia.)

MAJOR-GENERAL S. W. CRAWFORD, 1865.

in battle, it is not surprising that the Pennsylvania Reserve Corps occupies a unique position in the annals of Pennsylvania achievement and sacrifice in our civil war.

The command of the Reserves was first offered to General McClellan, and he had accepted, but on his way to Harrisburg he was stopped at Columbus, Ohio, where he was prevailed upon to accept the command of the Ohio State troops. It was then offered to General Franklin, but he declined, as he had been promoted to a colonelcy in the regular army. It was then tendered to General McCall of Chester county, Pennsylvania, a retired army officer, who proved to be an excellent disciplinarian and a most gallant soldier. General McCall earnestly devoted himself, and at once, to the organization for service of the division, to its drill and discipline, and gave to the Bucktails, or First Rifles, his especial care—a regiment to become famous as skirmishers wholly unique, and whose value in thick woods, tangled overgrowth, streams, and mountain-passes was unequaled anywhere. Three brigades were formed, under Reynolds, Meade, and Ord —names soon to become famous for ability and conspicuous service; and it cannot be questioned that the impression left by these able soldiers of the highest class in their discipline and instruction was long effective and contributed greatly to the reputation of the division.

Before the advance of our lines in front of Washington to a stronger position the Reserves were ordered to Langley, at Camp Pierpoint, beyond the Chain Bridge, where McCall's division constituted the right of the army, which it held until after the seven days' retreat on the Peninsula. Constantly in contact with the enemy, and always with credit to itself, it was preparing for the larger operations of war so soon to devolve upon it. A reconnaissance in force showed the presence of the enemy

in uncertain numbers near Dranesville, and an attack
from the direction of Centreville was anticipated, in regard to which McCall's division was warned.   Had the
reconnaissance to Dranesville resulted in holding that
place, the disaster to Baker and his command at Ball's
Bluff, and his subsequent rout, might have been avoided.

From intelligence received by a scout it was learned
that the enemy was in force at Dranesville, and that
his object was to forage in the unoccupied country in
his immediate front.   He had advanced his pickets in
front of his line, and was molesting Union men about
him, when it was determined to drive his line back
and take possession of the supplies of grain and forage
available.

On the 20th, Ord's brigade, with Easton's battery
and a detachment of cavalry, and with the Bucktails
as skirmishers, was ordered to move up the Dranesville
road.   Reynolds with his brigade, in support, was to
move in the same direction later, while Meade was held
in reserve in camp.   Ord reached Dranesville, and soon
developed the enemy, who opened fire with his artillery.
The brigade soon became closely engaged, Easton's battery coming rapidly into position and rendering most
effective service through the battle.   Ord's dispositions
were admirable, and he directed in person the operations
of his regiments, with Easton's guns and the Bucktails.
In an attempt to turn the left of our position the enemy
was repulsed by Easton's guns and the Sixth regiment.
There was close firing along the line, when an advance
was ordered and the enemy rapidly retreated toward
Centreville.   Meantime, Reynolds' brigade, followed
by that of Meade, had come up, but the battle was
over—a most successful affair, hardly to be dignified
with the name of a battle, and, in view of the immense
issues of the future, insignificant, but in its moral as-

pects immense. Young men gathered from all parts of Pennsylvania had assumed the panoply of war, and had gone into action and moved and fought with the confidence of veteran soldiers; and it was the first victory of the Army of the Potomac. Pennsylvania was thrilled at the achievement of her sons, and not only through her Governor, but through the Secretary of War, himself a Pennsylvanian, congratulations and commendations, official and private, upon the conduct of the division came in profusion.

The division now returned to its camp (Pierpoint) and made preparations to go into winter quarters. McClellan had been appointed to the command of the army, which for seven long months remained inactive confronting the enemy's lines. The Reserves under their competent officers were daily attaining efficiency in drill and in discipline and in preparation for battle—an efficiency that was never to leave them during their service. The whole heart of their State had gone out to them, and the patriotic Governor, who ever considered them his own special creation, never wearied in the exercise of his paternal care.

McClellan now moved from Alexandria to Fortress Monroe, and the advance of the Army of the Potomac began. To reach Yorktown and the Peninsula the army embarked by divisions. McDowell's corps, with the Pennsylvania Reserves, was in the rear. But while all was in motion, the President, learning that Washington had not been protected by a sufficient force in accordance with his orders, detached McDowell's corps and ordered him to report to the Secretary of War. This consequently kept the Pennsylvania Reserves from the Peninsula, and they accompanied their corps to Alexandria. Soon after another advance was made into Virginia to Falmouth and Fredericksburg. But when McDowell

arrived and was about to take up the line of march, he
received an order, directly from the President, forbidding
him to cross the river.   Here the Reserves remained for
over a month, going through all the phases and vicissitudes of military life, and becoming hardened and thoroughly fitted for the future service in store for them.
They were directly on the road to Richmond.   The gallant Bayard was made a brigadier-general on the 28th of
April, and the flying brigade was organized under his
command.

Again a forward movement toward Richmond was
ordered, and McDowell's corps had begun its movement
by the advance of Bayard's brigade, and everything
looked favorable to the speedy junction of McDowell and
his corps with the Army of the Potomac, when the President and his Cabinet arrived at Fredericksburg to confer
with McDowell as to the movement.   All was in readiness, the transportation secured, the men eager, and only
awaited the final order.   It was Saturday, the 24th of
May.   The next day being Sunday, the President objected to beginning a campaign on that day, when Monday morning was fixed upon.   Meantime a despatch was
received by McDowell revoking the order and changing
the whole plan of campaign.   Jackson had again burst
into the Valley of the Shenandoah and was in full march
northward.   The President personally interfered, Bayard
was quickly recalled, and the three divisions of Shields,
King, and Ord were hurried to the Shenandoah Valley
to meet him.   McCall with the Pennsylvania Reserves
was to hold Fredericksburg temporarily, some troops of
the cavalry only accompanying the expedition on their
march.   Bayard with his brigade encountered the enemy
in Jackson's rearguard, other troops, from Fremont's
command, joined him, and there was a brisk fight with
the enemy.   Bayard's brigade remained with Fremont.

Meantime the Reserves remained at Fredericksburg under McCall, when, on the 4th of June, McClellan called earnestly for reinforcements, and the Reserves were promised him to go to the White House. McClellan had assured the President that upon McCall's arrival with his division, if the state of the ground permitted, he would advance. McDowell moved promptly with the division of the Reserves alone. By the 14th of June the division was united at Tunstall's Station. Stuart's Confederate cavalry had threatened an attack upon the dépôt and had opened fire upon a train at the station. Upon the appearance of Reynolds with his brigade the cavalry retreated.

The Reserves, now united, mustered nearly ten thousand strong, of effective material. Fully organized, well drilled and equipped, under favorite and skilled commanders, they marched on the 17th with enthusiasm to take their place on the right of the army. It was the place of honor; they occupied it upon the 19th, and almost at once came under the fire of the enemy. It was a position which should have never been chosen, but which McCall with admirable sagacity and judgment at once made strong and formidable, taking advantage of the natural features of the ground and disposing his force with reference to the efficiency of its fire, putting two of his brigades in line and holding Meade's brigade in reserve.

The enemy was in plain view. At three o'clock he threw forward his skirmishers, which were at once driven back. Advancing his main body under cover of his artillery fire, he attacked the Reserves along their whole front. The fighting was long continued, and from the right centre to the left was hotly maintained. Various attempts were made by the enemy to find weak places in our line, but without success. The Reserves

maintained their position, inflicting great losses upon
the enemy, who finally retired at nine o'clock P. M.
McCall at once prepared for a renewal of the attack in
the morning, when he received McClellan's order to fall
back to Gaines' Mills. Jackson was marching from the
direction of Gordonsville upon the right flank and rear
of our army. This compelled an immediate change to
one definite side of the Chickahominy, the right bank.
The movement was executed with skill and success.
The Reserves moved speedily, and the spectacle of an
army with an impassable boggy stream flowing through
its centre was no longer seen.

The command fell back with regret, in perfect order,
behind the lines of Gaines' Mills at ten A. M., June
27th—a movement which the corps commander doubted
his ability to accomplish. Here it was held in reserve.
No veteran troops could have behaved with any greater
distinction than did the Pennsylvania Reserves in this
battle of Mechanicsville, and the glowing approbation
of their commander, McCall, was wholly deserved.
They had met most honorably every requirement of
their position with a devotion and courage worthy of
any troops in any army; and Mechanicsville will ever
remain one of their proudest achievements.

The withdrawal had been successfully accomplished,
and Porter's corps was in strong position at Gaines' Mill
by noon on the 27th of June, its flanks resting on the
creeks. The Pennsylvania Reserves, in justice to them
after their continued and gallant fighting, were held at
first in reserve and rear. But the enemy in strong
columns commenced his attack at four o'clock, and it
was so determined and persistent that the second line
had been moved up by the corps commander's order;
and the Second and Third brigades were ordered at once
to the support of the left centre, now severely engaged,

The conflict became desperate, and the men fought without regard to anything but the enemy in their front and the officers who commanded them. Other troops were moved up and much confusion prevailed. Again and again the enemy was repulsed, only to re-form, and, being reinforced, to again attack.

On our side the troops held their position bravely until every cartridge had been fired. One regiment on the left was repulsed and driven across the Chickahominy. Regiments of different corps were gotten together, led on a charge into the woods, and advanced against the enemy, when their flanks were assailed and broken, and in disorder they fell back to their old position. The Bucktails, by their unerring fire, forced a Confederate battery to change its position, and finally drove it from the field. One regiment that had gone to the relief of another then in line remained fighting until, its ammunition exhausted, with half its number captured, and with the enemy all around it, it was forced to surrender. Easton, after most heroic fighting, his support gone, his gunners killed at their pieces, his retreat cut off, lost four of his guns and two caissons.

The action had now become general, and for four hours raged furiously. The left, unable to withstand the repeated and desperate attacks upon it, had broken and was falling back in confusion, when McCall by his personal efforts partially restored order. It was now after sunset. The enemy, after forcing our left, had cut off the retreat of the Eleventh regiment and the Fourth New Jersey, to whose relief Reynolds had gone. While attempting to regain our lines the next morning he was captured with his adjutant-general. The enemy, believing that reinforcements had reached us, made no further attack. He had before displayed no such strength or determination. The Reserves fought against superior numbers and bravely, wholly "supporting the character they had previously gained," as was justly said by their commander. Reynolds had been everywhere, and in the exercise of that personal magnetism so characteristic of him was of the greatest influence in restoring order. We lost twenty-two guns in the battle, and the Pennsylvania Reserves alone had lost, including the affair at Beaver Dam Creek, fourteen hundred men. The enemy had been held in check, and this, the commanding general said, was all that he proposed, to secure his changed base on the James River.

But there was to be no rest yet for the division. On the 27th of June, after the affair at Gainesville, the Pennsylvania Reserves crossed the Chickahominy. It was late before their orders reached them to move to White Oak Creek as an escort and protection to Hunt's reserve artillery. It was an important and hazardous service, and it seemed to fall to the lot of the Reserves, as other details had done, without much reference to justice or routine. The transfer of so important an element of his fighting material might well occasion anxiety to the commanding general, and he had especially entrusted its care to McCall's division of Pennsylvanians. He had been satisfied with its brilliant service, and his unjust criticisms upon its action at New Market road had not yet been made.

The demoralization at Savage Station was great; everything was in confusion; nearly three thousand sick and wounded men were in tents and under any shelter that could be found, and all sorts of rumors of the approach of the enemy tended to demoralize the men. Upon their arrival the Reserves at once sought out and ministered to the wants of their comrades as far as they were able to do. The wounded and sick were to be left behind, and when this became known it occasioned a feeling that moved the stoutest heart. McCall had crossed the swamp with the artillery train, and had formed his division in line of battle, when he was relieved from his escort duty and ordered forward on the Quaker road toward the James River. The division moved with its corps. When on the march some confusion and delay took place in regard to the exact location of the Quaker road. The whole command was countermarched, except the Reserve division, to whom Porter, in command of the corps, sent no instructions, leaving the division in front and in sight of the enemy. His explanation was that he did not consider the division then under his command. The enemy had now discovered McClellan's intention to change his base, and resolved to go in pursuit. The army was formed in line of battle, and Sumner with the rearguard held Savage Station, the point of honor, and nobly repulsed a determined attack of the enemy.

Porter with his corps, including the Reserves, was in line of battle, with the remainder of the army across the roads and facing Richmond. The position originally taken by McCall was at the crossing of the Quaker road and the New Market road. Ordered back from this position, McCall received orders from McClellan himself to form his division on the New Market road, and to hold that position until our trains had passed on toward the James River. There was no continuous line of battle. The divisions were disjointed and McCall held the centre. He had formed his division with his usual ability. Meade with the Second brigade was on his right; Seymour on the left; Simmons with the First brigade in reserve, and his batteries were strongly posted. The Confederates had determined to seize the point where the Charles City and New Market roads crossed each other, and thus place themselves on our line of retreat. This movement, if successful, would have divided McClellan's army. Hill's

28

Confederate division, that had been repulsed by the Reserves at Mechanicsville, was again to attack, and McCall's division of Pennsylvania Reserves was again to meet it.

At half-past two o'clock the battle began by the driving in of our skirmishers. The enemy threw forward two regiments to feel McCall's line. Colonel Sickel with the Third and Colonel Harvey with the Seventh drove them back, when the enemy moved a large column upon our left flank and made a determined assault with his artillery and infantry. For two long hours the battle raged fiercely. The brave Simmons fell and the enemy was driven back. Our batteries, under Kern and Cooper, were well served, and a reckless and desperate charge made upon Randall's guns was bravely repulsed, the enemy coming up to the muzzles of the guns. Our men crossed bayonets with the Alabama troops, and a hand-to-hand fight occurred, a rare thing at any time in war. But there were no supports; every man had been put in; our lines were broken and could not re-form, and fell back in disorder. At once McCall began to re-form his line, to get his scattered men together, and to present again his front to the enemy. But all was changed: his brigade commanders had gone; his staff had all been disabled or killed, and even his personal escort wounded or dispersed, and he himself exhausted. While riding forward, unaccompanied by any of his staff, to look for one of his officers, he was captured.

At no previous battle had there been so many instances of hand-to-hand fighting, no such display of personal courage. Well might the enemy regard this battle as one of the most stubborn and long-contested that had yet occurred, and say, as Longstreet did, that if McCall's division had not fought as it did they would have captured our army. The Reserves had met the divisions of

Longstreet and A. P. Hill, among the best of the Confederate troops, and from eighteen to twenty thousand strong. The conduct of the Reserve division, as its commander said, was worthy of all praise. It had added to its laurels by as devoted and valiant a service as had ever been rendered by any troops. Meade had been wounded, but remained for a while, when he finally left the field. Seymour became separated from his command, and retired. In his official report the division commander thanks Colonels Roberts, Sickel, Hays, Jackson, and others. Three stands of colors, with two hundred prisoners, were captured, while the loss of the division in the three battles of the 26th, 27th, and 30th of June amounted to 3180; the killed and wounded amounted to 650 out of the 7000 who went into battle at Mechanicsville on the 26th of June.

The Reserve commander and Reynolds being now prisoners in the hands of the enemy, and Meade wounded, the command of the division devolved upon Seymour temporarily as the senior. Porter with the Fifth corps reached Malvern Hill only on the 30th of June, and took position to cover the passage of our trains and reserve artillery to the river behind Malvern Hill.

Lee, failing to break our centre on the New Market road, now determined to turn our left flank at Malvern Hill. A strong line was formed by our troops, and in front of it the enemy appeared on the morning of the 1st of July. Porter's corps held the left of the line. The Pennsylvania Reserve division was held in reserve behind Porter and Couch. In the attacks upon these commands the Reserves were not engaged. At the conclusion of the fight McClellan withdrew his army to Harrison's Landing, which had been previously determined upon, but which was received with regret by both officers and men,

The condition of the Reserves was not an encouraging one. Reduced in numbers, many sick, their officers gone, the severe service imposed upon them had affected their well-being and touched their morale. They were broken down, and their losses in men and officers had affected them; many were sent to hospitals only to die; many never again returned to their commands. But there was no giving up. Early in August, McCall, Reynolds, and the prisoners captured in the previous fights were exchanged and returned to the army. McCall's return was warmly welcomed by the division, but he too, broken down in health, was obliged to seek relief at his home. Failing to regain his strength, he resigned his commission, when Reynolds assumed command of the division, and was welcomed by the men with every expression of gratification and joy.

The government had now determined upon a new plan of operations. The Peninsula campaign had failed; a junction of the corps of Banks, Fremont, and McDowell had taken place, and Major-General Pope placed in command. While Pope protected Washington and made demonstrations toward Gordonsville, the Army of the Potomac was to be withdrawn from Harrison's Landing and to join him. The Confederates soon learned what was contemplated, and by the 18th their united forces were in Pope's front. An order to McClellan required him to withdraw his army to the Potomac. There was unaccountable delay. The Pennsylvania Reserves took the advance on the 11th of August, and by the 15th were *en route* to join Burnside. They were pushed forward with the greatest promptness, and on the 25th joined Pope's forces at Warrenton Junction, to resume their old position as a division of McDowell's corps. With Kearney's division they were the only organized troops that joined Pope until the 26th of August.

Pope was now on the Rapidan, but the concentration and force of the enemy on the south bank, the failure to receive reinforcements again and again demanded, both flanks exposed, and his communications with Fredericksburg threatened by which his relief was to arrive, compelled him to fall back to the Rappahannock. Lee followed with his army, and extended his line far beyond Pope's right. There was now constant fighting and skirmishing, and Pope's position again became untenable. The enemy was crossing to his left, when the river rose in floods and became an impassable barrier. Reynolds had now joined Pope, who fell back to Warrenton Junction and Manassas. Pope believed that he had thrown his force between Jackson and Longstreet, and he determined at once to force the fighting on the 28th and to attack Jackson. Reynolds, without waiting for formal orders from his chief, formed on Sigel's left, and on the march to Manassas came under the enemy's fire, which he repulsed with his artillery.

The Reserves, in connection with McDowell's other divisions and with Sigel, had succeeded in getting between Jackson and Thoroughfare Gap, and on the 29th Reynolds with his division was at once engaged with the enemy all day. On the morning of the 30th, Reynolds posted his division with all of his artillery on the left. Pushing forward his skirmishers and their support, he found a large force of the enemy ready for attack. He was ordered to resist this attack, and other troops were to support him. Porter's corps had been repulsed, and the Reserves were to form a line behind which it could rally. Heintzelman's corps was in retreat amid much confusion, leaving but one brigade of the Reserves under Anderson, with its batteries, to resist the attack. Here the command suffered great loss. Kern lost four of his guns; he himself was wounded and left on the field.

Colonel Hardin of the Twelfth was severely wounded.
The command now fell back by order to the right of the
Henry House, where Meade's and Seymour's brigades,
with Ransom's batteries, "gallantly maintained their
position." It was in this battle, when our left was forced
back and the troops on the right of the Reserves had
given way, that the brave Reynolds, seizing the flagstaff
of the Second regiment, dashed along his line, cheering
on his men with magnetic effect. The bridge over Bull
Run was saved to the army.

Thus ended another battle most creditable to the
Reserves, wholly sustaining their reputation. Well
might the army commander say in his official report:
"The Pennsylvania Reserves under Reynolds . . .
rendered most gallant and efficient service." In this
campaign they lost 4 officers and 64 privates killed,
31 officers and 364 privates wounded, which makes an
aggregate loss of 463 men.

The army had hardly become reunited in the defences
of Washington when the Confederates crossed the Potomac in force and marched toward Maryland. The Army
of the Potomac at once took the field. The Pennsylvania
Reserves were now a division in the First army corps,
commanded by Hooker. Meantime the Governor of
Pennsylvania had called out 75,000 of the militia, and
Reynolds had been relieved of his command of the Reserves and ordered to Harrisburg to assist the Governor.
General Meade now took command of the division, and
on the 13th of September they crossed the Monocacy.
The enemy, pushing northward, had taken position on
South Mountain. McClellan at once made his disposi-
tions to attack him, and if possible to throw Franklin
with the Sixth corps and Couch's division between
the main body of the enemy and Jackson at Harper's
Ferry. Franklin forced the enemy to take position on

the top of South Mountain, where he strongly posted himself at Turner's Gap. Burnside reported the fact to McClellan, when the whole army was ordered to move to the attack.

At one o'clock the Reserves were in position on our right, with orders to create a diversion in favor of Reno, who was pressed on our left by the enemy. They were to advance and turn the enemy's flank. Seymour's brigade, under Meade's order, took the crest of the first ridge, and, forming line of battle with the other brigades, advanced upon the enemy, the Bucktails leading. The enemy was engaged, and after determined fighting was driven from the walls and rocks and thick undergrowth. Reinforcements came up, but too late to open fire, when the enemy, who was not in large force, retired amid the loud shouts of our men.

The Reserves lost in this battle an aggregate of 392 officers and men. In his official report Meade states his indebtedness to the Bucktails, which he says "have always been in the advance," for ascertaining the exact position of the enemy. The battle was not renewed in the morning. During the night the enemy had fallen back across the Antietam Creek to Sharpsburg. Pushing through Boonesboro' and Keedysville, the enemy was found in force on the Antietam in front of Sharpsburg, and an attack in the morning was determined upon. The enemy had meantime changed his position to one of more strength, and had strongly posted his artillery.

Hooker with his corps, including the Pennsylvania Reserves, was to cross the Antietam and was to attack the enemy's left; Meade with the Reserves led the advance and opened the battle. The Bucktails soon found the enemy, and Meade at once ordered in Seymour with his brigade and posted his batteries. The engagement became general, when the remaining brigades were ordered up, and the fight continued until dark, with active artillery firing from Cooper's and Simpson's batteries. The opposing forces were almost hand to hand.

At daylight on the 17th the battle was renewed. Fresh troops had come up and the line was strengthened. The Reserves were at once engaged on the left. Cooper and Simpson, on the enemy's left flank, served their batteries actively. Warner with the Tenth Reserves was ordered to join Crawford's division of Mansfield's corps in his attack upon the enemy in the morning. The now noted cornfield was carried, then lost, again reoccupied with cheers, when their ammunition became exhausted, and the enemy, reinforced, pressed them again back and came on in heavy force; again the enemy was driven back, and not an inch of ground was lost.

The struggle was for the possession of the cornfield. Hooker with part of Mansfield's corps determined to take it. While in the act of initiating the movement he was wounded in the foot, and Meade took command of the corps, while Seymour assumed command of the Reserves. The Reserves were relieved at noon, after having been engaged for five hours and having exhausted their ammunition. Mansfield had now come up with all of his corps.

In his official report Meade gives to Ransom's battery the credit of repulsing the enemy in the cornfield at one of the most critical periods. He highly commends Seymour for his admirable service. In this battle the Reserves lost 573 men—9 officers and 96 men killed; 22 officers and 444 men wounded; and 2 missing.

Constant fighting and marching had now reduced the strength of the division to little more than a third of its effective strength. It was desired by Governor Curtin that it should be sent back to the State to be reorganized and recruited. This was not acceded to, and the work went on in the field; other regiments were added to the Second brigade. Colonel Biddle Roberts, who had done excellent service in every capacity, now resigned to assist Governor Curtin, and was placed on his staff. Reynolds upon his return was given the First army corps, while Meade went back to his division.

The army now rested at Sharpsburg and Harper's Ferry. But the President and authorities became anxious, and after repeated orders to move, the President, on the 6th of October, directed that McClellan should "cross the Potomac and give battle to the enemy or drive him southward"—a very positive military order, but in which the Secretary of War and the General-in-Chief concurred. At last, on the 26th of October, the army moved. The Reserves under Meade marched with their corps to Warrenton, arriving on the 6th of November. Meantime, McClellan was relieved from his command by Burnside unwillingly, and later resigned his position in the army. Seymour had been relieved and sent South. The army was now formed into three grand divisions, and the Reserves were attached to the left grand division, under Franklin.

In accordance with a plan of campaign of the new general, the army was to march to Fredericksburg by a forced movement, having made a feint toward Gordonsville. This was ordered, and on the 16th of November the movement commenced. By another blunder the pontoon bridges were not forwarded, and valuable time was lost while others were constructing, and the enemy had strongly occupied Fredericksburg. Finally, the river was crossed and the Reserves were placed on the extreme left of the army, and Meade was designated to lead the charge that was to break through the enemy's line. No description of their heroic service can be better than the testimony of General Meade himself: "The attack was for a time perfectly successful. The enemy was driven from the railroad, his rifle-pits, and breast-works for over half a mile. Over three hundred prisoners were taken and several standards, when the advancing line encountered the heavy reinforcements of the enemy, who, recovering from the effects of our assault, and perceiving both our flanks unprotected, poured in such a destructive fire from all three directions as to compel the line to fall back, which was executed without confusion;" and he subsequently says that "the best troops would be justified in withdrawing without loss of honor." The list of his losses, which he subsequently corrected, was not less than 14 officers and 161 men killed; 59 officers and 1182 men wounded; 12 officers and 425 men captured or missing.

It was the old story again of hesitancy and slowness of movement upon the part of the supporting forces at a critical time. No support, all in confusion from their attack, the enemy all around them, their work accomplished, their ammunition gone, broken, destroyed almost, they were driven from the hills to the low grounds, where they re-formed, and had left 176 killed, 1197 wounded, and 400 missing. Jackson of the Third brigade was killed while in command of his men: a most excellent and gallant officer was thus lost to the division.

No proper account of the battle can fail to mention the service of Captain O'Rourke of the First regiment, who had command of the ambulance corps, and a voluntary testimonial to his coolness, energy, and efficiency was tendered to him by the division and brigade surgeons. On Monday the army recrossed the river, having lost ten thousand men. Hooker relieved Burnside. The Reserves were now encamped at Belle Plaine. Meade had meantime been promoted to a major-generalcy, and was as-

signed to the command of the Fifth corps, while Colonel
Sickel, and subsequently General Doubleday, took temporary command of the division.

The effort to withdraw the Reserves from the army to
recruit them was again made, and was again unsuccessful.
Hooker reorganized the army and prepared for a forward
movement. But before this, on the 8th of February, the
Reserves under the command of Sickel were ordered to
Washington and assigned to stations in the defenses
under the command of Heintzelman, and were thus
absent from Chancellorsville. They were placed on duty
to guard the railroads, and the troops they relieved took
their place as the Third division of the First corps of the
Army of the Potomac. Finally, they were withdrawn
from the railroad and assigned to duty at Upton Hill,
Fairfax Courthouse, and Alexandria. Strong recommendations for their withdrawal to rest and recruit were
again made to the authorities. Meade, just before his
relief from their command, had made a strong representation to Franklin, and Colonel Sickel had made a similar statement to Governor Curtin; but the Secretary of
War did not see his way to consent, as similar applications had been made by other States, and all could not
be granted. Everything was now done to recall the ab-
sentees, those who had recovered from wounds and sick-
ness, and to recruit and refit the command. Brigadier-
General S. W. Crawford, an officer of the regular army
and a Pennsylvanian by birth, who had served at Fort
Sumter, who had commanded a brigade and division
after Cedar Mountain, and who had been severely
wounded at Antietam, although not yet wholly recovered from his wounds, was in Washington, and upon the
request of Governor Curtin, Senator Cameron, and myself was placed in command of the division on the 3d of
June, and made his headquarters at Upton Hill, with the

First brigade under McCandless. Here the division rested through the month of June, preparing for further service.

Meantime, elated with his success at Chancellorsville, the enemy under his ablest general had crossed the Rapidan and was moving northward. As soon as the movement was known Hooker promptly crossed the Potomac at Edwards' Ferry and the Point of Rocks on the 24th of June, and moved upon Frederick City, where he got his army together. As soon as it was known among the Reserves that the enemy was moving in the direction of their State some of the regiments at once asked for orders to accompany the Army of the Potomac into Maryland. Crawford earnestly and repeatedly urged, both by letter and in person, upon the government and upon the Governor of the State the necessity that the Reserves should be ordered to join the army. On the 20th of June he went at night to Hooker's headquarters, a considerable distance off, and in person induced him to ask for the division. This was successful, and at once, upon the receipt of the order, Crawford moved his command on the 25th of June toward Leesburg, crossing the Potomac at Edwards' Ferry to the Monocacy, leaving his camp and garrison equipment and his trains to follow him.

Early on the 28th the division reached Fredericksburg. Meantime, Hooker had been relieved and Meade assigned to the command of the army. This caused the greatest joy and satisfaction to the Reserves, who loved the general who had shared all of their dangers and successes with them. At Fredericksburg, Crawford reported at first to General Meade, who expressed his gratification at the return of his old division, which again became the Third division of the Fifth corps, under General Sykes. The division joined the corps on Rock Creek in the rear of our right, after a severe night-march to Hanover and Bonnoughtown, and prepared at once for the coming struggle. As it crossed the boundary-line of Maryland at Silver Springs its commander addressed it in a few stirring words of congratulation and· encouragement. At three o'clock the corps moved to take its positions on our left. The Reserves arrived upon the field so promptly as to elicit the commendation of the corps commander.

After some contradictory orders, made necessary by the enemy's movements, the Reserves were drawn up in line of battle on the slopes and near the crest of the Little Round Top, on the edge of the woods and undergrowth. Fisher's brigade had been sent to Big Round Top to support Vincent, when Crawford retained the Eleventh regiment under Jackson, attached it to McCandless's brigade, and took personal command. Seeing the advance of the enemy over the wheatfield and his approach to the Round Top, the retreat and confusion of our troops, and the falling back of the Second division of Ayres's regulars, Crawford, who had been left to act in accordance with his own judgment, rode forward and ordered the command to advance. The line moved at once, after opening fire; the Bucktails and the Sixth regiment, being in the rear of each flank, were subsequently deployed, and the line moved forward. Seizing the colors of the First regiment, near which he was, Crawford took them upon his horse and led on his men. The enemy was advancing irregularly, and had crossed the stone wall on the side of the wheatfield, when he was met by the Reserves and driven back to the stone wall, for the possession of which there was a short and active struggle, when he was driven across the wheatfield and made no further attempt at any advance.

On the left, Colonel Taylor of the Bucktails was killed

while leading his regiment. The line of the stone wall was firmly held by the Reserves until the afternoon of the next day, after Pickett's charge, when Crawford, in carrying out the direct orders of General Meade, who with other general officers was present, directed an advance. During the night the enemy had established himself in the woods opposite the Round Tops. Anderson's brigade of Hood's division lay in line, his left flank resting on the wheatfield, while Benning's brigade was in the rear in support. The presence of these troops was unknown to Meade or to Sykes. Crawford in person directed McCandless's movements. The command moved steadily, but in a wrong direction, when orders were sent to McCandless to halt, change front, and move toward the Round Top. When he entered the woods, striking the flanks of Anderson's brigade, which was behind temporary breastworks, that brigade gave way, involving Benning's brigade in its flight, and retiring to a distance of a mile, where it strongly entrenched itself along the general line of the army.

It was the last of the fighting upon the field of Gettysburg, and done by Pennsylvania troops, as the battle had been opened by the Fifty-sixth Pennsylvania regiment on the right. Had the force of the enemy been known, it were foolhardy to send such a force unsupported under such circumstances. Meade himself declared that there was no force in the woods but sharpshooters and stragglers only. The result was the capture of over two hundred prisoners, the battle-flag of the Fifteenth Georgia regiment, and the retaking of a great portion of the ground lost the previous day by our troops, and the recovery of one gun, two caissons, and over seven thousand stand of arms. Our picket-line was largely advanced.

And thus ended the battle of Gettysburg, the Pennsylvania Reserves adding largely to their well-earned reputation upon the soil of their own State. Their losses were between two hundred and three hundred men. The enemy maintained his front until Sunday night, when he fell back to the Potomac and strongly entrenched at Falling Waters in Virginia. The army followed, and on the 14th a reconnaissance was made by three selected divisions of the Second, Fifth, and Sixth corps, under Caldwell, Crawford with his Reserves, and Wright. The enemy had retreated. The Reserves alone followed to the river with the cavalry. The army soon after recrossed the Potomac and advanced into Virginia, manœuvring and skirmishing for position, while detachments were sent to various points of importance.

While on the Rappahannock, on the 28th of August, advantage was taken of a moment of inaction to present to General Meade, upon the part of the officers and men of the division, a costly sword of the finest workmanship, with sash and belt and a pair of golden spurs. A large number of distinguished people had been assembled. General Crawford in a few appropriate and stirring words made the presentation. General Meade replied, referring touchingly to his association with the division, justifying its action at New Market road, and regarding its service generally said "that no division in this glorious army is entitled to claim more credit for its uniform gallant conduct and for the amount of hard fighting it has gone through than the division of the Pennsylvania Reserve Corps."

Finally, the enemy determined upon a forward movement, apparently to seize the line of the Rapidan. He occupied Culpepper and its vicinity in great force. It was the middle of October when Meade concluded that the enemy's intention was to seize the heights of Centreville. By a rapid movement Meade succeeded in seizing the strong position at Bull Run, where on the 14th the

Fifth corps under Warren came up with the Confederates under Heth at Bristoe Station and engaged the enemy, when the Pennsylvania Reserves fell upon the left flank of the enemy and completely routed him, capturing some pieces of artillery and a large number of prisoners. Lee then fell back to the Rapidan, extending to Bartlett's Mills on Mine Run. Meade then commenced his movement to attack Lee's scattered forces. This Lee anticipated, and concentrated on Mine Run, which he strongly fortified. Meade determined to attack, and sent Warren with a strong force to feel the enemy's line and flanks. Warren had 24,000 men under his command. All was in readiness, and on the 30th the batteries opened upon the whole line. But Warren, finding the enemy more strongly posted than he had anticipated, took the responsibility of suspending his movements until further orders. The attack was not made, and Meade again fell back across the Rapidan.

In these operations the Reserves had been sent in support of Gregg's cavalry, and were ordered to attack the position which had proved too strong for our cavalry. The Sixth regiment, under Ent, rapidly advanced, driving in the skirmishers, when the enemy retired—a work that elicited the approval of Sykes, not at all partial to the division. On the 3d they had moved to the right into the woods with the large body of infantry under Sedgwick, anticipating the storming of the enemy's works. It was intensely cold, and many perished then and from the subsequent effects. Finally, they fell back with the army to Bristoe Station and Manassas, where they guarded the Orange and Alexandria Railroad until the end of April, 1864.

Grant, who had on the 22d of March been appointed General-in-Chief of all the armies, made his headquarters with the Army of the Potomac. The army was again to move, and the Reserves now entered upon their last campaign. Sykes had been relieved and Warren placed in permanent command of the Fifth corps. On the 3d of May the army crossed the Rapidan, the Reserves crossing at Germania Ford, and they moved out to the old Wilderness Tavern on the 4th. On this day the Ninth regiment was relieved, as it had completed its term of service, and it was ordered home. Warren moved out toward Parker's Store, with Hancock on his left and Sedgwick on his right. The enemy moved promptly, and Longstreet was ordered to attack at the Wilderness Tavern, and fell heavily on Warren's corps. Griffith successfully resisted the attack, and was supported by some of Crawford's division of the Reserves, and also by the divisions of Wadsworth and Robinson.

The Reserve division had been ordered to Parker's Store on the plank road. Upon advancing the enemy was found in force. It was when the regiments under McCandless were supporting Wadsworth that a gap had been opened between the Reserves and the other divisions: the enemy pushed into this gap and nearly surrounded the Reserves, which were extricated with difficulty, McCandless coming in with only two of his regiments and losing many of his men. Colonel Bollinger with the Seventh regiment, pressing too far to the front, was surrounded by the enemy; he was wounded and captured with a large portion of his regiment. The battle raged with varying success. Warren advanced his division in the centre, with the Reserves on his right, with some losses. The attack upon the right of the Sixth corps had driven Shaler's and Seymour's brigades, and, the enemy getting into the rear, Sedgwick was cut off. At this juncture the Reserves were ordered to the support of Sedgwick. The country was most difficult of passage, but the men pushed on and found Sedgwick,

29

who had meantime restored his line, when the Reserves returned to their former position at Lacy Farm. The army again was in motion to the left, the fight of Gregg and Curtis at Todd's Tavern having opened the way to Spottsylvania. Warren's corps, with the Reserves in front, marched all night. The great effort now making was to secure the heights of Spottsylvania, which were gained by the enemy.

Meantime all of the divisions of the Fifth corps had come up, and the enemy had concentrated his forces to attack them. The Reserves and Coulter with Wadsworth's division were ordered to attack, which resulted in driving the enemy upon his second line of entrenchments. McCandless, commanding the First brigade, was wounded and left the field. After a short respite the Reserves were again ordered to form in two lines under Tally, and a determined assault on the enemy's lines was again made three times, but without success. Again and again the assault was renewed at different portions of the line and with varied success day after day. The enemy had been driven from the Wilderness, his right flank turned, and Spottsylvania relinquished. Meade on the 13th issued a complimentary order to his army, and announced the enemy's loss to be 18 guns, 22 stands of colors, and 8000 prisoners.

Again a movement to the left was made, and again the enemy was encountered, and assaults, again and again repeated, were made, fighting along the whole line often for days at a time. The enemy, losing a position, would make desperate efforts to retake it; and "so terrific," says a writer, "was the death-grapple that at different times of the day the rebel colors were planted on one side of the works and ours on the other." On the 14th the Fifth corps changed its position, and the Reserves became again the extreme right of the army. Again marched to the left, they were constantly engaged, until the rains and impassable roads gave the army a temporary respite.

On Thursday, May 19th, an attempt was made to turn our left. Tyler's heavy artillery regiments were the only troops at the point threatened. They were new and had just arrived from Washington, but they behaved gallantly and repulsed the enemy, when Crawford with his Reserves was sent to their support and to take command. They moved at once, but the enemy had rapidly retreated. Spottsylvania was now to be abandoned, and once more a flank movement to the left decided upon. On the 22d the Fifth corps marched toward Bowling Green, Crawford's division in advance. On Monday, the 23d, the Fifth corps removed to the North Anna. The enemy had fortified his position on both flanks. Griffin's division had crossed, and the Reserves were formed on his left. The enemy assaulted the lines, but were repulsed. Warren had taken a strong position. On Tuesday the Reserves were ordered to advance to support Hancock. Early on Tuesday, General Warren had ordered Crawford to send a small detachment along the river-bank to open communication with Hancock's troops. This detachment was finally supported by another regiment under Colonel Stewart. It was a hazardous movement. Crawford had asked to move with his division. The enemy was in force, and had wellnigh cut off the regiment sent in advance, when Warren, seeing that his orders had isolated the regiment, directed Crawford to move to its position. Crittenden's division of Hancock's corps had not crossed, and seemed to have gone astray, when Crawford and his Reserves opened communications, and Crittenden crossed, followed shortly by the rest of his corps, to a firm position on the south bank.

Finding the enemy's position too strong for attack,

Grant on Thursday recrossed the North Anna. The Reserves moved with their corps in advance, crossed the Pamunkey at Hanover, advanced on the Mechanicsville road, and entrenched. By night the whole army had concentrated, when the enemy took up a new line to oppose the advance. On the 30th of May the Fifth corps crossed the Tolopotamy. The Reserves moved forward on the Mechanicsville road to connect with Griffin, who, finding himself a mile north of the enemy's outposts, determined to seize the road by a vigorous movement, and advanced upon Mechanicsville. The Bucktails in their advance drove back the enemy's cavalry to Bethesda Church. Hardin's brigade was advanced, but exposed his flank, when Crawford ordered Kitchen's brigade of heavy artillery to support him. Together these brigades drove back the enemy's right wing and centre. Fisher with the Third brigade was now ordered up to defend the right, and the whole division was posted on strong and irregular ground and light defenses were thrown up hastily. Two pieces of Richardson's batteries were placed in position on Hardin's left and two on his right.

Crawford had hardly made his dispositions when the enemy opened with his artillery, and soon after his infantry advanced, and the whole line engaged. In this attack on the Fifth corps Crawford with the Reserves was on the left. On came the enemy with his assaulting column, opening with artillery and infantry fire. Three times the attack was renewed, and as often repulsed. The men, now veterans, reserved their fire until the enemy's lines were close to them, and thus secured the result. The enemy was driven back with loss. The Reserves then advanced, captured seventy prisoners, and compelled the retreat of the enemy in confusion; a colonel, five commissioned officers, and three hundred privates were left upon the field. The Richmond papers, in commenting upon this affair, pronounced it "sad and distressing."

This brilliant success of the Pennsylvania Reserves marked the close of their service. They had fought a successful battle when within a few hours they were to be free. All around them were souvenirs of their early and devoted service, Beaver Dam Creek and Mechanicsville, and now the whole was crowned by a brilliant success due alone to them and to their officers. On the 31st of May the Reserves were relieved from all further service with the army. Taking farewell of Warren, they crossed the Tolopotamy, and soon after, on June 1st, departed with the remnant of that brave and devoted body of men who had been the first to offer themselves to the government. But even now they were not all to return. Nearly two thousand men re-enlisted to follow the fortunes of the army. About twelve hundred officers and men were all that returned to the State. The two thousand that were veteranized were organized into two regiments, the One-Hundred-and-Ninetieth and One-Hundred-and-Ninety-first, by General Crawford at Peebles Farm, and remained in service till the end of the war. Before their march their general issued the following farewell to the faithful men who had so nobly borne themselves under his command:

Soldiers of the Pennsylvania Reserves: To-day the connection which has so long existed between us is to be severed for ever.

I have no power to express to you the feelings of gratitude and affection that I bear to you, nor the deep regret with which I now part from you.

As a division you have ever been faithful and devoted soldiers, and you have nobly sustained me in the many trying scenes through which we have passed with an unwavering fidelity. The record of your service terminates gloriously, and "the Wilderness," "Spottsylvania Courthouse," and "Bethesda Church" have been added to the long list of battles and of triumphs that have marked your career.

Go home to the great State that sent you forth three years ago to battle for her honor and to strike for her in the great cause of the country; take back your soiled and war-worn banners, your thin and shattered ranks, and let them tell how you have performed your trust. Take back those banners, sacred from the glorious associations that surround them, sacred with the memories of our fallen comrades who gave their lives to defend them, and give them again into the keeping of the State for ever.

The duties of the hour prevent me from accompanying you, but my heart will follow you long after you return, and it shall ever be my pride that I was once your commander, and that side by side we fought and suffered through campaigns which will stand unexampled in history. Farewell!

Upon their return to the capital of their State they were received by the civil and military authorities and the people with a welcome and a demonstration wholly unprecedented. Nothing was omitted to show them the loving appreciation in which they were held, how warmly their services had been appreciated, and of the affection in which they must ever be cherished, and the State pride that was to continue to follow them; and all this was renewed at their homes. After a short rest many of the officers and men returned to the army in various regiments and batteries, and remained until the end of the war.

The Second brigade had been divided at Alexandria, and two of the regiments had been ordered to West Virginia, where they served creditably in all the relations they were called upon to fulfill under General Crook. Their term of service having expired in June, they were in turn transferred to their State to be mustered out of service. An effort was made to preserve the organization, but failed, as the authorities at Washington could only act for all regiments and organizations. Before separating at Harrisburg the Reserves sent for their old commander, McCall, and abundantly testified to him their enduring confidence and affection.

And thus passed into history the record of one of the most extraordinary bodies of men that had ever assembled for any single purpose. I have from time to time alluded to the peculiar conditions, the peculiar associations and characteristics, and their constant and heroic source. It is not now intended to enlarge upon this. To no other body of troops was it given to secure so entirely distinct a reputation that will go into history. Whatever credit may arise to them as a simple division, they will be known as the Pennsylvania Reserve Corps, as under that appellation they achieved their fame. To this title they ever adhered with a tenacity that assured it. Give them that, and you might add the name of any body to the division, and, although in accordance with orders, they were called by the name of the general commanding them, they ever retained among themselves their favorite title of Pennsylvania Reserves.

And what a peculiar soldiery they became! For all purposes of drills and discipline and in preparation for battle they ever gave the readiest acquiescence and obedience; but to all the special detail that went to make up the technical soldier they never would and never did yield until the last. They believed that they were ever citizens in arms for the nation's life, and they never lost sight of their coming return to their homes and the pursuits of peace. As to their service, it makes but little difference as to the necessity of their employment: the fact remains that they were constantly called upon for every variety of service, thrown into critical positions without hesitancy, and their services but poorly acknowledged. There was no murmur or complaint; they accepted every detail of the service required of them from Dranesville to Bethesda Church, and how they performed it let the official reports of their commanders and the sad lists of their losses attest.

It is not pretended that in this imperfect sketch anything like justice has been done to the living or the dead. Most is merely reference; honored names that will be remembered in history have not been mentioned, and many instances of personal valor unrecorded. If, however, the memory of their deeds has been recalled at all, and has again awakened a feeling of appreciation and gratitude upon the part of their fellows, with praise for those who yet survive and an affectionate memory for the self-sacrificing dead, then my object will not have been wholly lost in recalling the memory of their conspicuous service to the minds of a new generation.

APPENDIX.

THE NICOLAY-McCLURE CONTROVERSY.

LINCOLN AND HAMLIN.

[From *The Philadelphia Times*, July 6, 1891.]

THE death of Hannibal Hamlin, one of the few lingering picturesque characters of the political revolution that conquered armed rebellion and effaced slavery, has inspired very free discussion of the early conflicts of Republicanism and of the relations which existed between Lincoln and Hamlin. Hamlin was one of the central figures of the first national Republican battle in 1856; he was the first elected Republican Vice-President; his personal relations with President Lincoln were admittedly of the most agreeable nature; his public record while Vice-President had given no offense to any element of his party; and his then unexpected and now apparently unexplainable defeat for renomination with Lincoln in 1864 has elicited much conflicting discussion.

Looking back over the dark days of civil war, with their often sudden and imperious necessities in field and forum, and in political directions as well, it is often difficult to explain results in accord with the sunnier light of the present; and as yet we have seen no explanation of the rejection of Vice-President Hamlin in 1864 that presents the truth. Most of our contemporaries which have discussed the question have assumed that the defeat of Hamlin was accomplished against the wishes of Lincoln. This point is taken up in the elaborate *Life of Lincoln* by Nicolay and Hay, and they assume to settle it by stating that Mr. Lincoln was accused by members of the Baltimore Convention of preferring a Southern or a new man for Vice-President, and Mr. Nicolay communicated with Lincoln on the subject and reported a denial of Lincoln's purpose to interfere in the contest.

The *Evening Telegraph* of this city, usually accurate in the presentation of political history, states that "it was not the President's (Lincoln's) doings that his trusted and cherished coadjutor was deposed; it was a piece of politics, pure and simple; a mistaken attempt to placate Southern feeling before the time was ripe for it." In the same article it is assumed that "if Mr. Hamlin had been renominated President Lincoln would have lived through his second term," and the motive for Lincoln's assassination is ascribed to "the fact that a Southern man was to succeed as a result of his (Booth's) murderous deed." The theory that Lincoln was murdered to bring a Southern man to the Presidency is clearly refuted by the well-known historical fact that of all men North or South no one was at that time more execrated in the South than Andrew Johnson.

It is true that Hamlin, an entirely unobjectionable Vice-President and a leader with peculiar claims upon the Republican party, was rejected as Vice-President by the Republican Convention of 1864 to place a Southern man in that office, and it is equally true that it would not and could not have been done had President Lincoln opposed it. So far from opposing it, Lincoln discreetly favored it; indeed, earnestly desired it. The writer hereof was a delegate at large from Pennsylvania in the Baltimore Convention of 1864, and in response to an invitation from the President to visit Washington on the eve of the meeting of the body, a conference was had in which Lincoln gravely urged the nomination of Johnson for Vice-President. It was solely in deference to Lincoln's earnest convictions as to the national and international necessities which demanded Johnson's nomination for the Vice-Presidency that the writer's vote was cast against Hamlin, and other Pennsylvania delegates were influenced to the same action by the confidential assurance of Lincoln's wishes.

It should not be assumed that Lincoln was ambitious to play the role of political master or that he was perfidious to any. His position was not only one of the greatest delicacy in politics, but he was loaded with responsibilities to which all former Presidents had been strangers. His one supreme desire was the restoration of the Union, and he would gladly have surrendered his own high honors, and even his life, could he thereby have restored the dissevered States. The one great shadow that hung over him and his power was the sectional character of the ruling party and the government. It weakened his arm to make peace; it strengthened European hostility to the cause of the Union;

and it left the South without even a silver lining to the dark cloud of subjugation. Lincoln firmly believed that the nomination of Johnson, an old Democratic Southern Senator who had been aggressively loyal to the Union, and who was then the Military Governor of his rebellious but restored State, would not only desectionalize the party and the government, but that it would chill and curb the anti-Union sentiment of England and France, and inspire the friends of the Union in those countries to see a leading Southern statesman coming from a conquered insurgent State to the second office of the Republic.

Such were Lincoln's sincere convictions, and such his earnest arguments in favor of the nomination of Johnson in 1864, and but for Lincoln's convictions on the subject Hamlin would have been renominated and succeeded to the Presidency instead of Johnson. It is easy, in the clear light of the present, to say that the nomination of Johnson was a grave misfortune, and to speculate on the countless evils which could have been averted; but the one man who was most devoted to the endangered nation, and who could best judge of the sober necessities of the time, believed that it was not only wise, but an imperious need, to take a Vice-President from the South, and that is why Hannibal Hamlin was not renominated in 1864.

MR. NICOLAY'S DENIAL.

[Telegram given to Associated Press.]

WASHINGTON, July 7, 1891.

MRS. HANNIBAL HAMLIN, Bangor, Me.:

The editorial statement from *The Philadelphia Times*, printed in this morning's news dispatches, to the effect that President Lincoln opposed Mr. Hamlin's renomination as Vice-President, is entirely erroneous. Mr. Lincoln's personal feelings, on the contrary, were for Mr. Hamlin's renomination, as he confidentially expressed to me, but he persistently withheld any opinion calculated to influence the convention for or against any candidate, and I have his written words to that effect, as fully set forth on pages 72 and 73, chapter 3, volume ix. of *Abraham Lincoln: A History*, by Nicolay and Hay.

Permit me, in addition, to express my deepest sympathy in yours and the nation's loss through Mr. Hamlin's death.

JOHN G. NICOLAY.

THE EXTRACT NICOLAY REFERRED TO.

[From Nicolay and Hay's *Life of Lincoln*, vol. ix., pages 72, 73.]

The principal names mentioned for the Vice-Presidency were, besides Hannibal Hamlin, the actual incumbent, Andrew Johnson of Tennessee and Daniel S. Dickinson of New York. Besides these General L. H. Rousseau had the vote of his own State, Kentucky. The Radicals of Missouri favored General B. F. Butler, who had a few scattered votes also from New England. But among the three principal candidates the voters were equally enough divided to make the contest exceedingly spirited and interesting.

For several days before the convention the President had been besieged by inquiries as to his personal wishes in regard to his associate on the ticket. He had persistently refused to give the slightest intimation of such wish. His private secretary, Mr. Nicolay, was at Baltimore in attendance at the convention, and although he was acquainted with this attitude of the President, at last, overborne by the solicitations of the chairman of the Illinois delegation, who had been perplexed at the advocacy of Joseph Holt by Leonard Swett, one of the President's most intimate friends, Mr. Nicolay wrote a letter to Mr. Hay, who had been left in charge of the executive office in his absence, containing, among other matters, this passage: "Cook wants to know confidentially whether Swett is all right; whether in urging Holt for Vice-President he reflects the President's wishes; whether the President has any preference, either personal or on the score of policy; or whether he wishes not even to interfere by a confidential intimation. . . . Please get this information for me if possible." The letter was shown to the President, who indorsed upon it this memorandum: "Swett is unquestionably all right. Mr. Holt is a good man, but I had not heard or thought of him for V.-P. Wish not to interfere about V.-P. Cannot interfere about platform. Convention must judge for itself."

This positive and final instruction was sent at once to Mr. Nicolay, and by him communicated to the President's most intimate friends in the convention. It was, therefore, with minds absolutely untrammeled by even any knowledge of the President's wishes that the convention went about its work of selecting his associate on the ticket.

McCLURE ANSWERS NICOLAY.

[From *The Philadelphia Times*, July 9, 1891.]

The ignorance exhibited by John G. Nicolay in his public telegram to the widow of ex-Vice-President Hamlin is equaled only
by his arrogance in assuming to speak for Abraham Lincoln in
matters about which Nicolay was never consulted, and of which
he had no more knowledge than any other routine clerk about
the White House. I do not regret that Mr. Nicolay has rushed
into a dispute that must lead to the clear establishment of the
exact truth as to the defeat of Hamlin in 1864. It will surely
greatly impair, if not destroy, Nicolay's hitherto generally accepted claim to accuracy as the biographer of Lincoln, but he
can complain of none but himself.

I saw Abraham Lincoln at all hours of the day and night
during his Presidential service, and he has himself abundantly
testified to the trust that existed between us. Having had the
direction of his battle in the pivotal State of the Union, he
doubtless accorded me more credit than I merited, as the only
success in politics and war is success; and the fact that I never
sought or desired honors or profits from his administration, and
never embarrassed him with exactions of any kind, made our
relations the most grateful memories of my life.

In all of the many grave political emergencies arising from the
new and often appalling duties imposed by internecine war, I
was one of those called to the inner councils of Abraham Lincoln. He distrusted his own judgment in politics, and was ever
careful to gather the best counsels from all the varied shades of
opinion and interest to guide him in his conclusions; and there
were not only scores of confidential conferences in the White
House of which John G. Nicolay never heard, but no man ever
met or heard of John G. Nicolay in such councils. He was a
good mechanical, routine clerk; he was utterly inefficient as the
secretary of the President; his removal was earnestly pressed
upon Lincoln on more than one occasion because of his want of
tact and fitness for his trust, and only the proverbial kindness of
Lincoln saved him from dismissal. He saw and knew President
Lincoln; the man Abraham Lincoln he never saw and never
knew; and his assumption that he was the trusted repository of
Lincoln's confidential convictions and efforts would have been
regarded as grotesque a quarter of a century ago, when Lincoln
and his close surroundings were well understood. His biography

of Lincoln is invaluable as an accurate history of the public acts of the Lincoln administration, but there is not a chapter or page on the inner personal attributes of the man that is not burdened with unpardonable errors. Nicolay was a plodding, precise, mechanical clerk, well fitted to preserve historical data and present them intelligently and correctly; but there his fitness as a biographer ended.

I now repeat that, in obedience to a telegraphic request from President Lincoln, I visited him at the White House the day before the meeting of the Baltimore Convention of 1864. At that interview Mr. Lincoln earnestly explained why the nomination of a well-known Southern man like Andrew Johnson—who had been Congressman, Governor, and Senator by the favor of his State—would not only nationalize the Republican party and the government, but would greatly lessen the grave peril of the recog nition of the Confederacy by England and France. He believed that the election to the Vice-Presidency of a representative statesman from an insurgent State that had been restored to the Union would disarm the enemies of the Republic abroad and remove the load of sectionalism from the government that seemed to greatly hinder peace. No intimation, no trace, of prejudice against Mr. Hamlin was exhibited, and I well knew that no such consideration could have influenced Mr. Lincoln in such an emergency. Had he believed Mr. Hamlin to be the man who could best promote the great work whose direction fell solely upon himself, he would have favored Hamlin's nomination regardless of his personal wishes; but he believed that a great public achievement would be attained by the election of Johnson; and I returned to Baltimore to work and vote for Johnson, although against all my personal predilections in the matter.

Mr. Nicolay's public telegram to Mrs. Hamlin, saying that the foregoing statement "is entirely erroneous," is as insolent as it is false, and the correctness of my statement is not even inferentially contradicted by Nicolay's quotation from Lincoln. On the contrary, Nicolay's statement given in his history (vol. ix. pages 72, 73) proves simply that Nicolay was dress-parading at Baltimore and knew nothing of the President's purposes. True, he seems to assume that he had responsible charge of the Executive duties, as he says that "Mr. Nicolay wrote a letter to Mr. Hay, who had been left in charge of the Executive office," asking whether Leonard Swett, "one of the President's most intimate friends," was "all right" in urging the nomination of Judge-

Advocate-General Holt for Vice President. Had Nicolay ever learned anything in the White House, he would have known that of all living men Leonard Swett was the one most trusted by Abraham Lincoln, and he should have known that when Swett was opposing Hamlin, Lincoln was not yearning for Hamlin's renomination. Then comes Lincoln's answer to Nicolay's bombastic query, saying: "Swett is unquestionably all right;" and because Lincoln did not proclaim himself a fool by giving Nicolay an opportunity to herald Lincoln's sacredly private convictions as to the Vice-Presidency, he assumes that he has Lincoln's "written words" to justify his contradiction of a circumstantial statement and an executed purpose of which he could have had no knowledge. When Leonard Swett was against Hamlin, none could escape the conclusion that opposition to Hamlin was no offense to Lincoln. I saw and conferred with Swett almost every hour of the period of the convention. We both labored to nominate Johnson, and Swett made Holt, who was an impossible candidate, a mere foil to divide and conquer the supporters of Hamlin. Had Lincoln desired Hamlin's nomination, Swett would have desired and labored for it, and Hamlin would have been renominated on the first ballot. The convention was a Lincoln body pure and simple, and no man could have been put on the ticket with Lincoln who was not known to be his choice. It was not publicly proclaimed, but it was in the air, and pretty much everybody but John G. Nicolay perceived and bowed to it.

Of the few men who enjoyed Lincoln's complete confidence, Charles A. Dana was conspicuous, and his statement is as credible testimony as could now be given on the subject. He was trusted by Lincoln in most delicate matters political and military, and he logically tells of Johnson's "selection by Lincoln" for the Vice-Presidency in 1864. With Dana's direct corroboration of my statement added to the strongly corroborative facts herein given, I may safely dismiss John G. Nicolay and the dispute his mingled ignorance and arrogance have thrust upon me.

A. K. M.

NICOLAY TO McCLURE.

To the Editor of *The Philadelphia Times:*

I will not reply to your personal abuse; it proves nothing but your rage and wounded vanity at being exposed in a gross historical misstatement.

You asserted that President Lincoln opposed the renomination of Hannibal Hamlin for Vice-President. I refuted that assertion by calling attention to the written record wherein Lincoln in his own handwriting explicitly states to the contrary. You now reassert your statement, or, to put it in other words, you accuse President Lincoln of acting a low political deceit and with his own hand writing a deliberate lie. The country will not believe the monstrous implication.

Allow me to restate the facts. I was at the Baltimore Convention as a spectator. The chairman of the Illinois delegation, Hon. B. C. Cook, had a conversation with me about the course of certain disaffected leaders in Illinois. That conversation I reported to the President in a letter to Major Hay, my assistant private secretary, in part as follows:

"What transpired at home and what he has heard from several sources have made Cook suspicious that Swett may be untrue to Lincoln. One of the straws which lead him to this belief is that Swett has telegraphed here urging the Illinois delegation to go for Holt. . . . Cook wants to know confidentially whether Swett is all right; whether in urging Holt for Vice-President he reflects the President's wishes; whether the President has any preference, either personally or on the score of policy; or whether he wishes not even to interfere by a confidential indication."

Upon this letter President Lincoln made the following indorsement in his own handwriting :

"Swett is unquestionably all right. Mr. Holt is a good man, but I had not heard or thought of him for V.-P. Wish not to interfere about V.-P. Cannot interfere about platform—convention must judge for itself."

This written evidence is quoted in our history, and no amount of denial or assertion to contrary can overturn it.

In trying to evade its force you assert that Lincoln called you to Washington and urged the nomination of Johnson, and that you returned to Baltimore to work and vote in obedience to that request, against your personal predilections. Let us examine this claim. The official proceedings of the convention show that you were one of the four delegates at large from Pennsylvania, the others being Simon Cameron, W. W. Ketchum, M. B. Lowry, while the list of district delegates contains the names of many other eminent Pennsylvanians. The proceedings also show that you acted an entirely minor part. You were a member of the Committee on Organization and presented its report recommending the permanent officers which were elected. With that presentation your service and influence ended, so far as can be gathered from the proceedings.

Of other Pennsylvania delegates, William W. Ketchum was one of the vice-presidents of the convention. E. McPherson was on the Committee on Credentials, A. H. Reeder on the Committee on Organization, M. B. Lowry on the Committee on Resolutions, S. F. Wilson on the Committee on Rules and Order of Business, S. A. Purviance on the National Committee, while General Simon Cameron held the leading and important post of chairman of the Pennsylvania delegation. So again, among those who made motions and speeches were Cameron, Thaddeus Stevens, A. H. Reeder, C. A. Walborn, Galusha A. Grow, and M. B. Lowry, but beyond the presentation of the routine report I have mentioned your name did not give forth the squeak of the smallest mouse. Is it probable that Lincoln among all these men would have called you alone to receive his secret instructions?

It is a matter of public history that Simon Cameron was more prominent and efficient than any other Pennsylvanian in the movement in that State to give Lincoln a second term, and that on the 14th of January, 1864, he transmitted to the President the written request of every Union member of the Pennsylvania Legislature to accept a renomination. This and his subsequent open and unvarying support left no doubt of Cameron's attitude. How was it with you? I find among Lincoln's papers the following letter from you:

FRANKLIN REPOSITORY OFFICE,
CHAMBERSBURG, PA., May 2, 1864.

SIR: I have been amazed to see it intimated in one or two journals that I am not cordially in favor of your renomination. I shall notice the intimations no further than to assure you that you will have no more cordial, earnest, or faithful supporter in the Baltimore Convention than your obedient servant,

A. K. McCLURE.

To the President.

That is, only a month before the Baltimore Convention you felt called upon to personally protest against accusations of party disloyalty. But this is not all. When the time came to make the nominations for Vice-President, Simon Cameron, chairman

30

of the Pennsylvania delegation and one of the earliest and most persistent friends of Lincoln, himself nominated Hannibal Hamlin for Vice-President, while the whole vote of Pennsylvania was on the first ballot cast for Hamlin's nomination. So also the Illinois delegation cast its entire vote for Hamlin on the first ballot. Does it stand to reason that Lincoln called upon you to defeat Hamlin and nominate Johnson, and gave no intimation of this desire to the chairmen of the Pennsylvania delegation and of the Illinois delegation?

And once more, is it probable that if Lincoln had desired the nomination of Johnson he would have allowed Swett, "one of the President's most intimate friends," to urge the nomination of Holt? Dare you venture the assertion that Lincoln was deceiving Cameron, deceiving Cook, carrying on a secret intrigue against Hamlin and another secret intrigue against Holt, and that on top of the whole he was writing a deliberate lie to us? That may be your conception of Abraham Lincoln, but it is not mine. That may be your system of politics, but it was not his.

JOHN G. NICOLAY.

McCLURE TO NICOLAY.

[From *The Philadelphia Times*, July 12, 1891.]

To JOHN G. NICOLAY:

The public will be greatly surprised that such an undignified and quibbling letter as yours addressed to me could come from one who claims to be the chosen biographer of Abraham Lincoln. It must so generally offend the dispassionate opinion of decent men that answer to it is excusable only to expose several severely-strained new falsehoods you present, either directly or by the suppression of the vital parts of the truth.

Had you known anything about the inside political movements in the White House in 1864, you would have known that my letter to Lincoln, quoted in your defense, was written because of a suddenly-developed effort in this State to divide the lines drawn by the then bitter Cameron and Curtin factional war for and against Lincoln. The Cameron followers claimed to be the special supporters of Lincoln, and attempted to drive Curtin and the State administration into hostility to the President. My justly-assumed devotion to Curtin was the pretext for declaring me as either restrained in my support of Lincoln or likely to be in the opposition. The moment I saw the statement in print I wrote the letter you quote to dismiss from Lincoln's mind all apprehensions about either open or passive opposition from Curtin's friends. Had you stated these facts you would have been truthful. As you probably did not know of them, you may be excused for not stating them; but your ignorance can be no excuse for the entirely false construction you put upon my letter.

Equally—indeed even more flagrantly—false is your statement of only a minor part of the truth about the action of the Pennsylvania delegation at Baltimore in 1864. You say that General Cameron cast the solid vote of the State for Hamlin. Had you told the whole truth, ignorant as you seem to be of the force of important political facts, you would have known that your assumption that Johnson had no votes in the delegation was untrue. Had you desired to be truthful, you would have added that General Cameron cast the solid vote of the delegation for Johnson before the close of the first ballot. Were you ignorant of this fact? or have you deliberately attempted to so suppress the truth as to proclaim a palpable falsehood?

The Pennsylvania delegation was personally harmonious, although divided on Vice-President. In the Pennsylvania caucus an informal vote put Johnson in the lead, with Hamlin second and Dickinson third. Cameron knew that Hamlin's nomination was utterly hopeless, and he accepted the result without special grief. He urged a solid vote as a just compliment to Hamlin, and it was given with the knowledge that it could not help Hamlin and that a solid vote for Johnson would follow. The solid vote for Johnson was the only vital vote cast for Vice-President, and that record, accessible to every schoolboy, you studiously suppress to excuse a falsehood.

I was a doubly-elected delegate to the Baltimore Convention, having been first unanimously chosen as a district delegate without the formality of a conference, and when a district delegate I was one of two delegates elected at large on the first ballot by the State Convention. What I did or did not, or how important or unimportant I was as a member of the convention, is an issue that I have not raised or invited. I stated the simple fact that Lincoln had sent for me, had urged me to support Johnson, and that I had done so. Had Lincoln chosen to confide his wishes to another than myself, I would not have imitated his secretary and charged him with deceit and falsehood because he did not tell me all his purposes. He did not trust you with what you probably could not have understood had he told you, but that is no reason why you should accuse him of deceit, intrigue, and "writing a deliberate lie." He wrote you the exact truth in the only paper you have as the basis of your inexcusable misconception of his language. In it he says that "Swett is unquestionably all right;" and the only thing he could have been right about in the matter was in his active opposition to Hamlin's renomination. Your history is quite right in quoting Lincoln, but he cannot be justly held responsible for the want of common understanding of one of his biographers more than a quarter of a century after his death.

For answer to your undignified and unmanly efforts to belittle my relations with Lincoln, I refer you to your more discreet co-biographer, Mr. Hay. He refused to sustain your interpretation of Lincoln's note on the Vice-Presidency. He added that the dispute is a question of veracity between you and me, and he speaks of me as "evidently armed with his enviable record of close intimacy with our illustrious Lincoln." One of you is lying on this point: is it Mr. Hay or is it you?

Had you sought the truth as an honest biographer, you could have obtained it without offensive disputation, not only from me so far as I knew it, but from such living witnesses as Charles A. Dana and Murat Halstead, and from the recorded testimony of General Cameron, Colonel Forney, and others who know much of Lincoln and but little of you. Instead of seeking the truth, you flung your ignorance and egotism with ostentatious indecency upon the bereaved household of the yet untombed Hamlin, and when brought to bay by those better informed than yourself, you resent it in the tone and terms of the ward-heeler in a wharf-rat district battling for constabulary honors. I think it safe to say that the public judgment will be that it would have been well for both Lincoln's memory and for the country had such a biographer been drowned when a pup. Dismissed.

A. K. M.

NICOLAY TO McCLURE.

WASHINGTON, July 11, 1891.

To Col. A. K. McClure, Editor *Philadelphia Times:*

I will not allow you to retreat in a cloud of vituperation from full conviction of having made a misstatement of history. I need only to sum up the points of evidence.

You allege that Mr. Lincoln called and instructed you to oppose Hamlin and nominate Johnson.

1. This is proven to be a misstatement by Lincoln's written words: "Wish not to interfere about V.-P.; cannot interfere about platform—convention must judge for itself."

It is not a question between your assertion and my assertion, but between your assertion and Lincoln's written word.

It is proven to be a misstatement by the testimony of Hon. B. C. Cook, chairman of the Illinois delegation, who says : " Mr. Nicolay's statement that Mr. Lincoln was in favor of Hannibal Hamlin is correct. The dispatch which is published this morning was sent to me in reply to an inquiry to Mr. Lincoln in regard to the matter. It read: 'Wish not to interfere about V.-P. Cannot interfere about platform—convention must judge for itself.'

"I went to see Mr. Lincoln personally, however. There are always men who say the Presidential candidates prefer this man or that, and they do it without the slightest authority. It was so in this campaign. It was reported that Andrew Johnson was Mr. Lincoln's choice, and it was my business to find out whether it was or not. We were beyond all measure for Mr. Lincoln first, last, and for all time. Had he desired Mr. Johnson he would have been our choice, but he did not.

"As the dispatch indicates, Mr. Lincoln was particularly anxious not to make known his preferences on the question of his associate on the ticket. But that he had a preference I positively know. After my interview with him I was as positive that Hannibal Hamlin was his favorite as I am that I am alive to-day. The fact is further proven by the action of the entire Illinois delegation, which was a unit for Mr. Hamlin, and, as I stated before, we were at his service in the matter."

2. It is proven to be a misstatement by Colonel Hay, who says: "I have nothing to say about Mr. Nicolay's assertion nor about this telegram, but I do corroborate the statement that Mr. Lincoln withheld all opinion calculated to influence the Baltimore Convention of 1864." And further: "I stand simply by the proposition contained in our *History*. . . . For several days before the convention the President had been besieged by inquiries as to his personal wishes in regard to his associate on the ticket. He had persistently refused to give the slightest intimation of such wish. . . . It was therefore with minds absolutely untrammeled by any knowledge of the President's wishes that the con-

vention went about the work of selecting his associate on the ticket."

3. It is proven to be a misstatement by the action of Simon Cameron, chairman of the Pennsylvania delegation, in nominating Hamlin as a candidate for Vice-President and casting for him the whole fifty-two votes of the Pennsylvania delegation.

4. It is proven to be a misstatement by your own action in the Baltimore Convention, when, at the first vote for Vice-President, after the supposed instructions which you claim to have received from Lincoln, and having, as you say, "returned to work and vote for Johnson," you as a member of the Pennsylvania delegation voted for Hannibal Hamlin for Vice-President. If you did this willingly, you betrayed Lincoln's confidence and instructions which you alleged to have received. If you did it unwillingly, you proved yourself a political cipher—a pretended agent to manipulate a national convention who had not influence enough in his own delegation to control his own vote. The first roll-call was decisive in showing Johnson's strength against the Pennsylvania vote (yourself included), and it shows that you contributed nothing for, but everything against, the result you say you were commissioned to bring about. Subsequent changes still on the first ballot (for there was no second) were simply the usual rush to make the choice unanimous, in which Pennsylvania did not lead, but only joined after the rush became evident, just as Maine and Illinois did.

JOHN G. NICOLAY.

TESTIMONY OF LEADING POLITICAL ACTORS.

LINCOLN ADVISES JUDGE PETTIS.

[From *The Philadelphia Times*, Aug. 1, 1891.]

HON. S. NEWTON PETTIS, who was an active supporter of Lincoln at the conventions of 1860 and 1864, and who has been Congressman, Judge, and Foreign Minister, was personally advised by Lincoln in 1864 to support Johnson for Vice-President. The following is his testimony on the point:

MEADVILLE, July 20, 1891.

HON. A. K. McCLURE:

DEAR SIR: Your favor of last week reached me at Washington, asking for a copy of Mr. Hamlin's letter to me in 1889, and instead of a copy I enclose the original, which you can return to me at your convenience.

You will remember the circumstances connected with it, for we spoke about it shortly after. On the morning of the meeting of the Baltimore Convention in 1864 which nominated Mr. Lincoln, and immediately before leaving for Baltimore, I called upon Mr. Lincoln in his study and stated that I called especially to ask him whom he desired put on the ticket with him as Vice-President. He leaned forward and in a low but distinct tone of voice said, "Governor Johnson of Tennessee."

In March, 1889, I spent an hour with Mr. Hamlin in Washington at the house of a friend with whom he was stopping while attending the inauguration of President Harrison in March of that year.

Among other matters I casually mentioned the expression of Mr. Lincoln the morning of the meeting of the Baltimore Convention in 1864, not supposing for a moment that it was anything that would surprise him. You can imagine my annoyance at the remark that it called out from Mr. Hamlin, which was: "Judge Pettis, I am sorry you told me that." I regretted having made the statement, but I could not recall it.

Later in the year I noticed a published interview had with you in which you had made substantially the same statement from Mr. Lincoln to you very shortly before the meeting of the convention, which I clipped and with satisfaction enclosed to Mr. Hamlin in verification of mine to Mr. H., stating that your statement to the same effect as mine made to him in the March before had relieved me from fear that he, Mr. Hamlin, might have sometimes questioned the accuracy of my memory, and the letter I now send you was Mr. Hamlin's reply.

Yours very truly,

S. NEWTON PETTIS.

HAMLIN'S LETTER TO PETTIS.

THE following is Mr. Hamlin's letter to Judge Pettis, the original of which is now in our possession:

BANGOR, September 13, 1889.

MY DEAR SIR: Have been from home for several days, and did not get your letter and newspaper slip until last evening. Hence the delay in my reply.

When I met and conferred with you in Washington, and you told me of your interview with Mr. L. (Lincoln), I had not the slightest doubt of your correctness. The remark that I made was caused wholly because you made certain statements of Mr. L. which I had seen, but which I did not believe until made positive by you. I was really sorry to be disabused. Hence I was truly sorry at what you said and the information you gave me.

Mr. L. (Lincoln) evidently became some alarmed about his reelection and changed his position. That is all I care to say. If we ever shall meet again, I may say something more to you. I will write no more.   Yours very truly,

                                               H. HAMLIN.

HON. S. N. PETTIS, Meadville, Pa.

LINCOLN, CAMERON, AND BUTLER.

THE following letter from General Butler, and the added extract from his magazine article on the same subject, explain themselves:

                                    BOSTON, July 14, 1891.

MY DEAR SIR: A few years ago I was asked to write, as my memory serves me, for the *North American Review*, while under the editorial management of Mr. Allen Thorndike Rice, my reminiscences of the facts in relation to the interview between Mr. Cameron and myself which took place at Fort Monroe some time in March, 1864, as I remember. It might have been a little later, but it must have been before the 4th day of May, 1864, because I went into the field on that date, and did not see Mr. Cameron during the campaign. My recollection is that the article was entitled "Vice-Presidential Politics in 1864." I should say that the article was written five or six years ago.

I cannot now add anything that I know of to what I said then. I meant to tell it just as it lay in my memory, and certainly did so, wholly without any relation to Mr. Hamlin, because I understood it had been determined on by Mr. Lincoln and his friends that somebody else, if it were possible, should be nominated instead of Mr. Hamlin. Of the reasons of that determination I made no inquiry, because the whole matter was one in which I had no intention to take any part.   Yours truly,

                                         BENJ. F. BUTLER.

A. K. McCLURE, Esq.

GENERAL BUTLER'S STATEMENT IN MAGAZINE.

[From the *North American Review* for October, 1885.]

"Within three weeks afterward a gentleman (Cameron) who stood very high in Mr. Lincoln's confidence came to me at Fort Monroe. This was after I had heard that Grant had allotted to me a not unimportant part in the coming campaign around Richmond, of the results of which I had the highest hope, and for which I had been laboring, and the story of which has not yet been told, but may be hereafter.

"The gentleman informed me that he came from Mr. Lincoln; this was said with directness, because the messenger and myself had been for a considerable time in quite warm friendly relations, and I owed much to him, which I can never repay save with gratitude.

"He said: 'The President, as you know, intends to be a candidate for re-election, and as his friends indicate that Mr. Hamlin is no longer to be a candidate for Vice-President, and as he is from New England, the President thinks that his place should be filled by some one from that section; and aside from reasons of personal friendship which would make it pleasant to have you with him, he believes that being the first prominent Democrat who volunteered for the war, your candidature would add strength to the ticket, especially with the War Democrats, and he hopes that you will allow your friends to co-operate with his to place you in that position.'

"I answered: 'Please say to Mr. Lincoln that while I appreciate with the fullest sensibility this act of friendship and the compliment he pays me, yet I must decline· Tell him,' I said laughingly, 'with the prospects of the campaign, I would not quit the field to be Vice-President, even with himself as President, unless he will give me bond, with sureties, in the full sum of his four years' salary, that he will die or resign within three months after his inauguration.'"

CAMERON'S DECLARATIONS.

THE following is an extract from an interview with General Cameron taken by James R. Young, now Executive Clerk of the Senate, in 1873, revised by Cameron himself and published in the New York *Herald* in the summer of that year:

"Lincoln and Stanton thought highly of Butler, and I will now tell you of another fact that is not generally known, and which will show you how near Butler came to being President instead of Andrew Johnson. In the spring of 1864, when it was determined to run Mr. Lincoln for a second term, it was the desire of Lincoln, and also that of Stanton, who was the one man of the Cabinet upon whom Lincoln thoroughly depended, that Butler should run on the ticket with him as the candidate for Vice-President. I was called into consultation and heartily endorsed the scheme. Accordingly Lincoln sent me on a mission to Fort Monroe to see General Butler, and to say to him that it was his (Lincoln's) request that he (General Butler) should allow himself to be run as second on the ticket.

"I, accompanied by William H. Armstrong, afterward a member of Congress from the Williamsport district, did visit General Butler and made the tender according to instructions. To our astonishment, Butler refused to agree to the proposition. He said there was nothing in the Vice-Presidency, and he preferred remaining in command of his army, where he thought he would be of more service to his country."

A LATER CAMERON INTERVIEW.

THE following interview with General Cameron, taken by Colonel Burr a few years before his death, was carefully revised by Cameron himself. It is not only a repetition of General Butler's statement, but it tells how, after Butler declined the Vice-Presidency, Lincoln carefully considered other prominent War Democrats, and finally agreed with Cameron to nominate Johnson:

"I had been summoned from Harrisburg by the President to consult with him in relation to the approaching campaign," said General Cameron. "He was holding a reception when I arrived, but after it was over we had a long and earnest conversation. Mr. Lincoln had been much distressed at the intrigues in and out of his Cabinet to defeat his renomination; but that was now assured, and the question of a man for the second place on the ticket was freely and earnestly discussed. Mr. Lincoln thought, and so did I, that Mr. Hamlin's position during the four years of his administration made it advisable to have a new name substituted. Several men were freely talked of, but without conclusion as to any particular person. Not long after that I was requested to come to the White House again. I went and the subject was again brought up by the President; and the result of our conversation was that Mr. Lincoln asked me to go to Fortress Monroe and ask General Butler if he would be willing to run, and, if not, to confer with him upon the subject.

"General Butler positively declined to consider the subject, saying that he preferred to remain in the military service, and he thought a man could not justify himself in leaving the army in the time of war to run for a political office. The general and myself then talked the matter over freely, and it is my opinion at this distance from the event that he suggested that a Southern man should be given the place. After completing the duty assigned by the President, I returned to Washington and reported the result to Mr. Lincoln. He seemed to regret General Butler's decision, and afterward the name of Andrew Johnson was suggested and accepted. In my judgment, Mr. Hamlin never had a serious chance to become the Vice-Presidential candidate after Mr. Lincoln's renomination was assured."

JOHNSON'S SECRETARY SPEAKS.

MAJOR BENJAMIN C. TRUMAN, a well-known Eastern journalist, and now manager of the California exhibit for the coming Chicago Fair, testifies in the following conclusive manner on the subject:

CHICAGO, July 25.

MY DEAR MR. MCCLURE:

We met in New Orleans the year of the fair, as you may remember. I am the man recently quoted in the *Tribune* in relation to the Lincoln-Hamlin controversy, but I did not wish to volunteer conspicuously in the dispute. I was private secretary of Andrew Johnson in Nashville in 1864. I saw and handled all his correspondence during that time, and I know it to be a fact that Mr. Lincoln desired the nomination of Johnson for Vice-President, and that Brownlow and Maynard went to Baltimore at request of Lincoln and Johnson to promote the nomination.

Forney wrote to Johnson saying that General Sickles would be in Tennessee to canvass Johnson's availability, and that Lincoln, on the whole, preferred Johnson first and Holt next. I do not know that General Sickles conferred with Johnson on the subject, and it is possible that General Sickles was not advised by

Lincoln at the time he sent him on the secret mission what he had in view, for Lincoln may at that time have been undecided in his own mind. It is certain, however, that after General Sickles returned and reported to Lincoln, Lincoln decided to favor the nomination of Johnson.

I went out to Tennessee with Johnson in March, 1862, and had charge of his official and private correspondence for four years. I wrote at his dictation many letters to Mr. Lincoln, and was cognizant of all Mr. Lincoln's communications to him.

When he was made Military Governor and Brigadier-General, I was appointed on his staff along with William A. Browning of Baltimore, who died in '66. It was Colonel Forney who obtained the position for me, and he was in close confidential relations with Johnson during the entire period I speak of.

Very truly,

BEN C. TRUMAN.

JONES SPEAKS FOR RAYMOND.

HENRY J. RAYMOND was editor of the New York *Times* in 1864, of which George Jones was then, as now, the chief owner, and their relations were of the most confidential character. Raymond was the Lincoln leader and the master-spirit of the Baltimore Convention of 1864. He framed and reported the platform; he was made chairman of the National Committee; he wrote the Life of Lincoln for the campaign; and it was his leadership that carried a majority of the New York delegation for Johnson even against Dickinson, from Raymond's own State, because he was in the confidence of and acting in accord with the wishes of Lincoln. Raymond has long since joined the great majority beyond, but Jones thus incisively speaks for him:

SOUTH POLAND, ME., July 17, 1891.

MY DEAR COLONEL McCLURE: Your letter has been forwarded to me here. I have read the contention about the Vice-Presidency, and do not hesitate to say that you are absolutely in the right in your statement of the facts.

I had many talks with Raymond on the subject. Dickinson's friends never forgave him, although he made Dickinson U. S. District Attorney afterward to compensate him for the loss of the Vice-Presidency. Seward and Weed were also with Raymond in that fight.   Faithfully yours,

GEORGE JONES.

MARSHAL LAMON'S LETTER.

CARLSBAD, BOHEMIA, August 16, 1891.

HON. A. K. McCLURE:

DEAR SIR: The question of preference of President Lincoln in 1864 as to who ought to be placed on the national ticket with himself is one of doubt, I observe from reading the American newspapers, and one which has, since the death of Ex-Vice-President Hamlin, given rise to much controversy. At this distance of time from the exciting events of that period I had thought that no fact was better established than Mr. Lincoln's politic preference as a strategic skirmish from the beaten path to give strength to the party and discouragement to the South. He was decidedly in favor of a Southern man for Vice-President. And of all men South, his preference, as he expressed himself to prudent friends, was for Andrew Johnson. This he could not consistently make public, for he occupied a delicate position before the people, and was apprehensive of giving offense to Hamlin's united New England constituency.

To discreet and trusted friends with whom he deemed it prudent to confer he urged that such a nomination would disarm our enemies of the Union abroad, and be a check to the recognition of the Confederacy by England and France to a greater extent than anything in our power to do at that time, and if judiciously and quietly effected would, in his opinion, in no wise jeopardize the success of the party.

He believed that the election of one of the candidates on the national ticket from an insurgent State, from the heart of the Confederacy, that had been restored to the Union and had repented of the sin of rebellion, would not only be wise, but expedient; and Johnson being a lifelong representative Southern man, who had been Governor, a member of Congress, a United States Senator, and was then Military Governor of the State of Tennessee, it was fitting, and would have more influence in proving the success of the Union arms against the Confederate rebellion than anything that had been accomplished.

I recall to mind the fact that Mr. Lincoln sent for you, Mr. Editor, the day before the National Convention was to meet, for consultation on this veritable subject. To the best of my recollection, you were not in sympathy with the scheme; that you opposed it and declared yourself in favor of the old ticket of 1860; and I am confident that at first you were opposed to the nomination of Johnson. But after some discussion and hearing Mr. Lincoln's earnest reasoning in favor of his position, you yielded your prejudices and seemed convinced that there was philosophy and, perhaps, sound politics in the proposition. The late lamented Leonard Swett of Illinois was also sent for and consulted before the convention met; Mr. Lincoln always had great faith and confidence in Mr. Swett's political wisdom. The proposition took Swett by surprise. He had made up his mind that the old ticket of Lincoln and Hamlin would be again renominated as a matter of course. Swett said to him: "Lincoln, if it were known in New England that you are in favor of leaving Hamlin off the ticket it would raise the devil among the Yankees (Mr. Swett was born in Maine), and it would raise a bumble-bee's nest about your ears that would appall the country." Swett continued about in this strain: "However popular you are with the masses over the country, you are not so with the New England politicians, because of your tardiness in issuing your Emancipation Proclamation and your liberal reconstruction policy. You must know that you have not recovered from what these people think two great blunders of your administration. In view of these facts I think it a dangerous experiment."

Lincoln was serious, earnest, and resolute. He produced arguments so convincing to Swett that he shortly became a convert to the proposed new departure, and in deference to Mr. Lincoln's wishes he went to the convention as a delegate from Illinois, and joined Cameron, yourself, and others in supporting Johnson.

I recollect that Swett asked Mr. Lincoln, as he was leaving the White House, whether he was authorized to use his name in this behalf before the convention. The reply was, "No; I will address a letter to Lamon here embodying my views, which you, McClure, and other friends may use if it be found absolutely necessary. Otherwise, it may be better that I should not appear actively on the stage of this theatre." The letter was written, and I took it to the convention with me. It was not used, as there was no occasion for its use, and it was afterward returned to Mr. Lincoln, at his request.

Mr. Lincoln was beset before the convention by the friends of the Hamlin interest for his opinion and preference for Vice-President. To such he invariably dodged the question, sometimes saying: "It perhaps would not become me to interfere with the will of the people," always evading a direct answer.

However this conduct may subject him to the charge by some persons of the want of open candor, the success of the party and the safety of the Union were the paramount objects that moved him. He did not, by suppressing the truth to those whom he thought had no right to cross-question him, purpose conveying a false impression. If this is to be construed as duplicity, be it so; he was still "Honest old Abe," and he thought the end justified the means.

About this time, and for a short time before this convention was held, Mr. Lincoln was exceedingly anxious to bring Tennessee under a regular State government, and he argued that by emphasizing it by the election of Johnson to the Vice-Presidency (not that he had any prejudice against Mr. Hamlin) in no way could such rapid strides be made toward the restoration of the Union.

If the nomination of Johnson was a mistake, a misdemeanor, or a crime, the responsibility of it should rest where it belongs. Mr. Lincoln was undoubtedly blamable for the blunder. It may be that more calamitous mistakes happened in the lives of very many eminent and good men during those troublous times of our country's history.

With all my affection, admiration, love, and veneration for Mr. Lincoln, I have never been one of those who believed him immaculate and incapable of making mistakes. He was human and in the nature of things was liable to err, yet he erred less often than other men. He had amiable weaknesses, some of which only the more ennobled him.

It is no compliment to his memory to smother from the closest scrutiny any of the acts of his life and transfigure him by fullsome deification, so that his most intimate friends cannot recognize the Abraham Lincoln of other days. The truth of history requires that he should be placed on the record, now that he is dead, as he stood before the people while living. Whatever mistakes he made were made through the purest of motives. All his faults, all his amiable weaknesses, and all his virtues should be written on the same pages, so that the world may know the true man as his friends knew him. With all the truth told of him he will appear a purer and better man than any other man living or any man that ever did live.

With all that can truthfully be said of him, Abraham Lincoln has reached that stage of moral elevation where his name alone will be more beneficial to humanity at large than the personal services of any other man to the people of any country as their Chief Magistrate.   Respectfully,

WARD H. LAMON.

A CABINET MINISTER TESTIFIES.

[Gideon Welles, in the *Galaxy*, Nov., 1877.]

MR. HAMLIN, who was elected with Lincoln in 1860, had not displayed the breadth of view and enlightened statesmanship which was expected, and consequently lost confidence with the country during his term. Yet there was no concentration or unity on any one to fill his place. His friends and supporters, while conscious that he brought no strength to the ticket, claimed, but with no zeal or earnestness, that as Mr. Lincoln was renominated, it would be invidious not to nominate Hamlin also.

The question of substituting another for Vice-President had been discussed in political circles prior to the meeting of the convention, without any marked personal preference, but with a manifest desire that there should be a change. Mr. Lincoln felt the delicacy of his position, and was therefore careful to avoid the expression of any opinion; but it was known to those who enjoyed his confidence that he appreciated the honesty, integrity, and self-sacrificing patriotism of Andrew Johnson of Tennessee.

GENERAL SICKLES' STATEMENT.

[General Sickles' Interview in *New York Times*.]

"WHEN I went South to visit Governor Johnson this sentiment was in the air," continued General Sickles. "I knew of it, but I considered from my past position that it would be indelicate for me to invite the President's confidence on purely political matters. It was not my mission to undertake to bring about changes in Mr. Johnson's methods of administration which should affect his standing before the Baltimore Convention. The result of my visit may have had some such effect: I do not say that it did not. I reported to Mr. Lincoln and to Mr. Seward.

"Now, what was the situation at Baltimore? Mr. Leonard Swett was President Lincoln's shadow. Whatever Mr. Swett did represented and reflected Mr. Lincoln's views. In the Baltimore

Convention Mr. Swett at once came out for Judge Holt, a Border-State man. Mr. Nicolay sent word to Mr. Hay, who had been left to keep house, asking if the President approved of this. Now note Mr. Lincoln's reply:

" ' Swett is unquestionably all right. Mr. Holt is a good man, but I had not thought of him for Vice-President. Wish not to interfere.'

" That tells the whole story. Mr. Lincoln knew that Mr. Swett, in bringing out a Border-State man, was doing precisely right. The indorsement on that note was for Mr. Nicolay's eye. He was not one of the President's close advisers. He was but a clerk. He was not the man whom President Lincoln would send to Baltimore to take a hand in shaping the convention. A tyro in politics would see that if the President wanted a thing done, his own secretary would have been the last messenger sent to do it. It would have revealed the President's hand if Mr. Nicolay had been given a mission in the convention.

" Colonel McClure, Governor Andrew G. Curtin, Simon Cameron, and others of that stamp were the men whom Mr. Lincoln relied on. So that while the indorsement on the note gives Mr. Nicolay documentary evidence for his position, that very remark, ' Swett is all right,' gives Colonel McClure good ground for his position if there were nothing else.

" Mr. Seward and Mr. Stanton were close advisers of Mr. Lincoln. They spoke their sentiments in favor of a Border-State man. That they advised the choice of Mr. Johnson I do not know, or that the President had chosen Mr. Johnson I do not know, but the one expression, ' Swett is all right,' is the key that unlocks all the mystery there is in this present controversy."

31

INDEX.